Library Staff Development
and
Continuing Education

Library Staff Development
and
Continuing Education

Principles and Practices

Barbara Conroy

1978

Libraries Unlimited, Inc.
Littleton, Colorado

LIBRARIES UNLIMITED, INC.
P.O. Box 263
Littleton, Colorado 80160

Library of Congress Cataloging in Publication Data

Conroy, Barbara.
   Library staff development and continuing education.

   Bibliography: p. 277
   Includes index.
   1. Library education (Continuing education)
2. Library personnel management. I. Title.
Z668.C737   023'.5   78-18887
ISBN 0-87287-177-0

PREFACE

The growth of learning opportunities for library personnel is exciting to observe or to be a part of. Staff development and continuing education are becoming not only popularly accepted but also popularly done. The need exists, the interest persists, but the ability to produce quality learning experiences is sometimes lacking. This book is intended to provide a guide and reference book for practitioners and educators responsible for planning for the learning of others. Then, hopefully, more quality learning opportunities will be more available to to library personnel.

Sound theory is presented in a practical guidelines approach focused on systematic planning, involved implementation, and useful evaluation. Each Guideline includes principles and precepts, criteria and examples to aid those responsible for library staff development and continuing education. These are intended as tools for those starting a program, those wishing to review and perhaps to revitalize an existing one, or those wanting to coalesce existing isolated, sporadic activities into a program. The use of questions, alternatives, suggestions, and models is designed to help a program developer tailor learning to a wide variety of situations. The tools presented here can be used by conference planners, proposal writers, program developers, individual learners, educators, and institute and workshop planners. Issues are pointed out since these often present shoals to the pilot. Some parts of the book are for reflection, some for application to a situation, some for providing open doors to new alternatives, some for leading to further exploration in other resources.

This manual does not intend to make a science or regimen of what is generally known and practiced as "common sense." Rather, the intent is to articulate that common sense in such a way that inexperienced people can become skillful producers of learning opportunities. The three Parts describe the interrelated functions of program, planning, implementation and evaluation. Bibliographies at the end deliberately cite non-library literature to make program developers aware of and familiar with those resources. Footnotes and references scattered throughout the text pinpoint sources of particular value in relation to specific topics. The boldface terms are defined and described in the Glossary. Narrative program models in the appendix describe the guidelines applied to specific examples.

Planning, implementing, and evaluating are not mutually exclusive processes. Following the steps of assessing needs and establishing objectives, the order of the subsequent steps is not, in all cases, the same as in the guidelines presented here. Rather, the most logical order depends on the particular situation and people involved. Since the basic steps would be similar, these guidelines could be used for planning a single learning activity. The premise throughout the book, however, is that a learning program, composed of a number of related activities, is more likely to meet existing and future needs than is an assortment of sporadic, isolated activities without program coordination.

The book can assist the library practitioner to produce learning activities for colleagues. It can serve as a reference book for the staff developer in a library, as a guidebook for the committee responsible for an association's continuing education program, or as a checklist for the program evaluator or administrator. Most practitioners, however, have little practical experience with teaching or program planning. In fact, few library directors have had much experience with personnel development as such. Formal library education rarely includes the whys and hows of the processes of staff development or of continuing education. The need for this kind of work has been seen for some time.

Two earlier publications are part of the heritage of this work. The Staff Development Committee of the American Library Association published its "Guidelines to the Development of Human Resources in Libraries: Rationale, Policies, Programs and Recommendations" in *Library Trends* (vol. 20, no. 1, July, 1971, pp. 92-117). In 1973, Conroy's *Staff Development and Continuing Education Programs for Library Personnel: Guidelines and Criteria* offered the first such broadbrush treatment of the subject done within and for the library field. (Produced for ERIC. Boulder, Colorado: Western Interstate Commission for Higher Education, 1973. ED 083 986.) This book is a comprehensive, in-depth expansion of the latter booklet.

Many individuals and groups have aided the author in this lengthy task. Of particular importance have been: Larry Allen, Audry Kolb, Miles Martin, Julie Virgo, and Barbara Weaver. To them go my thanks for their ability, interest, and support.

Barbara Conroy

TABLE OF CONTENTS

LIST OF FIGURES

INTRODUCTION: In Search of Learning

Knowledgeable, able library personnel are essential if libraries are to meet the information needs of their clientele. Effective libraries require skillful, efficient people who work well with colleagues and with the public, who plan and develop sound programs of service, and who deal with emerging organizational problems. Intended to improve the competence of library personnel, learning opportunities can improve the quality of library service. In some cases, such learning occurs spontaneously, but, for the most part, sound learning opportunities must be planned and conducted carefully in order to achieve worthwhile results. Systematic programs of staff development and continuing education offer the strongest possibility for increasing knowledge, improving skills, and changing attitudes of library personnel through quality learning opportunities.

In the comprehensive study, *Continuing Library and Information Science Education*, the authors point out specifically the importance of that knowledge, those skills, and those attitudes:

> People are essential to the process of connecting the need for information and the information resources. People have to be prepared to acquire, organize, and deliver information in fields which do not remain static in terms of their needs or operation. People have to be able to effectively manage these information organizations to provide for society's needs to know. People have to know how to responsibly raise and deal with issues confronting their own professional field, to resolve them in humane and effective ways, and to persevere on matters involving professional principles. [1]

Thus, all categories of library personnel in all types of libraries have needs to learn, often for a number of reasons. The daily tasks and major issues that confront individuals require them to apply their knowledge and skill appropriately to each situation. The standards for personnel performance and institutional accountability are increasingly demanding, and without consistent and deliberate efforts, obsolescence is inevitable. Prompted by personal needs and desire for change, then, personnel mobility flows upward, laterally, geographically, and by specialty. And, finally, technological and societal change are rapid and unavoidable, and inevitably affect libraries and their personnel.

Such needs have prompted increased interest in staff development and continuing library education for library personnel to the point where these are now central, rather than peripheral, concerns. In fact, the National Commission on Libraries and Information Science, reflecting this increased interest, highlights as a priority one of its *Goals for Action*: "To achieve a technological upgrading of libraries and information centers will require new approaches to recruitment, personnel development, continuing education, technical training, trustee orientation and other matters relating to human resources." [2] At present, many efforts of libraries, state library agencies, library schools, and library associations are directed towards enhancing the abilities of practitioners who create and maintain effective patterns of library service. Likewise, individuals actually working in libraries are more aware of their own learning needs and those of their colleagues. Often, they take individual or organizational steps to meet those needs.

In spite of this interest, however, present efforts are not adequate. Although the number and the quality of learning opportunities are slowly improving, the degree of stated concern is not matched with action to meet the needs. In spite of being identified as an essential concern, learning appears to be classified as "useful" rather than "urgent" when priorities are designated and organizational resources are allocated. Most efforts to meet learning needs are sporadic and uncoordinated; responsibilities are usually ill-defined and not fully assumed. The designated resources are not adequate to meet the need. Administrative leadership does not consistently extend access to existing opportunities to all personnel, nor does it reward or recognize their participation. Library personnel rely on scarce external motivational factors rather than intrinsic values to provide incentives for their participation as learners. And, finally, the skills required to systematically develop personnel are not widespread in the library field, and little of this technology is available within the literature of librarianship.

These factors have forestalled attempts to meet the need for learning. As a result, present opportunities for library personnel to learn are generally inadequate in quality and insufficient in quantity. They miss achieving the necessary impact; they fail to make the best use of available resources within and outside the library field. Continuing the present uncoordinated approach will perpetuate the problem at an ever increasing rate as the need becomes greater.

Yet, an all-out effort, a crash program to remedy the situation is unfeasible and unrealistic. A steady, constructive, two-pronged approach is possible, however. First, deliberate and thoughtful efforts can be made by library personnel to develop new learning programs, to upgrade existing ones, and to coordinate those with each other. Second, convinced and capable individuals can work to improve the present situation by preparing the way, building the resources, setting the precedents, and developing the attitudes to enable the changes.

Although individuals, libraries, library agencies, and associations are making some of these efforts, at the present time, chance plays the leading role both for the producer and the consumer of learning opportunities. Too essential to continue in this unpredictable manner, learning as a deliberate and planned effort needs support, ability, and commitment to move beyond chance to consistent, reliable endeavors. Statements of interest and endorsement may support the precepts of learning for library personnel. But, this interest and endorsement have not yet served to clearly define or to adequately fulfill the responsibility to produce and maintain the effective learning opportunities needed in librarianship.

Indeed, increasing demands and proliferating activities have served to focus attention on this issue of responsibility. In the mid-1960s, Samuel Rothstein first raised the question in his article "Nobody's Baby: A Brief Sermon on Continuing Professional Education."[3] Since then, the issue has been explored in greater depth by those people who recognize and describe the areas of responsibility as they seem to be demonstrated, and those who present recommendations as to where they think those responsibilities ought to lie.

Now, the dilemma is no longer that learning for library personnel is nobody's baby, but rather that it is considered to be everybody's baby. The responsibility for continuing education and staff development is generally acknowledged to be shared by the individual, the library, the state library agency, the library school, and the library association. But, present efforts reveal that the ways in which the responsibilities are to be divided is not so universally agreed. Learning activities conducted by these various groups are sometimes at cross purposes and even in competition for learners, facilities, and funding. Although simple, clean, and clearcut distinctions between specific responsibilities of various segments of librarianship may not be possible to designate or assign, clarification of the question of responsibility is a major issue for librarians to address.

An important finding reported in *Continuing Library and Information Science Education* is the lack of defined responsibilities and coordinated efforts. These are major hindrances that prevent learning opportunities adequate in number, kind, and distribution. This survey of informed laymen and experts throughout librarianship and library education reveals that substantial progress has been made, however, to sort out what needs to be done and who should do it. This study and other sources in library literature indicate that the concern is being addressed and that some areas of agreement have already been reached.[4] From those sources come the following brief descriptions:

1) The basic responsibility for self-direction and self-development is that of the individual. That is, each person must identify his or her own needs for learning, establish personal goals, then supply the internal energy and drive as well as contribute some of the time and money necessary to obtain learning. Accepting the concept of life-long education, the individual can encourage and assist the learning of colleagues, and can serve actively on committees and task forces to work for increased learning opportunities. Individuals who actively seek to develop new means to meet their learning needs remain open to useful opportunities that already exist.

2) The employing library accepts learning as an integral and vital function of the organization, actively interacting with the goals, planning, and operation of the library. The library administration knows personnel and organizational needs and the relation between them, is willing to commit staff time and library budget for learning, and provides incentives for staff members who actively participate in learning. Quality education programming is aided by evaluating the results of current efforts and by participating in cooperative learning programs that share resources with other libraries and groups.

3) The state library agency is responsible for coordinating learning efforts on a state-wide basis and getting adequate support for them. It often identifies priority continuing education needs within the state, and conducts those activities not done more appropriately by others, linking individual libraries with national and regional plans. Staff, information, and consulting services are also seen as a logical extension of state library responsibility, enabling libraries and library personnel to gain access to existing opportunities and to produce their own learning activities.

At state, regional, and national levels, library associations are primarily responsible for identifying the larger learning needs within the library field. Often in the best position to look ahead at tomorrow's needs as well as those of today, associations organize and implement efforts to disseminate new information and produce new skills. This includes committing conference time and resources for learning purposes as well as establishing committees and assigning staff with specific responsibilities for continuing education. By making information, access, and opportunities available, they can encourage active participation of their members in learning activities. They establish standards and guidelines for learning opportunities, produce journals and publications, and identify resources to help practitioners learn.

4) Library schools with graduate or undergraduate programs can offer courses designed for practitioners as well as for those entering the field. In addition, the schools are a resource, providing faculty for learning activities sponsored by other organizations and supplying information about continuing education opportunities for others. They are often in the position of cooperating with or supporting groups producing learning opportunities. Library schools serve as an arena where experimentation, evaluation, and research can occur. Perhaps most importantly, library schools are in a unique position to alert students to their need and responsibility for continued learning and to help them build the skills and attitudes they will need for their continued self-development.

The 1970s appears to be the decade when these roles and responsibilities have become more distinct and taken root. To a large extent, each library, agency, and association must decide consciously its own role and responsibility for learning, since commonly accepted standards or specifications have not yet been developed. Presently, no standard of quality, no regular channels of production and distribution exist. Areas of responsibility will become more clearly articulated as individuals and organizations seek to clarify their own scope, to identify their expertise, and to work with other groups producing learning opportunities. From this search is now coming the realization that learning and growth for people at all staff levels are perceived as a right as well as a rite, as a privilege as well as a demand, as a responsibility to contribute as well as to consume.

The acceptance and practice of these responsibilities assumes that rich, full programs of learning are produced by various sources and coordinated for quality and predictability. Such an aim, however, raises another dilemma. To achieve this desirable state requires a certain amount of bureaucratic structure, financial support, and relinquished autonomy. And, to many, these requirements may be drawbacks to moving ahead to initiate or support learning programs. At local, state, regional, and national levels, time and thoughtful and constructive efforts will be necessary to find appropriate ways to achieve the desired aim.

From the early days of librarianship, three approaches have existed to build competency levels of library personnel. First, pre-service education prepares people to enter the field. Second, in-service training or staff development offers learning within the work setting. And, third, continuing education includes supplementary learning activities related to but apart from the work setting. The first of these three is well defined. Until recently, however, little distinction was made between in-service training or staff development and continuing education. This lack of distinction has served to confuse the issue of responsibility for learning and has delayed initiatives that could have resulted in sound educational programming. Some individuals, some libraries, even some learning opportunities may challenge this categorization. But these distinctions help define and resolve issues that otherwise may be bypassed or sidetracked.

The distinction between staff development and continuing education can be made on the basis of several apparent differences between the two. The focus of staff development centers on the needs of the individual library and on the learner's function in that library. To be effective, staff development activities must be closely integrated with other of the library functions and with the work context as a whole, dealing with its problems and potential. Even so, personnel with their individual needs and interests are involved as persons, not just positions. Continuing education, on the other hand, focuses on the learner as a person, and that individual is primarily responsible for translating and applying his or her learnings to the work situation. Continuing education generally addresses common needs shared by a number of libraries. It relies on the learner to transmit his or her learning to a particular work/library situation. Although areas of overlap do occur, this distinction is particularly useful to plan for learning. This distinction is accented throughout this book, especially in Part I (Planning the Learning Program).

Staff Development is a purposive effort intended to strengthen the library's capability to fulfill its mission effectively and efficiently by encouraging and providing for the growth of its own human resources. Its general purpose is to assure that library personnel are motivated, productive, and skilled in their jobs, and that they understand and can implement library purposes and policies. Staff development affirms the ability of both the individual and the library to grow. It can prepare the individual and the library for the future, enabling each to contribute to the growth of the other. As a series of interrelated activities continued over a period of time, staff development can motivate, sustain, and reinforce learning and the application of that learning on the job, thus contributing to the capability of the staff team as well as to the individual staff member. Possible staff development activities include: orientation of new staff, a supervisory skills short-course for department heads, a briefing session on computer use for reference inquiries, a film on the use of audiovisual equipment, a coaching system of on-the-job training. The library both sponsors and uses each of these activities with the intention of benefitting both that organization as a whole and its personnel as individuals.

Continuing education, on the other hand, consists of those learning opportunities utilized by individuals in fulfilling their need to learn and grow following their preparatory education and work experiences. It intends to deepen understanding or build skills of the individual learner, usually through short-term methods that concern only one segment of a larger topic. Producers of continuing education seek to contribute to the effectiveness of many libraries within a broad context. They do so by addressing generally shared library issues and concerns and encouraging individuals to learn and to take what they have learned back to the library. Continuing education is often used to enable library science to anticipate societal trends and technical advances, such as networking, data bases, adult independent learners, and cable TV. It can also help library personnel cope with more traditional concerns, such as management, library buildings, supervision, budgeting, or reference services. Examples of continuing education activities would include institutes, workshops, conferences, home study courses, programmed learning packages, job exchanges, and publications. Continuing education assists individuals, and through them, their libraries, to prepare for new responsibilities, to deal with emerging issues, to use new technologies, and to evolve change.

For staff development, the employing library initiates learning opportunities justified by the needs of the library and/or the interests of staff members. The choices and balance of learning activities are closely tied to the organizational view of their job relatedness and personnel potential. A major strength of staff development is the depth and impact that can be achieved, since a series of learning experiences for specific people can be closely tied to personal and library needs and sustained over a period of time. And, if staff development is an integral part of the library, setting goals and making steady, measured progress toward those goals is possible.

Continuing education efforts, however, are produced by a state library agency or a library association that senses its responsibility and seeks to address the urgency and importance of the needs it perceives. The selection of what activities to attend and how to apply the resulting learnings rests primarily with learner and employer. Continuing education offers the opportunity for vital interchange among people from different libraries, with different roles and responsibilities. This interchange can stimulate and motivate individuals towards further learning, broader vision, and application of new ideas in their own libraries. Since few libraries are fully self-sufficient in producing their own staff development programs, they often tap continuing education opportunities existing outside the library to complement and supplement learning activities within the library.

Thus, both staff development and continuing education are significant for library personnel. The effective development of the library's human resources is indeed a survival issue, for the ability of libraries to meet the information needs of their society depends on the people who staff them. In describing human resources development as "the optimization of people," Gordon Lippitt indicates that this field, evolving over the last twenty-five years, has produced "a considerable array of fine techniques, methods, and 'programs' ... and ... a body of experience with the process of developing human resources."[5] Human resources development brings the disciplines of personnel training and development, adult learning, program planning, and organization development together. It emphasizes the view of the person as an individual with common and unique needs working in an organization with a mission to accomplish. Linking learning with work, it acknowledges that the possibility of growing towards greater effectiveness is unending. Now a distinct entity, the information and expertise that results from this expanding body of knowledge can, if utilized, serve well the growing need for sound staff development and continuing education efforts in librarianship.

Aware of the impacts possible through the development of human resources, many in librarianship are active, building staff development programs in libraries and encouraging continuing education activities statewide and nationally. The potential impact from concentrated, well-planned staff development efforts tends to attract, prepare, and retain a committed core of capable people, able to work as a team. Concentrated on a particular staff in a particular library or library system, staff development utilizes the gamut of learning and working opportunities to develop, apply, and reinforce the growth of personnel. The abilities of individual staff members are strengthened, thus improving overall library effectiveness. Personnel are more clear in their understanding of their own place in the organization and how their jobs relate to those of others. Substantial organizational changes, such as changed decision-making responsibilities or a new management style, are often initiated by staff development. Staff development strives for both individual and organizational outcomes, and for short- and long-range achievements.

The impact of continuing education, however, tends to be somewhat more diffuse. Although increased effectiveness of libraries and personnel is again the desired outcome, continuing education embraces a broad concept of the present situation and a vision of the probable future. Anticipating how the present and future will affect libraries requires a long-range view beyond the scope of a single library. Major changes in librarianship, such as the concepts and techniques of outreach or networking, have been sparked or sustained through farsighted learning activities. Continuing education is a direct and effective means to develop and demonstrate leadership capabilities in library personnel. As with staff development, continuing education intends that library staff members will apply what they learn both to their existing tasks and to new assignments. By so doing, they strengthen their own performance and the effectiveness of the library.

Although valuable results can come from isolated efforts, solid benefits are more likely to be achieved from planning rather than from hope and chance. A systematic approach to staff development and continuing education increases the possibility and predictability of significant outcomes. Such an approach offers the strength of sound planning and avoids the waste of dispersed and uncoordinated action. Considering the entirety of learning as such, a systematic approach analyzes needs, sets goals and objectives, develops and implements plans to accomplish those objectives, and evaluates the effectiveness of the effort. With this approach, the quality of educational events is consistently higher, with effective and efficient use of resources, such as people, facilities, funding, and materials. There is minimal duplication of administrative or educational efforts. Planning and evaluation information is accessible and can be used to determine cost effectiveness and accountability as well as to plan future efforts using the experience and results from previous ones. Systematically planned learning activities correlate more closely with on-going processes of identifying needs, fostering self-directed study, and providing a sequence of learning levels. Most importantly, of course, the objectives are more likely to be achieved.

As part of a systematic approach to staff development and continuing education, this book specifically distinguishes between a learning program and activities. A **program** consists of a coordinated variety of learning activities that are sequentially planned over a substantial time span and are directed toward defined objectives. **Activities**, on the other hand, are discrete but coordinated components of a program designed to produce results that help to achieve program objectives as well as more specific educational objectives. Learning activities include a wide range of possibilities: conferences and conventions, institutes and workshops, orientation and job rotation, fellowships and scholarships, self-study and publications. Any combination of these might make up a given program with the selection of activities depending, in large measure, on the anticipated impact on program objectives. A successful learning program evolves through sound planning, integrated implementation, and on-going evaluation. Each of these vital functions is more effectively accomplished through a systematic approach.

For example, the goal of a continuing education program of a library association over a three-year period might be: develop an awareness to the potential within the concept of interlibrary cooperation and to produce the ability to achieve that potential by developing the necessary technical and human skills. The activities planned for that program might include: conference presentations and demonstrations, regional workshops on networking and group decision-making, a series of informational articles in the association's quarterly publication, dissemination of information about learning opportunities outside the region that are related to the topic, and availability of a consultant to help with problem-solving found essential in working out networking decisions. Such a program, of course, presumes that the association's decision-makers are clear and in agreement as to the association's priorities, that the need actually exists, and that resources are available to be tapped. This example illustrates the systematic approach to a priority need with a number of activities responding to that need.

In spite of the soundness of such a systematic approach, reflex response to specific and isolated needs with specific and isolated activities is still common. Habitual reflexes of this nature prompt individuals, libraries, agencies, and associations to bypass the systematic development of a thoughtful program designed to meet priority needs first and to plan long-range and coordinated efforts. The knee-jerk response to an emergency need is occasionally appropriate and may be an inevitable interim phase on the way to developing a more systematic approach.

Improved learning opportunities can become increasingly available, however, if those seeking to create or sustain programs of learning for library personnel utilize a systematic approach to program planning. Given the present need and the prevalent approach to programs and activities employed by individuals, libraries, library schools, state agencies, and library associations, each of these areas of responsibility would be more assured of the immediate and long-range results they desire by using this approach. Skilled library personnel, able to effectively respond to the information needs of the library's clientele is the outcome sought through learning programs.

Identifying possible results is only part of the picture, though, when considering a learning program, no matter how systematically it may be planned. Two issues exist in relation to staff development and continuing education. Confronting both consumers and producers of learning, the realities of cost and incentive are factors that cannot be ignored.

A major reason often given by individuals and organizations for not engaging in learning activities is: "It costs too much." Certainly organizational resources within a library, agency, or association have limits. Likewise, personal resources, including time, are precious to the individual and must be allocated among a number of priorities. When the cost of learning is viewed as an investment rather than an expense, however, it appears in a different light.

Over the last twenty years, business and industry have done much to distinguish between cost and investment in relation to the training and development of personnel. The general conclusion has been that *not* to develop the organization's human resources entails significant costs, such as lower productivity, poor safety, organizational ineffectiveness, low morale, and personnel turnover. Quality programs of staff development actually can improve service and productivity, often at a savings. And, from the perspective of the individual, an investment in learning can produce greater job satisfaction, mobility, interest, and salary. These benefits, of course, must be balanced against the allocation of personal time and money to other personal priorities. These various investment factors, when identified, help direct decision-making.

Outright costs also must be considered. For the producer of a learning program, the cost of planning and administering the program; the cost of space, training materials, equipment and overhead; and the cost of evaluation can be anticipated. The learner or employer often absorbs salaries for staff time, and sometimes for travel and living expenses as well as fees. Some costs will be obvious and can be easily predicted, but others will be less visible. Initially, such costs are often difficult to predict. Concern with costs also brings forth a definite responsibility for accountability: where do the funds come from? where do they go? what good do they do? what else could they be spent for? The ability of the individual and the organization to understand learning as an investment, and then to weigh the alternatives and budget the resources is vital.

Three practical suggestions can help extend the benefits and reduce the costs for learning for an individual or organization. First, a sound, on-going evaluation effort that reviews activities and functions will determine what is worthwhile and can enable culling what is not. Second, activities planned to achieve more than a single purpose will increase the result for roughly the same cost. Third, strong capabilities within the organization or individual for self-learning will give long-range results, assure that the learning will have strong impact, and decrease the cost. Those people engaging in learning efforts need to know the full range of costs and to understand what can and cannot be realistically expected from learning. These costs must then be compared with the implications of the costs of not helping personnel grow.

The second issue that learners and producers of learning must address is incentives for learning. Incentives motivate personnel to engage in learning and motivate libraries, agencies, and associations to produce learning activities. Often termed rewards and recognition, they are the benefits that result from engaging in learning activities. For the learner, incentives might be salary increment, promotion, certificates, academic credits, esteem, or personal satisfaction. For the producer of learning activities, the incentives might be improved library service, increased production, exercise of leadership, or professional acknowledgement. Incentives prompt involvement in learning, but they vary in their importance depending on the learner and on the producer. The issue is not whether rewards and recognition are valued, but rather, what is suitable, acceptable, and equitable recompense in exchange for being actively involved in learning.

Presently, individuals continuing their learning after their pre-service education do so voluntarily rather than by mandate or requirement. Libraries, agencies, and associations produce learning activities guided by their sense of organizational mission. As with other fields, however, growing emphasis at the state level is being placed on the possibility of required certification of librarians. At the national level, recognition systems are being studied. These efforts are likely to give direction to future incentives for learning as well as to increase the pressure for institutionalization of learning for library personnel.

In the meantime, however, incentives are largely unmandated. Learners view the anticipated benefits against the effort and expense as they make their decisions. Libraries, agencies, and associations work toward their organizational goals, fitting in learning opportunities where they seem appropriate and needed. Each of these issues (cost and incentives) is controversial and unresolved as yet. Although leaders in librarianship seek desirable directions, the present situation is relatively undetermined, without standards and regulations.

Even though learning for library personnel is largely self-determined, there is no lack of interest and action. Activities proliferate, and library literature evidences their increasing importance. Individuals actively seek their own learning and help others to do the same. Libraries engage in staff development more consciously and deliberately than ever before. Leading state agencies have long had active programs of continuing education and many are increasing their activities. Other states are following their patterns or designing new approaches.

All levels of library associations (state, regional, and national) are increasingly focusing on continuing education as a major organizational purpose. They are producing more continuing education within or in addition to conferences, and they are forming new organizational components or charging existing ones with increased responsibility for continuing education. The Continuing Library Education Network and Exchange (CLENE) now exists, offering the first solid hope of a nation-wide possibility for leadership in learning.

These many efforts on all levels to increase learning opportunities in librarianship indicate the value of human resources in this total picture. For a long time, efforts have been directed toward current and pressing concerns, such as building functional physical facilities, developing collections of value and substance, seeking stable funding sources, and adapting relevant technology to library functions. Knowledgeable and able people are certainly vital to accomplish each of these. Increased interest in staff development and continuing education reflects this awareness of and need for able human resources. The growing interest and activity, however, may not be sufficient for the future. The isolated, uncoordinated activity approach has been done to the end point of its effectiveness. Learners demand more value for their time and money, library directors are more concerned with accountability for funds, educators are more interested in quality outcomes, agencies and associations are more interested in results for their investment. A high standard of program development, in contrast to the continued production of activities, will take some time to evolve. But, in view of the need, the present, not the future, is an appropriate time to work toward that goal.

NOTES

[1] Elizabeth W. Stone, Ruth Patrick, and Barbara Conroy, *Continuing Library and Information Science Education: Final Report to the National Commission on Libraries and Information Science* (Washington, D.C.: Government Printing Office, 1974; also published by American Society for Information Science), pp. 1-2.

[2] National Commission on Libraries and Information Science, *Toward a National Program for Library and Information Services: Goals for Action* (Washington, D.C.: Government Printing Office, 1975), p. 44.

[3] Samuel Rothstein, "Nobody's Baby: A Brief Sermon on Continuing Professional Education," *Library Journal* 90:2226-2227 (May 15, 1965).

[4] Significant works on areas of responsibility for providing learning opportunities for library personnel include: American Library Association, Library Administration Division, Staff Development Committee, "Guidelines to the Development of Human Resources in Libraries: Rationale, Policies, Programs and Recommendations," *Library Trends* 20:97-117 (July, 1971); Association of American Library Schools, "A Position Paper by the Study Committee on the Role of the Association of American Library Schools in Continuing Library Education" (Paper distributed at 1972 annual meeting, Chicago, Illinois, January, 1972); Peter Hiatt, "The Educational Third Dimension, III. Toward the Development of a National Program of Continuing Education for Library Personnel,"

Library Trends 20:169-83 (July 1971); Allie Beth Martin and Maryann Duggan, *Continuing Education for Librarians in the Southwest: A Survey and Recommendations* (Dallas, Texas: Southwestern Library Association, 1973); Joseph F. Shubert, "Continuing Education in Ohio," *Illinois Libraries* 56, no. 6:471-76 (June 1974); Grace T. Stevenson, "Training for Growth—The Future For Librarians," *ALA Bulletin* 61:278-86 (March 1967); Elizabeth W. Stone, *Continuing Library and Information Science Education*, pp. 2-78 to 2-82 (1974); Elizabeth W. Stone, "Continuing Education: Avenue to Adventure," *School Libraries* 18:37-46 (Summer 1969); Elizabeth W. Stone, *Continuing Library Education as Viewed in Relation to Other Continuing Professional Education Movements* (Washington, D.C.: American Society for Information Science, 1975); Elizabeth W. Stone, "Continuing Education in Librarianship: Ideas for Action," *American Libraries* 1:543-51 (June 1970); and Ruth E. Warncke, "Continuing Education: Whose Responsibility?" *Minnesota Libraries* 24:59-65 (Autumn 1973). In addition to these specific references, most state library agencies and library associations have bylaw statements, position statements, or committee charges that reflect their perceived responsibility. Also, libraries and state library agencies often have policy statements or procedures that indicate their stance.

[5] Gordon L. Lippitt, "Criteria for Evaluating Human Resource Development," *Training and Development Journal* 30, no. 10:3 (October 1976).

PART I–PLANNING THE LEARNING PROGRAM

The success of any learning program depends to a great extent on the soundness with which it is planned. A successful program or activity can be traced to adequate planning more often than to any other single cause. Conversely, an unsuccessful program or activity may result from inadequate planning, even though other reasons are usually cited when events do not work out well. Knowing what to plan reduces the number of unknowns, assures more cohesive implementation, and increases the possibility for successful results. Planning can allow people to predict and sometimes forestall problems and thus keep to a minimum the risks and unforeseen circumstances likely to occur during implementation.

Planning is the process of making deliberate decisions in order to develop the means that will be used to accomplish the desired end(s). Fundamental to assuring a systematic approach, planning requires a portion of the investment of time, effort, and funds earmarked for the program. In addition to an ability for effective problem solving and program administration, planners need a tested belief in the planning process itself. And, a firmly rooted patience must bolster this belief. Without the ability, the belief, and the patience, planning may be difficult to justify since, from the outside, it often appears that little is happening.

Many people, impatient to "get to the doin' part," become frustrated because planning does not show "progress" as readily as does implementation. Actually, the planning process is itself not as apparent as is implementation of the activities themselves. In fact, the question often asked of those who produced a successful program or activity is, "What did you do?" and not, "How did you plan?" Ironically, the well planned program will appear easy and successful when implemented, even though the planning process seemed long and tedious at the time.

As a process, rather than a one-time event, planning requires an initial phase that addresses the questions:

What is the present situation?
What is the desired situation?

and a continuous phase that asks:

What is required next?

Planning for staff development and continuing education puts these three basic questions into the context of a fourth:

In what ways will these plans affect learning or be affected by learning?

Although initial planning is more easily identified as planning per se, it is, in fact, only the first step of the planning effort. Maintaining a viable program requires successive planning efforts.

Initial planning serves to develop program objectives from identified needs. These objectives then guide the development of a program of activities. Implementation of those activities, in turn, can achieve the objectives. The result of the initial planning process is a flexible outline that includes a description of the situation and needs, a statement of program objectives, an action plan of steps and activities designed to accomplish those objectives, and provisions for an evaluation process involving continuous planning.

Continuous planning, on the other hand, incorporates the discoveries and results from program implementation and evaluation into further decision making. Also termed developmental planning, it is closely linked with evaluation, for planners review the experiences and results of implementation, revise their original plans, and use the available information to aid them in making decisions on subsequent steps. Since planning may be based on inaccurate assumptions and misinterpretation of the evidence of need, initial planning must be flexible and open to modifications as they become necessary. Of course, planning is sometimes more ambitious than implementation is feasible. Then, the principle modification becomes that of scaling back.

Planning is the first point of program quality control, for planners attempt to anticipate possible problems, to predict what will happen, and to prepare for those planned results and their probable implications. Planning is also the first opportunity to correlate program aims with organizational goals, since an effective program must be a part of the fabric of the organization, joined with its purpose, direction, and functions. An integral part of the organization rather than an "easy-on, easy-off" frill, the contemplated program will build on existing organizational strengths, utilize available resources, and address gaps in personnel or library performance. As Figure 1 illustrates, the program, with its goals, objectives, and activities has a two-way relationship with the goals, objectives, functions, facilities, staff, and structure of the organization, whether that organization is a library, an agency, or an association. Changes in the organization will affect the program, and, conversely, changes in the program will influence the total organization.

Figure 1

The Learning Program in the Organization

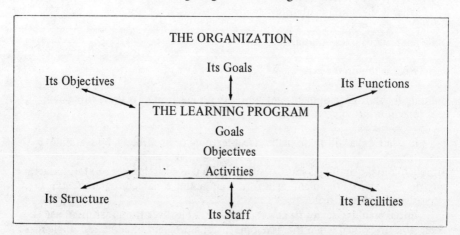

Likewise, the *ways* in which planning is accomplished must suit the organization's distinctive style. Usually, the most satisfactory and lasting way to achieve a reciprocal relationship between a program and its sponsoring organization is through active involvement of people in the organization. Such involvement is also an effective and desirable way to accomplish planning and implementation.

A major precept throughout this book is that continuous involvement is important both to the individual and to the organization. Results from the learning program will affect the use of the library's human resources and, at the same time, enable individuals to reach toward their own goals for learning and growth. Thus, a broad and deep impact both on the organization and on individuals is intended. The desired extent of this impact calls for a commensurate commitment to and involvement in the planning process.

Broad involvement during planning may have several advantages. Major program decisions involve choices of topic, instructional method, scheduling, allocation of resources, the kind and extent of dissemination of information, and priorities. Those decisions must be accurate, balanced, and comprehensive. Thus, since decisions made from a single person's perspective are necessarily limited, the use of multiple viewpoints in considering important decisions reduces the likelihood of overlooking significant factors.

Also, when a number of people contribute to planning, this reduces tremendously the risk of failure caused by non-acceptance of the program once it is announced. Not only are decisions based on a broader perspective, but the involved individuals can then inform those less involved about what is being done and why. Thus, when those who may participate in the program and those who may be responsible for implementing it are involved in some way in the planning, the program is likely to be more fully understood and accepted.

Involvement can provide continuity for the program as an on-going function as well. This continuity may become very important as circumstances change, new information comes to light, or present program staff members leave. New program directions may be called for or adjustments in the original plan may be required. If a number of people were involved in the planning process, they might then be prepared to make sound recommendations for any such changes and to effect a smooth transition. Again, they function as interpreters, able to explain changes to others less involved.

Finally, broad involvement in planning can in itself be an important learning activity. Planning, as a collaborative effort, can involve individuals who share among them knowledge of libraries, colleagues, and issues. As they work together addressing needs, ways to meet those needs, and essentials for the program as such, they become familiar with the planning process in relation to the specific program at hand. Later, it is reasonable to expect that they will be able and willing to apply what they have learned to other areas of responsibility, having gained practical experience and having seen the value of group involvement in planning demonstrated. Specifically, three areas of learning can be achieved through involvement: learning about the planning process in general, learning about planning specifically for a learning program as such, and learning about the abilities and perspectives of other people in the organization. Direct, obvious benefits come to the organization through the application of these learnings. In addition, the library, agency, or association may benefit from the insights and leadership that surface in participants, even if those qualities previously had been neither recognized nor utilized.

Involvement capitalizes on the opportunities offered by the planning process for people to deepen their commitment, to gain an array of perspectives, to become aware of potential implications and available resources, and to avoid inappropriate or duplicated efforts. The learning program, whether staff development or continuing education, will have a flavor of its own, depending both on its leadership and on those involved in working on the program. This flavor becomes evident during the planning process, the shape of which is determined as much by the organizational context as by those people who guide it.

An involved, supportive style for program planning and implementation relates directly to the principles of adult learning. Thus, such a style will reinforce the primary learning function of the program. Certainly, though, the degree and method of involvement are important factors in establishing a climate for a program. If a number of the program's activities are to include participative learning opportunities in a supportive, non-threatening climate, that approach can be initiated by involving potential learners in the planning process. Those so involved can provide a sense of the appropriateness of particular topics or methods for the larger group for whom the activity will be intended as well as an idea of that group's receptivity. Conversely, as stated above, those involved in planning can share their understanding of the program and its activities with those less involved. This exchange not only leads to better decisions but also creates a setting congenial to further planning and to in-depth learning.

For some libraries, agencies, or associations, involvement of staff in planning will be natural, already developed and functioning. For others, such involvement may be an alien concept resisted in principle and practice. For those seeking to move from the latter approach to the former, staff development or continuing education programs can be employed to facilitate that move. Individuals in organizations contemplating new involvement, however, must avoid easy assumptions that disregard the present nature of their organization. Thus, a word of caution: since the precept of involvement is emphasized throughout this book, descriptions and examples emphasizing involvement will require a good deal of adaptation to be useful in organizations lacking that approach and not consciously desiring to develop it. Consequently, where such suggestions are made, they might be wisely ignored, since false gestures of involvement, unable to be sustained later, should not be used at all.

When achieved, involvement generally provides for better decision making, continuity, understanding, and learning. Yet, the concept of participatory planning requires the leadership, endorsement, and commitment of the program's sponsor or producer and the active support of those to be involved. To be credible, this precept will need to be stated and then consistently demonstrated. Its value is significant, as is its cost.

Where its value is known, however, the specifics of how to achieve involvement become important. A staff development program within a single organization might employ several means of involvement. The continuity of the library and its staff members enables consistent contact with the same people during both initial planning and continuous planning, as well as during implementation. Thus, the results of involvement tend to build in a library, adding a cumulative dimension not possible in a continuing education program through a state agency or library association. With a continuing education program, potential learners are often not known, and, when known, time or distance may restrict their involvement in planning. Their involvement is no less important at this time, just less feasible. Where broad involvement is desired and feasible, however, ways can be found to achieve it.

With or without such involvement, though, methods used to accomplish planning vary. Naturally, organizational parameters define for planners those certain boundaries within which they must work. The planning responsibility may be centered on a single planner or on a staff planning team. The assignment may be broad and open or restricted to a narrow range of responsibilities. The structure for planning may be set or it may permit a good deal of flexibility. Procedures to be used for program planning may be exactly prescribed or left undefined.

Added to these organizational limits are the individual differences of those who will affect or do the planning. Each person will have certain characteristics, values, skills, abilities, and ways of working with others. And, a third set of factors to consider consists of more vaguely defined external influences, such as current priorities in librarianship; crisis situations in the nation, state, or community; and judicial and legislative mandates. These organizational, individual and external elements will each significantly affect the planning process of the learning program.

Along with the consideration of these elements, several typical patterns of program planning can be weighed when making the important choices for planning a learning program. A frequent approach is the use of a planning group with either advisory or decision making responsibilities. Working together, members of the group may identify the program's purpose and direction. One person often coordinates the group's work, convenes meetings, reports results, and provides a central point for communication and administration. Sometimes, that individual also administrates the program and has responsibilities for other duties and decisions as well.

Typically, such a planning group will address the following questions: What results are sought? For whom? When? How will results be achieved? What resources will be needed? How will they be used in the program? What specific evaluative information will be required for subsequent planning? When will this information be needed?

At first, these questions will apply to the development of the program; later, they will apply to specific activities as they actually are planned. The planning group may be responsible for setting long-range general planning directions, supplemented with technical or ad hoc committees that develop learning designs, materials, and logistics for specific activities. Official confirmation of the planning group's authority together with continuing active encouragement from administrators on all levels, is essential to make that group effective.

Library staff development programs often use a planning committee of personnel drawn from within the library itself. The blend of their unique subject knowledge, planning skills, and library perspectives will strengthen the ability of that group to produce a sound plan with a balanced approach. Individuals with previously undeveloped or undemonstrated capabilities can also be included along with those of proven abilities. If possible, potential participants in the program should be included. Representatives of various categories of personnel should be included as working members, but not solely because of their positions. And, since support and encouragement of administrators on all levels will be essential for the success of the resulting plan, administrative involvement will be important.

Continuing education programs through agencies and associations may use a combination of their own staff and the constituency or membership of the client group to compose a planning group. As governmental agencies, state libraries often have a traditional, designated procedure by which they plan. Such procedures have a built-in consistency and continuity. Although not insulated from personnel or institutional changes or from budget cutbacks, agencies can usually plan with some security for the future, providing for alternatives when changes must be made. The agency has a documented tradition, a present mission and locale, and a dependable (if not predictable) future. Also, the state library agency can tap other agencies, at state, regional, and national levels, for specialized assistance.

Most professional library associations, on the other hand, are characterized by frequent changes of personnel and of procedure. New officers and appointees bring fresh ideas of program needs, objectives, and priorities; they also have different methods of approaching continuing education and program planning, as well as varied contexts and contacts with which to work. Plans, priorities and place of operation can shift with each term. Since the results of a program planning process are limited in time, adequate planning may be difficult to justify. Lack of continuity is a major disadvantage.

With the exception of national associations with established continuing education structures and staff, library associations are essentially volunteer organizations encompassing a variety of personal and professional causes. For the most part, local, state, and regional associations function without firmly established structures, procedures, or staff. They have no permanent central location of association records and few permanent tangible resources. Once started, a continuing education program risks being jeopardized by a lack of follow-through effort or by the availability of the interest and expertise required to sustain it. The learning program may fluctuate from top to bottom priority within a few years. Skilled individuals may build the educational capability of the organization for a couple of years only to have that effort regress with successors. These factors impede the ability to plan consistently or long-range. Sound planning, however, is most likely to occur when it is accepted as an important function of a priority program, when it has consistent commitment from association leadership, and when established procedures require and provide for sound means for planning.

Whether for staff development or for continuing education, the integrity and quality of the planning process will be a major influence on any program's success. Thus, the planning process should not be bypassed or regarded as unimportant. Nor should it be advocated solely as a pro forma gesture, one without real substance. Rather, active and deliberate efforts are required to establish the planning process, identifying what needs to be done and how best to do that. Then, initiative is essential to coordinate the steps that bring together the people and other resources necessary to plan. Particularly at first, these arrangements are best if kept flexible, allowing for necessary modification.

These active and deliberate efforts to assure planning are important, for planning serves to "build in" the essential qualities and conditions that will assure a program's success. Planning must take into account both the motivations and incentives that are important to learners and the hindrances that may prevent them from learning. Planners must also strive to match the program to organizational aims. Planning can make the most of existing organizational strengths and can capitalize on available opportunities. Foresighted planning can anticipate results from the program and the implications inherent in those results.

Most important of all, a soundly planned program can ensure the necessary links between learning and the application of that learning on the job. Planning, when well done, can direct the program in such a way that the intended, cohesive impact is made on both the library and the learners. Planning increases the possibility that this impact will be feasible and desirable. Without adequate planning, successful implementation of any program as a whole (or of its activities) is unlikely. Thus, throughout planning, preparation is being made for implementation.

GUIDELINE 1—GATHER NEEDS INFORMATION

Needs are dynamic, constantly shifting and evolving, buffeted by organizational, societal, and technological changes, sparked by current causes and issues, activated by personal priorities and job shifts. The generalized needs that come from these varied sources all have implications for a learning program, as do more specific organizational circumstances. For instance, because of changes in the library, its personnel may suddenly have new tasks that require new skills. Or, individuals may seek to prepare themselves for future responsibilities or to follow growing areas of their own specialized interests. Often, visionary leadership with a broad view of the library field may foresee a trend and wish to prepare for its impact by increasing the awareness of library decision makers about the implications for libraries. Further, more action-oriented leaders may wish to involve library personnel both in learning about changes and in helping to plan for coping with them. Each of these factors is likely to result in some needs for learning; thus, each will have some influence on the learning program.

This Guideline accents the importance of identifying needs as a beginning step in planning a learning program. It presents the various types of needs in both descriptive and chart form, and it describes the areas in which those needs may be identified. Several methods and techniques are suggested, together with criteria for selecting those most appropriate for gathering needs information. A systematic approach to needs assessment is suggested with details on how to develop such an action plan. Guideline 2 describes the analysis of the gathered information.

Importance

Gathering and analyzing needs information is an essential and early phase in planning for staff development and continuing education programs. Identification of patterns of learning needs will indicate the scope and direction of the contemplated program as well as how roles and responsibilities might be allocated. Through discovering the needs of the library personnel for whom it is responsible, the library, agency, or association can verify whether the contemplated program is indeed congruent with the organizational purpose. Also, identifying overall needs offers a rough benchmark against which the accomplishments of the program can later be measured. Without knowing the actual needs, assumptions are likely. And, if they are inaccurate, use of those assumptions will result in planning a misdirected program. Although more detailed needs information may be required later when planning for particular activities, early identification of general needs directs the initial development of the overall program.

Unless solidly based on actual needs, planned activities will fail to interest and attract learners. Obviously, without learners, established program goals and objectives will be unmet. Most studies concerning education for practitioners have found directly or by implication that potential learners seek to match learning opportunities with their perceived job-related needs. In a landmark study, Stone identified the close relationship of the content of a learning activity to the learner's work situation as the primary motivation prompting librarians to participate in continuing education activities. Other factors, such as the method, accessibility, cost, scheduling, and expected rewards are also significant for the person and the library, but less so than the relationship between the content of the activity and the on-the-job need.[1]

The process of needs assessment also offers an early and important opportunity to inform and involve library personnel, some of whom may be potential learners. This first step can build interest and expectations for later program activities as well as identify the needs of which those activities should be based. The assessment can begin two-way communication between learners and the program planner(s). Often, the extent of involvement at this point consists of responding to printed forms or to interviews. In other instances, involvement might include helping to plan for needs assessment or gathering and analyzing information.

For both the organization and the learner, however, the investment in assessing learning needs is justified only if effective action results. Without necessary follow-through, studies of needs may go out of date, their value unrealized. Library personnel, asked about their learning needs, begin to expect that some means will be provided them to help meet those needs. If nothing happens following that needs assessment, the credibility of both the organization and the program may be impaired.

Definitions

A successful program is designed to respond to real learning needs. **Needs**, in the specific context of staff development and continuing education, can be defined as the lack of essential knowledge, skills, or attitudes that, in turn, prevent satisfactory job performance or interferes with an individual's potential for assuming different or greater responsibilities, now or in the future. Identifying learning needs presumes: 1) that real needs exist, and 2) that those needs can be answered, at least in part, by some kind of education or training. Some identified needs may require something other than education or training as an effective response, such as new equipment, organizational change, or career redirection.

The needs that require learning, training, or practice on the part of the individual learner, however, are those primarily addressed by a learning program. **Needs assessment** is the process that identifies those needs systematically by gathering and analyzing available information. In contrast, identifying needs by chance usually leads to a pattern of short-range, troubleshooter efforts aimed to remedy an immediate problem or crisis. A program based on such a random approach has only a remote chance of making a significant, long-range impact on either the learners or the library. Thus, substantial investment to meet such randomly identified needs is usually questionable. If needs are identified through a careful, sustained assessment using sound methods and techniques, however, further investment in developing and implementing a learning program is more likely to provide a satisfactory return.

The term "need" is not one that can be easily or clearly defined. Monette, viewing the concept of educational need, suggests that the fuzziness around the term is due to its indiscriminate application. Specialized uses such as "felt needs" to describe self-perceived interests, or "real needs" to indicate an observer's view of another person's needs, result from efforts to determine the best ways to assess needs. Monette goes on to state:

> Given the variety of uses to which it has been subjected, the
> concept of need may soon become worthless for program
> planners unless it is defined more narrowly. Perhaps educa-
> tional need might be defined either from the point of view
> of the individual learner, as a desire/want/interest; or, from
> an external perspective, as an objectively determined deficiency
> in knowledge, skills, or attitudes.[2]

With this caution in mind, areas of need, types of need, and methods by which needs can be determined are explored herein.

Areas

Learning needs in librarianship rise from three broad areas: the individual, the library, and the community. The most tangible and easily identifiable needs are usually those of people working in libraries. Often, their performance in relation to their present or future responsibilities is inadequate because of insufficient information or ability. Even the finest education and experience must be updated continually to prevent obsolescence. And, what the individual already knows through education and experience must be tailored to fit new situations and changed circumstances. Thus, the individual has needs to learn.

In the second area, the needs of the library include those issues and concerns that involve its ability as an organization to achieve its present mission and objectives, to fulfill its institutional responsibilities, and to prepare for its anticipated future directions. More specifically, library needs that provide focus for a learning program include those components that function ineffectively or those faced with substantial change in personnel, function, or workload. Or, needs may result from attempts to plan and effect deliberate organizational change, with administrators facilitating that effort through a learning program. An example of this is the shift many libraries are making from traditional styles of management to participative management. This kind of organizational change requires strong staff development efforts to assure the possibility of the transition as well as to support and sustain the change once made.

For a staff development program, those learning efforts designed to respond to such needs may be sustained, specific, and at considerable depth. A continuing education effort channeled through an agency or association, on the other hand, must address such needs through individual staff members at a learning activity spanning a relatively short period of time. This approach relies on those individuals to then apply their learnings upon their return to their libraries.

The third area of need relates to the community, that is, the clientele that the library serves. For libraries contemplating staff development, the term community would include the town, the school, or the university in which that institution is located. Significant change in its community affects the library, its services and its staff. For example, university reorganization may directly affect the library's structure, roles, and responsibilities. Staff development efforts will be needed to assure continued library services to students and faculty, who will also have to adjust to their new functions. Or, pronounced population shifts and deterioration of a central city may alter public library services and shift personnel and functions more heavily to a branch system. Staff development then would be essential to prepare staff for the anticipated changes.

For agencies or associations planning for continuing education, community needs will be somewhat different, not in principle but in nature. In this case, the community is the society and the role of librarianship within that society with needs arising from service trneds, legislative changes, national crises, and the ideas of library leaders. The impact of these needs on individual libraries and library personnel is most often achieved at that level by agencies and associations with programs of continuing education activities. For example, national and state affirmative action legislation affects libraries, and an association-produced institute might assist library personnel to understand and plan for this impact. Or, interlibrary loan code changes may be addressed by regional state library workshops, which could teach new procedures as they are instituted. Thus, the community has needs that can be addressed with staff development and continuing education efforts.

These same three areas provide the motivations that nurture and reward the investment required by staff development and continuing education. The staff member whose need and desire to do a better job are met by learning opportunities provided through the library is thus motivated to expend the time and effort required to learn and the initiative to apply those learnings on the job. When the library's needs are met through planned learning activities, administrators are encouraged to continue or even expand such programs to answer new needs. The community, seeing evidence of improved services, is more likely to give the library priority and needed support.

These three areas of general needs provide, in turn, an overview for understanding more specific types of needs and the sources and methods that may be used to discover those needs.

Types

Specific types of needs can be grouped within a general construct to present a brief picture of needs that might exist in a library. In Figure 2, examples of typical needs of library personnel are arranged within a framework of six categories. This chart can aid in planning ways first to identify and then to meet those different types of needs. This construct is a useful tool for gathering and analyzing needs information and later for planning the program and learning activities. The three kinds of learning have been identified by Paul Hersey and Kenneth M. Blanchard as skills needed at various levels in *Management of Organizational Behavior: Utilizing Human Resources* (2nd ed., Englewood Cliffs, NJ: Prentice-Hall, 1972, pp. 6-7).

Action Plan

Gathering information about the various learning needs of library personnel may be a very simple task: assembling various reports and documents that indicate current needs; supplementing that with interviews of key people whose perspective

Figure 2
Categories and Examples of Typical Needs in Libraries

RESULTS EXPECTED → KINDS OF LEARNING ↓	KNOWLEDGE (Awareness of facts, ideas and concepts relevant to a task, a function or an organization)	SKILLS (Ability to apply knowledge proficiently in a manner appropriate to the situation)	ATTITUDES (A position, and often behavior, that indicates an opinion, disposition, or manner with regard to a person, a thing, or a situation)
CONCEPTUAL (Ability to formulate, understand, and apply concepts and ideas)	–organizational structure –available community resources –present directions of librarianship –own position description	–how to plan for a new service program –how to catalog a book –how to select materials	–awareness of self –image of self –value of others –desire for quality work –sensitivity
TECHNICAL (Ability to apply a particular art or skill)	–the audio-visual equipment market –new book selection tools	–how to keypunch –how to operate equipment –how to file –how to use audio-visual equipment –how to produce a slide-tape presentation	–receptivity to using new methods –receptivity to an altered work flow pattern –acceptance of the importance of the personal value of work
HUMAN (Ability to understand and work effectively with others)	–cultural differences –sociological principles –communication principles –how people behave	–how to supervise –how to do a reference interview –how to counsel adult learners	–view of mankind –importance of the value of interaction with others –feelings of prejudice

is thought valuable; then analyzing that information to develop program objectives and its design. On the other hand, gathering needs information may be a complex, involved procedure that involves a survey questionnaire of all staff members, the correlation of that with their job performance, and, finally, the preparation of personnel profiles for individuals as well as overall patterns including the entire library staff.

For a staff development program, the assessment of needs will be focused on the personnel in that library. The assessment might be done by an individual on the staff or a committee or, perhaps, a consultant from outside the library. The responsibility might be limited to needs assessment, or it might entail planning for and even implementing the program. For a continuing education program, needs information may be routinely gathered by agency field consultants or association representatives as an integral part of their normal functions. This information then would be tabulated and forwarded to a single individual responsible for needs assessment or for planning a program. Or, an agency or association will sometimes launch a special needs assessment project, with staff to study the needs of a specific target group of library personnel. Such a study could be in cooperation with other interested organizations (such as a library school or research group) able to use the results for their own purposes.

Whether the assessment is simple or complex, a systematic approach can guide its planning and implementation, enabling it to produce usable information to develop and maintain the program. Four questions can help in planning for gathering the needs information:

- What information is required?
- Who can supply that information?
- What are the best ways to acquire the information?
- Who should gather the information, and how, when, and where should it be gathered?

The answers to these questions can help in evolving a plan to discover the needs existing in a given situation. Once gathered, the information then must be analyzed, the second step in needs assessment.

What information is required? The needs assessment process can identify several categories of information useful to program planners. Perhaps the most important single kind of information obtained from the needs assessment will be the topics that are needed for learning activities, such as supervisory skills, library applications of automated techniques, or public relations. An initial definition of topics or themes indicates general program direction, but it may not be specific enough in itself to be a basis for planning the actual activities. A later assessment effort will be called for if the initial assessment was not sufficiently specific. For example, an expressed need for "communication" may, for some individuals, refer to interpersonal communication skills and, for others, may mean they want to know how to plan and manage organizational communications effectively within a single library or a system of libraries. When specific needs like these can be pinpointed early, later efforts for further needs assessment may be saved. Often, however, this degree of specificity is not possible initially.

In addition to this specificity, another important dimension of the topic is the level of need. For example, one topic might be required by those seeking basics at a beginner level of awareness. Or, an altogether different aspect of the same topic may be required by those with some background and experience, and yet another by those with more advanced knowledge and skills. Determining the appropriate level of need often requires some perspective on how aware the person is about his/her need to know. Often, a particular expressed need can be correlated with both the work responsibilities and the type of learner to understand the level of need. Asking for information such as a job title can be helpful for staff development in a single library; for continuing education, this is rarely clearcut, specific, or commonly shared, since job labels vary extensively among libraries and titles often conceal more than they may reveal in relation to an individual's need. Especially useful for needs assessment for continuing education, however, will be information about the potential learner's past experience with the topic, either as a result of a job assignment or through a previous learning opportunity.

In addition to the identification of topic, other important kinds of information gathered during the needs assessment phase are helpful to program planners. Preferred methods and formats for learning (such as workshops, lectures, demonstrations, or home study) may be useful. To aid later scheduling of activities, comments about feasible timing might be elicited (such as one session at an annual conference, a week between school terms, or two days in the spring). Agencies and associations may ask about preferred locale for learning activities, thereby giving direction to their decisions about the geographical pattern of continuing education activities. When correlated and analyzed, these various types of information give guidance in program planning.

Who can supply that information? This, in turn, raises other questions, such as: Who really knows the needs? Who is available to be asked? Who will be willing to respond? What indirect sources are valid?

Two approaches are possible. One approach obtains information directly from the potential learner, and this is supplemented by the views of colleagues, supervisors, and others. The other approach uses indirect sources such as library literature, documentation, surveys, and research. The first approach begins to involve people in the program even before activities are conducted, building anticipation for the program. The latter is often more easily done, usually less expensive. Sometimes both approaches are used to cross-check or supplement each other.

The direct approach seeks the individual's view of his or her own needs. Since people usually have a sense of their needs and interests, such self-assessment can provide a useful, valid starting point. Several considerations are important to note, however. First, individuals rarely can identify or clearly define their full needs, either in relation to a topic or in relation to the extent of their own knowledge and abilities. Second, an individual may identify as needs what are actually only wants or interests. Third, self-perception tends to be more accurate for immediate, tangible needs than for issue-oriented needs. And, finally, some individuals find it emotionally difficult to admit having needs at all, for, in their view, needs may be equated with a personal inadequacy.

Often, to round out the information obtained from a self-assessment, the perceptions of colleagues, supervisors, and supervisees can provide additional information. Administrators, with their overview of library needs, may help to define potential needs of staff by indicating anticipated as well as existing work requirements. Personal and job perspectives, work experiences, and attitudes, as well as personalities, will condition the responses from different individuals. Thus, responses can be expected to vary from one another, yet all must be seen as equally valid. These differences will tend to balance each other when the gathered information is analyzed.

The second approach, that of using indirect sources, may be the quickest and most feasible means to establish the general needs on which to build a program. Library literature provides a cross-section of issues, problems, and concerns in the library field, many of which have implications for staff development and continuing education programs. Journals and newsletters report results of needs assessment surveys of particular groups of library personnel. Observations and comments of those who work with a wide array of libraries are recorded in periodicals and give general information about possible needs in typical problem areas. The reported results of work groups and committees often identify areas of change, such as plans for new service programs, modified standards and policies, and changing federal and state priorities.

Several surveys and studies have, in recent years, focused on the learning needs of library personnel. Some of these have looked generally at the entire field. Others have used a more selective approach, defining a specific group perhaps for a particular purpose.[3] The general studies have indicated a remarkable unanimity as to the topics most often identified by practitioners as being useful to them:

- administration and management—systems analysis, philosophy and techniques of management, planning and programming, motivation, supervisory skills, budgeting.

- new technology—automation, applications of machines in libraries, computer basics, centralized processing, the impact of technological innovations on libraries.

- non-print media—media uses and applications, management and collection of media, creativity and innovation with materials, technical skills with media.

- human relations—communications, group dynamics, leadership development, interpersonal attitudes and abilities.

- updating—impacts of changes and trends in society and in the library field, innovations and their results, evaluations of new approaches to old problems.

These findings might provide a basis for assumptions as to the range or types of need that a program might address. Such assumptions can then provide a way to identify those specific needs unique to the staff in a particular library or the membership of a particular association.

These studies are useful, not because their findings can be substituted for a needs assessment in a given situation, but because the findings establish parameters within which to guide and focus a more specific needs assessment than would otherwise be possible. If such assumptions are made, close checking throughout assessment should be made to see if discrepancies appear that might show the assumptions to be faulty.

To supplement the direct information from people themselves and the broader approach of using surveys and studies from library literature, the people doing needs assessment for staff development can tap several other sources of information within their organization to provide information quickly and economically. Some of the sources most readily available are meetings, records, reports, plans, policies, and procedures. From these sources might come direct indications of needs. Or, implications for needs might be seen in changes that occur within the organization.

Many current and regular procedures may already provide information about the needs and problems of personnel. For example, regular and special meetings are held in every library as part of accomplishing the organizational business. These meetings can indicate staff needs for new knowledge, skills, or attitudes, since they often center on a problem, a crisis, or a new policy. Existing records and reports can also provide needs information as they signal difficulties and accomplishments. Annual progress reports show trends and directions, thus indicating areas of growth for different groups of personnel. Budget figures and user complaints can point out areas where efficiency and effectiveness might be improved. Personnel records, including appraisal interviews and evaluation forms, may indicate the learning needs of individuals on a regular and consistent basis.

In addition to these already existing sources of needs information, special efforts fitting the regular organizational procedures may be used to obtain needs information. For example, an annual personnel questionnaire about learning needs may be instituted as a regular procedure. The advantage of such a special survey is that it draws attention and helps personnel focus on the need for learning and growing. At the same time, it evidence the organization's commitment to the learning program. Another example of a special effort is when new plans, policies, and procedures result from dealing with problems that confront staff members individually or the library as a whole. Since these changes often modify responsibilities or require new organizational structures or new staff skills, special attention would be warranted in looking at the implications of these changes for personnel learning needs.

A key consideration in looking for sources of information is, of course, the people for whom the learning program is designed. Certainly, the entire staff of a library is essential for the effective delivery of library services. Yet, educational programming efforts, especially those through agencies and associations, often address only the needs of the professional librarian, leaving the needs of paraprofessional personnel either unmet or met only through staff development efforts. Some learning activities, such as learning interpersonal communications techniques or acquiring information about technological developments, are just as applicable to the paraprofessional as to the professional. Sometimes, however, paraprofessionals are eliminated from relevant learning experiences because of regulations and actual statements of eligibility requirements. Or, their participation may be discouraged more subtly because of inferences in program publicity or simply through established practices. Programs of staff development and continuing education that seek to improve the competencies of library personnel cannot justifiably exclude any level of personnel. Thus, needs on all staff levels need to be assessed to obtain useful, reliable results.

What are the best ways to acquire the information? This question opens the exploration of alternative techniques that can be used to gather information about needs. Before specific techniques are considered, though, a basic strategy must be selected. Two are possible. One is a thorough, one-time survey of the needs of the group for whom the learning program is being planned. The second is a phased continuum of needs assessment techniques extending over a period of time, using early findings for initial program planning and implementation, and the later information to guide program modifications and subsequent activities.

The one-time strategy provides a solid base of in-depth needs information useful for planners as they begin to develop the program. Since such a survey will not sustain a viable learning program without provision for continuity, a continuing means of needs assessment should be planned to assure that the program addresses current needs. The second strategy employs a variety of techniques to acquire and assemble needs information, often using functions and procedures already in place rather than an isolated, special effort. Both strategies, however, should provide for keeping the results of the needs assessment over the period of time they will be needed for initial and continuous planning and for evaluative purposes. Also, each strategy should establish a continuous needs assessment process to provide for subsequent program planning.

Staff development offers many possibilities for keeping in touch with needs. Patterns of needs emerge and predictability is possible to a certain extent since communications are relatively quick, easy, and continuous. Indeed, identifying needs is often an automatic and integral part of the functions of the library. Once needs are identified, later observations can reveal those that have been sufficiently answered and those that require further learning opportunities. Identification of needs may come about as a useful by-product of an organizational analysis or a job analysis, a performance appraisal system, or a human resources study. For example, an analysis of a library as a whole reveals operating problems, patterns of work flow, conditions that reduce effectiveness and efficiency. Or, an examination of jobs in depth finds unrealistic job specifications, illogical task assignments, or unreasonable production expectations. Or, a focus on individual staff members turns up discrepancies between wants, needs and abilities; an imbalance of requirements and the capacity of the individual; or personnel problems previously ignored. Being alert to these opportunities is an economical way to discover learning needs in a library without the need for elaborate special efforts.

Direct efforts aimed only at needs assessment for a learning program might also be desirable, however, particularly in trying to start a new program. This special emphasis can be useful to draw interest and involvement from the staff and to reveal the library's commitment to the program. In such instances, a survey by questionnaire of staff members might be an initial step. This might include all personnel or a selected sample. The questionnaire might be followed then by selected interviews and a review of performance appraisals for staff members at all levels. To continue this initial effort, regularly scheduled discussions in staff meetings could address potential staff development topics of general value. The personnel office or a staff committee might be responsible for receiving staff development suggestions directly, or an intentional effort might be made in all performance appraisals to explore the needs of each individual for staff development opportunities. This combination of methods and techniques makes the most of the advantages of staff development within a library.

This integrated approach is less possible, however, for continuing education, since keeping track of patterns of the learning needs of library personnel in many different libraries is difficult. Agency personnel and association officers are usually fully occupied with their regular duties, which may not be closely connected with learning needs of library personnel. Sometimes having a single individual assigned the responsibility for discovering learning needs is useful, but the reduced scope of contacts usually hampers the completeness of the effort. Most often, unless a concentrated effort to assess needs is made a priority, the essential step of assessment may be bypassed due to its complexity.

The survey tends to be the most popular method of assessing needs for continuing education programs, but even when the agency or association has a clear concept of its responsibility to do needs assessment, three difficulties arise. Planning a survey well enough to result in the appropriate scope and depth of information is the first challenge. Individuals receiving questionnaires or being interviewed then must be informed and convinced of the importance of responding. And, finally, the fact that program planners are not in frequent or continuous contact with potential learners prevents follow-through on an initial learning needs survey and inhibits real continuity in the assessment process. Because of these difficulties, state and regional associations are not likely to have continuous, consistent processes. National associations with a firm priority of continuing education, though, have staff and committee arrangements that build in the possibility of necessary follow-through. Likewise, state agencies may provide for continuity of the assessment process through regular policies and procedures.

In some situations, needs assessment efforts for continuing education might be coordinated with another organization. For example, if both the state agency and the state library association would benefit from identifying learning needs, they might combine their efforts. Such a joint endeavor could provide greater depth than either might manage if working alone, would eliminate duplication of effort, would bring the influence of both sponsors to the task, and would effect significant economy. In some instances, a joint needs assessment leads to cooperatively sponsored learning activities.

Criteria

Whatever approach is devised, whatever methods and techniques are selected, specific criteria can aid planners seeking to make appropriate choices for a particular organization in a particular situation with particular staff capabilities. The following criteria can guide selection:

- Needs assessment should gather only usable, valid information.

- Needs assessment should be a sustained process. Since individuals, libraries, and librarianship change, it is to be expected that their needs will also change.

- Needs assessment should include all levels of personnel. Everyone will have needs, even though the type and urgency of those needs will vary.

- Needs assessment should utilize a number of different sources and employ a number of different techniques to minimize unchecked bias, to catch gaps, and to balance different perceptions.

- Needs assessment should identify future as well as present needs.

- Needs assessment should look at all types of learning needs: broad, general needs as well as more specific staff attitudes, expectations, knowledge, and skills.

- Needs assessment results should be made available to those from whom it was gathered. Personnel should be informed of both the purpose and procedures of the needs assessment and the use of the information that is collected from them.

- Needs assessment should be feasible. Feasibility includes considerations of time, cost, use of available resources, and choice of techniques acceptable to those whose needs are being assessed.

- Needs assessment method and techniques should be congruent with the organization's style of doing things.

If these criteria are applied to the various needs assessment alternatives being considered, the decisions reached about the approach, methods, and techniques are likely to be more sound.

Methods

One or more general methods must be selected to gather and analyze needs information. Only after a methodology has been chosen should techniques be determined. When techniques, such as questionnaires and interviews, are selected without yet knowing the approach or method, needs assessment usually becomes a series of single, uncoordinated efforts resulting only in isolated needs being met through scattershot activities. The selection of specific techniques follows the identification of the information that will be required, the sources from which that information will be obtained, and the general method that will be used to obtain that information.

Generally, methods focus on the needs of the individual, the job, or the library. Although there may be very great differences between how planners for staff development programs and those for continuing education programs might discover these three types of needs, the distinction is helpful to make when weighing the advantages and disadvantages of both methods and techniques. The method emphasizing the learning needs of the individual would accent contacts, measurements, and techniques that would draw out individual needs. Methods with job-centered focus would examine the nature and functions of tasks, required skills, and interrelationships among different jobs. Exploration of the needs of a library as an organization would concern problems and potentials in relation to that institutions present and future directions. A staff development or continuing education program might include more than one such focus in a single program, although usually one focus will take precedence.

For the method that focuses on the individual, various self-assessment or testing techniques might be used to supplement normal performance appraisal information. A way for the individual and his or her supervisor to trace progress is important both to assess present needs and to identify new ones as they arise. Personal goal setting is the prime base for the needs assessment oriented to the individual. In addition to personnel appraisal techniques, career development and life-work planning can help to establish directions for the individual's growth through learning.

The job-oriented focus is often selected as primary, and currently advocated as a definitive method for achieving this focus is functional job analysis. This method seeks to discover any gap between actual and desired performance by defining the various competencies required for each task and function in the library. Then, present personnel performance is measured and compared with the required level. Variances found then provide the basis for different efforts. Identifying learning needs is but one use of this method, since it leads to an analysis of the competency of both individuals and the organization as well as the performance of specific jobs. Applied to the management of human resources in the library, job analysis can serve to guide the recruitment, assignment, and appraisal of personnel as well as the training needed.

Although this method is being used to some extent at the present time, most libraries are not yet prepared to make such an expensive effort. Recent studies have defined and described the necessary procedures for this process and have identified tasks and levels of performance for specific types of libraries. [4] As these tools and techniques become more a part of the management and utilization of library personnel, this method will become easier to adopt and adapt to additional situations. As more libraries use this method, the possibility of using commonly identified needs for continuing education may become just as feasible as the use of needs for staff development is now.

The growth of organizational development as a field over the past fifteen years has begun to influence libraries, and some people now view the library itself as a primary focus. The diagnosis and planned change of the library as an organization has implications for staff members and for their responsibilities. [5] Consequently, as needs are identified by a careful look at the library, some will inevitably have implications for a learning program. Again, the possibilities for staff development within the library are the most obvious, but as more and more libraries view themselves objectively as organizations, any patterns of commonly shared needs that emerge may indicate directions for continuing education programs also.

Each focus point—the individual, the job, and the library—has an emphasis perhaps more suited to one situation or another. Yet they all share some important and common characteristics. Each requires extensive staff involvement, sustained administrative commitment, allocated support, and some degree of technical expertise with the method itself. Each holds a holistic view, placing learning needs within a larger framework. And, each has available a body of knowledge and people with expertise to help utilize the method successfully.

In spite of these factors, however, most needs assessment done in libraries at the present time consists of an assembly of techniques selected to obtain needs information essential to plan for learning activities. Using one of these methods supports the idea of a learning program, one integrated with the organization and with learning activities designed to fulfill the aims of the program. But, the element of what is feasible, what is actually likely to be able to be done, often overwhelms what may be most advisable. As a consequence, most needs assessment methods are constructed from the problems and prospects of a particular library, agency, or association foremost in mind. These methods are constructed from a variety of techniques rather than from an overall methodology.

An obvious consequence of this formulation of a needs assessment methodology is any program's lack of ability to address the full range of needs of the individual, the job, or the library. Yet, a learning program, held back from being developed by methods less than desirable because of their lack of feasibility, may never be begun and emergency needs may never be met while waiting for the possibility of the best method to be set in place.

Thus, most "methods" now in use consist of a variety of techniques, preferably used over a period of time in order to cross-check and verify initial findings, and to distinguish between immediate priority needs, long-term needs, and needs of minor consequence. Although less than a perfect approach, it does allow related needs to be met through combined activities, assuring that results can be achieved through the various segments of the program and that the results and implications of earlier activities become part of later planning.

Techniques

Careful selection of specific techniques to be used either for the needs assessment for the program or for that of specific contemplated activities is important. This selection usually includes considering each possibility in light of where and what sources of information are available, when the information will be required in order to make essential decisions, and how well the technique meets the criteria listed earlier. Selection requires review of alternatives and possible modification to assure an appropriate fit for the specific situation. Looking ahead at the feasibility of analyzing information gathered through the various techniques is essential, not only to determine whether the information can be analyzed, but also whether the information, when gathered and analyzed, will actually provide a basis for action.

Pretesting techniques, forms, and procedures can be an effective way to discover needed modifications. Pretesting is a trial run of a technique with a few individuals before its full and final implementation. This preview can indicate the effectiveness of the technique in obtaining needed information, the general intelligibility of written instructions, and the timing required for the mechanics of implementing the procedure. Feedback from individuals involved in a pretest then can be used to improve the technique or to justify selection of a better alternative.

The questionnaire is the most commonly known and frequently used technique. Although its format may vary depending on the information sought, the questionnaire is designed to elicit responses of varying kinds that will later be tallied and analyzed. Some questionnaires ask for a self-analysis of learning needs, others gather the respondent's opinions and perceptions of the needs of others or of those problems and issues confronting the library that may have implications for what staff members must know or do. A questionnaire in the form of a checklist of possible training needs will make the respondent's task easier and speed the analysis of the information. On the other hand, the checklist approach can also restrict, stratify, or distort the information simply because of its restricted content or format. Figures 3 and 4 provide examples of both types of questionnaires.

Figure 3

Checklist Questionnaire for Needs Assessment in a Library (Sample)

For each of these areas and each of these categories, indicate whether there is a high (H), medium (M), or low (L) level of need.

Areas of Need	For yourself	For your subordinates	For your colleagues	For your supervisor	For your administrators

A. Technical knowledge with skills
   Materials selection
   Collection organization/maintenance/
      preparation
   Reference
   Audiovisual and microforms
   Media production
   Data processing
   Other (specify)					

B. Public service knowledge and skills
   Community needs and resources
   Interpersonal and group communica-
      tions
   Human relations
   Other (specify)					

C. Knowledge of organizational goals					
D. Planning skills					
E. Problem solving skills					
F. Management skills					
G. Supervisory skills					
H. Public relations skills					
I. Professional issues and concerns					
J. Other (specify)					

Adapted from: WICHE/USOE Institute for Training in Staff Development (1975-1976).

Figure 4

Open-ended Questionnaire for Needs Assessment in a Library (Sample)

Individual Needs

1. Which of your present job responsibilities require that you acquire more knowledge or skill in order to be able to improve your effectiveness? (List the responsibility and indicate the area of knowledge and/or skill that you need.)

2. What knowledge or skills do you anticipate you will need in order to prepare for your future job responsibilities?

3. What areas of personal growth interest you most? In what ways are they job related?

Organizational Needs

1. List the current problems you see now facing this organization, then rank them in order of their importance or urgency, using 1 for most important, 2 for second most important, etc.

2. What are some problem areas you anticipate the organization will face in the future?

3. What capabilities will your organization require in the future that it does not now have?

Adapted from: WICHE/USOE Institute for Training in Staff Development (1975-1976)

The questionnaire is popular because of its distinct advantages. It is relatively easy and inexpensive to develop, to administer, and to analyze. When anonymous, it offers the opportunity of free expression. It can be used to gather information from a large number of people scattered over substantial distances. Conversely, the questionnaire brings some disadvantages also. Its over-use and misuse have damaged its credibility with those asked to respond. Poorly designed questionnaires or a lack of action following the circulation of a questionnaire will try the patience of those hoping for results. Questionnaire format may inhibit full response or the ability to draw out larger issues or problems.

Initial questionnaires, designed to elicit the needs of individuals, may require follow-up to discover more specific needs before training activities can be planned. Figures 3 and 4, for instance, would certainly need some qualification of the broad categories included. Information about library needs must be sought from various points of view, bringing in all levels of employees. Sometimes it may be necessary to ask for identification of respondents in order to understand the responses or to carry the needs assessment process further. Other techniques may be used to balance information resulting from questionnaires or to delve more precisely into the nature of the needs being identified. Many sources on needs assessment describe and illustrate suggested questionnaire forms and include tips on how to administer and analyze them.

The Delphi is a variant of the questionnaire. It employs a series of forms in a prescribed sequence. Results from each form of the sequence are tallied and analyzed, then used to develop the basis of the next form. Thus, each form refines and specifies the identified needs, thereby providing better information on which to plan. The Delphi is often used for forecasting future trends, needs, strengths and resources, but easy adaptation provides for identifying current and future needs, including those for learning. The written Delphi can accommodate problems of time and distance, and it can bring wide-ranging opinions and perspectives together to permit sound and feasible planning. The Delphi must be carefully tailored to the specific circumstances of a particular situation, but its use over the past few years has provided a number of resources to help accomplish numerous adaptations with some skill.[6]

Tests can be used to measure the level of knowledge, skills, or attitudes, and many validated tests are available for various areas of knowledge or levels of skill.[7] However, three qualifications are important. One, few libraries have identified those behaviors needed by personnel specifically enough to be able to select, apply, and interpret appropriate tests. Two, most tests must be professionally administered and interpreted to be valid, which raises the cost considerably. Three, strong resentment of tests is prevalent generally and resistance to testing can be expected from those to whom they are to be given. The risk of destroying a favorable climate in order to get solid test results may outweigh the value of the test results information. Thus, tests are not often used for needs assessment in the library field.

Individual or group interviews can reveal both individual and library needs. Used by a skilled interviewer, they are more reliable than forms to "read" the interest and commitment that individuals have in learning possibilities. If interviews are well planned and carefully designed, the information gained can be relevant and relatively easily analyzed. Interviewing offers the advantage of eliciting comments, opinions, qualifications, and clarifications not otherwise possible—freer response than a form if the climate of the interview is appropriate. However, interviewing is expensive in the time it requires first to schedule and conduct the interviews, then to analyze the wealth of information it produces. Sometimes, this expense limits the number of people who can be interviewed and that compromise may not be advisable in some situations. Also, the results from interviewing are often difficult to quantify and interpret, again adding to the cost.

The group interview can cut some of that cost by providing fruitful, two-way exchanges of information with more than one person at a time. This can be just as effective as individual interviews in obtaining information about needs. To be productive, interviews must be well planned and those conducting the interviews must be open to ideas and suggestions. The interview exchange can give the learning program direction and impetus and is a good way of demonstrating the style and climate that participants might expect of the program.[8]

An outside consultant brought into the program-planning process at the point of needs assessment might bring any of these techniques into the situation. The consultant is a strong possibility when the program planners are uncertain as to how to proceed or simply do not have the time or skills for particular assessment techniques. Those techniques used by the consultant could then be used later without the continued involvement of the consultant if the program planners can observe or be trained in the use of them.

Any of these deliberate formalized efforts for assessing needs can be usefully supplemented with less structured approaches to utilize information already available. For example, in a library, routine observation and direct discussion of personnel needs in everyday situations are usually considered as part of the manager's or supervisor's job. Performance evaluation forms and appraisal interviews often provide an initial indication of development needs for an individual or a position. For the most part, these sources are already in place in most organizations. In an agency, consultant field visits provide insights into and perhaps indications of learning needs. The overview from an agency perspective can suggest broad needs affecting present or future library services. In an association, annual reports may be combed to reveal the issues and concerns faced by library personnel, and conference meetings can be observed with an eye to the needs they will bring to the surface.

The best method and techniques for gathering needs information will depend a great deal on the situation. The aim is to obtain the information in order to provide a base for planning the program. Often a combination of techniques enables cross checking and verification of the information, and, at the same time, encourages the involvement of more people in the process. Indeed, gathering needs information is often the initial contact of library personnel with the learning program. Consequently, the assessment is important both for the information it gathers and analyzes and for its approach and appeal.

Who should gather the information and how and when and where should it be done? Approaching needs assessment systematically is essential to assure that the required information is obtained and that that information is accurate, able to be used in developing a program that will remedy the lack of knowledge, skills, or attitudes now preventing individuals or the library from accomplishing their respective tasks. An action plan can guide the needs assessment process by identifying the information that is needed, the sources of the information, and the methods and techniques by which needs are found. A plan for needs assessment serves to correlate the learning program with other organizational functions within the overall context of the library, agency, or association. It provides for a coordinated approach to discover initial and subsequent needs and, then, to plan for responses to them.

An action plan brings together the answers to the four questions asked in this Guideline. These answers are then restructured into a framework necessary to implement them. Who is to be responsible for planning and implementing the needs assessment? The action plan might charge an agency staff member, an association committee, a library task force, or an outside consultant with the responsibility. The method and techniques that are planned for gathering and analyzing the information must be outlined with a schedule of when and where they are to be implemented. This indicates the sequence and relationship of the various steps in the assessment process so that its implementation can be done effectively and efficiently, taking into account the various factors that will be important in a particular situation. The action plan spells out both the initial steps to assess the needs for learning and the coordinated, continuous means of gathering needs information that will be required to plan effectively to meet needs as they change or emerge over time.

For example, an agency about to launch a continuing education program might designate an agency staff member to coordinate planning with an advisory group composed of library personnel and other agency staff members who have frequent contact with libraries and library personnel throughout the state. A consultant may be hired to design and analyze the assessment, although the implementation of that assessment may rest with agency personnel having responsibilities in the field. The plan may specify the sources of information, the timing and sites where the information is collected, and the coordination of the needs assessment with other on-going organizational functions.

The formulation of an action plan for needs assessment provides a look at the feasibility of the needs assessment, helps to assure that an all-out assessment effort does not upset necessary and routine functions, and provides for internal consistency and coordination of the assessment itself. Such an approach may be standard practice for a library, agency, or association and the application of it to the needs assessment of the learning program may be natural. For those organizations and individuals not accustomed to this approach, however, several sources might be helpful. Craig's *Training and Development Handbook* (1976) has a lengthy section on the assessment of needs. Leonard's *Assessment of Training Needs* (1974) and Brown's *Assessing Training Needs* (1974) both provide systematic approaches to the process.

Summary

Needs assessment involves gathering and analyzing information about the learning needs of library staff members. This information provides a basis for planning and implementing the learning program. Without a sound knowledge of the areas and types of needs of the library personnel, no staff development or continuing education program will be able to meet the needs that do exist. A systematic approach to needs assessment has many immediate and long-range advantages. Such an approach considers what information is required, the sources of that information and how to obtain it. These specifics are then formulated into an action plan that enables smooth and consistent implementation as the result of careful and logical planning. Selected on the basis of fundamental criteria and taken together, the specific methods and techniques of gathering needs information reveal both general and specific needs. Then, this information is analyzed to reveal its patterns and to guide the direction of the program. In turn, the program itself or the specific activities within the program are designed to meet the identified needs.

GUIDELINE 2—ANALYZE INFORMATION ABOUT NEEDS

Analysis links the needs information and the outline of the learning program. Often the amount of data that has been gathered from forms, interviews, and surveys is overwhelming. In order to be understood and used, this information must be organized; it requires review and interpretation before definite decisions are made or action is taken regarding the program. Analysis of the available information gives the first firm indication of the scope and depth required for the program, indicating priorities and providing the first realistic view of the levels of expense and involvement that must be considered. This is the point where major decisions can still be made soundly and economically.

Lack of sound analysis can impair the potential program in two ways. It can lead to poor decisions with regard to the direction, scope, or nature of the program during the planning stages. Often this mistake is not discovered until later, when it becomes very expensive to remedy. Also, it can fail to convince decision-makers as they ponder whether to go further or to abandon the efforts to start or continue a learning program. If it is not well analyzed, needs information may be discounted, not considered at all, or used only to support already formed assumptions. If analyzed too slowly, the information becomes out of date; inadequate analysis can distort the information leading to errors in judgment. The importance of prompt, thorough analysis should never be overlooked.

The techniques used to gather information will identify many different needs among library personnel. Some relate to present or future individual job responsibilities. Some are tied to personal interests or desires not closely linked with an individual's job responsibilities. Some highlight library problems, reflect concern about the trends and challenges within the library field, or result from change in the community within which the library functions. Careful planning for the assessment will assure that the essential information about needs will be available for analysis and eventually for program planning.

This Guideline describes ways to classify and analyze needs information, making distinctions between various categories of needs. It also covers the specifics of how such information can be analyzed, reported, and used. The importance of designating priority needs is emphasized as well.

Responses to Identified Needs

Organizing and analyzing the gathered needs information requires definition and grouping of needs in generalized patterns. These patterns provide anonymity for individuals yet allow planning for ways to meet their needs. Basically, of course, analysis identifies personnel needs (what must be known or done) in relation to set standards of effectiveness. People work in relation to their understanding of those explicit or implicit standards that define the desired or required level of performance. In addition to this understanding, staff interest and ability also influence performance. The patterns that surface during the analysis of needs will reflect the standards, interests, and abilities of the individuals and/or libraries where those needs are identified. Often, needs assessment also turns up previously unknown personnel resources, pinpoints information useful in long-range planning, or raises key issues for further or future exploration.

Characteristically, a wide range of needs will be found even though the assessment intentionally aims at discovering only needs for learning. Three questions are useful in determining the needs a learning program might address:

- What is the difference (i.e., gap) between the present situation and the situation as it should be?

- What is required to remedy the situation or solve the problem?

- How can learning, training, or practice feasibly be used to help close that gap or improve the situation?

The answer to the first question identifies the gap between the present situation (i.e., what is) and the desired situation (i.e., what should be). For example, the present situation might be inadequate quality of the library's public service. The specific difference might be between the existing level and the desired or required level of satisfactorily answered reference inquiries. Improving the situation may call for more reference materials, more available telephones, or better trained staff members at the information desk. Materials and telephones are needs with some training implications but only in a secondary sense. Efforts through a learning program, however, might improve the situation by training reference staff to improve their individual and collective competency. Needs analysis would ascertain which solution would be most effective and feasible.

Those identified needs that call for learning—more knowledge, better skills, changed attitudes—are the basis on which the objectives for the learning program are formulated. They give direction for a new or an on-going program, and indicate appropriate strategies for the design of learning activities. But, not all needs revealed by the assessment process will indicate learning as the best or only response. Alternatives might include the rearrangement of existing space; reassignment or termination of personnel; modification of organizational relationships, lines of communications or procedures; acquisition of new or different equipment, and these must be considered. For example, if "slow and inefficient circulation of materials" has been identified as a problem, one possible solution would indeed be to improve the training of circulation personnel. However, alternative solutions might include modifying existing procedures or acquiring new equipment. Either of these alternatives would require training as part of the response but much different training than originally thought. Analysis, then, becomes the logical step to distinguish between those needs that require learning as a response and those that do not.

Often, assessment will discover needs that will require more than an educational opportunity to fill. A learning program is primarily focused on those needs for learning that have been identified. Yet the learning program must be connected with the other functions of the organization. An essential distinction must be made between learning and non-learning needs. Learning needs are those that indicate that someone needs to know something, to do something differently, or to develop improved attitudes. These needs can be fully or in part met with learning opportunities. Non-learning needs, on the other hand, require something other than learning to remedy. In some cases, non-learning needs might have to be met before the indicated learning needs can be addressed. Often, even non-learning needs have implications for learning in whatever solution is devised. Figure 5 indicates examples of learning and non-learning needs.

Figure 5

Examples of Learning and Non-Learning Needs

Learning Needs	Non-Learning Needs
how to use new forms, changed procedures	new procedural forms
how to maintain audio-visual equipment	audio-visual equipment
how to supervise staff	improved staff scheduling procedures
how to organize and delegate tasks and functions	more time available to do what needs to be done
how to develop or apply innovations in library services	development of library networking policies
how to improve individual and group capabilities with creative problem-solving	re-organization of the library, agency, or association

If no distinction is made between these two types of needs, a blurring of program purpose and function is likely. Needs for learning will require planning and methods that will enable individuals to learn. Needs for communication, problem-solving, or decision-making, however, will require planning and methods that allow those to occur. As these are sorted out in the needs assessment process, non-learning needs can be referred to appropriate individuals or groups in the library, agency, or association. The remaining needs for learning form the crux of planning for the learning program.

Analysis

The analysis of the gathered, classified, and tabulated information depends on the unique circumstances and situation of the library, agency, or association. To be useful and convincing, the analysis of needs should address the following questions:

- What are the needs? Who has those needs? What kinds of training will be required for each group?

- What problems can training be expected to alleviate? What results can be expected from a learning program?

- What alternatives to training are feasible?

- What size and scope of program appears essential? What appears to be the most logical means to meet the indicated needs? What is the contemplated cost of the program?

- Is the program feasible?

- What support exists for the learning program? What constraints will it face? What is the priority for the program itself? How urgent is it in relation to other organizational functions? How will the program link with other functions?

- What are long-range implications?

- Who should be involved in the planning, implementation, and evaluation if a program is to be developed? What direction and focus should the program have? What are the recommended next steps?

Other factors are important in determining whether or not to move into an ambitious program for staff development on the basis of identified needs. These factors are also unique to each particular situation. Some that are often influential include: the climate of the organization, its history and "personality," the present attitude of administrator(s) and staff toward the program or learning in general, the availability of resources, and the depth of both stated and real commitment to growth and development and education. The importance of a thorough and convincing needs assessment becomes most apparent after it is done, at the time decisions about the program are made.

Often the analysis presents key considerations together with recommendations to the decision-makers in the library, agency, or association. How well the analysis is done will significantly influence subsequent decisions about the program. How the analysis is received and what happens as a result of it will also provide an indication of how ready and willing the organization is to be supportive of a learning program. Convinced commitment on the part of decision-makers will be essential if a program is to move beyond needs assessment into actually producing learning activities for library personnel.

Procedure

Classification and tabulation are two tasks required to make the gathered needs information usable for making decisions regarding any program. Classification surfaces the patterns of needs. Tabulation enumerates and sometimes ranks needs and who has them. For example, three specific needs may be in book selection, supervisory skills, and communications; the people with those needs may be heads of departments, supervisors, and library technicians. Analysis brings this kind of information together with the other factors that will influence subsequent decisions about the program.

Once gathered, information must be analyzed quickly and easily, but effectively and accurately. If careful planning for the gathering of needs has included looking ahead to the task of analysis, the techniques used for obtaining information may also be instrumental in analyzing it. In other words, the design of forms and interviews may ease the collection, recording, and interpretation of the information gathered. For example, a checklist questionnaire can be easily responded to, and also can be quickly tabulated for analysis. If the form is well designed, with a sense of order, a complete rationale, and a classification outline as its basis, the compilation of needs will be relatively simple. For such questionnaires, a blank form then can be used to tally the responses quite easily.

Open-ended questions and interview responses will be less easily analyzed. When done, however, they may offer more depth and perspective than that possible with a checklist. Generally, patterns of response will evolve. These then can be recorded as key words or phrases with hatch marks used to indicate the number of similar responses. In addition to this kind of tally, significant conditions or qualifications made by respondents are important to note. These comments might be jotted next to the appropriate keyword or phrase.

The Delphi process requires an analysis to be made between each of the three or four successive forms that are used, since each form is based on the analysis of the earlier one. Each analysis serves to draw even more cohesiveness and specificity from the information supplied by the respondents. The resources indicated in Guideline 1 define the process of analysis of Delphi instruments step by step.

Patterns of responses from interviews can be initially categorized the way notes are taken at the time of the interviews. This grouping is sometimes easier if separate sheets are kept for each question rather than for each interviewee. Longer responses can be noted with the help of the interviewee if the interviewer asks questions to clarify or to summarize at the appropriate points during the interview. Although it doubles the amount of time required for analyzing the interviews, tape recording interviews can provide the opportunity of accurately recapturing what was said and allows the interviewer's attention to be devoted solely to the interviewee at the time of the interview. The resources indicated in Guideline 1 provide additional direction and detail.

Needs information obtained from specialized methods (such as personnel surveys, job analysis, or organizational development) require special forms, manuals, and procedures, and, sometimes, outside expertise to describe or demonstrate how to gather and analyze the information. Since these methods yield more comprehensive information than simply needs for learning, special efforts may be required to reveal those needs that relate specifically to the staff development or continuing education program. Again, the resources indicated in Guideline 1 can be more specific for each of these methods.

Information from documentation such as records and reports requires a method of recording and analysis that will allow the identification of the source as well as the information from that source. One possibility is for notes to be taken, a list of needs indicated by each source. Or, photocopies may be taken of relevant sections of records or reports and the needs information marked directly on the copy. If several of these indirect sources have been used either to provide a base of information or to supplement more direct approaches, the information from all sources must be dovetailed into the patterns that emerge.

The patterns that result from the analysis of information about needs must be brought together to draw conclusions about the nature of the program required to meet priority needs. If the total population was surveyed, the tabulation will indicate the largest number of needs and where those needs lie. If a sample was drawn, generalizations must be made on the basis of that sample.

A major outcome from the assessment process is the indication of the kinds of needs that exist and what groups of people have those needs. This information must then be viewed in the context of the responsibilities assumed by the library, the agency, or association for a learning program for library personnel. These two essentials—information from the needs assessment and the organizational responsibility—will indicate the program's direction directly or by implication. The procedures that bring about this situation include defining the categories into which information fits, drawing conclusions from the information, and assuring that the information is in usable form for those people actually making decisions and planning programs.

Basic Categories

Assembling needs information in categories aids analysis and can facilitate later planning. The categories selected will naturally vary with the uniqueness of the situation and the organization. Individuals working with needs analysis may prefer fewer, more, or different categories than those suggested here. Yet, these are offered as basic, useful groupings relevant to most needs assessment circumstances. Patterns, generally, help focus and clarify areas of need.

The most important basic category, after distinguishing the learning from the non-learning needs, is that of identifying needs on the basis of whether they will require knowledge, skills, or attitude changes. The distinctions among these three are important since different educational and training approaches are used to address these three types of needs. Basically, **knowledge** refers to the awareness of facts, ideas, and concepts relevant to a task, a function, or an organization. **Skills** refers to the ability to apply knowledge proficiently in a manner appropriate to a given situation. **Attitude** is a position, and often behavior, that indicates an opinion, disposition, or manner with regard to a person, a thing, or a situation. Figure 2, page 11 (in Guideline 1) gives a number of specific examples of each of these groups.

The depth to which the knowledge, skills, or attitudes are sought is significant. If it can be determined at the point of analyzing the data, that information should be indicated. For example, a need may be indicated as "better reference service." This need may refer to a broader knowledge of reference tools available in the library as a whole or to those in a given subject area. At this level of need, a satisfactory response might be to explain and generally describe reference tools at a meeting including staff members who have indicated that need.

However, if these tools are expected to be used with proficiency by those individuals, a more detailed explanation will be necessary, together with the opportunity to practice using them with supervision and review. Further, if the indicated need actually refers to a necessity for changing attitudes toward reference service in order to increase staff receptiveness to all library users, a broad range of approaches would be essential to enable the attitudinal and behavioral changes sought.

Another category differentiates between individual and organizational needs. Individual needs are those that arise from a person's lack of ability in a particular position or for a particular task. Organizational needs, on the other hand, are related to the ineffectiveness or inefficiency of a library function. The first are those needs that individuals must have answered to be more effective, the second, the needs the library must have answered to be more effective. Again, this categorization helps in subsequent planning of learning activities, since the selection of educational approaches and alternatives may depend on this difference. With few exceptions, the analysis of needs is done in relation to a position, an area of responsibility, or a function rather than on a personal, named basis. For example, supervisors in technical services might need to know how to delegate responsibilities, or, public service librarians might need to know how to communicate with patrons better. This approach is preferred to designating what "Pat Smith" may need to learn. Some examples of individual and organizational needs are given in Figure 6.

Figure 6

Examples of Individual and Organizational Needs

Individual Needs	Organizational Needs
improvement of written and oral communications skills	more effective communication between departments
awareness of organizational operations and procedures	clarified organizational structure and functions
improvement of group skills	more effective group decision-making at faculty meetings
ability to evaluate current programs	improved public image
ability to find and use non-print media	creative use of interlibrary cooperation and networking

Separating long- and short-range needs provides a useful category in some instances, as indicated by the examples in Figure 7. This distinction can be used to help determine immediate priorities and, at the same time, to plan ahead for responding to likely future needs.

Figure 7

Examples of Long- and Short-Range Needs

Long-Range	Short-Range
switch to telecommunications communications methods	use of the newly-installed telephone centrex
increased opportunities for community library control	knowledge of existing community groups
planning for a new library building	planning for moving into a new library building

Another category of possible use is the distinction between needs that point to learning activities that must be planned for individuals as such and those that are suitable for group learning activities. Generally, if only a few individuals need training, continuing education opportunities away from the library might be the best answer. However, if several people need to develop their competencies in similar areas, it is often useful to plan group learning activities.

For example, an individual learning opportunity might be accounting, cataloging, or the initial awareness of a new subject area. To a great extent, these can be learned alone, through self-study, observation, or on-the-job instruction. However, group skills, such as communications, human relations, or participative problem-solving cannot be learned as effectively alone as in a group situation.

Classifying needs as information is gathered is useful in preparing for further analysis and for formulating the program objectives. The categories described here are not the only ones that are useful and are not necessarily valid or applicable in all situations. In fact, the lines of distinction may blur when the data actually is being classified, and the relevance of some groupings may not be meaningful until later. But, some sorting process is necessary to begin to see patterns, trends, or directions that the learning program will be designed to address.

Inevitably, more needs will be identified than can be accommodated feasibly by a program. Thus, a designation of priority needs is essential. **Priority needs** are those of the greatest urgency and necessity, the needs that can most justifiably claim individual and organizational investment of time and money. Specific procedures and criteria by which priority needs are designated will vary with each situation, and often they are implicit or "automatic." Some questions that cover common ground for selecting priorities include:

- What is the urgency of the need as perceived by the individuals who expressed the need?

- How central is the need to those respondents or to the groups whom they may represent?

- How congruent is the need with the possibilities that could be offered by a continuing education program?

- How congruent is the need with the mission of the agency or association?

- How practicable for the learners will the response to the need be?

- Are opportunities presently available through other sources for meeting the need?

- Does the need require actual learning activities provided by the agency or association, or might disseminating information about existing learning opportunities suffice?

- How feasibly can the need be met with the resources available to the continuing education effort?

These questions can be used to test each category of need to determine which needs deserve priority status.

The responsibility for designating priority needs is an important consideration. In some cases, those responsible for the needs assessment might be the most logical choice to do this, on the grounds that they are familiar with the findings. Or, priorities might be designated by the program director or the administrator of the library, agency, or association. Another alternative is to elicit from potential learners their perceptions of priority needs. In a staff development situation, this might be done through a "voting" procedure or through open discussions in a meeting where the assessment findings are presented. These approaches would not be possible for a continuing education program, but a follow-up contact with those surveyed might first describe the findings and then request respondents to indicate the most urgent, essential needs of all those identified through the initial survey. Since priority needs will shape the future allocation of organizational resources as well as its present directions, administrative involvement in setting priorities is important.

Drawing Conclusions

Classifying and tabulating the gathered needs information leads to conclusions that, in turn, become decisions about what is needed, what is possible, and what will be done. Only when solid and accurate information from careful analysis is in hand can sound decisions be made that will guide subsequent steps. The decisions about what will be required emerge from working with the data. What is possible and what will be done incorporate a broader picture of the capabilities and commitments of the library, agency, or association.

The capability of a library, an agency, or association to successfully initiate and maintain a learning program depends, to a large extent, on knowing what is feasible. The question of feasibility is usually not considered while the needs assessment is being planned or while the information is being gathered. However, it comes immediately to the fore when the issue is whether to drop the idea or to proceed with it. In considering what is feasible and what is not, two questions are helpful:

- Are the available resources adequate to what is required?

- Does the program fall within the scope of the organization's mission?

Response to the first question considers resources as a very inclusive term, embracing not only the people, the money, the time, and the ability to produce learning activities, but also the organization's ability to influence participation in activities and to assist in the application of learnings during or following those activities. In other words, what is possible for the library, agency, or association to accomplish, given its restrictions of time, money, mission, and interests? For example, an association's goal may be to improve the professional competence of its members through continuing education opportunities. Yet, limitations of staff and funds may prevent the association from producing learning activities. But, a more feasible approach may be determined to link the needs found to an increased awareness on the part of library personnel of available learning opportunities. This increased awareness might be accomplished by disseminating listings of opportunities produced by other groups, by encouraging local colleges or adult education programs to produce courses related to the identified needs, or by co-sponsoring educational efforts being produced by others.

The second question again touches the issue of where the responsibility lies for staff development and continuing education. The array of needs identified by an assessment process may prompt distinctions to be made. For example, training in circulation procedures would clearly be the library's province for its own staff. However, teaching specific skills and techniques for use with a particular circulation system might fall to the manufacturer's sales representatives. Or, if a state-wide reciprocal borrowing agreement is negotiated by the state agency, it logically may fall to that agency to train staff members in the commonly shared procedures, particularly if an agency's goal is to actively support all interlibrary cooperation efforts.

Although its first application can come in relation to the number of needs that have been expressed and identified, feasibility is a test that must be applied throughout the planning and implementation of any program. An organization with abundant resources may wish to encompass a large number of the needs discovered. A less well-endowed organization may be very selective about its priorities. Once implementation is begun, the scope of what has been undertaken becomes apparent, and the question of feasibility will again be raised. Sometimes during implementation, stated commitments made early in the needs assessment phase pale when the responses are eager, enthusiastic—and demanding. Cutbacks in resources or inflation or loss of key (and convinced) personnel can also affect feasibility.

Decisions

Culmination of the needs assessment process brings the crucial decision of whether or not to embark on the learning program. With the completed analysis of the findings, the establishment of priorities, and the test of feasibility, this essential decision must be made. If that decision is not to proceed, the risk of lost credibility and dismayed frustration is likely to be felt by those library personnel who contributed to the assessment and had their expectations raised by being asked about their needs.

If, on the other hand, the decision is to go forward with developing the program, the next decision that must be made is that of how extensive an effort will be attempted. Decisions to then follow include: what is to be done with the needs information? who should be involved in planning? what is the most advisable phasing of the program? what is its direction and focus? These decisions are considered in later Guidelines.

In the meantime, though, an immediate next step would be to inform key persons of the findings of the needs assessment. Many of them would have been likely to have already been involved in the decision-making process to that point, and those who are to be in charge of the program will certainly need an in-depth report for planning purposes. A formal written report of the analysis of the assessment is helpful both to document recommendations and to provide a basis for subsequent planning. Such a report could include indications of discerned patterns of needs, the groups of people who have those needs, which needs have priority, and any recommendations for action. A brief description of the methods used for the assessment may be helpful for later reference. Copies of forms, schedules of interview questions, and other documentation should, of course, be kept on file.

An implicit obligation exists to let personnel know the results of the assessment in return for their time, thought, and effort. Since interest and commitments from all levels of staff will be essential for the program's successful implementation, the analysis information should be disseminated widely. Potential learners will be interested in the results of the assessment in which they were involved. Administrators, naturally, will need to know the findings because of the many decisions that will necessarily have to be made and because of the value of such a study to the organization overall.

Making needs assessment information available provides other advantages. Additional comments and reactions from personnel can be elicited, thereby providing a double check on the results of the analysis. If the assessment also involved potential learners directly, it is likely to interest and motivate individuals to follow the progress of the program's development. The means to do this might be direct mailing of an informational brochure, an article in a newsletter, or a report to a conference session. Reporting needs assessment information follows through, then, on the initial involvement of individuals in the learning program.

For a staff development program, the analysis could be presented in an informational report circulated to all personnel together with a request for further comments. Or, the findings might be presented to a staff meeting or at open hearings for the staff, where comments and questions would be exchanged. Such meetings in themselves would be staff development activities, offering the advantage of providing a deeper mutual understanding of the organization and its personnel and their needs. These means could also show the interest and support of the staff and the administration for the program, and the style of presentation would serve to introduce the program.

The people responsible for developing and implementing the needs assessment and those responsible for making decisions at the conclusion of the assessment should be selected on the basis of their availability, interest, and skill. A library may have to tap an outside resource to help with the assessment. Within an agency, expertise from other staff members or from sister agencies may be available. Associations may have staff members or general members who are able to do a needs assessment. Often, the responsibility falls to a committee.

When the same individuals plan an assessment, analyze it, and are also responsible for developing the ensuing program, this offers advantages of in-depth familiarity and commitment. On the other hand, disadvantages include their being so involved with the entire range of procedures that the program tends to reflect unquestioned personal assumptions and preferences. This, in turn, can create a strong sense of ownership or possessiveness on the part of those consistently involved.

Once the basic needs assessment has been completed and plans have been made for developing a learning program, provisions should be made for subsequent, regular procedures that will continue to assess needs and to report that information to program planners and those responsible for particular activities. Continued needs assessment is essential for planning and evaluation, as both individual and organizational needs are dynamic.

The wealth of needs information gathered is brought into organized form through analysis. This enables the use of the information as the program is developed initially. Continued needs assessment provides for later program development which is also essential. Often in planning learning programs, needs are assumed to be known and the planning proceeds on those assumptions. When they are accurate, no problem arises and much time and effort are saved. Where they are not accurate, however, poor decisions may result, and these may well be very costly.

Summary

Analyzing needs assessment information is vital to make it useful in the necessary decision-making process about the potential learning program. Procedurally, this analysis includes classifying and tabulating the information about needs gathered earlier. Classification aids the formulation of patterns; tabulation records where the needs are indicated to be. Together, these steps enable the establishment of priority needs and an initial view of the anticipated nature of the program.

Once the information is drawn together, thoughtful review should be concerned with the feasibility of the program and guide decisions about the steps necessary to develop the program. A written report of the analysis includes the patterns of needs found, the priorities of needs, and recommendations for action. The dissemination of such a report can be an important follow-through that prepares library personnel for the activities in the program to follow.

GUIDELINE 3–DEVELOP OBJECTIVES

If, at the conclusion of the initial needs assessment, the decision is made to go forward with planning a learning program, the next step is to develop program objectives. Objectives are essential since they furnish a blueprint for action and are the most basic decision-making tool for guiding a program's successful implementation. They are vital for the design, management, and evaluation of the program, keeping it "on track." Formulating objectives is not merely a ritualistic exercise. Program efforts with solid objectives are more likely to have a solid impact on the organization and on the learners than such efforts conducted in a slapdash or haphazard fashion.

Sound and realistic objectives provide a secure base for program developers to make the many decisions that will be necessary at each stage of the program. They are the foundation for reliable evaluation measure to discover what results from the program. The process of developing them helps to organize thoughts, communications, and decisions and helps to clarify assumptions, either confirming them as accurate or prompting their modification. Objectives assure that the attempts and achievements of a program can be articulated, linked with other organizational functions and activities, communicated within and outside the library, agency, or association. When objectives are real, known, and understood, individuals who are involved are more likely to hold clear, realistic, and feasible expectations of the program, and are less apt to be misled, then, later, frustrated and disappointed. Honest objectives can be relied on throughout program development and on-going decision making.

Important as objectives are, program planners and implementers often bypass the task of developing them. Formulating objectives is a difficult task requiring clear thinking and focused attention—and time. Yet, the time and effort "saved" in bypassing the process of carefully developing objectives will likely be required in trying to remedy mistakes or failure resulting from the lack of them. Planners may assume objectives to be implicit and mutually understood; yet, if this assumption is erroneous, high risks are incurred: faulty planning, misdirected implementation, impossible evaluation, and misunderstood intentions. Or, planners may devise objectives for the program, then set them aside as they get on with the job, and thereby run many of the same risks as in not having developed them at all. Developing objectives is a process requiring commitment, discipline, and skill. Once they are developed, using them presents an equal challenge.

Ineffective learning programs with negative results can often be traced to inadequate planning or to nonexistent, poorly developed, or assumed objectives. Without defined program objectives to indicate consistent direction for the functions of planning, implementation, and evaluation, the chances are high for random and uncoordinated efforts, inappropriate use of resources, and confused communications. Misunderstandings are likely to affect the credibility of the programs, as learners are not informed of the nature or depth of the activity, instructors do not know to what end their efforts should be directed, and others do not understand what the program is doing or expected to do. Nonexistent or poorly stated objectives prevent reliable evaluation. Assumed but unstated objectives foster the belief that they are substantial enough to use for planning, implementation, and evaluation. Without sound objectives, ineffective or even counterproductive results from the learning program may be expected.

The development of objectives follows directly from the need assessment since program objectives must be rooted in learning needs. Consequently, identifying needs and developing sound, stated objectives are essential first steps before planning learning activities, selecting resources and learners, or weighing evaluation possibilities are feasible. These two essentials—needs assessment and objectives— then, form the basis for all subsequent steps. Neither of these essentials, however, are one-time processes. Rather, both will be dynamic, evolving over a period of time, accommodating modifications, meeting new circumstances. For example, current training activities will unearth new needs as well as answer present ones. Current objectives must be changed then because they have been achieved or because they have become inappropriate. Or, perhaps organizational changes require personnel and position reorganization in the library, calling for extensive new training efforts based on needs that did not previously exist.

Once needs are identified and objectives are developed, however, the next steps depend on whatever order is appropriate to the situation and to the opportunities available. Usually a natural ebb and flow occurs in planning the program and activities begin to take definite shape. No prescribed order is suggested for bringing together the components of the program and its activities. Rather, the order will vary depending on each situation with its unique constraints and opportunities.

This Guideline describes the process of developing objectives, their importance, and their function. A distinction is made between the objectives for a program and those for activities, illustrating the relationship between the two with definitions and examples for both staff development and continuing education programs. Criteria are given for each. Alternative methods and types of objectives are described, citing resources for further study.

Definitions

Encompassed by a general statement of **purpose** that defines the aim or goal of the program, two kinds of objectives are necessary: those for the program itself and those for the learning activities that are part of the program. As defined previously, the learning program is a variety of learning activities that are sequentially planned over a substantial time span and directed toward defined objectives. **Program objectives** describe the intent, function, and outcomes expected from the total learning program. Comprehensive and broad, they are based on the general needs found in the assessment.

Activities, on the other hand, are discrete but coordinated components of a program. They are based on more specific needs, usually those needs related to the topic or to the learnings expected to result from that activity. Thus, **activity objectives** are instructional or learning objectives that specify the kind of behavior expected to occur in learners and/or the changes expected in the library as a result of the activity. Examples of activities include workshops, orientation, job rotation, or management training seminars.

Both program and activity objectives are developed from the learning needs identified in the assessment. General and organizational needs are the basis for program objectives; more specific needs for knowledge, skills, and attitudes are the source for activity objectives. These relationships are shown by Figure 8.

Figure 8

Development of Program and Activities Objectives

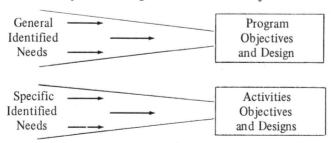

Following the needs assessment and the decision to engage in a learning program, program objectives can be developed simultaneously with those for early activities. This offers the advantages of maintaining a clear distinction between the two and, at the same time, assuring that they are congruent with one another. Developing these jointly is not always possible or feasible, however. Sometimes, program objectives are developed together with the program design, and those for the activities evolve later. Or, a program may develop out of previously isolated, independent activities, each of which may have its own set of objectives.

Often, activities are more likely to have stated objectives than is the program as a whole. However, when this practice is sustained over a period of time without an effort to unite these under a program framework with stated objectives, the long-range effectiveness of such isolated activities will diminish, and activities may become a random series of unconnected events promptly only by crisis situations. This, in turn, prevents staff development or continuing education from becoming an acknowledged function and responsibility of the organization.

Types of Objectives

The process of forming objectives is vital for the success of a program or its activities. Thus, both the type of objectives and the method by which they are developed is important. An appropriate selection from among the possibilities will depend on the norms and standards of the library, agency, or association and upon the inclination of the individual or group responsible for the development of the program. An organization may encourage or even mandate a certain type of objective or a certain process by which objectives are to be formed. The experience of individuals and their comfort with certain types of objectives will influence what is developed for the program. Here, no one "right" way to develop objectives is designated, and no one "right" type of objectives is prescribed.

For those new to program planning, however, the use of simple and direct objectives for the program and activities is recommended rather than striving for ultimate perfection and definitiveness. Basically, objectives should be clear and understandable, able to be communicated and feasibly implemented. Both objectives and the process for developing them are likely to be revised as the program and its activities develop. The emphasis here is on assisting those who normally tend to work without objectives to begin the process of working with them; for those whose work is already guided by objectives, the perspective offered here is intended to enrich their ability to develop even better objectives.

Operational objectives are those that state *what* is intended to be done. They describe what functions will be performed and, in some instances, how those functions will be done. They often describe what the program staff will do rather than what is expected of the learner. Examples include:

Program: The program will teach library skills and keep library personnel aware of new developments.

Workshops will be held to meet needs of library personnel.

Activity: Participants will be encouraged to learn about [topic].

A catalog of continuing education opportunities will be distributed widely to increase staff awareness of learning opportunities.

Operational objectives are perhaps the easiest and most natural type of objectives for the inexperienced person to develop and implement. And, they do give guidance for implementation as well as planning. However, they usually can not be measured. Thus, they serve as a starting point for forming objectives where none have been developed before. For program planners starting here, however, it is recommended that as soon as the importance of objectives and the precedent for having them is established, the move is made to a more adequate type of objective.

Unlike operational objectives, which describe how the program or activity will be done, results objectives attempt to describe what the situation will be when the program or activity is accomplished by delineating the results that are sought. Examples include:

Program: On the basis of identified learning needs, library personnel will meet established performance standards related to their jobs as a result of engaging in staff development activities in appropriate learning formats.

                Measures established to determine library effectiveness will be increased by 10% in one year due to involvement of staff in learning activities.

Activity: Using appropriate interviewing and search techniques, participants will accurately respond to 80% of reference inquiries asked.

                As a result of increased awareness of opportunities available, more library personnel will engage in continuing education activities.

This type of objective is more abstract and relies on the ability to formulate concepts as well as describe action. The most direct and simple approach to developing results objectives is to ask: "What do we want to happen from this activity (or program)?" The answers to this question form the basis for results objectives. (Qualifying definitions and criteria must be stated at some point as well.) Although they are difficult to formulate, results objectives can be measured by observing overt behavior, by examining level of performance, or by the conditions resulting from the program or the activities.

For those wishing to use more specialized types of objectives, several available sources may be helpful. A variant of the results type of objective is the behavioral objective, widely used in all levels of education. Robert Mager, the basic source for developing behavioral objectives, affirms that objectives should "in all instances be able to identify correctly the performance, the conditions and the criterion of acceptable performance."[9] His programmed text, *Preparing Instructional Objectives* (1975) is a course itself in how to develop learning objectives that require the demonstration of achievement as the prime measure. Behavioral objectives state the desired outcome in terms of observable achievements and established performance criteria so that any person will know the extent of its being done successfully.

Mager sums up the importance of establishing objectives with the succinct comment: "In short, if you know where you are going, you have a better change of getting there." And, in speaking of objectives for learning activities, he states that objectives are useful "in providing a sound basis (1) for the selection or designing of instructional content and procedures (2) for evaluating or assessing the success of the instruction, and (3) for organizing the students' own efforts and activities for the accomplishment of the important instructional intents."[10]

Tying the familiar concepts of behavioral objectives with the hierarchies of learning objectives defined by Bloom, Krathwohl, and others in *Taxonomies of Educational Objectives*, Norman Gronlund advocates stating broader instructional results. He acknowledges that the results of learning may not fit necessarily nor exclusively into cognitive, affective, or psychomotor domains, but may overlap. In his view, objectives should provide direction for both instructor and student without being overly restrictive about the nature of instruction.[11]

However, Davis and McCallon rely strongly on the *Taxonomies*, but use them in the definitions of general learning objectives (GLO) and, at a different level, for specific learning objectives (SLO). The general learning objectives are used to organize a "disconnected string of specific objectives."[12] However, a specific learning objective "describes as precisely as possible what the learner will be able to do as a result of a learning activity or series of learning activities which focus directly on a particular previously identified need."[13]

Where applicable, the development of learning objectives through a "learning contract" offers new ground particularly meaningful in continuing education. An outgrowth of experimental study formats in nontraditional education, contract learning is based on a negotiated agreement among the learners, the instructor, and the organization. The contract, strongly rooted in objectives, acknowledges that both learner and teacher are responsible to some degree for learning and that both personal objectives and organizational requirements can both be achieved. Malcolm Knowles stresses the importance of objectives and evaluation as well as the many learning possibilities that are possible with this method.[14]

And, finally, the management by objectives (MBO) approach, becoming widespread in libraries, requires that objectives be carefully determined and that the level of achievement be based on the measurement of performance in relation to those objectives. George S. Odiorne, on authority in the field, has written *Training by Objectives; An Economic Approach to Management Training* (Toronto, Canada: Macmillan, 1970), which can usefully be applied to staff development and, more limitedly, to continuing education. Two good sources of general MBO principles are Anthony P. Raia's *Managing by Objectives* (Glenview, Ill.: Scott, Foresman, 1974) and Dale D. McConkey's *MBO for Nonprofit Organizations* (New York: AMACOM, American Management Assoc., 1975). For libraries, agencies, and associations influenced by this method, continuing education and staff development both can evolve through this process as integral functions of the organization.

Whichever type of objective is preferred, program and activity objectives will need to be congruent with each other and with the program's purpose. Of course, planning is the stage at which congruency can most feasibly be assured. Implementation and evaluation will often require modification, and adjustments may have to be made in the objectives or the activities or in the program. Since they will be used throughout all phases of the program, time spent carefully developing sound program objectives is an investment in quality learning activities and good program administration. Objectives for activities are essential to allow prompt and valid decision making in the production of each learning event.

Examples

The distinctions between purpose, program objectives, and activity objectives may be more clearly seen with examples that illustrate the differences between them. These examples are relatively simple and straightforward and are suggested for use as patterns for those responsible for forming objectives. They are not intended for adoption by any library, agency, or association, since the development of objectives must be a process internalized within the individual and organization in order to be real and valid.

A Staff Development Program in a Library of Moderate or Large Size

Purpose: The ability of the library to serve its public will increase by providing access to a wide variety of work-related learning opportunities for all staff members.

Program Objectives: The capabilities of staff members to fulfill their present responsibilities will improve through quality in-house learning opportunities.

Staff will prepare for advancement into additional and future responsibilities with staff development opportunities.

Staff use of relevant continuing education opportunities will develop work-related interests and abilities.

A library with these program objectives might plan the following activities: a job rotation sequence for all new people entering Librarian I positions; redesign of the annual performance review form and interview to focus on areas for potential growth of each staff member; a regular staff seminar series to draw information about available learning opportunities to the attention of the staff; a bulletin board in the staff room for posting brochures, literature, and exhibits about staff development and continuing education opportunities.

Each of these activities should have objectives congruent with the program objectives to support and guide the development of the activity. For example, the activity objectives for the staff seminar series might be:

- Staff members will learn about present continuing education activities available in the region.

- Staff members will know about library policies and procedures that encourage and support staff development efforts.

- The personnel officer or other knowledgeable staff member will guide those staff members who request assistance in selecting appropriate growth opportunities.

- Staff members who have recently participated in useful learning experiences may use this opportunity to share with others what they have learned and how they have applied those learnings.

Those objectives would be sufficient to provide direction for planners to produce seminars and to communicate the intent of the seminars to the staff. If, in the future, the series proved no longer useful, the objectives could be changed or the series dropped.

A Continuing Education Program
in a State Library Agency

Purpose: Effective learning opportunities for all levels of library personnel in all types of libraries will upgrade the general level of library service throughout the state.

Program Objectives: Administrators, library personnel and trustees will become aware of the value of engaging in continuing education.

Sound planning and evaluation methods will assure continued long-range programming as well as quick response to emerging learning needs.

Available information about continuing education opportunities related to the identified needs of library personnel will enable them to select and participate in continuing education.

The agency will produce educational activities to meet priority learning needs with those methods which are most acceptable and effective.

Several activities might be planned to accomplish these objectives. For example, the program might include a series of traveling workshops on such topics as interlibrary loan procedures, proposal writing, book selection and weeding, or materials repair and preservation. The agency might also arrange for the purchase of slide tape and video-tape training packages on supervisory skills, management concepts, and communications. Also helpful to achieve these objectives would be supportive activities such as producing a newsletter listing continuing education opportunities. Assigning agency staff members the responsibility for developing an evaluation plan to be implemented throughout the program, and planning active efforts aimed at administrators and trustees, with the intention of raising their awareness of the tangible results of participating in continuing education activities as well as about presently available opportunities open to library personnel.

Many of these activities will need stated objectives to provide direction for their design and implementation. For example, the objectives for a regional workshop on materials repair and preservation might include:

- Participants will define and illustrate the basic criteria for selecting materials for repair.

- Participants will achieve and demonstrate basic skills in working with mending materials and tools,

- Participants will practice what they have learned by working with materials actually needing repair.

- Participants will learn basic training techniques to enable each to teach mending and repair techniques to other staff members.

And, the objectives for developing a continuing education newsletter might be:

- It will list essential information about regionally available continuing education opportunities related to identified needs.

- It will publicize brief reports from participants indicating opportunities and results they believe were most important.

- It will update information about continuing education activities being planned by the program staff at the agency.

- It will offer collegial information exchange based on the prime interests and concerns of other groups interested and active in staff development and continuing education.

With such objectives, workshop participants and instructors will know how to prepare and plan, and the newsletter editor will know what information to seek and include.

A Continuing Education Program
of a Library Association

Purpose: Individual and library effectiveness will increase through the use of continuing education opportunities.

**Program
Objectives:** Learning opportunities will develop an active continuing education leadership, able to plan and produce quality activities.

The association will encourage and support efforts of interested groups wishing to engage in or produce continuing education activities for library personnel.

The continuing education program will plan and launch five activities each year intended to answer priority needs unmet elsewhere.

The efforts of the continuing education program will coordinate with efforts by other groups in order to fully utilize available resources and to minimize duplicate efforts.

Activities to accomplish these objectives might include: involving interested key library personnel in planning learning activities; using educational programming as the basic approach for conference planning around current themes that reflect library issues; exploring the incentives and motivations that prompt potential learners to engage in continuing education; sponsoring a given number of workshops and institutes per year in addition to the conference program; directing staff or committees to review information coming from other groups involved in continuing education and to communicate with those groups exploring the ways in which future cooperation might be effected.

Again, many of these activities will require stated objectives. For example, the effort to use educational planning as a deliberate approach for conference programming might utilize the following objectives:

- All units of the association will maintain high quality programming by using effective techniques of adult education as the means by which they approach the issues they wish to present at conference.

- Committee and association members will attend briefing sessions on educational techniques to enable them to plan and implement various formats for conference sessions.

- Program staff will evaluate all conference sessions and feedback will be compiled, analyzed, and provided to planners of subsequent conference sessions.

These objectives indicate an association's intent and the assistance it can provide to achieve more effective educational programming through association conferences.

These three sets of examples present an array of illustrations of purpose, and program and activity objectives for a library, an agency, and an association. The purpose is the general aim or goal of the program. The program objectives are more specific than the statement of purpose but still relate to the whole. They should address the staff development or continuing education function within the library, the agency, or the association. They might describe what the program is intended to accomplish, define the responsibility and accountability for it, establish the extent of the program, or provide a base for necessary policies and procedures. Activity objectives are quite specific, indicating what will be learned or done. Both program and activity objectives should be measurable. These three basic elements of the learning program are the result of initial planning, and they open the door to subsequent planning and implementation.

Criteria

Even for experienced planners, objectives are not easy to develop. For program objectives, the following criteria are generally applicable to assure a sound basis for planning and evaluation of a learning program.

- Program objectives should be based on identified learning needs.

- Program objectives should indicate honestly and clearly the intent and desired results of the program (i.e., the intended achievements, the difficulties it should help resolve, the differences it anticipates in the individuals or the library as a result of the program).

- Program objectives should be clear, concise, and feasible.

- Program objectives should be written and easily available.

- Program objectives should be the basis for decision-making during planning and implementation of the program.

- Program objectives should be the basis for evaluating the program, and thus should be able to be measured in some way.

- Program objectives should elicit some "stretch" and challenge for the organization and the learners involved.

- Program objectives should express those actual and realistic commitments that the organization is willing to fulfill.

For activity objectives, the following criteria are applicable:

- Activity objectives should be based on specific identified needs.

- Activity objectives should indicate the groups that require training, the training needed, and the results expected.

- Activity objectives should be clear, precise and specific.

- Activity objectives should be written and available to each learner.

- Activity objectives should be feasible, realistically attainable, and capable of completion.

- Activity objectives should be the basis for decision-making during planning and implementation of the activity.

These criteria can serve as a checklist against which to test the objectives being developed for a program and/or activities.

These additional criteria apply both to the program objectives and to the activity objectives. First, since a number of objectives are usually developed, priorities should be assigned to them. These priorities will assist on-going decision making, much of which is likely to be done under more stress than is present during initial planning. Decisions on priorities will help determine the most urgent aspects to consider when choices about scarce resources are made. Lower priority objectives may have to be delayed or set aside when time or resources are found to be in shorter supply than expected.

A second additional criteria is that of flexibility. Although objectives should not be changed for casual reasons, modification should be possible on the basis of discoveries made during planning, implementation, or evaluation. In other words, objectives, once formed, should not be regarded as being immutable when strong indications show they need to be altered.

Thirdly, objectives should be congruent with and supportive of the goals of the library, agency, or association. Objectives should also acknowlege and encourage the goals of learners who are to be involved in the program. If the program or activity objectives conflict with individual or organizational goals, the motivation of those individuals or that organization to support the learning program may be threatened. Individuals who see no room for achieving their personal goals in the program may not be sufficiently interested or attracted to participate as fully as as was hoped. The organization then may discontinue its support if staff development efforts do not further its aims.

These criteria apply in general to whatever type of objective is being developed for a learning program. The type selected will depend, of course, on the requirements of the organization and the comfort and ability of the individual(s) responsible for developing those objectives. Within those parameters, the criteria discussed above can be used to check whatever objectives are developed.

Method

Considering the importance of the objectives, the method by which program objectives are developed can be vitally important. The method, essentially, is the means selected to decide on the objectives either for the program or for specific activities. The methods selected should be appropriate both to the learning program and to the library, agency, or association that supports it. Substantial differences exist for staff development programs in a library and continuing education programs through a state agency or a library association, as illustrated in the following discussions of each type of effort.

Staff Development Programs

A substantial staff development program is likely to have considerable impact within the organization. Consequently, the selection of the most appropriate and feasible method for developing program objectives should be carefully chosen. Various methods are possible, no single one suiting all situations, and the choice of the most appropriate method for a particular organization at a given time can be guided by several determinants. General determinants include:

- the organizational size, climate, and style,
- how quickly decisions must be made,
- the depth of personnel involvement expected to result from the program, and
- the cost, including staff time, which is allocated for program development.

In some instances, additional determinants may be relevant.

Three methods are possible: 1) the staff members working as a total group, 2) a committee for staff development, or 3) an individual or office responsible for staff development. The first alternative, the use of the staff as a total group developing the program objectives is feasible and preferable if the staff numbers between three and fifteen people, and they have a history of working together productively. The group as a whole, focusing on their needs, would decide what was most vital for the program to accomplish. The cost, in terms of the collective staff time spent on the task, would be high and the decisions would not be rapid. However, for long-range commitment and in-depth involvement, this method might be worth the cost.

In a larger organization, one that had had occasional staff development activities for some time without developing a coordinated program, the most appropriate approach might be a committee made up of people representing the various perspectives, experiences, and levels of responsibility within the library. The committee could meet to formulate objectives based on the results of both the needs assessment and their own observations and practices prompted by the previous staff development activities. Once objectives are stated in writing, the committee might present them as a draft for consideration by the staff as a whole or by the administrator. Suggested and necessary modifications could then be incorporated in a final statement of objectives. Using this method, decision-making would be faster than in the first method suggested and the cost would be reduced. If staff members reviewed the draft objectives, they would have been involved somewhat and would have some understanding of the developing nature of the program.

A third alternative might be used in an organization where the assigned responsibility for staff development rests with a single individual or with an office. In this case, the person in charge might develop statements of program objectives either alone or with the help of an advisory group. Then, those objectives could be submitted for consideration and comment by staff as well as by the administrator. This method provides the quickest decision-making at the least cost in terms of personnel time. Involvement would be increased with the advisory group, as would the required time and cost.

The method selected to develop program objectives may warrant being extended to design the program and to develop activity objectives and, in some cases, to implement the program. Or, those people involved in planning the program might determine that a different method would be more suitable for implementation. However these later tasks may be assigned, the needs assessment information and the major issues that were considered in developing the program objectives should be forwarded to assure adequate background knowledge.

The advantages and disadvantages of each of these methods must be weighed, whether the methods are being considered for working out the program objectives and design or as the means through which the program will be implemented. Each organization has its own style and personality. The method selected to develop and carry forward any staff development program should be congruent with and appropriate to that style.

The decision to involve all personnel in such key roles is an important one. Involvement of the whole group in planning will build expectations and will develop commitment and a sense of personal ownership in the program. This broad involvement usually offers a balance of perspectives and a rich resource of information as the group works toward consensus decision-making. A program planned and implemented in this way will maintain a close connection with personnel needs. Staff members so fully involved tend to be highly motivated to participate in learning activities. They also tend to be very aware of the shared responsibility for staff development—the responsibility of both employer and employee.

Such in-depth involvement consumes extensive personnel time, lengthens the time to make decisions, and increases the cost. However, this cost is offset if, throughout the process of assessing needs and developing objectives, administrators and personnel are aware that the entire process offers an opportunity for staff development. Learning the planning process first-hand can effectively develop staff resources within the library. Individual staff members can then extend the benefits of their learning even further as they deepen their knowledge of the organization, its needs and resources, and as they develop the ability to work well with their colleagues. These learnings, however, do not automatically occur; a conscious effort is required to help individuals understand the principles and process as they go through it.

A greater focus for the development of a program occurs when an individual or an office in the organization has the primary responsibility. This situation offers the advantages of quick decision-making, central coordination and communication, and focused responsibility and accountability. An individual may be the most effective and efficient way to translate staff discussion and ideas into action and to assure follow-through on necessary administrative details—if it is the right individual. A potential disadvantage includes the possibility that that individual might hold a narrow view of the library and the needs of its personnel, or that (s)he might become insular and lose touch with personnel needs, thereby lessening the relevancy and immediacy of the program's efforts for participants. Without constant, clear communication with personnel, a person in such a position may become too distant. Another disadvantage occurs when the individual or office conducts the program *for* rather than *with* the library staff.

The representative committee provides a middle ground. On a large staff, it may provide the only feasible means for involvement. Its advantages include an assigned responsibility for major functions of coordination, decision-making, and communications. The committee is less restricted than the abilities of a single individual, yet it provides more focus and continuity than full participation of the whole staff. Either of the two other alternatives might benefit from including a committee structure. It would serve to narrow the scope of the full involvement method, making it more efficient and less costly, and perhaps it could improve decision-making abilities. It would broaden the perspective of the single individual responsible for staff development and could provide for a consistent link with personnel, testing the ideas of that single individual. Such a committee is often an effective channel for transmitting information about the program to staff and conveying information about their needs, reactions, and interests back into the program planning process.

An example can be used to illustrate a method that both combines the maximum advantages of and offsets some of the disadvantages of the approaches described earlier. Soon after the needs of the library's personnel are assessed, the Staff Development Librarian convened a meeting of the newly formed Staff Development Committee to begin work on developing program objectives based on the findings of the needs assessment. Those people invited to the meeting included a representative of the library administration, professional and paraprofessional representatives from the service and function areas in the library, a representative from the Library Staff Association, and two individuals who had been instrumental in planning and conducting the needs assessment.

Prior to the meeting, the Staff Development Librarian distributed informational material from the needs assessment analysis, and personally discussed the purpose of the meeting and the indicated tasks of the committee with each Committee member individually. At the two-hour meeting, the Librarian briefly reviewed the findings of the needs assessment and described the Committee's function as that of evolving a program of staff development; then discussion was opened on two key questions: 1) Is this information accurate, sufficient and useful? and 2) Given this information, what do we do now? Initial and tentative program directions were formulated and written down, then were assigned priorities. This constituted a first draft of the program objectives. Three activities thought to be the most feasible and necessary were selected on the basis of urgency of need, availability of resources, and level of concern. The time and place were set for the next meeting.

In the meantime, the Staff Development Librarian took the results from the discussion, developed a second draft of the program objectives in the agreed-upon priority order, and attached the group's recommendations about the three suggested activities together with a time-table of necessary actions to produce those activities. This material was distributed to Committee members a few days prior to the next meeting with a cover note requesting that each elicit comments and reactions from other staff members.

In the second meeting, Committee members refined the original program objectives, modifying the original draft on the basis of their own direct feedback and the ideas and suggestions they had heard from other staff members. Then, discussion focused on the activities—the selection of topics and suggestions for format and tentative schedule—as well as the objectives for those activities. The objectives were reviewed in light of the program objectives to see if any modifications needed to be made. Each of the Committee members offered to serve on one of the three ad hoc subcommittees responsible for developing further plans for these initial activities. Additional staff members, including potential participants, were asked to serve on the basis of their interest and abilities.

Following this meeting, the Staff Development Librarian developed for all staff members a memorandum containing the polished program objectives, an outline of activities, and information about Committee and subcommittee assignments. The memo invited suggestions and comments about the program and activities as each staff member saw them in relation to personal needs and goals.

Subsequently, the Staff Development Librarian attended the meetings of the ad hoc subcommittees and a month later, convened a meeting of the Staff Development Committee to consider the feedback received regarding the program objectives and the planned activities. Although they were basically confirmed in their original form, some modifications seemed advisable. The revised program objectives, together with brief progress reports of the ad hoc subcommittees, were then communicated to the entire staff through an article in the Staff Newsletter and a notice posted on the Staff Development Bulletin Board.

In this example, the major result of the efforts of the Staff Development Librarian and the Committee was the development of objectives for the program. These objectives provided guidance for all staff development efforts in the library. In addition, planning for three activities was well underway, evidence of the progress made thus far. A firm structure, the Staff Development Committee, had been established. The precedent of using ad hoc groups to plan and produce activities had been set. This pattern of involvement and action, serving as a two-way communications liaison with the entire staff, could then build a credibility with the staff that the program would require. This process of using a combination of assigned individual responsibilities and the involvement and advice of a representative committee capitalized on the advantages offered by the centralized and the full staff approaches. It involved staff members and yielded definite accomplishments. The example also shows how early decisions on initial activities can help determine the final shape of the program.

Continuing Education Programs

An agency or association contemplating a continuing education program, however, would proceed differently because of their differences in focus from an individual library's staff development program. The following four questions can help decide the appropriate and feasible method to develop objectives in a particular situation. The same four questions can then help determine the method for developing activities objectives, since many continuing education activities are planned and produced under ad hoc circumstances.

Who should decide on the objectives? The development of the continuing education program or specific activities may be a task assigned to either an individual or a group within the organization. Expertise or knowledge not presently available may be required. Individuals and groups with an interest and ability in program planning or adult education or library concerns may be involved as well as the actual staff of the association or agency. Agencies that have personnel responsible for producing educational activities might also use an advisory group for assistance. In associations, usually a continuing education committee is responsible for program planning even if the association itself has available staff.

How should the objectives be developed? The needs assessment may have indicated a broad or narrow scope and the specific method chosen could well be used to assure either of these directions through planning the involvement of individuals and groups with special interests and expertise. The responsibility assigned to those individuals or that group should be explicitly defined, distinguishing between advisory and decision-making functions.

When should objectives be developed? The continuing education program may be an immediate priority of the organization and require prompt attention, or it may be wise to await administrative mandate and funding or grassroots demand. The effort to develop objectives may be coordinated with efforts by other organizations working towards similar aims. The program may require rapid decision-making to take advantage of available funding.

How is the program to be linked with the mission of the agency or association? The continuing education program may be used to further other organizational purposes. The present pattern of organizational integration will be a strong influence. Conflicting purposes and competition for resources may restrict the program. Communication, coordination, and decision-making linkages will be required for the program and may be included usefully in the development of objectives for the program.

The careful consideration of these ingredients will evolve the method by which the objectives, and perhaps the program planning itself, can be determined. Usually some decisions are already made by the organization, stipulated either by association bylaws or by an official agency charge. However, within the established bounds, planning decisions that include the development of objectives may be made with a number of alternative procedures. The choice of the most suitable one depends on the organization's size and its available resources and expertise.

A frequent pattern, particularly with agencies, is the assignment of responsibility for continuing education to a single individual or office. Continuing education may be a full time function for that individual or one of several tasks. Since the likely users of continuing education activities are widely dispersed throughout a state, a region, or the nation, a central locus for coordination and communication is important. Sometimes this individual develops program objectives and objectives for each activity based on information from the needs assessment and contacts.

Another pattern, seen more often in associations, is a permanent committee responsible for continuing education planning and programming. This group is often composed of representatives of the library personnel for whom the program is intended. Sometimes such a representative group is supplemented by library school faculty members or by individuals with expertise in educational programming and in training and development work. Such a group is often self-selecting on the basis of their interests and commitment to continuing education. In most cases, a standing committee may continue to exist although the changeover of members on the committee may be frequent. The group's effectiveness often depends heavily on its membership and leadership, so the consistency of continuing education programming is often uneven both in quality and in enthusiasm.

An ad hoc committee may be formed by either an agency or an association to assume the responsibility for developing a plan for the program, even though they may not be responsible for implementing it. The development of objectives on the basis of needs assessment is often seen as a logical unit for the work of an ad hoc group. The use of either an ad hoc or permanent committee involves factors of time and costs that are often divided between the committee member and his or her library/employer. Between the two, they usually contribute time, effort, and funds to support the required meeting time and travel. Success with this pattern relies on the interest and ability of those who are to implement the objectives.

A fourth pattern combines the organization's staff member who is assigned the responsibility for final decisions about the objectives and an ad hoc or permanent committee responsible for advisory functions. This pattern can be extended into subsequent planning, implementation, and evaluation efforts concerned with the continuing education function. It offers several advantages: it keeps the staff person in touch with opinions and changes and events at the grassroots library level; it helps to assure widespread awareness of the program; it incorporates more resources to supplement the staff person; and it develops continuing education leadership and expertise beyond the confines of the agency or association staff.

Basically, the decisions about what action to take with regard to developing objectives and program design from needs assessment rests with those people within the agency or association having the decision-making responsibility. However, that responsibility may be delegated in various ways. Wherever the responsibility rests, once decisions about program objectives have been made, they should be forwarded immediately to the individual or group assigned the task of program planning in written form. If those who have developed the objectives will also be responsible for implementing them, the next step is program design.

Most of the differences between methods of planning for staff development programs and those for continuing education result from the fact that staff development efforts are produced for learners with whom there can be continuous contact and a sustained relationship, whereas continuing education efforts are produced for learners who are often unknown prior to a specific activity and with whom there is little likelihood of contact after that activity. Certainly, these factors influence the process of developing objectives as well as the nature of the program.

The type of objectives developed and the process itself are important determinents of the quality and manageability of the program. To expect a program to be successfully sustained and to reap solid results without its being guided by objectives is unrealistic. Individual activities, short-term efforts, and superficial impacts can be made, of course. But in-depth results will come only with solid planning built on sound objectives.

Summary

Developing objectives is the key factor that will enable a program of staff development or continuing education to move from knowing what the staff members needs are to meeting those needs. Lack of objectives and poor planning are costly and frustrating. Developing objectives is difficult and because of that, it is sometimes bypassed. But the importance of good objectives for both the learning program and its activities is a strong argument in favor of making the effort.

Several types of objectives are possible to select from, depending on the norms of the organization and the preferences of the individuals involved. The library, the agency, and the association also have options for the method by which objectives might be developed. The various methods seek to capitalize on the strengths of the organization and the opportunities it offers as well as to make up for its disadvantages.

Sound, stated objectives are essential to give stable and consistent direction for planning, implementation, and evaluation of a program and its activities. Clear direction and communication are more easily achieved when the process of developing objectives has been done thoroughly and well.

GUIDELINE 4—IDENTIFY RESOURCES

Consistent use of quality resources in a learning program provides a significant strength and may be a determining factor in the degree of success achieved. Traditionally, library personnel show great skill and resourcefulness in meeting the needs of their library users. This same ability can be used to discover and employ the resources required for the learning program. **Resources** are defined for use here as the means needed, available, and/or used to produce a program or its activities. Resources include information and financial support, people, facilities and equipment, and materials and supplies. The two most basic of these are information and funding. From these, the others can be gained.

Benefits from the appropriate selection and wise use of resources are many. Early identification of resources helps to guide the development of a sound feasible program design. Program costs can be estimated. Program planners who identify and tap a wide range of available resources can then consider possible alternatives more efficiently when a sudden change may affect original plans. Careful use of resources can build the credibility of the program. Conversely, the effect of an inadequate presenter, faulty audio-visual equipment, or a noisy room on a learning activity has been demonstrated often enough to have been noted by everyone. The major benefit of any program, of course, is the quality of the learning experiences. And, quality resources can create and sustain high levels of creativity, energy, and enthusiasm in learners and can improve the ability of program planners and educators to produce effective activities.

Usually, however, a balance and a blend of the maximum use of the best resources and the creative use of available resources is necessary. The former is desirable, the latter is possible. Each library, agency, or association will have special strengths within itself that can be tapped, and it will have helpful contacts established outside. These will aid in the identification, discovery, selection, and use of resources as well as in their care and management. They will be needed repeatedly, for the question of resources will be raised again and again throughout the program. An early view of the resources that are anticipated follows the identification of needs and objectives that will direct the program. Later, each activity will require that resources be considered again as it is planned, implemented, and evaluated.

This Guideline describes the resources required for a program and its activities. Some of these resources are used by the learners themselves, others are needed by those who plan, implement, or evaluate the program. Various types of resources are described, and criteria are suggested to aid in the identification and selection of them. This Guideline concerns resources in general. Other Guidelines in Part II describe more specifically those resources essential for the administration of the program (Guideline 6) and its educational function (Guideline 7), those used to involve the learner (Guideline 8), and those required for specific methods and techniques (Guideline 9). Guideline 10 illustrates how resources are brought together for implementing learning activities.

Basic Criteria

One approach to the identification and use of resources is that of reviewing the available resources and building the program and activities on that base. In some cases, the available resources and the needs for either content or instructional methods will fit closely enough to justify this approach. However, wise use of the available resources rarely means the exclusive use of them. Rather, consistent or dominant use of a single method or topic may indicate that not all viable alternatives are being considered. Available or free resources may guide program planning to some extent, but they should not eliminate viable alternatives that may be more relevant to the purposes and style of the learners or the requirements of specific topics. The other approach would be to plan the use of desired quality resources to the full extent they are needed and then to trim plans back to fit the budget of time and funds available. Whichever approach is used usually depends on the prevalent style of the organization and the personal preference of the planners.

Basic criteria, used with either approach, can help identify and select resources, and such criteria also can aid planners to judge a particular resource, to choose between different ones, or to explore alternatives. For reviewing resources that can be anticipated this early, suggested criteria, in the form of questions, include:

- Is the resource actually available? (Does it exist? Can it be used at the time and place needed?)

- Is the resource appropriate to the use for which it is intended?

- · What expertise is required to use it? (Is this appropriate? Feasible?)

- Is the cost reasonable? (Is the cost commensurate with the value for the purpose? Does the available budget make it possible?)

More specific criteria are detailed in relation to the different types of resources that will need to be identified and selected. These criteria refer to resources in general. Other Guidelines are concerned with particular resources more specifically.

Categories and Types

The various types of resources can be grouped into two general categories. Some resources are intended for the use of the individuals or groups who are responsible for planning, implementing, and/or evaluating a program and activities. They may never be seen by learners. Other resources are intended for the direct use of the learners involved in those activities before, during, or after the activity. For example, office space, a typewriter, and filing cabinets may be needed by those who administer the program and its activities; a flip chart, a film, or a demonstration model may be required by the educator in producing a particular activity. The learners, on the other hand, will use the role descriptions and cases as materials to help them learn, but will also need tables and chairs as well. The first category described identifies those resources required to produce learning events and activities. The second are the resources learners require to aid their ability to learn from those activities. Although at first glance this distinction may seem unimportant, it proves helpful to clarify which resources are being sought to meet whose needs. The distinction also clarifies decisions in assigning responsibilities or in budgeting, since the purposes are different.

These categories of use can be applied to each of the various types of resources. Information and funding are basic resources which, when available, enable other resources to be identified, selected, and used. Both information and funding are essential to explore alternatives and to guide decisions that must be made among those alternatives. People to plan, implement, and evaluate the program and/or its activities are also vital. The facilities and equipment and the materials and supplies are important supplementary resources that may be more obvious when they are inappropriately selected or unwisely used than when they are adequately employed.

Information

Librarianship is based on the precept of the value of information as a key resource on which to base decisions and action. The importance of information is equally vital in relation to the learning program and its present and potential activities. The usefulness of information as a resource depends on how accurate and accessible it is and on how well it is organized. Information can come from diverse sources and can have multiple uses in the program. It needs to be consistently acquired, carefully stored, and quickly available.

Information essential to those people responsible for producing learning activities and for managing a program will vary with each situation to some extent. Although most of the heavily used materials will be in print form, (books, periodicals, pamphlets, and other documents), microfiche and cassette tapes are becoming increasingly important as training aids. A carefully selected and well used collection on program planning, adult education, and training techniques will reward the required investment with quality programming. Contacts with people who have knowledge in these fields is a less tangible but no less valuable resource to provide this information when needed.

More specifically, some major sources of information valuable to program planners include handbooks and manuals on educational methods, evaluation techniques, needs assessment procedures, and training exercises. Directories of meeting sites, resource people and instructional materials and equipment are basic. Checklists of arrangements and procedures necessary for implementation of typical training activities are helpful, as are brochures showing different training designs, resumés of potential resource people, and bibliographies covering those prime topic areas that are priority needs to be addressed in the program. Plans, surveys, reports, and studies that indicate learning needs, training designs, and evaluation findings are helpful to provide ideas. Documentation of the program's past activities, records of learner participation, and plans for present and future activities are invaluable and might include memos, contracts, minutes of planning meetings, and returned questionnaires. Records of contacts with resource people, if kept up to date, will build a bank of sources to additional information, available to be tapped as needed.

Outside the field of librarianship, major sources of information resources include professional associations such as the American Society for Training and Development and the Adult Education Association. Both organizations issue practical publications and regular journals with helpful articles, book reviews, and advertisements. Each has state or regional affiliates that schedule regular meetings and workshops focused on topics of interest to staff developers and continuing educators. In addition, these organizations provide useful personal contacts with others with similar aims. Materials from related fields of personnel, administration, continuing professional education, and training media are also helpful. The bibliography in the Appendix of this book lists specific books and periodicals of particular value.

Information about specific activities or the program as a whole, policy and procedure statements, and file copies of informational and educational materials used in conjunction with the program's activities may be needed for reference by program planners, either for on-going planning or to respond to inquiries. Generally, bookshelves, files, and folders can house these informational resources near the administrator responsible for the program.

Funding

Funding is the second basic resource needed to support any program. The money required depends on how extensive and how intensive the program is intended to be for how many people over what period of time. Funds allocated for the program depend, for the most part, on the commitment within the organization to it, and the money that that commitment makes available. If a proposed program is based on carefully assessed needs and clearly developed objectives, it is more likely to justify adequate allocation of funds.

When the direction and scope of the program emerges, initial figures indicating required funding may be estimated. Definite estimates, however, are possible only from program plans that describe what will be done, when and where, and the facilities, equipment, and instructors needed. These figures become more firm as plans are developed more specifically. Even so, the actual total cost is likely to be greater than originally anticipated.

Competition for funds is keen at all levels and in all organizations. Not only must strong justification be presented to obtain funds, but also a definite responsibility for accountability exists. Where the money goes and what results occur are ever-present concerns for those people responsible for administering organizational resources. To sustain a program over a period of time, solid and consistent response to the concern for accountability will be important. Funds will be needed to continue the program as well as initiate it, so program planners would be well advised to view the need for funds from a long-range as well as an immediate perspective. Administrators and program planners both need to understand the results that can realistically be expected from the program and what can not. When promises glow too brightly and are not fulfilled, continued funding may be jeopardized.

At the outset, particularly, it will be difficult to predict accurately and to justify costs. Establishing a budget will be unique for each organization, since sources of funds vary, accounting procedures differ, and categories depend on organizational factors. In some cases, the program might be a separately identified effort with a budget detailing total and itemized costs separately for each activity. In other instances, a program budget might be more appropriate with cost categories such as educators or learning materials or equipment for all activities grouped together. The full range of direct and indirect operational costs for the program is wide. In considering the need for funding, as many costs as possible should be estimated, the logical sources to bear those costs should be considered, and ways to trim costs should be identified.

For a staff development program, many kinds of costs are incurred: the cost of planning and administering the program; the cost of staff involved in the activities (that is, salaries covering learners' time in the activities, and perhaps travel and living expenses for off-site activities); the cost of space, materials, equipment, and overhead; the cost of evaluation. Program costs should be integrated and managed within the total organizational picture, and records and reports should be required of the staff development function just as they are of any other part of the organization.

As with staff development, some continuing education program costs will be obvious and can be easily foreseen and anticipated, while others will be more indirect and concealed. Obvious items include the costs of developing the program and activities using staff time and travel, consultants, materials, facilities, and supplies. Less obvious are items such as administrative overhead, planning and evaluation meetings, and communication expenses.

The major source for staff development program funds is the regular organizational budget of the library. Funds, however, might also be sought from the parent organization (that is, the municipality, the university, the library system),

Friends groups, or grant funds from state, regional, or federal sources. Assured continuity of funding is desirable but often not possible. For programs of staff development or of continuing education, the conditions under which funds are obtained should not inhibit the program from performing to accomplish its objectives. Neither the funding source nor the program should have to compromise its own purpose and objectives either to give or receive the funds.

Financial resources used for continuing education may come from many sources. State agencies often use a combination of regular state funding allocations in concert with federal funds from the Library Services and Construction Act, the Higher Education Act, or others. Associations combine registration fees from participants or their libraries, dues income, and, in some cases, state, federal or private funding sources to offset the costs to the sponsor and/or the learner. Co-sponsorship is sometimes used to pool resources but may also bring constraints in implementing and planning, since each additional organization introduces additional factors, some of which may jeopardize cohesive programming in exchange for easing the cost.

Less direct possibilities also exist. Often associations tap interested professional people who will work voluntarily on its educational activities. Sources of contributed materials and facilities also ease the financial strain on associations. Presently, a growing movement is gaining favor. Association funds previously committed to scholarships are being re-directed to continuing education activities in the belief that pre-service education is less a need now than is the improvement of skills of those already in the field.

Agencies and associations often require individual learners or their libraries to share some expenses. Staff time is almost always a required contribution, and often travel and living expenses are paid by the learner or library. Institutes and conferences are rather typical examples of this. This manner of sharing costs differentiates between the production of the activity (the agency or association) and attending the activity (the individual learner or library). However, with staff development, the cost is borne by the library to a greater extent than continuing education is borne by the agency or association. Available funds will influence a learning program significantly and budgeting is a major early concern. Various ways to trim costs are possible. For example, activities developed for one program might be exchanged with another organization with similar needs. Or, the use of available activities, such as civil service training activities, learning packages, or community adult education, extend the learning possibilities without entailing development costs. Or, these might be adopted and then adapted in new ways by the library, agency, or association to assure closer correlation with library concerns. a sound, on-going evaluation effort, as a key part of the program, can review program activities and functions to cull those that are not worthwhile. Employing the capabilities and talents of people already on the staff rather than using outside consultants can stretch program dollars. Already developed designs and materials can sometimes be substituted for the expensive process of developing new ones even when the activity is produced by the library, agency or association. And, finally, if activities are planned to achieve more than a single purpose, the number of results and benefits may be increased without extending the cost significantly. Making the best use of the funding available also may assist in justifying continued funding possibilities.

People

Identification of the human resources sought for the program and for specific activities requires the definition of the knowledge, skills, and attitudes that such people will need to do the job. Much of the success of any program hinges on the calibre of the people involved, both those responsible for administering the program and those responsible for the instructional functions within the activities. Some individuals put together the various components in such a way that maximum learning and growth can occur in spite of limited resources. Others, even with a wealth of resources, may be unable to construct and manage a viable program or even a specific learning activity.

Able people are required to manage a program. They need skills of administration, communicating clearly in person or on paper, coordinating details and follow-through, planning flexibly, and accommodating unexpected turns of events. The knowledge needed by such people would include a broad understanding of the particular organization and the people in it, as well as the knowledge of how adults learn and the techniques that can best enable that to happen. The attitudes needed would include a belief in the inherent capability of individuals to learn and apply those learnings, patience and understanding with the individuals involved in the program, and an openness to one's own personal growth. Guideline 6 details the capabilities needed for managing a program.

Competency is also a prime requirement for those responsible for instructional functions. Specialized knowledge in a particular subject area through study or work experiences is important, as are knowledge of effective training techniques and the ability to work well with learners. Specific descriptions of the various kinds of people needed for different purposes in the instructional portion of a program are given in Guideline 7.

The present staff of the library, agency, or association should be considered first in assigning responsibilities for managing a program. They have the advantage of knowing the organization and its needs and of demonstrating their abilities and knowledge and work habits, advantages particularly important in the selection of personnel for program administration. Most often, the additional skills needed by present staff members assuming such program responsibilities are those of educational programming and training techniques. The former can be learned; the latter may be found in individuals rich with the experience and the attitudes that will help others learn.

Similarly, staff members can often contribute to the instructional or training functions of the program. Particularly in a staff development program, this may have many advantages. For example, the supervisor with a skill for on-the-job instruction in one area might teach others the essential steps in that process. Or, a particular interest or ability of a staff member may be relevant to the subject or methodology of an activity. Those who serve as educators in staff development activities deepen their own knowledge and experience through that experience. As well as being a sound long-range method of development, utilization of present staff is cost effective. Charles Kozoll emphasizes the importance of using outside resources to supplement internal personnel only when particular skills or knowledge are not available or for very specialized reasons such as to give impetus or new direction, or, perhaps, to provide a useful evaluative viewpoint.[15]

Thus, only when it has been determined that the present staff members do not have the needed competencies should the search for outside resources begin. The search for these needed competencies may center on the position of program administrator or may be for educators and resource people for special activities or events. For the former, as a regular position, a job description will be necessary and the search would be conducted as others are for the organization. Special emphasis might be given to recruiting through training and development or adult education channels. Often outside people are engaged on an ad hoc basis, their services bound by a time limitation and by a specified area of responsibility. Usually termed consultants, they might be used to conduct a survey of needs, to help design the program, or to evaluate parts of the program in action. Educational specialists may be engaged to present specific and unique information at an activity, to demonstrate skills or equipment not available within the organization, or to conduct a particular learning activity.

The usefulness of ad hoc educators or consultants depends on two key factors: 1) their personal and professional abilities, and 2) the clarity with which their responsibility has been defined. The first factor includes what they know, what they can do with that knowledge, and how well they can help others learn. The second factor is concerned with how well the organization has defined what it needs and what it wants specifically from the consultant. Although the consultant is partially responsible for assuring this clarity, the prime responsibility rests with those in the organization having the task of preparing the consultant for the assigned job.

Sources for finding consultants range widely, too widely perhaps to be much help in careful selection. The most frequently used source is word-of-mouth about who has been used in similar circumstances with good results. Library associations, state library agencies, and library schools, as well as other libraries, can often provide suggestions. Outside the fields of librarianship and education, consultants helpful for developing a program would include people from business and industry, community and government, college and university, public service fields, training and development and adult education organizations. For individuals sought as resources for specific training responsibilities, the basic concern is with the area of expertise, such as electronic data processing, networking, communications, and interpersonal relations.

Facilities and Equipment

Facilities house the program and/or its activities. Equipment includes the apparatus required to administer the program or instruct. Strong organizational commitment to the program and sufficient funding to support that commitment might provide ample facilities and equipment for staff development, such as a room in which training activities and planning and evaluation meetings can take place; a well-equipped office for the program staff; bulletin boards for posting announcements, brochures, and schedules; reliable access to copying services; and ample audio-visual equipment for instruction.

Where this ideal situation does not exist, modifications will be necessary. If training activities and meetings are not frequent and routine, a suitable community room in the library or perhaps in a nearby agency or bank could be used, as long as it could be scheduled when needed. On a campus, an appropriate classroom or conference room might be available at the required times. Although facilities needed for conducting learning activities ideally might include a carpeted room with provisions for flexible seating and multiple audio-visual possibilities, under less ideal circumstances, the physical facilities might be a community meeting room with borrowed audiovisual equipment and a portable flipchart.

The requirements for learning facilities and equipment for continuing education activities through a state agency or a library association would be similar. For agencies and associations, however, the locale is likely to vary, since agencies often conduct continuing education activities regionally and associations change conference sites and institute locations. Thus, agencies and associations are more likely to use a given site only once, or, at most, a few times, whereas participants in a library's staff development program would become familiar with the same site(s). For both programs, physical facilities for learners are important to the learning potential. Adequate rooms with comfortable furniture and appropriate provision for instructional aids do facilitate learning. The atmosphere of the facility as well as the physical structure can have a significant effect.

The equipment for learning includes the hardware and educational technology required for the educational methods used. These are often essential to increase learning and include such items as film projectors, recorders, videotape equipment, demonstration units, flip charts, and flannel boards. Equipment is often closely associated with facilities because of the close relationship between the two, since certain facilities may enable or prohibit the use of some types of equipment. Regularly used equipment may warrant purchase, whereas special equipment used only for a few training activities might well be borrowed or rented.

A staff development program, whether administered full-time or part-time, is likely to have a stable and equipped office headquarters. For a state library agency, this is also true, even though the various learning activities actually may be conducted at different sites throughout the state. Regional and national library associations with assigned personnel for continuing education also may have a permanent base from which programs are administered. Many state library associations, however, do not have a stable office to administer a program or consistent facilities for conducting learning activities. This naturally limits the extent and ability of the program. Office facilities may be the contribution of the home or work site of the person having primary responsibility for that year's continuing education activities. Thus, extensive files and informational materials cannot be collected, and equipment usually must be obtained from a variety of sources rather than being readily available to the program. Publicizing the office locale is also difficult because of frequent change. These limitations may inhibit the desired range of activities, but, nonetheless, quality learning and administration can still occur. Detailed information about facilities and equipment can be found in Guidelines 9 and 10.

Materials and Supplies

Materials are the educational aids used to initiate, facilitate, or reinforce the learning process. They may be used before a learning activity to prepare the learner, during the activity to help the learner understand and apply principles being presented, or after an activity in order to reinforce the learning. Custom-designed materials are usually preferred, for they are most closely related to the needs of the learner and the type of activity. Although the development of materials is usually most effective if done in the final stages of planning for an activity, handouts, bibliographies, background readings, and case studies can be collected in anticipation of their possible adaptation and later use.

The design of materials for activities is a significant cost factor in the development of a learning program. Sometimes entire **learning packages** exist and may provide substantial savings. A learning package is a collection of focused resources to help people learn. For example, a priority staff development need shown in a library might be for supervisory skills. If the municipal or state government has developed a supervisory skills training package that is scheduled regularly for its personnel, that package, after careful review of its appropriateness in meeting the needs of the library, might be used with library personnel. This approach might offer cost savings over the development of a new activity as well as the added benefit of an opportunity to build library contact with local governmental offices and personnel. Or, a commercially available package on supervisory skills might be purchased for use in the library.

When such packages can be discovered and found useful, the saved time, energy and money can then be shifted into developing a needed activity for which no package exists or an activity that cannot be done as well outside the organization. Other examples of such ready-made packages include commercially produced short-courses; professional and trade association meetings and seminars; business and technical school courses; civic and university organization programs; national, state, and local library association conferences; and state library workshops. Some of these present content information for a basic level of awareness, some focus on building specific skills, and some offer a sequence of gradually more advanced work on a specific topic.

Supplies, like materials, will depend on the implementation of activities in order to define a library's specific need. The size of the program, the preferences of its management, the kinds of activities that are developed, and the needs for communication within the library, agency or association are all prime determinents of what supplies will be required. Supplies often furnished to learners include paper, notebooks, pencils, and folders.

Materials and supplies are also required for the administration of the program. Some of these materials overlap with the informational resources covered earlier. Collected during planning, these may provide useful models for planning groups to consider or for educational staff to adapt. Some materials may be developed that describe either the program itself or the individual activities that make it up. These might be supplied to staff members or distributed to association membership to encourage participation. State agencies that include listings of continuing education opportunities in periodic newsletters help make continuing education activities available for staff development programs.

Supplies that might be needed for the administration of a program would include paper stock for copying and correspondence, newsprint for planning as well as instructional purposes, and forms for registration or record-keeping or evaluation. Smaller items such as markers, chalk, cassettes, and nametags will also be needed. Guideline 9 includes more detailed information about materials and supplies in relation to the implementation of the program.

Resources Inventory

While planning a program or an activity, key questions arise that require the identification of resources. For example:

- What do we, as planners, need to help us plan well?
- What kind of expertise is needed?
- Who has that expertise?
- Will training materials be necessary to prepare learners and make the most of the learning experience?
- What facilities and equipment will be required?

The answers to these and other questions give an initial indication of the resources that will be needed.

One means of acquiring or managing the many resources that may be needed is to inventory or list them during the planning process. If done during planning rather than at the point of actual need and use, such a list can be helpful in several ways. If an essential resource is found to be unavailable at one stage, planning may redirect the nature of that particular activity. An inventory will make quickly obvious the alternatives that may exist and prompt further consideration of alternative means to accomplish the ends sought. An inventory can be a helpful guide to select priority purchases, to decide when to rent or borrow, to determine which needs can be delayed, or to assist with budgeting of the activity. In addition to the list of what is needed, a second step can be annotating the list with indications of which resources are known to be available through normal channels and which will require special contacts to locate and obtain. These annotations can also specify where and how the resource might be located if it is presently unavailable. This list is particularly helpful in working with a planning group for it pools information and contacts from many people and serves as a checklist for follow-up as planning evolves into implementation.

If the planning process involves a group of people, a surprising number of resources will be known among the members of the group: a committee member may have special but unrevealed skills, equipment may be available to be borrowed from a university or government unit, facilities may be obtainable from a business or institution. Other resources may not be known to be immediately available when found to be needed, but may be revealed through contacts suggested by group members based on their knowledge or personal experience.

Resources File

Another useful tool that can aid the management of program resources is a resource file consisting of folders in a filing cabinet or cards in a box with resources noted at the time of their discovery. The information is then available to be used when needed. The file could indicate, by category of resource, those known to be available. For example, under equipment might be indicated the source, the conditions for use, and the contact person through whom it can be obtained. If a resource has been used previously, the file can be annotated as to important qualifications or conditions that were found during its use. Or, a file might be arranged by topic, indicating resource people, training packages, or workshop designs for the various areas of need that are priorities for the program, such as supervisory skills, affirmative action, interpersonal communications, networking. Often, a file of annotations for self-instructional courses and programmed learning possibilities can encourage personalized self-study.

These files provide a base for building a valuable resource bank which could save time, effort, and money. Perhaps the files described would not be of great value the first year, but after that time and with consistent additions and updating, they could be a valuable aid in planning for activities and in keeping a record of what resources have been used and with what results.

Summary

Quality resources, well selected and well used, strengthen staff development efforts. Taking a careful look at the need for resources during planning will help to guide program design, determine the feasibility of the program and identify alternatives that may be needed for later decision-making. Some resources are required by those who are responsible for planning and implementing the program, some for those who seek to learn from the activities. Although these two categories of use are different, both need the same types of resources. The basic criteria that can be used to identify and select specific resources include: availability, cost, appropriateness, and feasibility. The inventory list and the resource file are tools that can aid the management of resources.

Two basic resources are information and funding. Information is essential for decisions and action. Its usefulness depends on its accuracy and accessibility. Funding is necessary to support the program. Cost depends on how extensive and how intensive the training will be, on how many people will be involved, and on time available. Paring costs will help to extend the use of available funds.

Human resources are responsible for administering the program and for the educational functions. Utilization of the present staff is economical and, at the same time, is an effective method of staff development. Outside resources will always be needed for specializations. Physical facilities, equipment, materials, and supplies all depend on implementation for final decisions. They may be difficult to predict during early planning, although they must be anticipated to some extent in order to be budgeted then. The steady accumulation of information might well be collected in a resource file, which would prove useful as long as kept up to date.

GUIDELINE 5—DESIGN PROGRAM

The quality and success of the learning program depends on the awareness, knowledge, and skill of the planning and implementation of it. The program itself brings together the components, the resources, and the capabilities of the library, agency, or association in addressing its staff development or continuing education function. Guided by program objectives that were developed from the needs assessment, the design of the program itself provides the basic framework into which learning activities are set. The **design** is the planning of a sequence of learning events, activities, and processes in such a way that the established program objectives can be accomplished effectively and appropriately.

The program design brings identified needs and program objectives to meet those needs together with the outline of activities to be done in order to achieve the objectives. More specifically, the design shows the relationship of the various learning activities as to sequence and scheduling. It also indicates the management of the program, such as how decisions are made and communicated and how evaluation information will be obtained and used. A major result of initial planning, the design provides directions for implementing the program over a given time period, designating those efforts presently being done and those contemplated for the future. The process of designing such a plan includes decisions about the many components that make up the program.

This Guideline describes each of these components: topics, learners, methods, resources, scheduling, and management. Principles, key questions, and criteria are suggested to aid planners making decisions about these components. Various approaches to designing a program are offered as are the policy implications for the program. General principles are indicated and specific alternatives suggested. The focus here is on the program's design. The design of specific activities is the emphasis of Guideline 10.

Basic Principles

Program planning principles aid in developing a quality program and enabling its successful implementation. If these tenets are woven into the program design either implicitly or explicitly, they will more likely guide its implementation. Important to be considered at the point of shaping the design, they are framed here as questions to encourage their use not only for developing a new program but also to review or evaluate an existing program:

- Is the design based on the identified needs of individuals and the library?

- Does it provide for redirection when new needs emerge or when present ones change?

- Does it acknowledge individual and organizational goals and provide possibilities for each to be achieved?

- Does it operate generally within prescribed organizational constraints yet provide some opportunities to experiment beyond present organizational bounds?

- Does it integrate staff development with other library functions?

- Does it build on existing strengths and present activities that are relevant to program objectives yet expose personnel to ideas and methods beyond those now available within the library?

- Does it operate within the realm of feasibility, as determined by the level of competence and the available resources of the organization?

- Does it seek and utilize learning resources and opportunities relevant to identified needs whether those are within or outside the organization?

- Does it provide for building knowledge and skills through a succession of activities that offer both balance and growth for the present capabilities of individuals and the library?

- Does it provide a range of learning opportunities that will enable a variety of learning and methods for learning for all levels of personnel?

- Does it assure that the learning process can be a conscious one so that personnel are encouraged and enabled to learn more continuously in a self-directed manner?

- Does it provide for necessary assistance to the learner before, during, and after learning activities to assure maximum effectiveness of the learning process?

- Does it assist the individual and the library to relate available learning opportunities with on-the-job application of those learnings?

- Does it schedule activities to meet the needs of the learner and the library at the appropriate depth and scope?

- Is it considered flexible, able to adjust to changing circumstances, emerging priorities, evaluative findings?

- Does it assure the gathering and use of evaluation information to measure results and enable continuous program review?

- Is it educationally sound, incorporating the tenets of adult learning?

Learning

This last principle may need further definition and explanation for program planners with limited experience in present-day adult education. Leading adult educator Malcolm S. Knowles describes the concept of "andragogy," a new term used to describe the body of theory and technology that now prevails among adult educators in all fields. Andragogy is based on empirical evidence that leads to basic assumptions about adults as learners. As their premise, these assumptions draw the conclusion that adults as learners differ in some significant ways from children as learners (i.e., the body of theory known as pedagogy). Knowles has outlined "a process and a set of principles that apply in one way or another to all programs that have as their purpose the growth and development of adults . . . premised on the proposition that there is a unique technology of adult education, which in turn is based on certain assumptions about the unique characteristics of adults as learners. . . . " He lists these tested assumptions as:

1. "Adults . . . tend to see themselves as responsible self-directing independent personalities . . . and tend to resist learning under conditions that are incongruent with their self-concept as autonomous individuals."

2. The "adult enters into any educational activity with a different background of experience from that of his youth. . . . For this reason, adults are themselves a richer resource for one another's learning than youth usually are [and are] less dependent on the vicarious experience of teachers, experts and textbooks."

3. Adults, like youth, have phases of growth related to their social roles and their readiness to learn is based on the changes in the developmental tasks that confront them at particular points of their growth.

4. Adults "tend to enter any educational activity in a problem-centered frame of mind."[16]

In his many books and articles, Knowles describes the implications these principles have for those who plan programs in which adults are the learners.

In their research, Pine and Horne identified similar principles related to adult learning that support Knowles's concept. These are a further aid for program planners:

- "Learning is an experience which occurs inside the learner and is activated by the learner."

- "Learning is the discovery of the personal meaning and relevance of ideas."

- "Learning (behavioral change) is a consequence of experience."

- "Learning is a cooperative and collaborative process."

- "Learning is an evolutionary process."

- "Learning is sometimes a painful process."

- "One of the richest resources for learning is the learner himself."

- "The process of learning is emotional as well as intellectual."

- "The processes of problem solving and learning are highly unique and individual."

In reporting their findings in the adult education field following their exhaustive Operation Mainstream research project, the authors detail these principles and go on to describe the conditions that facilitate the learning of adults.[17]

More extensive resources in adult learning theory may be useful to locate research findings, to compare current with earlier theories, and to explore how what is now known about learning can affect staff development program planning and evaluation, and its implementation. J. R. Kidd in *How Adults Learn* (1973) is concerned with the cognitive, affective, and psychological aspects of the learning process, the teaching-learning transaction, and the role of the teacher/practitioner. *The Modern Practice of Adult Education* (1972) by Malcolm S. Knowles describes a comprehensive theory of adult education and learning and offers concrete assistance for program planners. Knowles's *The Adult Learner: A Neglected Species* (1973) details "the emerging theories about adult learning based on the unique characteristics of adults as learners." Lawrence Allen's previously cited study of *Continuing Education Needs of Special Librarians* (1974) was the first thorough introduction of the concepts of andragogy in library literature.

Since staff development and continuing education efforts are both based on the ability of library personnel to learn effectively, and since the learners are adults, these principles of program design and those with regard to adult learning are relevant and essential for application during planning and implementation.

The Design

The word design brings to mind scientific or technological principles being brought to bear on a problem, challenge, or discovery of some significance. Or, it conjures the emergence of an art form expressing truth and beauty. An educational design, like both of these images, combines creativeness and technique. Knowles and Davis, both known for their pragmatic approach to creating learning opportunities, have each drawn the parallel between educational design and art design. Knowles bases his concept on the belief that the aesthetic quality of any program directly affects its educative quality. He applies the elements of artistic design to program design and describes how the use of line, space, tone, texture, and color, all artistically combined, yields a satisfying composition that can produce effective learning.[18] In his approach, Davis states: "Every serious art form has an orderly way or arranging the elements; libraries are filled with critical books documenting it. Without apology, therefore, I call a good learning design a work of art and high art at that. . . ."[19]

More often, however, the program planner is less concerned about these concepts than about the pressure related to specific decisions about topics, methods, and the intended learner group for each activity of the program. At least the need for and availability of resources must be tentatively explored. A schedule of events is needed, with immediate activities more definitively planned than the long-range view. The design must accommodate operational constraints, those fixed elements such as physical facilities, funding and time limits, and the organizational style and work schedule. In addition to designating the frequency, sequence, and duration of the learning activities, decisions concerning program management also need to be part of the plan: the points of decision making, who makes what decisions, how those will be communicated and coordinated, who is accountable. The final design results from the process of bringing all of these various components together.

Figure 9 illustrates an abbreviated staff development program design for a medium-size library. This plan makes a clear distinction between the program's

Figure 9

Annual Plan for Staff Development Program
for the _____ Public Library

	JAN	FEB	MAR	APR	MAY	JUNE	JULY	AUG	SEPT	OCT	NOV	DEC
Learning Activities	*Supervisors' Clinic: On-Job Instruction		*Typing Skills Class, Business College			*Colloquium on Systems and Networking	*American Library Association Annual Conference		*State Library Conference		*All-Staff Workshop on New Information Handling Techniques and Electronic Data Processing Equipment	
	*All-Staff Meeting and Program					*All-Staff Meeting and Program						
Program Management	*Staff Development Committee Meeting—To Review and Evaluate Present Program					*Staff Development Committee Meeting: To Review, Modify, Program, and Plan Upcoming Events						
	*Present Report to Staff Meeting											
	*Update Report on Staff Development Published in Staff Newsletter				*Meeting of Ad Hoc Committee on Staff Workshop				*Meeting of Ad Hoc Committee on Staff Workshop			
	*Librarian I—Job-Rotation Change-Over						*Librarian I—Job-Rotation Change-Over					

learning activities and its management over a period of a year, showing how the various components link, alternate, and reinforce each other. Such a chart can be useful both to program planners and those who have responsibilities for implementing the design. For a staff development program, learners and managers in other parts of the organization will understand the program more clearly with such a chart. For a continuing education program, this kind of chart is valuable to describe the program to agency or association personnel and to library personnel who are potential learners themselves or who supervise potential learners.

Components

The strength of any program comes from the creative selection, balance, and use of its components. How well each of these components can be satisfactorily defined and interrelated with one another will depend, in large measure, on the adequacy of the assessment of needs and the establishment of objectives. Time and care taken at these earlier stages will now pay off by providing information and direction adequate to help assemble other program ingredients. The essential program components include:

- Topics for learning must be selected.
- Learners must be identified.
- Methods for learning must be chosen.
- Resources must be selected.
- Scheduling must be determined.
- Program management must be planned.

Program planning principles need to be used as constant checkpoints to assure that they are integral both to the program as a whole and to each of the individual components.

Decisions as to components are required at two levels. The first level is that of the program itself. The second is that of the activities making up the program. Decisions about components at the program level are far-reaching, broadly aimed. Those for the learning activities are more specific, relating to a specific topic for a given group of learners for a particular activity planned for anticipated results. At the stage of designing the program, initial decisions must be made with regard to components in relation to the program as a whole. In relation to the first few activities, components can also be usefully selected and defined at this stage. In fact, making such decisions for activities at an early point serves to test the validity of the decisions made for the program.

Topics for learning must be selected. The topics are the content, the subject matter, or the focus of the activities. Together, the topics compose the curriculum of the program and provide the motif of the program's design. The selection of topics is based on the results of the needs assessment and on the specified objec-. tives. Individual topics are the centering point for each of the various learning activities. Themes of priority topics will weave throughout the program, and their coordination and scheduling should be designed to make maximum impact with respect to those topics.

Topics should not be selected independently of such other factors as learners, methods, or resources, since these other components are essential to adequately treat that topic. For example, "communication" may have been found to be a prime need. Certainly, that topic may require several interconnected activities to meet the needs of different groups of learners. For some, communications with library users may be the need; for others, written communications such as correspondence or reports may be essential; for others, communicating with key community people may be important. To each of these groups the need for "communication" may mean something different. Or, the need may be for "management." Substantial difference may be found between the management knowledge and skills needed by the director of a small public library and those needed by the administrator of an academic research library, between those needed by a systems director for a region or state and those needed by a school library supervisor. Further definition of a topic's scope and depth must be made before definitive plans can be made about the other components. And, too, some of the topic's definition may come from decisions made in relation to other components.

Several factors are important in relation to the topic. Topics too generally defined may require further needs assessment to make them specifically useful for pursuit. On the other hand, the number of learners available for a narrow topic may make that activity unfeasible to produce. The degree of closeness in the relationship between the topic of a learning activity and the learner's library situation is often a surprisingly large factor governing its acceptance and ultimate usefulness. Thus, the results from a given activity are often directly related to its topic. Each of these factors may serve to limit learners' use of needed topics such as supervisory skills, communications, and human relations when they are offered and available outside the library context.

Key questions that can be used to clarify each topic selected as the focus for learning efforts include:

- How broad a scope is required for this topic to be applicable to the learners' library situation?

- What levels within the topic's scope are most crucial: introductory? for those with some experience? advanced?

- What learning opportunities already exist in relation to this topic? Are they available to library personnel?

- How urgent and important is this topic?

Program planners who define topics in relation to the other components of the program acknowledge the effect of those other components on the topic and, in turn, the effects of topic choice on components.

Staff development programs can capitalize on several potential advantages in relation to the topic for learning. The real level of need may be more easily observed, clarified, and demonstrated, since most libraries can provide a relatively accurate definition of need in relation to a given topic through an adequate needs assessment. A single topic can then be approached in a number of ways to meet the needs of different categories of learners within the library. For example, a skills workshop can be followed by one-to-one on-the-job instruction and subsequent problem-solving seminars to reinforce the learning gained through the original activity. Then, work relationships can link the different learning groups and different topics in the scheduled activities and in coordinated work assignments of learners. These advantages, if pursued, can provide a more coordinated approach to a given topic and can improve the possibility of substantial impact from the learning activities related to that topic.

Continuing education programs, however, must rely more on the observation of a sample of the potential learner group for defining a given topic. Topics for continuing education activities are more subject to trends in popularity than those in staff development. Also, they often need careful promotion when topics are controversial. The scope and level of topic must be very clearly defined to enable potential learners to select what activity will best suit their needs. Each potential learner will bring to the learning activity a slightly different expectation concerning the topic, with little opportunity beforehand to fully understand the program's particular definition(s) of that topic.

Learners must be identified. Learners are those whose needs will be met through the program's learning activities. They are expected to improve the library's effectiveness through the increased competency that results from their learning. The needs assessment identifies a number of learner groups, such as personnel responsible for the selection and use of audiovisual equipment, librarians involved with developing new service programs, or reference staff. Often the topics, roughly defined by the needs assessment, then can be more carefully delineated as learner groups are identified. Since each component significantly affects the other, the relationship between the topic and the learner group usually ends up being a close one.

The learners may be explicitly identified through needs assessment, or, more implicitly, on the basis of related needs and topics. The following questions may be useful to help further define learner groups:

- Whose job responsibilities require knowledge or skill related to the topic?

- What level and scope of job responsibilities do potential learners have?

- What experience and previous training have they had?

- What are the major motivating factors of the learner? of the employing library?

- What are the expectations of the learner? of the library?

- How many learners are likely to participate?

- Are there enough potential learners in relation to the topic to sustain a collective learning activity, or should individual approaches be offered?

These questions not only help define the learner group but also anticipate the view the learner may have of the activity. Both of these perspectives are useful in designing the program.

When the needs assessment has not provided sufficient detail to answer these questions, assumptions about learners are usually made based on either factual information or conjecture. Of course, the more information that is known, the more reliable the design decisions are likely to be. Sometimes, though, the additional time and expense necessary to obtain more information is not possible.

When it is justifiable, however, a more limited, more focused assessment of the specific learner group can be helpful, particularly for more detailed planning necessary for a particular activity.

A staff development program often derives strength from its advantages in relation to the learners. Although the actual individuals who will be involved in a particular learning activity may not be immediately known, the potential learners in the program are well defined. Continuous contact before, during, and after the learning activity can furnish both a sound definition of their needs and the opportunity to identify the level at which those needs must be met. Follow-through can determine the degree of learning that was achieved and has been applied on the job. Successive learning activities and processes then can provide an array of staff skills by building on previous learnings.

The on-going relationship between the learner and the library permits a continuing view of each individual's aims, abilities and growth. This view can be actively supplemented through supervision, performance appraisal procedures, incentives, and record-keeping to guide and support the continuation of a learning path for each staff member. Staff development can weave the learning and the application of that learning together. This reinforces learning and supports the learner who is attempting new or difficult behavior. For example, a one-day workshop on supervisory skills might be supplemented by job rotation and coaching to help the learner apply what was learned. These many advantages, if utilized constructively, offer continuous benefits to the staff development program.

In contrast, continuing education efforts through a state agency or library association usually offer a single activity for a designated category of learners on a specified subject. Often there is little, if any, prior knowledge of the individual learners who will be attending the activity. Limited contact previous to the activity impedes the preparation of the learner, and follow-through is also difficult and unpredictable. The learner group may be specified solely by the individual's interest or the library's concern with the topic, by geographic location and date, or by the type of library. Planning for continuing education activities can affect some of these factors, thus strengthening the program. But, in many instances, they will prove insurmountable, and the responsibility will fall to the individual learner to creatively counteract these disadvantages. Additional material on learners in staff development and continuing education programs is offered in Guideline 8.

Methods for learning must be chosen. The **method** is the mode of procedure, the form and format, or the type of approach to learning that will be employed for the various activities in the program. A method may consist of a single technique or of a combination of several techniques selected to meet the requirements of the topic, the anticipated results, and the qualifications and ability of the educator(s). A variety of carefully chosen methods will add interest and vitality to the program. The program itself is not likely to have a single established method, even though it may have guiding precepts and principles. Rather, its texture will be determined by the choices of methods to be used for the program's activities.

A wide range of alternative methods should be considered to assure that the most appropriate one is selected. Often, the method may be predetermined, such as the frequent inclination to "have a workshop." This tendency must be resisted to enable careful selection of the best method for the situation. Yet, the process of selection is often difficult, with many methods to choose from. Following is a list of possible learning activity methods that are particularly useful for staff development and continuing education activities. For each method listed, a primary purpose is suggested, a brief description highlights its principle value and use, and citations are given for further information. Some of these methods, such as job instruction or job rotation, may be centered largely within the library. Others, such as conferences, laboratory training, and institutes are most often produced by an agency or association.

* * *

Methods and Techniques to be Used in Designs
for Staff Development and Continuing Education

If the primary function is to present sources of information, ideas, or concepts, consider:

AUDIO MEDIA (Radio, tape recorder, telephone)
Information presented by mechanical device. May serve as a trigger for discussion groups. Current developments utilize call-in telephone capabilities to create question and answer or dialogue situation.
*[Anderson, pp. 87-104; Brown, pp. 207-213; Craig, pp. 43-1 to 43-23; Klevins, pp. 199-215.]

CLASS/COURSE
A series of sessions prepared by the instructor usually with a well defined subject and scope. Commonly focused on the dissemination of knowledge, but sometimes may include skills building or attitudinal training.
[Craig, pp. 33-1 to 33-13.]

CORRESPONDENCE STUDY/COURSE
A packaged program directed toward specific educational objectives. Can use a variety of print and non-print techniques. Self-directing. Relies on learner initiative and sustained interest over a period of time.
[Craig, pp. 38-1 to 38-14.]

DISCUSSION GROUP
Group of people talk about topic(s) of mutual concern. May be based on common background or experience. Often moderated by a designated discussion leader. Success may depend on skilled leadership.
[Dimock, pp. 17-19; Klevins, pp. 59-60; Kozoll, pp. 109-111; This, pp. 63-66.]

FILMS/TELEVISION/VIDEOTAPE
Useful for portrayal of realistic situations. Requires special equipment and technical knowledge. Needs to be selected carefully for audience level and relevance to what is to be learned. May be used to stimulate discussion. Videotape can record immediate events and provide playback for review

---

*Citations for sources noted in brackets are on page 79.

and analysis. Requires trained people to do taping and to
help learning result from what is taped.
[Anderson, pp. 69-85; Brown, pp. 179-206, 235-254; Craig,
pp. 43-1 to 43-23; Dimock, pp. 31-38; Klevins, pp. 183-188;
Kozoll, pp. 94-96, 101-102.]

FILMSTRIP/SLIDES

Projected still visual images, usually accompanied by an
audio tape or scripted message. Valuable for teaching
recognition and principles. Filmstrips have a locked-in
visual content and sequence. Slides more flexible. Requires
technical competence to produce, but little to use.
[Anderson, pp. 55-66.]

FORUM/PANEL

Two or more individuals conduct a discussion before an
audience. The individuals may be subject experts or experienced practitioners. Method can be used to explore a problem
in depth, present conflicting points of view or stimulate
audience interest. Usually requires a moderator.
[Kozoll, pp. 92-94.]

LECTURE

Information presented by an individual to a group for purposes
of instruction in a particular subject area. Relies on transmission of information. May be supplemented by use of
visuals and exhibits. Easily controlled time, scope and depth.
Impact varies with speaker credibility, with learner acceptance and the relevance of the topic and focus.
[Craig, pp. 33-1; Dimock, pp. 17-19; Kozoll, pp. 90-92;
Lynton, pp. 137-141.]

PROGRAMMED INSTRUCTION

A self-instructional method of learning which may use print
or non-print materials. A series of steps gradually increasing
in complexity lead the learner through a sequence: acquisition of information and testing for comprehension. Self-
paced. Relies on learner initiative. Gives immediate evidence
of learning. May include computer-assisted instruction.
[Brown, pp. 412-415; Craig, pp. 39-1 to 39-23; Lynton, pp.
168-172; Yarple.]

SEMINAR

A recognized expert meets with a small group of learners,
usually for the purpose of exploring a subject in depth.
Learners expected to prepare papers for discussion. Offers
the advantages of guidance and expertise with in-depth
discussion. Can be a one-time event or a series over a period
of time.
[Lynton, pp. 135-137.]

SYMPOSIUM/COLLOQUIUM

A presenter or group of presenters deals with a single subject. Usually opportunity for the audience to question and comment.

If the primary function is demonstrations and observation, consider:

CONFERENCE/CONVENTION

A conference is a gathering of people for exchange of points of view, and consideration of problems of mutual concern. A convention gathers people around areas of concern within the organization, including organizational governance as well as educational programs.
[Burke; Craig, pp. 34-1 to 34-24; This, pp. 43-63.]

DEMONSTRATION/EXHIBIT

May show a method or a result. Usually describes each step or element sequentially. Is often combined with an opportunity for the learner to try. May be on film. Exhibits may be of materials, equipment, or displays of step-by-step processes for reference and reminder.
[Brown, pp. 245-322; Dale, pp. 272-295; Klevins, pp. 62-63; Kozoll, pp. 97-100.]

FIELD TRIP/TOUR

Learners go to a site to learn. May be to a library or a school, a commercial service, a manufacturer. Often a guide will assist learners to understand what is going on. Required reading or other preparation aids the depth of learning.

If the primary function is to practice skills, techniques, and thinking processes, consider:

CASE STUDY

A realistic situation presented in verbal, written or film form to a group of learners. Work done individually, in small groups or in a total group. Designed to illustrate the principles. Gives a shared experience with built-in problems for learners to address.
[Craig, pp. 35-1 to 35-12; Dimock, pp. 19-24; Engle, pp. 34-70; Galvin; Kozoll, pp. 102-105; Lynton, pp. 128-131.]

CLINIC

Use of resource people and consultants interacting with learners to help analyze and discuss problems on a particular topic.

COMMITTEE/TASK FORCE

A group of individuals charged with a defined task. Often used for planning or getting something done. Lends itself to deeper understanding of the issue with which the committee deals. Opportunity to practice skills of working with colleagues. May be ad hoc in nature.

CRITICAL INCIDENT
>   Blends the methods of case study and role play. Focus is on
>   a simulated situation which requires the learner(s) to act in
>   such a way that will alleviate or solve the problem.

ROLE PLAYING
>   A simulated situation involving realistic incidents presenting
>   a problem situation which must be solved. The role play may
>   be structured with parts and scripts or with only roles desig-
>   nated which are then enacted spontaneously.
>   [Craig, pp. 36-1 to 36-14; Dimock, pp. 24-30; Engle, pp. 71-139;
>   Kozoll, pp. 105-107; Lynton, pp. 123-125; Maier.]

SIMULATION/GAMES
>   Contrived situation using a model that duplicates as many
>   real life situations as possible. Learners experience the situa-
>   tion, derive the principles that apply and exercise problem-
>   solving methods.
>   [Brown, pp. 349-374; Craig, pp. 40-1 to 40-14; Engle,
>   pp. 140-247; Kozoll, pp. 107-109; Lynton, pp. 123-125;
>   Zachert.]

If the primary function is to produce in-depth understanding, consider:

COACHING
>   Close supervisor/supervisee relationships to assure short-term
>   and long-range communication and learning opportunities.
>   Can be used to supplement, reinforce and monitor all other
>   learning experiences.

JOB INSTRUCTION
>   Teaches the nature and practice of a task or series of tasks.
>   Usually involves demonstration and observation followed
>   by supervised practice of the learner.
>   [Craig, pp. 32-3 to 32-24.]

JOB ROTATION
>   Shifting responsibilities and task assignments for personnel
>   to learn a broader range of competencies.

LABORATORY TRAINING
>   A residential program for the purpose of learning, usually
>   in the area of human relations skills, personal self-awareness
>   and group skills.
>   [Craig, pp. 37-1 to 37-15; Dimock, pp. 30-31; Klevins, pp. 189-
>   198, 217-234; Lynton, pp. 125-127; Pfeiffer.]

SABBATICAL
>   A period of freedom from regular assignments for purposes of
>   travel or study.

If a number of purposes and possibilities are intended, consider:

CONSULTATION
> Involvement of an outside expert who might be charged
> with observation, evaluation, or help in planning or imple-
> menting. Often used for organizational development work.
> May be involved a single time or make a series of visits over
> a period of time.
> [Craig, pp. 46-1 to 46-13.]

INSTITUTE
> A series of meetings around a central focus. Uses resource
> people and consultant staff as sources of information on
> the subject. Often employs workshop techniques.
> [Davis, Warncke.]

WORKSHOP
> Brings together a group with a similar background and common
> concerns about a topic. Instructors and resource people
> may be used but the bulk of the responsibility for learning
> rests with the participants. Often combines learnings of
> knowledge, skills, attitudes. Usually short and intensive.
> [Davis, Warncke.]

Sources Cited

Anderson, *Selecting and Developing Media for Instruction* (1976).

Brown, *AV Instruction: Technology, Media and Methods* (1973).

Burke, *Conference Planning* (1970).

Craig, *Training and Development Handbook* (1976).

Dale, *Audiovisual Methods in Teaching* (1969).

Davis, *Planning, Conducting and Evaluating Workshops* (1974).

Dimock, *How to Plan Staff Training Programs* (1973).

Engle, *Handbook of Creative Learning Experiences* (1973).

Galvin, *The Case Method in Library Education and In-Service
Training* (1973).

Klevins, *Materials and Methods in Adult Education* (1972).

Kozoll, *In-Service Training: Philosophy, Processes and Operational
Techniques.* (1972).

Lynton, *Training for Development* (1967).

Maier, *The Role-Play Technique* (1975).

Pfeiffer, *A Handbook of Structured Experiences for Human
Relations Training* (Vols. 1-5) (1969-1975).

This, *The Small Meeting Planner* (1972).

Warncke, *Planning Library Workshops and Institutes* (1976).

Yarple, *Programmed Instruction in Librarianship* (1976).

Zachert, *Simulation Teaching of Library Administration* (1975).

A general source for all methods is: Aker, *Adult Education Procedures, Methods and Techniques; A Classified and Annotated Bibliography, 1953-1963.*

* * *

This array of possible methods to consider may not make the choice easier for a given activity. The following key questions can be used to choose between alternatives:

- What results are anticipated from the use of this method?

- Is the method appropriate to the kinds of needs and/or problems that have been identified?

- Is it suited to meet the objectives set for the activity? the program objectives?

- Will it be able to provide the necessary knowledge, skills, and attitudes in the learner?

- How appropriate is the method for the topic? for the learner group?

- Is the method educationally sound in these circumstances? How does it employ the principles of adult learning?

- What does this method require of the learner? How feasible are those requirements?

- How will this method be perceived in relation to a learner's expectations and perspective? Is it acceptable to potential learners?

- To what extent is this method likely to enable the personal interests and aims of individual learners to be met?

- Does this method provide assistance to learners in the application of what they learn to their job situations? How closely related to real-life circumstances is the method?

- What possible unintended effects might occur from the use of this method?

- What resources will the method require? Are those available to the program?

- What alternative methods would be possible if adequate resources are not available to permit the preferred choice?

Selection from alternative methods is often neither rapid nor easy. In most instances, the answers to these questions will aid in that selection, but choices between alternatives often must be made. In such cases, each alternative must be

assessed for what it can realistically be expected to accomplish in return for invest-
ments required of both the learner and the organization. Thus, second-best alternatives should be held in reserve for use later if the first choice becomes unfeasible
for some reason, or if additional activities must be planned.

Both staff development and continuing education programs share a tendency
to become "locked in" to a pattern of overusing a particular method, such as workshops or institutes. This limits the variety of activities that might appeal to potential learners. This pattern often occurs because of organizational tradition or style
or because of the preference of the program planners. When the selection of methods
results from considering the questions listed above, however, patterns of overuse
can be broken more easily.

Staff development programs can capitalize on some advantages with regard
to methods. Regular library functions can be linked with specific learning activities
to increase the impact of both. Learners can be prepared for a variety of methods
new to them, or for ones that are unusual or complex. A series of different activities
can be constructed with graduated intensity or depth to guide the progress of
learners over a lengthy time period. These different activities can utilize more and
more in-depth methods as well as more involved topics. A similar careful sequencing
can enable the creation of potential educators within the library through apprenticeship opportunities that team an experienced person with one less skilled. These
advantages can creatively use a variety of methods in new ways to achieve greater
impact within the library than can be achieved with most continuing education
programs and activities.

Resources must be selected. Significantly affecting the program's success are
the resources, that is, facilities and equipment, information sources and financial
support, supplies and materials, plus human resources. Staff development and continuing education programs may tap or develop internal resources, may share
resources outside the organization. Each resource will be greatly influenced by the
other components of the design. For example, the method will influence the
choice of physical facilities, the learner group will affect the materials selected, the
financial resources available will alter the choice of equipment. Guideline 4 details
the considerations important for the selection of resources. Guidelines 6, 7, and 9
describe the use of various resources during implementation, including the important factors that must be weighed for selection and use of each of these resources.

Scheduling must be determined. Scheduling refers to the sequence, frequency,
timing, and location of learning activities. Its primary purpose is to enable the
intended learners to attend activities and to assure that the necessary arrangements
are made and logistics are worked out to produce each event and activity. Often,
the use of resources influences scheduling for the use of special equipment or sites;
or the availability of funds will direct the timing, frequency, or duration of learning
experiences.

If activities can be scheduled sufficiently in advance, potential learners can be
notified in time to allow for necessary arrangements to be made. Advance scheduling also keeps duplication of effort by other groups doing similar work in staff
development or continuing education to a minimum, since they can then plan to
avoid conflict with the topic or date. Careful scheduling can improve the management of work in both the program and the organization. It also allows a margin to
accommodate shifts to alternatives when that becomes necessary.

Key questions that can be used to set scheduling include:

- What is the most logical sequence of topics, learner groups, and methods of activities?

- When should each activity be offered to achieve the desired outcomes?

- Do dates/places of other events and activities affect similar learner groups?

- Are dates/places already scheduled to bring library personnel together for reasons compatible with learning activities?

- How often will each activity be needed?

- Where are potential learner groups located geographically?

- Does scheduling include consideration of both work flow in the sponsoring library, agency, or association and the convenience of the learner?

Sometimes, scheduling seems to be done in a vacuum and may consider only one facet, ignoring others. For instance, the agency's internal work flow may be closely correlated with the continuing education program's schedule, but the activities may conflict with other conferences, meetings, and events that are likely to involve library personnel who are also expected to participate in continuing education program activities. Or, the activity plans and calendar may be well defined and coordinated but simply not publicized, thus preventing learners from making advance plans. Poor scheduling can make even the highest priority needs impossible to meet because of conflicting dates or inaccessible locations.

Through scheduling, a staff development program offers the opportunity of integrating learning and its application. If program planners are alert, careful scheduling can balance both time and a cycle of learning and doing so as to benefit individual learners and the library. A balanced workload divides responsibility among personnel throughout the library, providing in itself an additional possibility for staff development. For example, in a public library system, branch and main building personnel may cover each other's responsibilities to permit absences for learning activities. Thus, personnel can develop a flexible potential with a greater range of skills and knowledge of learning functions than they might otherwise have.

A continuing education program's success often hinges on successful scheduling, for usually a workshop or institute produced by an agency or association must accommodate the requirements of a number of learners and their various libraries. Since many activities are held only once, individuals with conflicting responsibilities will be prevented from attending. Of course, association conferences are characteristically scheduled well in advance and well publicized to allow for attendees to plan ahead. Now though, advance distribution of continuing education calendars is becoming more prevalent, allowing library personnel to schedule topics, dates, and places to meet their needs.

Program management must be planned. Program quality, consistency, and continuity is influenced as much by effective program management as by learning activities. Program management includes identifying points of decision making, designating who makes what decisions, specifying how those decisions will be communicated and implemented, and providing opportunities for accountability. Important program qualities such as flexibility and involvement can be achieved through sound management. However, planning for good management is essential to enable it to occur throughout implementation.

The major functions of program management are decision-making, communication, and coordination. Decision-making prompts action, initiating as well as responding to circumstances. Thus, it is important to define where decision-making regarding the program rests, how decisions are made and by whom, what organizational structures influence them and, in turn, are influenced by them. Decision-making must be linked with communications, since information must be conveyed to draw an issue to general attention, to affect a decision, or to take action. Communication channels must exist within the program, between the program and other organizational functions, and between the program and learners and educators. Coordination effects the linkage between decision-making and communication functions, prompting both to be done at the appropriate time and place. Good communication aids sound decision-making and enables coordinated implementation of the decisions made.

In addition to these three functions, two qualities very important to program management should be threaded through each of the functions. One is flexibility, a valuable logistical and attitudinal asset enabling adjustment to current reactions and needs and preserving the relevancy of the program to learners' needs and expectations. The second is involvement, the inclusion of those affected by decisions in the decision-making process. Education, particularly of adults, is an interactive process through which behavior change is accomplished. If this is accepted as a basic tenet of the program, flexibility and involvement must be basic qualities in the management of the program in order to be congruent with this approach to learning.

These three functions and two essential qualities can be supplemented by additional important characteristics of program management. These should be kept in mind while building the program. And, once built and implemented, the program can be reviewed from time to time in view of them. First, the program should evidence quality through using the most assured methods and resources feasible, documenting planning and evaluation, building in realistic sequencing, and providing for sound alternatives where needed. Yet, the desire for quality should not prevent a willingness to experiment and to test new approaches. One result of striving for quality is to help achieve a credibility that will build esteem and trust, encouraging more individuals and organizations to engage in learning in relation to their work responsibilities and personal interests and goals. Motivation of learners can also result from the use of a variety of learning opportunities as distinguished from overuse of a few favorite methods, consistent personalities, or routine patterns. Program managers should strive to make the most efficient use of resources—not only those of the program, but also those of the sponsoring organization and those of the learners. In sum, these characteristics would describe the ideal learning program that could be achieved through effective management. Actually, however, few, if any programs will be able to achieve all of these desirable qualities. Yet, these provide valid aims for program managers to strive for.

During planning, particularly while working on the design of the program, the possibility of adjustment and modification should be foreseen. To enable changes, some means for evaluation will be necessary. Charles Denova stresses that without a specific plan for evaluation, the planning process is not complete, since formal efforts will not be as useful as they might be otherwise and informal efforts will be directionless.[20] Assembling the components will require shifting focus among them as more information comes to light to influence the decisions made about each one. Where and in whom the management function is vested is a vital issue. It may be unquestioned, determined by administrative fiat, through tradition, or as the result of circumstances. Or, it may be an unresolved issue, anticipated to emerge through the process of designing the program. In any event, an essential question that must be asked is: **"Who makes the decision about who makes the decisions?"**

A main consideration that guides the response to that question is the desired balance between efficiency and effectiveness. Often the expedient smoothness and spread of centering the program on a single individual or office is chosen over the less apparent advantage of building a depth of commitment and understanding through wider involvement, which divides responsibilities for different areas of decision-making, adjusting as the program develops. Most organizations, striving for both efficiency and effectiveness have determined that centralization of functions plus advice from a representative group achieves the desired balance. Others have a tradition and style that influence their choice. If this crucial question is not answered prior to the point when the design is developed, it must be answered then.

Helpful to aid in answering that question are other questions to answer in relation to various alternatives that may be considered:

- Where is/who has the essential information required to manage the program?

- What are the precepts about control of the program?

- What enforcement or implementation of decisions is possible in relation to each alternative?

- What are the requirements for communication?

- What is the source for financial resources and what restricts and conditions the use of funds?

The answers to these questions may change over a period of time. Consequently, these questions should be reviewed and repeated from time to time to test whether changes in answers affect the management of the program, just as changing learning needs affects the program's activities. Program management is described more specifically in Guideline 6 in relation to implementation.

When staff development or continuing education efforts are viewed as isolated, self-contained learning activities, the decision-making, communication, and coordination are administered on an ad hoc basis within the confines of that single activity. This approach tends to perpetuate itself, especially when most of the activities are based on individual interests related to a particular need, with a prescribed time limit. When the advantages of a program approach begin to outweigh those of the activities approach, however, the management of the program must be planned as carefully as the educational aspect.

More specifically, staff development programs should be integrated with other library programs since both learning activities and the program's management will directly affect the rest of the library. Thus, the complexion of the program will be similar to that of other parts of the library. The frequent contact of the program with its learners is a reinforcing element affecting program management, linking it with the library. The staff development program can grow with the experience gained over time by program planners. Because of its continuity, new people can come into the program planning and management process, bringing new ideas and energy without destroying what has been built.

Management of a continuing education program, however, may be a more complex arrangement. Frequently the agency pattern for the program is that the individual or office responsible for the program also has other assignments. The usual state or regional association pattern relies on an individual or committee operating on a volunteer basis. Thus, decision-making, communication, and coordination are difficult to pinpoint, for much depends on the ability of the individuals concerned, the demands of their other responsibilities, and the vision available to assist and support the program.

The design of a learning program brings these six components together in a framework that provides for future decisions and action. The design encompasses the overall program and, at least, its initial activities, with the provision for their implementation. This overview of the program components serves to introduce them for consideration as the design is being assembled. Later Guidelines on implementation cover these in greater depth.

The completion of the design signals the transition from initial planning into implementation and evaluation. Realistically, however, few programs will be launched with each of these components preplanned to the full extent. Rather, most program struggle, evolve, and develop, shaped by individuals, organizations, and circumstances. Thus, each program will be unique, with its planners directing not only its content and intent, but also its process.

Process

For the most part, the order in which these components are assembled will be governed by circumstance. Working on each activity, program planners usually begin with those components that are "givens," add those decisions that follow naturally, then spend most of the time in working out the remaining tougher decisions. For example, if a topic revealed by the needs assessment within a large research library was that of departmental budgeting, that would be the "given." The learners would naturally be staff members responsible for budgeting, and scheduling would depend on when they could be present and available. The tougher decisions might be the choice of educational staff and the methods to enable those learners to acquire the necessary skills.

This example also shows how closely related the components are. Obviously, initial or changed decisions in one component will affect some or all of the others. If, for instance, a one-day workshop were chosen as the method in this example, but the instructor selected was not able to do a workshop, either the choice of instructor must be altered or a different method selected. If the instructor were retained but the method was changed to that of a regular course in the curriculum, the scheduling would change from one that required one-day involvement of learners to one that enabled more frequent but shorter attendance. Thus, in planning for activities, the assembly of components shifts from one to another as later decisions confirm those made earlier, or cause them to be altered.

Planning for each activity requires bringing together necessary information, making decisions, and coordinating efforts that lead to actually producing the activity. On a different scale, a similar process is required to develop the program design. The various components are important but are not the only significant factors. The process by which those components are brought together will strongly influence the nature and style of the program.

If the program is assembled in unilateral isolation with little staff participation and involvement, potential learners may be initially skeptical or suspicious about it and apathetic and resistant during training activities. However, if involvement is invited and encouraged, and if potential learners are regarded as resources, as adults with ideas to contribute, then their interest and energy may be motivated toward developing the program and its activities. In addition, the program will then reflect the perspective of those who actually will be learning.

Characteristically, a number of eager individuals are interested in growth beyond the parameters of their assigned jobs, and these people can provide a core of involvement in a new learning program or one being revitalized. Planning, then, brings their ideas and abilities to the formulation of an individual activity, or perhaps the program itself. This core group provides a useful liaison with other personnel, communicating enthusiasm to motivate those not so excited to become involved in learning and growth. At the same time, involvement can keep program managers aware of the current situation, engaged with its problems and prospects, yet less vulnerable to unexpected elements and results. At the outset, often only the core group may evidence interest, concern, and commitment. Yet, early initiative shown by a few individuals plus sustained official encouragement of that initiative often provides the impetus necessary to interest and broaden involvement by others. Then, involvement can provide long-range program strength, assuring its continuation even though those responsible for the original program may move on to other tasks.

Policies

Through the process of program design, policies will evolve regarding the learning program. Generally, policies prescribe a preferred course of action used to guide decision-making with consistency and fairness. Sometimes, they are stated in written form and are used to govern and guide program operation in day-to-day operations. Often, however, they are unstated, yet regarded as being generally understood and used by personnel throughout the library, agency, or association.

Policies with regard to staff development or continuing education responsibilities often emerge as a new program is developed. Some policies may be identified before implementation, and they then can be incorporated into the planning process to guide initial activities. Early policies should be considered flexible until experience either confirms or modifies them. In the case of an on-going program being remodeled, old policies may have to be altered to fit new directions.

Policies are the basis for procedures. Together, policies and procedures are very influential in the conduct of various organizational functions, including staff development or continuing education. Thus, it is important for stated policies to include the precepts as well as the practices of the learning program. Clear policies, known and understood, can assure library personnel, agency staff, and association members that learning is encouraged, and in what specific ways it is possible. This, in turn, prevents inaccurate assumptions and misunderstandings about what is and what is not feasible. Productive use of policy statements is, of course, predicated on the assumption that they do indeed guide actual practice, and that such statements are modified when the practice is changed.

The following questions can guide program planners who are responsible for formulating policies, and perhaps procedures, that will guide the operation of the staff development program:

- What is the commitment of the library to staff development?

- What are the staff development responsibilities of the library director? of library personnel? of those directly responsible for the learning program?

- From what sources will funds for staff development come?

- Will library support be given for fees and/or expenses for staff development activities outside the library? What factors are to be considered in approving leave or funds?

- Is the selection of learners ordinarily to be on a voluntary basis (i.e., self-selection) or prescribed by others? If learners are selected by others, who will make the selection?

- What proportion of staff development activities are to be done on work time? on personal time?

- Are staff development specifications included in job descriptions as a requirement or expectation?

- What means of recognition are possible for learners involved in staff development efforts?

- Will staff development efforts be indicated on personnel records of learners?

- What communication and reporting responsibilities are required of program managers? To whom are they responsible?

Some modification will need to be made in adapting these same questions to policy formulation for a continuing education program. There, policies should indicate the roles and responsibilities of the agency or association, the library, the learner, and possibly other entities. Policies should indicate under what terms the organization itself will produce learning activities and under what terms known opportunities and needs will be referred to other organizations. In some cases, policies articulate assumptions. In other instances, they describe and prescribe practice. If used, however, they serve to guide decisions and actions affecting the program.

Policies, together with the design, embody the principles and components and process of the program. These draw the picture of the program at the close of the initial planning phase. Continuous planning will incorporate changes, respond to new needs, alter policies, and modify methods as required. Initial and continuous planning guided by program goals and objectives refine the program within its context of library, agency, or association.

Many similarities exist between staff development and continuing education programs. Differences do exist, however. A staff development program is intended to serve the needs of a consistent group of people working in a single library that sponsors the program. A continuing education program addresses the more generalized needs of library personnel who come from a number of different libraries to share a single learning experience. These basic differences will slant and condition the design, the principles, components, process, and policies of the program.

Summary

The design of the learning program fits the selected learning activities into meaningful relationships and provides for the necessary management functions that will assure the success of the program. It defines a sequence of learning events, activities, and processes in such a way that established program objectives can be accomplished effectively and appropriately.

Both program and activity design must be educationally sound, incorporating the basic principles of adult learning in all parts of the program. These principles will affect the process by which the design is accomplished and the policies that emerge to guide the implementation of the program. The result of program design is a plan that anticipates and directs subsequent program actions. The factors that went into the planning process will strongly influence the nature and style of the program's implementation.

Six components of the design will be assembled in different ways in different organizations by different individuals. They are, however, the basic ingredients to consider during planning. They include: the topics for learning, the learners, the methods for learning, the resources, scheduling, and program management. Sometimes these components evolve naturally through a series of decisions. Sometimes they are declared by administrative fiat. To allow effective program management and implementation, they all should be at least outlined during the planning phase.

SUMMARY OF PART I

Sound planning is essential to assure that any learning program will provide significant and healthy impacts on learners and their libraries. Planners collect information about learning needs, formulate objectives, and assemble the components that will be required to implement the program and its activities. Although it is a period that requires patience and skill, its importance is often overlooked because it may appear that nothing is happening during planning. Time, effort, and funds spent on planning return benefits as the program is implemented and evaluated. The adequacy of planning serves long-range as well as immediate purposes, causing both direct and indirect results from the program.

Usually done at the beginning of a new or revamped program, initial planning allows a library, an agency, or an association to pull together scattered, uncoordinated learning efforts into a program, or to prepare a new staff development or continuing education function. It identifies the needs and objectives, then sets plans for the program's implementation. This major thrust envisions and develops the program as a whole, establishing directions for subsequent efforts. Continuous planning, on the other hand, weaves throughout implementation and ties in with evaluation. It incorporates emerging needs, changing circumstances, and the evaluative information that results from putting the plan into action. Together, initial and continuous planning provide for the production of learning activities and the management of the program itself. Both types of planning will be essential to achieve the objectives envisioned.

Planning for the learning program begins with the assessment of individual and library needs. Those needs that indicate learning as an appropriate response form the base of the program's plan. The assessment identifies the gap between the present level of performance and that level desired or required. These needs must be identified and analyzed in such a way that essential resources can be found and a program design can be developed.

Planning for the needs assessment defines the kind of information sought and from whom that information will be obtained. Using a variety of sources and methods, the assessment will discover a number of needs that then must be tabulated and put into categories to be meaningful. Predetermining the categories of information sought is helpful to guide the selection of techniques for collecting and analyzing information. The resulting array of information must then be analyzed and interpreted. A continuous assessment process is important to keep in touch with changing needs.

The needs assessment gives an indication of the scope and nature required of the learning program. At this point, the library, agency, or association must decide about the feasibility of undertaking such an effort. If the decision is not to continue with the contemplated program, this is the most economical point to curtail further planning. On the other hand, if the decision-makers determine that the effort should be launched, provisions must be made for planning the entire program.

Sound objectives must be formulated based on identified needs. Needs assessment and the development of program objectives are essential and sequential steps before a successful program can be designed. Objectives will provide a blueprint for decision-making during the planning and implementation of the program, and they require definition of what is sought from the program and what is intended by it. They are vital to the evaluation of the effectiveness of the program.

Although often time-consuming and difficult, the development of program objectives is an essential task, that serves to clarify directions and assumptions. It also provides a common basis for understanding and communication, and forms a base for further planning and evaluation as well as guides implementation. Program objectives are broad in scope; they describe the intent of the total program.

Activity objectives are more specifically related to an actual event or activity. Although formulating program objectives is advisable during initial planning, it may be more logical to develop activity objectives later. Stated objectives, honest and clear, can be relied on throughout the development of the program of activities and the on-going decision-making required for sound planning, implementation, and evaluation.

After needs have been identified and program objectives have been developed, program planners arrange various events, activities, and processes in the pattern most appropriate to effect both learning and the application of learnings to the learner's work situation. Six components are essential in planning the program and each activity: topics, learners, resources, methods, scheduling, and management. Each of these must be planned in order to achieve the program and activity objectives most effectively and efficiently.

Consistent use of quality resources for each of these components will strengthen the program as a whole, particularly if resources are appropriately selected for each activity. A review of those resources available and those needed provides an early check of the feasibility and costs of various parts of the program. Resources include people, physical facilities and equipment, information and financial support, materials and supplies. Some resources are required by the procedures of the program, and some are needed by the learners. Although obtaining the latter can be delayed until more detailed planning for the activity is undertaken, the former should be identified during planning. Exploring the range of resources likely to be needed will also reveal available alternatives. important to be examined in early planning, and will assist decision-making about the nature and scope of the program.

The program design resulting from initial planning brings together identified needs, program objectives, and resources. Then, an outline fits these various learning activities into meaningful relationships with one another and includes the necessary management functions to assure the successful accomplishment of the program. The comprehensiveness of this planning can also include planning for broad involvement of people to be affected by the program. Such involvement will build their interest, motivation, and commitment for the program, increasing the chances for realistic expectations and credibility of the program and providing a valuable learning experience in itself. Another factor, adherence to the principles of program design and adult learning will further the possibility for a quality, consistent, and continuous program.

Although not a one-time event, planning is, essentially, a common sense process intended to reduce unpredictable factors and increase the chance of success. The rewards and benefits from sound planning occur throughout subsequent implementation and evaluation, making even the long and tedious process of planning worthwhile. Ironically, the program that is well planned looks easy by the time it is implemented.

NOTES

[1] Elizabeth W. Stone, *Factors Related to the Professional Development of Librarians* (Metuchen, NJ: Scarecrow Press, 1969).

[2] Maurice L. Monette, "The Concept of Educational Need: An Analysis of Selected Literature," *Adult Education, A Journal of Research and Theory* 27, no. 2:122-23 (1977).

[3] The most comprehensive recent study of learning needs of library personnel as well as their learning modes and methods is found in *Continuing Library and Information Science Education; Final Report to the National Commission on Libraries and Information Science*, by Elizabeth W. Stone, Ruth Patrick, and Barbara Conroy (Washington, DC: Government Printing Office, 1974; also issued by American Society for Information Science, Washington, 1974).

Other published studies have been more specialized:

Lawrence A. Allen, *Continuing Education Needs of Special Librarians* [SLA State-of-the-Art Review, no. 3] (New York: Special Libraries Association, 1974);

American Library Association, Association of State Library Agencies and Library Education Division, *Education of State Library Personnel: A Report with Recommendations Relating to the Continuing Education of State Library Agency Professional Personnel* (Chicago, IL: American Library Association, 1971);

American Association of School Librarians, "Summary Sheet of Responses Received from 'Questionnaire about Continuing Education for School-Library-Media Supervisors," *School Libraries* 18:53 (Summer 1969);

Neal Harlow, et al., *Administration and Change: Continuing Education in Library Administration* (New Brunswick, NJ: Rutgers University Press, 1969);

James J. Kortendick and Elizabeth W. Stone, *Job Dimensions and Educational Needs in Librarianship* (Chicago, IL: American Library Association, 1971);

Allie Beth Martin and Maryann Duggan, *Continuing Education for Library Staffs in the Southwest (CELS): A Survey with Recommendations* (Dallas, TX: Southwestern Library Association, 1974);

Elizabeth W. Stone, *New Directions in Staff Development: Moving from Ideas to Action* (Chicago, IL: American Library Association, 1971);

C. Walter Stone, Jack Belzer, and James W. Brown, *Needs for Improvement of Professional Education* (Syracuse, NY: Syracuse University, Center for the Study of Information and Education, 1973); and

Julie A. Virgo, Patricia McConaghey Dunkel, and Pauline V. Angione, *Continuing Library Education Needs Assessment and Model Programs* [Concept Paper, no. 5] (Washington, DC: Continuing Library Education Network and Exchange, 1977).

Additional, focused studies, articles, and reports can be found through *Library Literature* and the following extensive bibliographies:

Mary Ellen Michael, *Continuing Professional Education in Librarianship and Other Fields: A Classified and Annotated Bibliography, 1965-1974* (New York: Garland Publishing, 1975);

Ruth J. Patrick, *An Annotated Bibliography of Recent Continuing Education Literature* (ERIC Clearinghouse on Information Resources. Stanford, CA: Stanford University, October, 1976);

Patrick Penland, "Inservice Training," *Encyclopedia of Library and Information Science* (New York: Dekker, 1968-) 12:46-79 [4 page, 103-item bibliography concludes article] ; and

Elizabeth W. Stone, *Continuing Library Education as Viewed in Relation to Other Continuing Professional Education Movements* (Washington, DC: American Society for Information Science, 1974).

[4] The major effort in this area in librarianship has been the Illinois Library Task Analysis Project. This effort and several related efforts are compared and discussed in Myrl Ricking and Robert E. Booth, *Personnel Utilization in Libraries, A Systems Approach* (Chicago, IL: American Library Association, 1974). Other helps include: U. S. Department of Labor, *A Handbook for Analyzing Jobs* (Washington, DC: Government Printing Office, 1972); U. S. Department of Labor, *A Handbook for Job Restructuring* (Washington, DC: Government Printing Office, 1970); and U. S. Department of Labor, Bureau of Employment Security, *Training and Reference Manual for Job Analysis* (Washington, DC: Government Printing Office, 1965).

[5] A basic, clear overview is Wendell L. French and Cecil H. Bell, Jr., *Organizational Development; Behavioral Science Interventions for Organization Improvement* (Englewood Cliffs, NJ: Prentice-Hall, Inc., 1973). Other practical resources include: Jack K. Fordyce and Raymond Weil, *Managing WITH People; A Manager's Handbook of Organization Development Methods* (Reading, MA: Addison-Wesley Publishing Co., 1971) and Dave Francis and Mike Woodcock, *People at Work; A Practical Guide to Organizational Change* (La Jolla, CA: University Associates, Inc., 1975).

[6] Some useful resources that include the use of the Delphi in needs assessment are:

Andre L. Delbecq et al., *Group Techniques for Program Planning. A Guide to Nominal Group and Delphi Processes* (Glenview, IL: Scott, Foresman and Co., 1975);

Sonya Peterson, *Delphi Technique: A Working Notebook* (Dundee, IL: The A Corporation, 1972);

Alfred Rasp, Jr., *A New Tool for Administrators; Delphi and Decision Making* (Office of the Superintendent of Public Instruction, (Olympia, WA: Office of the Superintendent of Publication, 1973); and

W. F. Spikes, "The Delphi Technique and the Adult Educator," *Mountain Plains Journal of Adult Education* 4, no. 1:1-7 (1975).

[7] Basic sources for locating information about tests is available in Oscar Krisen Buros, *The Mental Measurements Yearbook*, 7th edition (Highland Park, NJ: Gryphon Press, 1972) and Buros's *Tests in Print II; An Index to Tests, Test Reviews and the Literature on Specific Tests* (Highland Park, NJ: Gryphon Press, 1974).

[8] Two articles describe structured group interviews and their use in needs assessment:

Suzanne H. Mahmoodi, Mary M. Wagner, and Sister Therese Sherlock, "Assessing Educational Needs of Minnesota Library Personnel: A Proposed Technique," *Minnesota Libraries* 25, no. 2:51-55 (Summer 1976) and

Barbara Conroy, "The Structured Group Interview: A Useful Tool for Needs Assessment and Evaluation," *Mountain Plains Journal of Adult Education* 4, no. 2:19-26 (March 1976).

[9] Robert T. Mager, *Preparing Instructional Objectives* 2nd ed. (Belmont, CA: Fearon Publishers, 1975), p. 3.

[10] *Ibid.*, p. 6.

[11] Norman E. Gronlund, *Stating Behavioral Objectives for Classroom Instruction* (New York: Macmillan, 1970).

[12] Larry Nolan Davis and Earl McCallon, *Planning, Conducting and Evaluating Workshops: A Practitioner's Guide to Adult Education* (Austin, TX: Learning Concepts, 1974), p. 82.

[13] *Ibid.*, p. 86.

[14] Malcolm S. Knowles, *Self-Directed Learning; A Guide for Learners and Teachers* (New York: Association Press, 1975), pp. 129-35.

[15] Charles E. Kozoll, *Staff Development in Organizations: Cost Evaluation Manual for Managers and Trainers* (Reading, MA: Addison Wesley, 1974), pp. 78-79.

[16] Malcolm S. Knowles, "Program Planning for Adults as Learners," *Adult Leadership* 15, no. 8:267-68, 278-79 (February 1967).

[17] Gerald J. Pine and Peter J. Horne, "Principles and Conditions for Learning in Adult Education," *Adult Leadership* 18, no. 4:108-110, 126, 133-34 (October 1969).

[18] Malcolm S. Knowles, *The Modern Practice of Adult Education: Andragogy Versus Pedagogy* (New York: Association Press, [1970]), pp. 129-132.

[19] Davis and McCallon, *Planning Workshops*, p. 109.

[20] Charles C. Denova, *Establishing a Training Function* (Englewood Cliffs, NJ: Educational Technology Publications, 1971), p. 123.

PART II—IMPLEMENTING THE LEARNING PROGRAM

    Implementation fulfills the planning process, transforming ideas into reality, moving the program design from concept into action. Implementation is the action part of the action plan. To those with no direct involvement in the program, implementation is likely to be more obvious than either planning or evaluation. Thus, a program might be described and characterized more often by its skillful workshops or job-exchange effort than by its ability to comprehensively identify and respond to a wide range of library staff needs with a variety of well-selected activities in a carefully planned sequence. A program's effective coordination, timely decision making, and clear communication may be overlooked by those unaware of all that is necessary to bring such a program to successful implementation.

    Implementation, however, includes all of these and can be defined as the process of assembling the decisions and ingredients essential to accomplish what is intended. It is the action being taken to help people learn, the production of events, activities, and processes that, when fulfilled, will achieve the program's objectives. Often viewed as the payoff for the sometimes tedious planning efforts, implementation results from initial and continuous planning, and, in turn, it produces evaluation information. Figure 10 shows the interrelationship of these three basic processes required of a program. Planning prepares for both implementation and evaluation. Implementation results in evaluation and in further planning. Evaluation affects both planning and implementation of the program.

Figure 10

**Interrelationship of the Basic
Processes of a Learning Program**

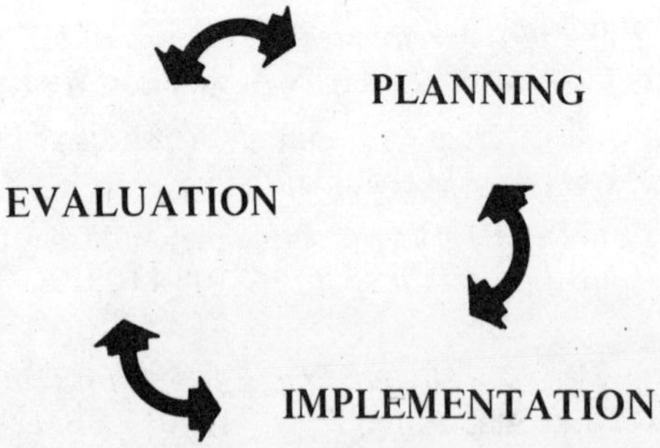

PLANNING

EVALUATION

IMPLEMENTATION

    Planning for the learning program does not suddenly conclude and implementation then begin. Rather, planning is ongoing, for new needs will emerge, objectives must be modified, unanticipated resources become available. Changes and discoveries made during implementation prompt new decisions, or, in some cases, reveal new problems. Continuous planning benefits from what occurs during implementation and what is revealed through evaluation, since in spite of good initial planning, not everything will be predictable. Implementation may also bring the unforeseen, which can surprise, delight, or frustrate. Difficulties with issues, problems, or logistics inevitably arise, but usually, the better the planning, the more likely that implementation will entail a minimum of problems.

Neither is evaluation delayed until implementation is completed. The process and results of implementation reveal the effectiveness of planning and demonstrate the organization's capability of putting planning into practice. On-the-spot decision-making during implementation incorporates both the planning and evaluation capabilities within the program. Evaluation can reveal the soundness of the planning process as well as measure the results of the implemented activities in relation to the expectations held for them. Both these aspects begin to become apparent during implementation.

Implementation, the first point at which a program's activities are set in motion, lived through, observed, and learned from, brings together planners, learners, educators, evaluators, and decision-makers together as individuals, as groups, and as functions. Here, the results of the planning process become tangible and evident. Here, also, is the opportunity for reflection and asking questions that may result in a change of direction or a remedy for an earlier oversight. A careful look at what happens during implementation can prevent mistakes from being perpetuated and serendipitous results from being overlooked. Implementation of the specific events, activities, and processes making up the program is, in effect, the implementation of the entire program. Program management must not only be capable of producing these individual events, activities, and processes but also of sustaining the program as a whole. Thus, production and management are essential elements of program implementation.

A learning program requires more than knowledge of libraries and educational design skills. The ability to manage the program is also essential since leadership and capability are necessary to develop and sustain the learning program beyond isolated learning activities. Inept program management will jeopardize the educational effectiveness of the program's activities. Even when staff development and continuing education efforts are attempted only with single and unconnected activities, sound management is important to assure logistics are smooth, resources are well selected, and communications are available. When accomplished by the same person(s), the details of scheduling and budgeting are clearly distinct from the educational function that includes learning design, educational strategies and techniques, and the measurement of educational outcomes.

Both educational and management functions must be adequately fulfilled to achieve a successful learning program. Implementation is likely to reveal just how adequately they are performed. Implementation brings together educational content and methods, the management abilities and attitudes, and learners in the learning environment. Both educational and management functions must work together to achieve the objectives. If one or the other function is not ably done, the possibility of learning is diminished, as is the achievement of the program or activity objectives.

These implications are serious and should lead program developers to direct their thought and effort towards assuring that both educational and management functions are in good hands. Not only must both functions be capably handled, but they must be congruent with one another. Both educational and management functions must be systematically approached with a conscious awareness of the importance of their being linked with a common philosophy and values within the program. An authoritarian management style and a learner-centered educational style would be incongruent, likely to be at cross purposes, as would the reverse example of participative management norms together with teacher-oriented educational approaches. The match between educational and management styles in the implementation of the program will be important to achieve program effectiveness and credibility. Figure 11 lists several areas that bear scrutiny in bringing these two functions into congruence.

Figure 11
Educational and Management Functions
of a Learning Program

THE EDUCATIONAL FUNCTION	THE MANAGEMENT FUNCTION
—educational precepts, methods and techniques	—management concepts, methods, and techniques
—decision-making about who is to learn what, and how, and when	—decision-making about who is to do what, and how, and when
—communications with learners and instructional staff	—communications, both internal and external, to the program
—assignment of instructional tasks and responsibilities	—assignment of tasks and responsibilities
—staffing requirements	—staffing requirements
—policies and procedures	—policies and procedures
—evaluation of learning	—evaluation of program
—budgeting	—budgeting
—routines, procedures, and forms	—routines, procedures, and forms
—reporting and recordkeeping	—reporting and recordkeeping

A staff development program within a library is relatively easy both to identify and to establish this congruency between the program and the library. The selection and appointment of continuing education program staff, however, is less clear-cut. State library agencies and large national or regional associations with established programs are able to be more definitive about their existing style. Associations, particularly those with no assigned continuing education program staff, may have difficulty achieving the needed congruency since they depend on member interest, ability, and commitment. Libraries, agencies, and associations must seek program staff with abilities and attitudes to match the precepts and practices of the organization; they must also endeavor to match the educational and management functions within the learning program.

Congruency is important to the development and maintenance of a learning program. In addition, implementation provides a testing ground for three other factors: balance, flexibility, and involvement. A common danger during implementation, one usually unseen at the time, is the possibility of upsetting the program's balance between learner needs and organizational needs. Sometimes the excitement and enthusiasm of individuals learning and growing can overwhelm the organizational goals that are also a necessary part of the program. Or, the planners and managers of activities may pursue their organizational charge so eagerly that individual interests and motivations get set aside in the pursuit of a grand master plan, one directed almost exclusively toward organizational goals. Balance must be maintained to serve both individual and organizational goals.

Although it is a desired quality in programming learning opportunities, the appropriate degree of flexibility may not be an easy ingredient for an individual or an organization to provide while implementing a program or an activity. Not the same as indecisiveness or ambiguity, flexibility refers to the ability to alter a previously made decision in the light of later information received. Information after the initial decision was made may reveal that original decision was not as feasible as originally thought. Then, if flexibility was anticipated from the planning stage, and if alternatives were considered at that time, possible program adjustments can be more easily seen and made. If, however, alternatives were not fully considered during planning, it will be difficult for program developers to review and select from those possibilities, particularly at a time of stress calling for change due to altered situation or circumstances. Implementation is a process that tests the willingness and ability of program staff to be flexible.

The factor of involvement is the third one tested during implementation. Stressed throughout Part I on Planning, that emphasis on involvement will continue in implementation (Part II) and evaluation (Part III). Implementation actually offers richer possibilities for involvement than does planning. Active inclusion of individuals as participants in the various stages, activities, and functions of the program can be incorporated at the point of implementation even if not utilized during planning. And, if involvement was practiced during planning, it should certainly be continued as those plans are realized.

Methods and means for involvement will need to be planned both to involve individuals as learners and to enable them to create learning experiences for themselves. Good adult education involves participants in learning more as active elements than as passive recipients of knowledge. This, in turn, influences the selection of participative educational techniques and the provision of other means of realistically and actively involving individuals and groups in the program—and of endeavoring to make that involvement itself a learning possibility.

The benefits from involvement are mainly evident during implementation: the understanding and acceptance of learners, the enriched resources brought to the learning opportunity, the increased ability to apply one's learnings, greater depth of learning, and the possibility of sustained interest, commitment, and support. Most of the results of involvement are long-range, but many have short-range usefulness also.

These three factors—balance, flexibility, and involvement—thread through the successful program. Together with congruency within the program and between the program and its sponsoring organization, these three factors may be found during implementation to be well planned for and integrated into the program. Implementation provides the test of the ability of the program and its staff to assure these qualities as an integrated part of the educational and management functions of the program.

Implementation gives evidence that something is being *done*. The character and capability of the program take shape during implementation; its successes and failures become apparent. Continued quality programming and getting desired results from the program are most likely to be achieved through alternating implementation with continued planning and reflection. A blitz approach to producing learning activities can preempt the possibility for program planners to profit from reviewing the results and implications of accomplishments. And, it can prevent learners from balancing their learnings with actual application of those learnings on the job. Implementation should provide opportunities for both evaluation and planning integrated with the events, activities, and processes produced for the specific purpose of learning specific knowledge, skills, or attitudes.

This chapter describes the major elements required to implement learning activities. Guidelines 6 and 7 describe how to select, assign, and organize the administrative and educational responsibilities for the program and its activities. Guideline 8 explores the reasons for involving learners and ways this can be accomplished if there is a commitment to that precept. Definitions, criteria, and checklists are offered in Guideline 9 as aids in the skillful use of resources to support the learning design. These aids indicate what resources are needed and how resources are employed during implementation. Concluding, Guideline 10 describes how these ingredients interact with each other during implementation and how they fit within the planning and evaluation processes.

GUIDELINE 6—DETERMINE ADMINISTRATIVE RESPONSIBILITIES

The program design resulting from the initial planning process defines essential roles and responsibilities required to establish and maintain a learning program. With the first steps of implementation, those roles become actualized through action taken to produce what was planned. Translation of program plans into program activities requires communication, coordination, and decision-making responsibilities separate from those of the educational function. Administrative responsibilities are those management functions that guide and direct the learning program of the library, agency, or association. The exact and specific nature of those responsibilities depends, of course, on the organization, the program, and the individual.

The program administrator is the person primarily responsible for directing the program; this person will be the manager who assures that direction and progress are maintained, that needed communication and activities are coordinated, and that the environment supports the important task of learning. Although of key importance, many of the functions and tasks of the administrator are behind the scenes and not directly evident. The administrator must orchestrate the ingredients of the program, provide for smooth and effective implementation, sustain continued planning, and employ sound evaluation. As the person who must know what has to be done, when, and how—and then be able to accomplish that—the administrator is the key person upon whom much of the success of the program depends.

This Guideline describes the three major areas of administrative responsibility: coordination, decision-making, and communication. The tasks that support these functions are detailed and a profile is drawn to indicate the essential skills and competencies needed by a program administrator. Various alternative structural arrangements for program administration are described for both staff development and continuing education programs, along with their advantages and disadvantages. The differences between staff development and continuing education in providing for administrative responsibilities, though similar in principle, may vary in practice depending on the situation.

Responsibilities

The program administrator must have a perspective on the entire program, a focus on how the various activities fit together to meet the present and future learning needs of people in the organization, an overview of the interplay between the educational and management aspects of the program. Up to the point of implementing each activity, the administrative role is predominant: working with a planning group, selecting instructors and methods, assembling and preparing materials, communicating with learners, arranging the many details necessary to produce a learning activity.

During the actual activity, however, the educator assumes the prime role, dealing with content and the most effective techniques to use in helping people learn, striving to achieve the objectives established for the activity. Then, following the activity, the program administrator again becomes preeminent, assuring necessary follow-through and utilization of evaluation information for subsequent planning. Even though the administrative responsibilities for the program should be separate from the educational responsibilities, the ability of the individuals filling these roles to work together is an important ingredient for the success of each specific activity and, ultimately, of the whole program.

The three major administrative responsibilities are: coordination, decision-making, and communication. These are characteristic for the manager of any department, service, project, or organization as well as a program. They may be clearly and definatively spelled out, or they may rely heavily on the perspective and initiative of the person in the position at the time. Whether formally or informally defined, those responsibilities must include some measure of coordination, decision-making, and communication.

Coordination is the appropriate and timely interrelationship of the various components of the learning program. It is essential to produce a learning activity with motivated learners, prepared instructional staff, adequate resources, and successful results. It requires organizing and setting priorities for the various tasks that must be done, doing that in such a way that they all get done well and on time. Coordination is important to integrate the program smoothly with other efforts of the organization, other assignments of personnel, other issues that must be addressed. The skill of the coordinating function can be seen not only in the successful results of a particular activity but also in the trouble-free nature of its implementation.

The decision-making responsibility, a second administrative function, is closely related to coordination. Decision-making refers to the willingness, ability and authority to determine issues, choices, and directions. In any program, many decisions must be made—some can be made coolly and reflectively before or after an activity, some are made under pressure during an activity. The ability to make good decisions depends on several factors: the information available on which to base the decision, the knowledge that comes from adequately understanding the problem, the experience of dealing with similar situations in the past, the feeling that comes from a sensitive intuition in tune with the situation and the people. Decision-making is linked with coordination because the coordinative function determines the decisions to be made, who makes them and when; the information on which the decisions will be made is then gathered through coordinative tasks. Decision-making refers to the fact that decisions *do* get made.

The decision-making responsibility of the administrator is influenced by both the style of the organization and the characteristic methods preferred by the person. Some administrators make decisions alone, then implement them. Others work closely with groups to explore alternatives, then make decisions jointly. Often major decisions must be channeled in a prescribed way through the organization for approval or modification. Even within that condition, however, the individual's decision-making style can have considerable lattitude. Although these functions may not be clearly defined in the case of a new program, implementation will serve to develop at least an outline, which may be further defined through policy statements and job descriptions to assure clear and mutual understanding of the range of responsibilities and the limits of authority. In the beginning, however, it will be important to set forth the expectations of the program administrator and those of the administrator of the sponsoring organization.

The third responsibility, that of communication, is essential to support the decision-making and coordination of the program. Communication refers to the process of transferring information from one person or group to another through a suitable means of transmission. Used singularly, it refers to the process itself. Used in the plural form, it refers to the individual transactions that transfer information. The administrator is the central focus for communication, the source and recipient of much information as well as a channel and disseminator.

Necessary, accurate, and adequate communication is complex for any administrator. The learning program administrator must deal with the following components of the communication process:

1) Individuals and groups that require information or have information:

- Learners *require* communications that are informational, supportive, and motivational, especially about the activity in which they will be participating. They will *need* to know its purpose and objectives, its methods, when and how to prepare for attending, as well as topical materials and handouts about the subject. They will need to see the program as growth opportunities rather than punishment. Learners *have* information about their needs, interests, and abilities as well as a perspective on how their anticipated learnings will apply to their job responsibilities.

- Colleagues and supervisors of learners *require* information about the involvement of their fellow staff members and how they might encourage and support the application of new efforts of the learner. Colleagues and supervisors of learners *have* information about their perspectives on learner needs and abilities as well as their view of the library situation and its needs.

- Educators *require* information about the learner group as well as the desired results from the activity and the facilities and equipment with which they will work. They *have* information about priority topics, educational techniques and materials, and their own abilities.

- Suppliers of materials, equipment, and services *need* information about what is required to produce the program's activities. They *have* information about availability, price, and viable alternatives.

- The library, agency, or association as a whole *requires* information about the successes and problems within the program, and the results from the various activities. The organization *has* information about present impacts from the program.

- The head of the organization will *require* information about what is planned and done, and also evidence of the results in order to justify further activity and to maintain or increase the program's priority and continuity. The head *has* information about how the program fits into other organizational functions, projects, and priorities.

- The library world *needs* information about the program and its activities to inform, interest, and attract new learners, to tell about accomplishments and results, and to increase staff development and continuing education capabilities and motivations. Librarianship *has* information about the larger context wherein those results fit and additional needs and priorities that learning opportunities might address.

2) The content of the communications:

- Informational material is needed about the activities presently being done, where, when, and how.

- Reports of what has happened are important, such as documentation of meetings, evaluation of activities, or reports on the program progress.

- Updates keep people informed; for instance, the results of requests for feedback, news of changed circumstances or emerging needs.

3) The logistics of communicating information:

- Information should usually be transmitted to where it is needed when it is available.

- Information should clearly indicate its source, its intended recipient, and its date.

- Direct and personal exchange with one-to-one or one-to-group contact is often the most accurate and understood but not always feasible.

- The telephone is quick, two-way communication but may be costly. Memos and correspondence provide a written record at moderate cost. Group mailings are standard for reports, newsletters, brochures, and forms.

Consideration of these factors influences the communication function of the program administrator. Although regular lines of communication are essential, the style and method selected will depend on the administrator's personal preference, the purpose for the contact being made, those for whom the information is intended, and the style and capability of the library, agency, or association. Administrators may use personal contacts, newsletters, announcements, bulletin boards, or the inevitable grapevine. In addition to initial communications, clarification may be required later, either through repetition or by using a different approach. The administrator must be alert to feedback indicating whether the message was received and understood.

Obviously, the coordination, decision-making, and communication responsibilities are closely interrelated with one another. Because of this, they are not easily divided and assigned to different persons. The responsibility for specific activities, such as a workshop or an orientation, may be delegated, but program administration as a whole requires a single focal point. The administrator must view the entire program, assuring the appropriate sequence of events, knowing who is to do what in the indicated time period, keeping track of when decisions must be made and by whom, plus necessary procedural details. Being alert to early signs that may signal trouble is important, as is the careful delegation of responsibilities. The administrator needs a clear concept of what is to be done, what must be centralized with the administrator, what can be assigned to others, what needs to be followed up.

Tasks

The responsibilities of coordination, communication, and decision-making call for a number of tasks. In most instances, the identification of tasks that must be done lies with the administrator, as does the setting of priorities and the delegation of who is to be responsible for which tasks. The scope of responsibility and authority in relation to delegated tasks must be defined and understood by the administrator and person(s) assigned those tasks. Coordinating program planning and evaluation processes, maintaining communication channels, and fulfilling record-keeping and reporting requirements in relation to the program as a whole are usually the responsibility of the administrator. However, those tasks in relation to a specific activity or series of activities may well be assigned to an activity manager.

The following questions may be used as a checklist in relation to the administrative tasks required for each event, activity, or process that is a part of the learning program:

- Has the planning process for the activity been defined and initiated? Have planners been identified and notified? If planning meetings are to be held, have they been scheduled with a preliminary agenda of essential matters to be considered? How will planning decisions be made? Who is responsible to communicate and implement those decisions? Are all necessary aspects of planning covered?

- Have educators been selected? What alternatives were considered? Are existing agreements satisfactory or would contractual arrangements assure clarity and specificity? What provisions are necessary for getting information and making decisions required before the activity?

- Will specialized staff be needed for their educational or technical expertise or for handling the extra workload? What skills will they need? What is the availability and cost? What contractual arrangements are necessary?

- Has the learning method been selected? What alternatives were considered? Does the selected method require a special site, equipment, or materials? If so, how will those be managed?

- Have the site and equipment been chosen? What alternatives were considered? How will it be adapted to fit the special needs of learners and activity staff? How will necessary equipment be located, reserved, delivered, and operated? Will the site pose travel problems for learners? Will facilities be needed for meetings between educational and administrative staffs?

- What educational aids will be needed? Who will prepare them and when? What materials will be required? When must they be supplied? In what ways do they support the learning sought?

- What information is necessary prior to, during, and following the activities for the learners, the educational staff, the administrator or manager? Will briefings be required? How will this information be communicated?

- Have the dates for the activity been checked for possible conflict with other events that affect those to be involved in the learning activity? Have the logistics of scheduling and workload been coordinated with other efforts of the library, agency, or association?

- Has the necessary funding been committed to the activity? Has the cost been determined? What cost-cutting efforts have been made? What financial and other records are required?

- Have plans been made for evaluation of the activity? What reporting and record keeping are required? What efforts must be made before, during, and following the learning activity? Who will need feedback and when? When, where, and how will evaluation information be collected? Is research to be done during the activity, or as a result of its outcomes? What provision is made to observe serendipitous outcomes?

Of course, the specifics in relation to each of these administrative tasks will depend on the nature of the activity. Each of the tasks outlined above will be covered in more specific detail in later Guidelines in this chapter. Essentials for conducting a workshop differ from those necessary to maintain an internship, even though both activities might be part of the overall learning program. The number and kind of administrative tasks is sufficiently demanding to warrant the recommendation that, under all but the most unusual circumstances, the administrator of a program should not also be responsible for the educational functions also.

During most learning activities, a single person ordinarily is not able to cope with both kinds of responsibilities simultaneously. The active presence of administrative staff frees the instructional staff to concentrate on the learners, the content, and the techniques of the design rather than to be concerned about administrative details. Problems may arise unexpectedly during the learning activity. If someone with administrative responsibility and capability is present, those needs can be accommodated with little interruption of the learning process. If, on the other hand, the administrator is also the educator, either the logistical or the learning issues will take priority, with the other needs perhaps remaining unanswered.

For each learning activity, careful attention must be given to the details of preparation and follow-through to assure that the activity goes smoothly. Equal attention must be given to enabling learners to learn. Except for the occasional extraordinary individual, these two functions cannot be equally well performed by the same person for the same activity. As the arranger of the facilities, finances and logistics, the administrator becomes familiar with the procedures and routines that are necessary. Knowing the key questions to ask and knowing what can be assumed to be needed, the experienced administrator will be able to catch early warning signals and act upon them even during the course of the activity. The need might be for additional newsprint or markers or for alternative arrangements for a delay in a session's adjournment. Though often viewed as expedient, to expect this capability of the educator(s) simultaneously with their conducting the learning process is neither advisable nor wise.

Skills and Competencies

The learning program administrator needs a number of skills and competencies to be able to adequately fulfill the three major responsibilities and the many specific tasks required. The probability of selecting an ideal person able to meet all demands is remote. It is, however, helpful to view the range of the knowledge, skills, and attitudes that are important for the administrator to have. Thus, a library, an agency, or an association can establish personnel requirements for a new position. Or, a present or potential program administrator can assess his or her own strengths and weaknesses in relation to what actually is needed in such a position. Areas that need strengthening could then be the basis of a personal learning plan for an individual interested in directing a staff development or continuing education program.

Major competencies desired of a program administrator include organizational ability, leadership and initiative, flexibility and creativity, problem-solving, and the ability to communicate. Since the administrative position blends both educational and administrative contexts, each of the competencies should be viewed from both perspectives. Each competency requires an area of knowledge, a range of skills, and an attitudinal approach.

Program administration is very like managing an ad hoc organization and must be understood in terms of its own organizational structure, particularly its functions of coordination, communication, and decision-making. As a mini-organization, a program exists within the immediate context of the sponsoring library, agency, or association, and within the larger context of librarianship. Thus, the administrator should be able to weave together a knowledge of librarianship, adult education, and management. That ability might come from formal academic study, from practical experience, or from both.

A well-managed program brings together the ingredients essential to produce quality learning experiences from library personnel. Rational thinking, sound planning, and adequate follow-through by the administrator will strengthen the entire program and increase the possibility of solid results from efforts made. Vision is important to accompany the administrator's overview of the program's present and future directions. Careful attention to details is important whether those details are assumed by the administrator or are delegated. The ability to work well with colleagues, individually and in groups, is particularly essential if broad-based involvement is a precept of the program. Overall organizational ability knits the program together, keeps its priorities in view, assures its progress.

Leadership and initiative are important skills to enable the administrator to start a new program or to develop a new thrust for an existing one. Both abilities are important to build and sustain an interest and commitment for specific activities as well as for the program itself. For a new program especially, the credibility of staff development and continuing education efforts often relies on the character and behavior of the program administrator. Leadership, not dominance, is essential to meet the tests of those who are suspicious or sceptical of the program. Initiative is important not only to begin the program, but also to actively seek out needs and resources, to find new ways to respond to those people seeking to learn and grow, and to interest and motivate those not yet involved. Leadership and initiative are vital to begin and to maintain the learning program.

Even with sound planning, though, some changes inevitably are necessary. Flexibility is the ability to cope successfully with those changes. Without the flexibility to move to viable alternatives, the program may not be as effective as it might have been in achieving its aims. The administrator will, at times, have to act quickly and logically to employ the most feasible and sound alternatives, acting coolly even under stress. When necessary changes create pressures impossible to surmount in making sound decisions, however, the administrator's usefulness will be limited, for often initial educational and management decisions must later be changed. Flexibility is essential in situations designed for the change and growth of people. The existence of a learning program assumes that change and growth are possible and valuable. If the administrator is not a flexible person, change and growth will be inhibited in others, either through rigid learning designs or through program management decisions that restrict opportunities. A flexible but decisive administrator, on the other hand, facilitates the development of the learning program.

Creativity includes the ability to see, to understand, and to employ the many different approaches that can prompt growth and learning. In addition, it makes possible the innovative use of limited resources, draws out the potential of learners and of instructional staff, and stimulates those involved beyond what is possible without a creative touch. A creative program administrator perceives how creative learning designs can increase the possibility of learning and can motivate interest in learning. A learning program done with flair as well as with substance will be more effective.

Problem-solving is a competency that enables the program administrator to cope with difficult situations that may rise from accommodating conflicting goals, from redirecting efforts or plans, from responding to emergency changes. Problem-solving requires an ability to perceive and identify the program, to explore and weigh alternative solutions, and to decisively settle upon the best single (or combination of) alternative(s) for a solution. If much of the program is based on group decisions, the administrator will require not only skills of individual problem-solving but also the ability to facilitate groups in that process.

Clear communication assures that the functions of the program work smoothly and effectively together. Articulate communications, both written and spoken, are important to assist the administrator to perform managerial responsibilities, especially in gaining acceptance and understanding for the program. Interpersonal communication skills, including active listening, are an indispensible asset. The ability to know and utilize organizational communication is equally essential for involving, informing, and convincing individuals within the framework of the library, agency or association.

In addition to these essential competencies, the program administrator requires at least basic knowledge in several areas. First, the administrator must understand the learning process, particularly as it applies to the adult practitioner. This knowledge, then, is translated into effective learning designs, and supportive administrative functions that enable learning rather than thwart it. Knowledge of how to manage is especially important for the administrator of a substantial and complex program. A well-managed program facilitates providing valid and relevant learning opportunities. A familiarity with librarianship, and with the people and resources involved in the program, is useful although that can be gained on the job. Thorough knowledge of the sponsoring library, agency, or association is important, particularly its purpose and operations.

And, finally, self-knowledge is vital. The administrator must also be involved in learning, willing to engage in frequent personal learning experiences. These will help assure needed competencies and, at the same time, may develop an empathy and understanding for the role of the learner. This implies that the administrator knows his or her strengths and weaknesses in relation to the administrative job, and continues to assess them throughout the experience of working with the program. It is important, although sometimes difficult, for a program administrator to also be aware of his or her own personal needs for development, willing and able to be a learner as well as the person responsible for enabling the learning of others.

The administrator's role develops in accord with the particular interests and abilities of the individual, the needs to which the program responds, and the immediate and long range aims of the sponsoring organization. The person and his or her competencies are a major component of the program and a factor in its success. But, the administrator as a person is not the only factor. Organizational commitment, learner acceptance, and procedural and budgetary constraints are all very real challenges to the administrator's abilities, calling for managerial and educational skills.

Two kinds of program/project management are possible. One is when the program is a permanent function of the organization. Then, resources describing organizational behavior in general are helpful. The second is when the program is intended as a temporary system. The following are helpful sources in such instances: Russell L. Ackoff and Fred E. Emergy, *On Purposeful Systems* (Chicago, Illinois: Aldine-Atherton, 1972); Joseph J. Moder and Cecil R. Phillips, *Project Management with CPM and PERT*, 2nd ed. (New York: Van Nostrand-Reinhold, 1970); and Alan T. Peart, *Design of Project Management Systems and Records*, (Boston, Mass.: Cahners, 1972).

Structures

This wide array of the essential functions and competencies, together with the extensive list of some of the more specific tasks that are required, indicates that a sizeable program will tax the time and ability of the individual responsible for the program. Just how program responsibilities are designated in relation to other organizational functions depends on the nature of the library, the agency, or the association, as well as on the abilities of the individual program administrator. Some of the important organizational factors that will need to be considered include: its present and future funding levels, its directions and priorities, its customary approach to staff development or continuing education, and the level of understanding possessed by its decision-makers in regard to the needs and potential of the program.

Another influential factor is the general approach that brings the program into being. In situations with no previous program, the effort to insert a full-fledged new program will require careful preparation of personnel as well as organizational structure to become an integral part of the library, the agency, or the association. The program cannot just drop into place and then begin its work. Other situations are those where the segments and activities of a learning program have existed but are, for the first time, being brought together into a program format of its own. Here, too, careful ground work is essential, including decisions about scope, authority, personnel, funding, and how the program will interrelate with other organizational functions.

The library, agency, or association interested in establishing a learning program might consider four basic patterns of structure. Whether putting a new program into place or restructuring an existing one, each of these alternatives might be viewed either as a temporary measure on the way to something more permanent, or as the final and firm commitment. With forethought and planning, one alternative can build successfully into another. The four patterns are:

1) An individual working full- or part-time alone can be expected to manage a simple program, given the appropriate experience, skills, and support. This, of course, depends on the availability of time, the nature of the planned activities, and the competence of the individual. Difficulties can be anticipated, however, if the

administrator is expected to manage the program and also be responsible for major instructional tasks for activities.

2) An administrator aided by a capable support staff can manage a sizeable and complex program. Other staff members or outside assistance can help with time-consuming tasks or those requiring special expertise. And, an advisory committee used for planning and/or evaluation is helpful, often increasing the program's viability. The communication and coordination with an advisory body will usually add to the administrative responsibilities but the return is usually worth the time and effort. An advisory group can also be used with the first pattern described.

3) Administrative functions for the program may be shared by a team of two, or perhaps three, people whose skills and specialities balance. Such a team can bring richer resources to the program and, if each works part-time with the program, the program is assured of strong organizational ties and awareness. In exchange for these benefits, this pattern requires additional time to plan and coordinate activities. Clearly defined lines of responsibility are important, as is the ability to work well together.

4) A committee of interested people is sometimes used to administer a program. This pattern has the advantage of involving people in the program, drawing together colleagues who are interested in and committed to learning. The group may also include individuals capable of designing learning activities and of managing a program. The committee and its head ordinarily share functions of coordination, communications, and decision-making. Ordinarily, this pattern is used to make a transition to staff appointments with assigned responsibilities since a program is usually limited in scope and quality when administered by a committee.

Selection of the way in which the program will be administered is a crucial one, for it determines how all the other elements will be pulled together to develop the program and to produce its activities.

The importance of appointed and funded positions must be highlighted. Whether for staff development or for continuing education, dependence on volunteer managers poses two significant problems: one, a great demand is likely to be made of the individual in the role of volunteer administrator. This will require personal sacrifice beyond what was originally envisioned and, probably, will restrict the extent and quality of the program that is possible under those terms. Two, when the position does not meet the expectations set for it, a real danger exists that the function as well as the position will be thought unworthy of further organizational support, and both will be set aside. Obviously reliance on volunteers is one way to initiate a new effort. From the start, however, planning should focus on the need for permanence, stability, and quality.

A wide variety of titles and job descriptions exist for administrators of learning programs in libraries, agencies, and associations. This variety may indicate the differences in organizational structure within each of these groups, or it may reflect an inexact and uncertain approach to this function in most organizations.

Current examples of administrative titles for staff development in libraries include: Staff Development Librarian, Staff Development Coordinator, In-service Training Director, Library Personnel Officer, Assistant for Personnel and Staff Development, Staff Development and Affirmative Action Officer, and Coordinator of Research and Staff Development. Titles for continuing education program administrators include: Director of Continuing Education, Director for Professional Development, Director of Education, Continuing Education Coordinator.

Similar to these differences in titles, the definitions of responsibilities and duties also vary considerably from organization or organization. Often, job descriptions are vaguely stated, apparently waiting for the development of the function as well as the staff. Literature on personnel policies in librarianship is less explicit about the importance of staff development and continuing education than is that of other professions, business, or industry. Yet, such policy statements are a constructive and concrete means to assure that this responsibility is turned into action on the part of the individual employee and the library, the agency, and the association. The function and the position reflect the priority of the learning program.

Since the program administrator's is the key role for the program, that person becomes the focus for staff development or continuing education. In turn, the library, agency, or association must articulate this responsibility, support and sustain it in order to be assured of a program with results in line with expectations. The administrator has the perspective of the entire program, bringing the many functions, tasks, and activities together to meet present and future learning needs. With an understanding of the educational function and with managerial abilities, the administrator must work together with the instructional staff to produce quality activities. Through time and experience, the role and responsibilities of the program administrator become clarified, taking shape from the situation and the people involved.

Summary

Program plans are translated into program activities through the skill and efforts of the program administrator. The administrator is a manager, primarily responsible for directing the program, and for assuring communication, coordination, and decision-making. The administrator must know what needs to be done, when and how—and then be able to accomplish that. The functions of the administrator and the tasks that fall to that person call for a number of competencies: organizational ability, leadership and initiative, flexiblity and creativity, problem-solving, and the ability to communicate. In addition to personal competencies, the success of the learning program also hinges on the willingness and ability of the organization to provide for the administration of the program, with designated responsibility and authority as well as support. Program administration usually includes the supportive and logistical arrangements necessary to produce the learning events, activities, and processes: assuring adequate meeting facilities, providing needed training materials and equipment, selecting and preparing educational staff and resource people and keeping required financial and personnel records. The number and kind of administrative tasks are sufficiently impressive to warrant the recommendation that under all but the most unusual circumstances, the administrator of a program should not also be responsible for the educational functions.

GUIDELINE 7–LOCATE AND SELECT EDUCATIONAL STAFF

The overriding responsibility of the educational staff is to enable individuals and groups to learn. Unlike the program administrator whose job is to guide and direct the program as a whole, the educational staff usually consists of individuals employed for specific activities in the program. Alone or as a team, they prepare and conduct the workshops, institutes, colloquia, or training sessions that make up the program. Most often, the involvement of each individual educator is for a single activity, or, at most, a series of related activities. Whatever the involvement, the primary job of the educator is to provide for the learning experience of the specified program activity.

The success or failure of each learning activity is commonly assumed to rest almost exclusively on the shoulders of the educators. Usually, they are expected to be all-knowing, able to put together and produce successful activities with little interference from the library, agency, or association sponsoring the activity. They are expected to be individuals whose knowledge, experience, and ability equips them to be aware of and knowledgeable about a given issue, problem, or subject area. For each activity, the educators are seen as the focus, the headliners.

These high expectations may be held by the learners, by the program administrator and planners, or by the educators themselves. Certainly, the educators must be viewed as a very important, indeed essential, component of the activity. A danger exists, however, if that is perceived as the *only* element enabling learners to learn. True, some activities rely heavily on the competence of the educator. Other activities may simply require a skilled and sensitive floor manager to encourage learning. Believing that the learning potential of the activity depends almost solely on the performance of one individual educator at one time and place diminishes the value of the many other factors that also enable learning. If all responsibility is placed on the educator, and if that person's performance does not meet the high expectations of it, other potentials for learning may be overlooked. Although quality educational staff may be the most important, and expensive, single ingredient used, that is not the only ingredient that enables learning.

This Guideline describes various specialists required for different types of learning activities, together with the basic categories, characteristics, and areas of expertise and responsibility appropriate for each of them. It describes the kind of information required to seek educational staff for learning program activities, including the sources to use in locating them, and the criteria useful in selecting them. Procedures that the administrator can use to engage and prepare educational staff for their responsibilities are introduced. And, finally, ways to cope with common problems that sometimes hinder the effectiveness of educational staff are suggested.

Definitions

Terminology becomes particularly confusing at the point of describing the educational function in staff development and continuing education. The labels are diverse: teachers, instructors, faculty, facilitators, leaders, trainers, consultants, and resource people. These terms seem less specific and predictable now than they were in the past, for the semantics and the practice of teaching/learning, particularly with adults, are changing. Presently in a transition period, these terms differ widely in their application. So do the concepts about the necessary qualifications, skills and behaviors these labels include. No matter by what terms they are called, these individuals, designated "agents of learning" by J. R. Kidd,[1] are essential for the implementation of the activities in the learning program.

Because of our past experiences and associations, each individual has a very personal picture of the appropriate role and behavior for the person responsible for enabling learning. The examples associated with our school days, however, are not necessarily the best models to help the adult practitioner learn. The confusion of terminology is further heightened by the differences between staff development and continuing education, the former with its roots in business and industry, the latter emerging from adult education. From these various sources come different terms and expectations for those responsible for the educational function of either the program in general or the activities specifically.

The most common terms, "teacher" and "instructor" have much carryover from narrowly defined roles of the past. Because of its limited range of approach, however, this traditional role does not adequately fulfill the principles of adult learning described in Guideline 5. In relation to his definition of roles required for human resources development, Leonard Nadler points out his difficulty with the terms "teacher" and "instructor." The need, he says, is no longer for lecturers imparting knowledge but rather for individuals performing a number of different functions that relate to meeting the needs of learners. Finding both terms inadequate, he uses the term "learning specialist" to include the interrelated responsibilities of instructor, curriculum builder, and methods and materials developer.[2]

Certainly, instructors, teachers, and faculty are responsible to develop their courses, advise students, engage in research, and become involved in campus and community activities. They are, however, more generally associated with classroom education than with learning efforts conducted at the work place or other out-of-school sites. These latter locales are more the concern of staff development and continuing education, whereas the classroom is traditionally the style of pre-service education.

Developed over the past thirty years, the terms "training" and "trainers" are now in frequent use. For the most part, they are understood in relation to roles and functions evolved first through business and industry, then through professional organizations such as the American Society for Training and Development. Lynton and Pareek use the concept and term "training" in relation to staff development for service-oriented occupations. Describing training as helping the practitioner aim for lasting improvement on the job, they explain the trainer's functions as:

> stimulating and motivating participants to wish to acquire certain kinds of knowledge and understanding and to practice certain skills because they recognize that they need them. Training then comes to consist

largely of well-organized opportunities for participants to acquire the necessary understanding and skill. The trainer appreciates that he is close to only some parts of the whole learning process and can in the final analysis hope to control only one: his own behavior. He is like a farmer who prepares the soil, plants good seed, and tends and nurtures the new growth. He does not harbor the illusion that he *makes* things grow or determines their ultimate size and shape.[3]

Training generally implies a wide range of functions. A trainer may design a variety of learning techniques for use within a given activity, prepare materials for exercises to assist learners, facilitate interactive groups working with problem-solving or decision-making situations, analyze organizational problems with training implications, build means to aid learners apply their learnings and to learn from their own experiences, and develop means to actively elicit feedback to guide the direction of the activity. The depth and range of skills possessed by capable trainers often leads to their deep involvement in the learning process itself.

Although "training" is now a generally accepted term in wide use outside the library field, recent experiences working with staff development and continuing education activities for library personnel reveal a strong and articulate minority opinion expressing resistance to the term on the basis that dogs may be trained but people are taught. The difficult but understandable discrepancy between the previous and current understanding of how adults learn can complicate the issue. Knowles pinpoints this dilemma when he describes the last decade as being a time when "there has been evolving a body of knowledge about how adults learn and a body of technology for facilitating that learning that is changing the role of the trainer and requiring that he or she know few things few teachers know. . . ."[4]

The term "educator" however, is an overall and inclusive term. Cyril Houle describes adult education as being "like many other major enterprises of mankind. A Smoky Mountain craftsman weaving rugs on a hand loom in his cabin is engaged in industry; so is General Motors; and between the two extremes of complexity lie countless producers of many kinds of wares, all of whom have their places in the total industrial enterprise of the nation."[5] Recent years have seen the field of adult education and the role of the educator broaden into new dimensions, use new techniques, and expand into new fields.

As with this analogy, the practice of staff development in libraries and continuing education through agencies and associations ranges broadly. For this reason, the terms "educator" and "educational staff" will be used in this book to designate individuals with the prime responsibility for the conduct of the learning experience those who enable learning through skilled and deliberate efforts, those "agents of learning" upon whom much of the success of each activity will depend. Where other terms are used, they will refer to more specialized roles defined either explicitly or within a revealing context.

Types of Educational Skills

In seeking the appropriate educator(s) for a particular activity, the program administrator or program planners must identify the skills required in relation to the job to be done. That, together with the application of more general criteria make the selection of educational staff more likely to be accurate and suitable. For most staff development and continuing education activities, three major skill areas can be identified. Each area has its distinct characteristics and unique uses. Most of the specialized terminology is drawn from adult education.

1) Individuals responsible for presenting information include the content or subject specialist with the skills of being able to speak and/or write articulately. These individuals are likely to make presentations or serve on panels or respond to questions or prepare written materials for learners. Their competency is usually in a specific area of knowledge or technical skill, for example, circulation equipment, systems management, or copyright. Here, this group of individuals will be identified as **content specialists.**

2) Individuals responsible for designing and implementing particular methods by which learning can take place are specialists in the techniques by which adults learn. They may or may not be content specialists, but their primary expertise lies in the appropriate design and proficient practice of one or more learning methods, such as simulation, computer assisted learning, audiovisual production, or self-instructional learning systems. These individuals may be from disciplines such as education or management or training and development. Most specialize in a particular type of method and, through continued application in new situations, develop a proficiency in adapting a method to a situation. Some use prepared learning packages, others prefer to design afresh for each new group and circumstance. Generally, these individuals are referred to as resource people or consultants. Here, they will be referred to as **methods specialists.**

3) Individuals responsible for managing the process of learning are specialists in applied behavioral sciences and/or adult education. They are skilled in "reading" groups and in eliciting "process" learnings from behavior and interaction, and may or may not be closely identified with the subject matter focus. These individuals are most often referred to as leaders, facilitators, or consultants. Often they are also skilled in the design and implementation of interactive or participative learning exercises from which process learnings come. These individuals are most commonly known as trainers or facilitators. Here, this group will be termed **process specialists.**

At times, of course, individuals may offer a blend of any two or even all three of these specialities. Or, if a particular activity needs more than one specialty, an educational team can be assembled that brings together the various areas of needed skills. Selection of the educational staff needed for a particular activity will depend on the responsibilities and functions required to produce the learning sought.

Each of these categories implies particular expertise. Those responsible for selection of the educational staff will need to specify the qualifications needed for the functions and responsibilities that are required for an activity. For example, a speaker on computer applications in libraries would not necessarily need process skills. However, an individual being asked to develop and produce a skills building workshop on supervision would need competencies in both content and process and might also need the ability to design such a learning experience.

In general, a content specialist should be up-to-date, accurate, comprehensive and aware of the full context of the subject matter as well as its possible applications and implications. A content specialist is most often asked to make a presentation that provides needed information, stimulation or a context for learning. A panel or symposium would assemble several content specialists to convey information from a variety of views or aspects of a problem or issue. The content specialist often uses audio-visual media, such as film, slide tapes, multi-media, or exhibits to supplement orally presented material. Used as a resource person, the content specialist can share, formally or informally, the particular study or experiences that may make him or her an authority. Sometimes the distinct area of knowledge of the content specialist is not presented directly (in person) to a group of learners but is channeled into instructional materials, learning packages, or briefing sessions for other resource persons or consultants to then be used directly by the learners.

The methods specialist is one whose expertise is primarily a technical one— the design of how the learning will be accomplished. Most presentation techniques are traditional and employ well-known methods that need little experience to implement. However, interactive and participative methods that incorporate content areas such as problem-solving, decision-making, communications, outreach and action training are becoming more frequently used. These often require special skills that may not necessarily be possessed by the content specialist.

The skill of eliciting learner involvement and participation through adept planning and design, together with competent practice requires extensive study and experience to do well. Methods specialists might be used to give advice on a particular technique or to personally manage that technique in action or to prepare materials to be used. Some of the methods that usually require skilled expertise are audience participation techniques, workshops, institutes, skill practice exercises, and simulations that include role playing, case methods, games, action mazes, and in-basket exercises. The specialist should be able to employ a wide range of techniques and adaptations using a number of methods. Some specialists, however, have a tendency to overuse a few techniques because of their own comfort and familiarity with a particular method rather than because of its relevance to the intent and the situation at hand. Another methods concern is that "fads" prevail for a time, certain methods become frequently demanded and used, and are offered as "the" method, before they are replaced by another approach.

The process specialist is becoming more and more in demand as interactive and participative methods of adult learning are increasingly used. These individuals facilitate *how* learning happens. Most such specialists function on the premise that learning is learner-centered rather than teacher-centered. This substantial shift in adult education is influencing continuing library education as the traditional role of the teacher evolves into that of a mediator for learning. The process specialist is the individual who establishes the conditions for interaction, observes what happens, and helps the learner to perceive and analyze that interaction in terms of basic principles. Learning comes through participation followed by an analysis of what occured. This type of learning is usually focused on skills and attitudes with a framework of basic principles and precepts bringing the theoretical constructs alive through their actual application and use by the learner.

The use of the process specialist is primarily for building skills of individual and group communication, decision-making, and problem-solving in the areas of supervision and management and public services. The process specialist needs to be knowledgeable and competent in "people skills" and in the art of helping people learn. A great deal of the test of such competence relies on the personal qualities of the individual specialist, for the learner must respect and trust the specialist to be able to risk exposing her or his present behavior and experimentation with new behavior. Process specialists are most often called faculty, resource persons, trainers, or consultants, and they are usually used to observe and guide learnings in support of the activity objectives. Some use predesigned packages that have been utilized and tested with other groups for like purposes. Others prefer to work in depth with precisely designated learners, needs, and organizations to tailor an activity to fit the specific situation. Each learning situation usually includes a presentation of content for context, structured exercises to promote interaction, and an analysis period. The analysis is shared by the learner and the specialist alike as they view what occurred in the interaction in light of basic principles and also how learning might apply to on-the-job situations.

Each of these specialists might be sought by program planners or the administrator to stimulate, motivate, and encourage learning to occur, and thus, to achieve the objectives for the activity, and ultimately, those for the program. Obviously, a wide range of roles is possible, but most of them add up to the specialist's ability to cope capably with the learning situation, whether that is a presentation of information, a demonstration of skills, response to questions, or facilitating the ability of the group to learn from its immediate process.

Although a substantial part of the success or failure of the activity is often attributed to the individual specialist(s), many elements actually contribute to whatever happens, such as the appropriateness of person and method of instruction, completeness in briefing educational staff, and accuracy of reading the needs of the situation and of the participants. Generally speaking, a high quality activity will be much more possible when the specialists are involved in the planning and evaluation processes related to the activity, as well as to the particular assignment they have during the actual implementation.

Educators usually specialize in particular content areas, skills, or issues in librarianship, and each often develops a personal style and competency with certain methods and techniques. Some specialize in institutes and workshops, others develop demonstrations and exhibits, others function as resource people with special knowledge on a given subject. It is the responsibility of the administrator or the program planners to select those skills that are required for the activity being planned.

An illustration of the importance of this responsibility would be a program in a medium-size public library where, over a three month period, the following staff development activities might be planned:

Activity 1:   a series of monthly problem-solving clinics for supervisory staff in which they can examine their supervisory styles and discuss alternative approaches to problems of personnel management.

Activity 2:   a half-day workshop with hands-on practice with film projectors, slide-tape equipment, and other audio-visual hardware for all branch personnel in order to prepare them for new equipment to be supplied to branches.

Activity 3:   an orientation session to brief new pages on the library as a whole and on the importance of effective page services.

Activity 4:   two repeated half-day sessions for interested public service staff members on the importance and practice of interpersonal communications.

Each of these activities would require separate educational objectives, each is directed toward a specific audience, each has different content, and each would need different methods and techniques. The same educator(s) would be unlikely to be equally skilled in the needed content areas and learning techniques of all four activities. The selection of educators would be on the basis of their specialities in relation to what was needed for producing the activity. In this example, the following might be the plans as they finally developed: Activity 1 sessions are planned, convened and evaluated by a group of supervisors, assisted by the trainer from the municipal Personnel Department acting as a resource person at the sessions dealing with shared problem-solving and the exploration of alternative styles and their effectiveness. Activity 2 uses an instructor from a local vocational education audio-visual curriculum to conduct the workshop at the school facilities, using the same types of equipment as those being purchased by the library. Activity 3 orientation is planned and conducted by members of a staff committee that designed a brief presentation about the role of the library in the community, more detailed presentations about each area in the library, and an extensive tour conducted before the library is opened for the day. Activity 4 brings in a facilitator from a local public service company (located through the local chapter of a professional association) to assist in planning the activity and to take primary responsibility for conducting the day. Library staff members are prepared to serve as discussion leaders.

This example shows a typical range of needs in a rather ordinary staff development program sequence. Obviously, many different capabilities are required. Even though the program administrator is not ordinarily recommended for educational functions, the need for a balance of skills from the three specialty areas and the usual limited budget would suggest that the administrator's abilities not be entirely disregarded. For instance, an administrator possessing a knowledge of instructional methods would be well prepared to design the learning methods to be used in an activity, working together with the content and/or process specialists.

In addition to employing specialists to work with specific learning activities that are part of the program, specialists might also be considered to assist in developing the program as a whole. This is, of course, the province of the program administrator and, where applicable, other program planners. However, for a sequence of management training, a content specialist could be helpful in planning, as could a methods specialist. A process specialist could be useful in assisting the group of program planners work more effectively together. These decisions

·rest with the program administrator, who will be consistently involved throughout the program. Involvement of specialists and educators in general will characteristically be brief and specifically defined, and usually limited in time and scope.

Criteria

The individual program administrator or program planner group responsible for selecting educational staff for a program's activities must identify the skills that will be needed by that staff. That becomes a basis to guide seeking and selecting educators. Other criteria are also helpful, however, to decide on the individual(s) with the strongest capabilities to meet the required responsibilities. More general qualifications and criteria can supplement the more specific indications given within each specialist category. Taken together, both general and specific criteria offer guidelines for selection of educational staff. Important criteria for educators involved in the learning program include:

- The understanding, acceptance, and practice of the principles of adult learning.

- A respect for the knowledge and experience of the learner, together with a willingness and skill to bring out the learner's perspective as well as to present new perspectives to the learner.

- An enthusiasm for the activity being planned, and an attitude of genuine interest for the organization and the individuals involved.

- Ability and willingness to plan well in advance, and an awareness that effective selection and use of methods and media are related to available "lead time."

- Proficiency at "reading" the group's ability to understand the content and to work with the methods and media used to implement the activity.

- Constant awareness of the objectives and intent of the activity and a willingness to respond with what is required and possible to accomplish these objectives.

- Expertise built on current and solid study and experience.

- Personal characteristics, such as being patient, ethical, emphatic, non-manipulative, honest, and direct, as well as the ability to communicate and to listen.

- Willingness and skill to balance the needs of the learners, the requirements of the organization, and the constraints and possibilities of the situation.

- Availability and fee in relation to the organizational scheduling and budgeting possibilities.

Additional criteria may, in some cases, be developed by planners or the administrator in relation to particular and unique circumstances that may exist within the library, agency, or association, or within the program itself.

The importance of each of these qualifications will depend on the requirements of the activities being planned. For a brief presentation on a limited subject, content knowledge would be the most important along with desirable personal characteristics. Other factors might not be as essential. For an intensive day-long, interactive group activity, however, all of the above criteria would be very necessary to assure the success of the activity.

The job of any educator engaged to produce a learning activity for a staff development or continuing education program will vary a great deal with the circumstances. In some instances, the educator will be responsible for developing objectives, design, materials, and logistics. Another time, those decisions will be made by the program administrator and the only function of the educator is to prepare content-oriented material and show up on time. Sometimes the educator's expertise is acknowledged and used; other times it is not. The match between the program's needs and the definition of the educator's responsibility is usually in the hands of the administrator, as is the selection.

Sources

Locating the needed specialists from which to choose the educational staff for an activity is often a challenge and can test the skill of the administrator or program planners. Content specialists will most often come from the field of librarianship, for instance, library school faculty or library practitioners whose study or experiences especially qualify them.

Method and process specialists are often drawn from outside the library field, perhaps from higher education, from special projects, or from business, trade, industrial, or professional organizations. The American Society for Training and Development and the Adult Education Association are helpful sources, for they are active nationally and have regional and local chapters able to give suggestions and leads in response to requests. Many areas have community adult education organizations worthwhile to explore. Individuals with methods and process skills often engage in independent consultant work, either in addition to their present job or as a full-time enterprise.

Directories of consultants and resources can provide a starting place for seeking any specialists that are sought. Suggestions and ideas can come also from individuals involved in planning for the activity. Articles, brochures, announcements, and personal contacts are rich sources for identifying potential educational staff as well as for design ideas and useful supportive instructional materials. (Much of this information can be maintained until needed in the files described in Guideline 4. Such a file can save much time and energy when seeking appropriate possibilities for educational staff.)

Individuals involved for some time in staff development and continuing education work with library personnel often form informal networks of contacts. Thus, professional colleagues could be asked for ideas and referrals. From this source can come suggestions as to individuals who have been observed to perform well in activities of similar nature in the past or who otherwise have demonstrated their skills or knowledge (through writings or service on official boards and committees). Individuals being contacted for their interest and availability in serving as educators for an activity may also provide referrals to others with the same speciality. This is particularly true if the availability, schedule, or geographic location of the original contact are not exactly suited to the needs of the program.

In light of some of the suggestions made here, those people responsible for selecting educational staff should also be aware of four cautions. First, when considering the use of able practitioners who possess knowledge and skill in the content area sought, the willingness and the ability of that individual to impart that knowledge or skill to others should also be carefully reviewed. Second, it is not necessary to automatically subscribe to the assumption that the use of the distant "expert" is preferrable to the use of local talent. Sometimes, it is true, a name and fame may enhance the value of the learning activity, and automatic credibility will be worth the added cost. Other times, however, equally knowledgeable and skilled people may be available locally. Third, when considering suggestions and recommendations on the basis of reported observations, it may be that those observations may indicate more about the perception and values of the person reporting them than about the actual level of expertise of the specialist being observed or the relevance of that person to the contemplated activity. And, finally, limited program budgets often place constraints on fees offered to educators. Sometimes association members or agency or library staff with a special interest in the activity will be asked to serve as educator on an unpaid basis. Occasionally, though, the same individuals are overused due to their convenience, willingness, and availability. Essentially, this amounts to professional exploitation and raises the question of fairness.

Special note may be made here of the advantages offered when the educators for a library's staff development program are selected from that library's staff. Using staff members for educational functions may offer cost savings, although it must be noted that their services are not "free" just because no fee is paid in exchange for services. Use of library personnel, however, offers other advantages, such as their familiarity with the organization, their availability for the all-important preparatory and follow-up work, the possibility of their involvement with a planning committee to assure a clear understanding of what is needed, and of course, the in-depth learning on the part of selected staff member(s). Kozoll underlines some of the advantages of using library personnel as educators for staff development activities:

> Keep in mind that your own staff's responsibility for training new personnel can increase their own efficiency. There is nothing like explaining something to a person that reinforces your understanding of knowledge, techniques or processes. Staff involvement in the training process means there is a higher level of information exchange among people and a cutback in reliance on outsiders for delivering what perhaps insiders know best.[6]

Not only is the depth of knowledge of those working to help others learn tremendously increased, but benefits also are extended more broadly. Building the concept of self-sufficiency can help promote good morale. Increasing the library's ability to do much of its own training and development work spreads to incorporate teaching and learning processes more naturally as a part of each job, with staff members better able to help each other learn and work together more easily. But, perhaps the strongest advantage is the economic benefit. Developing library staff capabilities to plan, conduct, and evaluate learning activities is a long-range advantage, since it increases the depth of learning of those individuals, assures that the learning activities are closely work related, and reduces the reliance on outside educators.

Several benefits can be expected from using an outsider in a staff development program. Unique expertise can be brought into the library, with objective and up-to-date knowledge, the ability to help people learn new skills or change their behavior. Familiarity with a subject in depth can be gained, as well as knowledge of how other libraries handle such problems and perspective on different ways to learn. Often the outsider brings a degree of experience and prestige that, together with greater freedom of action, offers more latitude and gains more credibility. Sometimes the outside educator will say just what has been said by inside educators previously—but it will now be heard and believed.

In order to avoid the potential disadvantage of using the less-qualified inside educator in preference to a well-qualified outside one, deliberate efforts must be made either to recruit or to prepare staff members with required skills. Time as well as special preparation and opportunities, will be needed for such individuals to develop their educational potential. Large libraries and large library systems might well consider building a balanced educational team assigned with the responsibility of staff development. Smaller libraries would be more likely to use interested and able staff members who are responsible for staff development and learning activities for only part of their time. Study, supplemented by apprenticeship work with other educators, can provide the basics. That can then be enriched through experiences with a variety of training techniques.

Even if a deliberate and concentrated effort is directed toward special preparation of selected individuals from the library staff as potential educators, some reliance on outside resources will still be necessary. The program administrator and planners will have to plan for full use of the library's staff, thereby increasing their knowledge of the content of the activity and their ability to plan and/or conduct learning activities. And, planning will also have to make efficient and effective use of outside educators, using them for their unique knowledge and ability to stimulate, interest, and convince.

A staff development program, then, can blend the advantages of using "insiders" and of using "outsiders" to enrich the learning possible from a given activity. Educators from outside the library offer advantages such as fresh approaches, valuable insights and perspectives, and different educational techniques. These can serve to "open up" the staff to new ideas and ways of doing things. Some of the outside educator's contributions will be in relation to content: but the outside educator also introduces learning methods and processes, and these can then be observed and perhaps adapted for later activities conducted by inside educators.

A continuing education program, of course, will consistently use outside educators for the learning activities sponsored by the agency or association. Often, however, a "stable" of educators may form almost a "core curriculum" in the sense that a regular group of educators are used for repeating the same content or method, or perhaps for a series of activities. Usually, the program planners for continuing education draw on their sources and resources to engage the appropriate outside educators.

The sources from which these insiders and outsiders are drawn will vary greatly with the situation, since no one resource will meet all the needs of the

particular program will need to be built, probably beginning with the needs
assessment phase.

Problems

In locating, selecting, and working with educational staff to implement
learning activities, various problems are possible. Anticipating them may enable
preventative measures, usually more pleasant and desirable than the prescriptive
approach. One problem often encountered is that not enough potential educators
can be located to make a sound selection. Locating appropriate educators is
generally a time-consuming task and should be expected to be so. Perhaps the
sources tapped, the people contacted for ideas, the directories and files were not
adequate. Alternatives must be identified. For example, the search might go
beyond the library field if those resources are limited, or the possibility of using
skilled practitioners can be explored. Or, if some of the necessary knowledge and
skills are not available, the design of the activity might be altered. Or, if enough
lead time exists, additional efforts might be made to locate more possibilities.

A second problem arises when the selected educator requires a fee in excess
of the amount allowed in the activity budget or in excess of the perceived value
of that person or specialty. If, after discovering just what services the indicated
fee entails, it is still thought excessive, alternative educators can be sought or the
design can be changed. If neither of these alternatives are feasible, the educator
may be asked to reduce the number of services provided and scale down the
fee accordingly. When this is not possible, additional services that might be of
value may be requested to be included at the originally stated fee. For example,
the educator might be asked to meet with the planning committee to discuss his
or her speciality at a deeper level than will be presented at the activity. Or, the
educator might be asked to participate in a post-activity evaluation discussion to
share perceptions about the ways the activity met or did not meet its objectives.
Or, the educator might be asked to incorporate apprentices drawn from the
participant group or the planners into the implementation of the activity. Each
of these approaches would provide increased learning opportunities at no extra
cost.

Two problems sometimes occur after the educator is located and selected.
One is after being notified of the selection, the person in charge of the activity
may not hear further from the educator, either to confirm or cancel the arrangements made. If no word is heard of further preplanning work in process, a phone
call would be an appropriate follow-through move to assure that communications
have been clear about the expectations held of the educator by the program
planners. The second occurs when the performance has not met the expectations
held for it, either in terms of outcome or in relation to the plans and agreements
made. One way of keeping expectations realistic is to keep in close touch throughout the planning period so anticipations by both the administrator and the educator are understood. For paid educators, the fee payment can be held until after
the activity and, if a contractual agreement was signed, there may be reason to
adjust the fee in relation to the actual performance if it did not meet the standards
set in the agreement. Fewer options are possible for educators who agree to

perform without fee. Often a very delicate matter, the resolution of that issue depends on personalities and situation.

Problems are not always encountered in relation to the educational staff. A new program is more likely to meet with difficulties in discovering potential candidates from which to select, in achieving an equitable agreement that will assure the activity the skills and production that is needed, in providing the specialists the information essential for them to plan and perform well. With more experience, each of these difficulties is less likely to occur. Decisions on educational staffing are a major decision faced during implementation.

Procedures

To locate and select educational staff, the program administrator and/or the planners of the activity must define the requirements for the desired educational staff. This includes clarifying the objectives the activity is designed to accomplish, the essential scope and depth of content needed, the responsibilities required of the educator(s), the feasible dates and fees, and the particular methods and techniques desired. Kozoll speaks strongly in relation to this point:

> Keep in mind that there is no one person or group of persons who are best able to deliver relevant training. Start from the content to be discussed, the best form to present that content and then the best people to do it. Starting from the opposite side means that you are often limited by the personnel who cannot make the adjustments to move from a lecture of a leadership presentation mold to one requiring far greater staff involvement.[7]

Without clear and definite specifications in mind, the search is likely to be aimless, using time and effort to little avail. Locating the most appropriate persons becomes risky and the likelihood of subsidizing someone's soapbox or of reinforcing the latest fad is great. Another danger is that the sole basis for reaching an agreement with an educator becomes that person's knowledge of his or her speciality, thus placing the planner(s) at a disadvantage. Since the search is difficult and time-consuming, often it is wise to enter that search with basic ideas of what is required as well as with some flexibility.

Whether to use library staff as educators or to bring in outside educators to conduct the activity is a decision to be made based on those advantages most important in each particular situation. Sometimes the choice is very obvious and quickly made; sometimes it depends on how the in-house and outside educator possibilities compare; sometimes both are combined in a team, gaining the advantages of both approaches. The interest and ability of the in-house person can be observed over a period of time and, in many ways, can be cultivated by encouraging in-depth study, experience, or apprenticeship in a particular area of interest. Then, when the level of that person's capability matches a learning activity, he or she can be involved throughout the planning and conduct of the activity. Except for these few remarks, the procedures described below pertain to locating and selecting outside educators. Adaptation of these different steps may also be relevant for using internal library staff as educators.

Individuals whose education, experience, and/or ability are in line with what is needed for the activity are located through the previously indicated sources. To the extent possible, these alternatives then can be measured against the criteria for selection. For those individuals who seem feasible and should be considered, an initial contact by correspondence, telephone, or in person will establish whether the person is interested and available. For those not eliminated by these two requirements, the next step is to request a resumé or vita and a tentative reservation on the date(s).

At this point, references may be requested. Especially helpful would be those from individuals in libraries where similar work has been done recently. Also, the individual being considered may have publications that may reveal that person's knowledge, perspective, or attitudes. Or, the person's work may be observed at an up-coming workshop, conference, or committee meeting. Then, information from the individual, the references, the writings, and possibly the observation can be measured against the criteria to see which persons should be considered further.

Direct communications with each of those people still being considered will further aid in the final selection. Correspondence is the most often used method. It is also the least expensive and, sometimes, the least satisfactory. A telephone or in-person interview can better describe what is needed, elicit more information about the person, and begin a possible working relationship. However, a letter may be used to initiate and expedite the interview by specifying the areas and questions to be discussed, by setting a time and date to reserve the educator's time and attention. During communications with potential educators, the interviewer, usually the program administrator, will need to explain clearly and in depth the objectives of the activity, the results needed and wanted, the scope and depth of content or types of methods and techniques sought, and the expected roles and responsibilities of the various individuals involved in the activity, with particular attention given to those of that educator.

The educator should be asked questions to reveal the level of interest and the study and experience qualifying him or her for this activity. Such dialogue can explore ideas, suggestions, and alternative techniques or designs, thus providing information about the educator's degree of flexibility and skill. This can also broaden the program administrator's ability to design future activities or to consider the educator for future activities. Throughout this initial exploration period, it should be made clear to each person being considered that the selection process is not completed and that no commitments are implied until the selection is made.

All of the information gathered must be reviewed and tested against the requirements of the responsibilities envisioned for the activity as well as against the criteria developed to select such staff. The final selection may be the task of the administrator alone or may include the help of an advisory or decision-making group. The choice should be made of the individual(s) with the top qualifications, falling within budget and schedule constraints. Once made, selection should be promptly communicated to both the selected person(s) and to the others considered, allowing the latter to release the reserved date and thanking them for their interest.

A clear-cut, specific letter of confirmation will be needed to outline the responsibilities of the selected educator(s) and the expectations held for the activity, the time schedule for communications and decision-making deadlines, and the date and fee arrangements. This or subsequent contacts will need to confirm or provide new information such as:

- the issue or problem as presently perceived and the results sought from the activity that will aid in solving the problem,
- the objectives that have been established for the activity, and for the program,
- the anticipated number and nature of the group of learners,
- learner needs and how those were identified,
- general information about the sponsoring organization and its purposes,
- the method to be used,
- the type of evaluation that will be used to ascertain the activity's accomplishments,
- at what point a final decision will be made regarding the possibility of not doing the activity.

The initial or subsequent contacts will also need to ask for information *from* the educator(s). This can be guided by such questions as:

- What content do you plan to cover and how?
- How do you see the design of the activity?
- How do you plan to get participant response?
- In what ways do these elements (content, design, participation) achieve the objectives?
- What room arrangements and equipment will be needed?
- What materials and supplies will be needed?
- What preparatory and follow-up activities do you suggest for learners?
- When and where would feedback be helpful? From whom, how, and when should it be obtained?

Although written correspondence often is adequate for a record of agreement, a contract may be advisable or required by the library, agency, or association. As this information is agreed upon, informational materials may be composed, reproduced, and disseminated to interest and inform potential (or already selected) participants.

These contacts begin to define the working relationship and responsibilites of both the program administrator and the educator(s) selected for the activity. The administrator lays out the specifications for the activity, the educator suggests design and technique specifics; the administrator approves or suggests modifications, the educator responds. This begins a dialogue preparing both for the actual implementation of the particular activity.

Then, just prior to the activity, a briefing session will be helpful to bring everyone up to date, review plans, clarify logistics, anticipate problems that may arise, and check timing. For a speech or presentation, this briefing would be short. If the activity is a long workshop, however, or if a group of specialists have agreed to work as a team with interrelated roles, a full day's meeting before the activity may be necessary to assure that it is smoothly planned and that the group members are prepared to work in concert with one another. For an extended activity, additional educational staff meetings may also be necessary during the activity. This information should be part of the preparation for the activity, and the staff and administrator should both be aware of these time demands.

During the early stages of planning, the program planners or the ad hoc committee working with a specific learning activity are the most involved, usually along with the program administrator. Then, as the activity comes closer and closer to implementation, the educational staff role becomes predominant, and the planning and administrative roles are less evident, though still significant. At the point the activity actually takes place, the educational staff is actively working with the learners, and the administrator fulfills a back-up role, assuring that things go smoothly and as planned. Guideline 10 describes this flow of roles in relation to specific examples of responsibilities.

Summary

The importance of the educational staff to the success of each activity, together with the cost entailed, warrants careful selection and preparation of those serving educational roles. Although known by many titles, educational staff fall generally into three categories in relation to their function: (1) content specialists, primarily responsible for presenting topical or subject information, (2) methods specialists, who design and implement particular methods and techniques that prompt learning to take place, and (3) process specialists, who manage the process of participative learning. Some educators combine two or even all three of these specialty areas. The program administrator, often working with program planners, is responsible to find and effectively use educators in relation to the needs of the program's activities and learners. The quality of the learning activity is often assumed to rest exclusively with the educational staff. This is not fully accurate, however, for that staff is but one part of the total learning activity. Neither should their importance be underestimated. Once potential educators are located, they must be carefully considered in relation to basic criteria. Then, procedures for the final selection and preparation of the selected educator are important to bypass potential problems. Educators for staff development may be drawn from the library staff or from outside the library. Continuing education almost always draws on outside educators for learning activities.

GUIDELINE 8—INVOLVE LEARNERS

Throughout the learning program, a major focus is on the learners: how much have they learned? what have they learned? how are they applying their learnings? what happens as a result of what they learn? The degree of program or activity success is measured by how much is learned and, of that, how much is applied on-the-job. Adult education theory and practice reveal that for the greatest amount and depth of learning, learner involvement is essential. Involvement is needed, should be planned for, and must be real. Real involvement is purposeful, directly related to the learning desired. It is not "busywork" intended to help pass time or keep learners awake.

Rather, **involvement** is the active inclusion of individuals as participants in the various stages, activities, and functions of the learning program. Often, it "just happens naturally," particularly in organizations where the prevailing style is one of participation and involvement. However, where it is not so likely to occur naturally, the means to encourage and enable involvement will have to be planned in order to assure that it happens, and that it supports the intended learning efforts.

Involvement of learners may be sought in the process of developing the program or its activities. Or, it may be sought within a learning design utilizing participative techniques. It may, of course, be sought both ways. Where previously not the mode, steps to involve learners must be gradual, beginning with what is natural and comfortable to the potential learners. Approached abruptly, individuals and groups may demonstrate a caution and reserve that inhibits the free and open participation anticipated by planners, administrators, and educators. Attitudes of wariness and suspicion are only strengthened when involvement is mandated or when efforts to involve learners are made too quickly. Generally, staff development offers many more opportunities to involve the learner gradually and consistently than does continuing education.

This Guideline defines and describes learner involvement as a basic precept of the program, exploring why it is important and what results can be expected from it. Various means to effectively involve the learner are described and a planned approach to assure learner involvement is advocated. Responsibility, opportunity, and attitude are essential factors to successfully achieve learner involvement.

Rationale

Most of the rationale justifying an active and adept effort to involve the learner in the educational process is based on what is now known about how adults learn. In contrast to past practice that regarded the learner as merely a passive recipient of knowledge, present trends in adult education and continuing education led by modern theorists and educational practitioners advocate an active learner-centered focus. Thus, new approaches to helping people learn consider the whole person of the learner as the primary element in the learning process. The emphasis now is on learning rather than teaching.

Studies and writings abound in the literature on adult learning testifying to the importance of the active involvement of learners in their own learning. Knowles, Miller, Miles, Kidd, Nadler, and Mager all have written articulately and extensively about the need for learner involvement. Hedley Dimock's research also supports the value of involvement, as he found that:

> The major factor that separated the successful from the less successful programs was the degree to which the learners participated in the program. By participation I mean the extent to which they were actively

involved in making decisions about what they would do in the program and then were active in taking responsibility and carrying out activities related to their own learning. The training methods were not at all as important as a training design which encouraged the active participation of the learners.[8]

As a result of his research, Dimock's primary assumption is that "the training process is a cooperative process and all learners (participants and trainers) should participate in planning the program and be involved in the process of making other decisions which affect them." As an educator, he expresses concern that this assumption has been used to "support a non-planning approach to training where it is hoped that educational experiences will just happen."[9] And, he emphasizes, the opposite is true, participation often takes more planning rather than less.

At least two separate rationales can be given in support of learner involvement, neither excluding nor contradicting the other. One is most passionately advanced by Carl R. Rogers, whose "whole approach obviously exists in a personal context, a philosophical context, a context of values."[10] In *Freedom to Learn*, he affirms a deep philosophical belief in the potentiality and wisdom of the human being together with the tenet that individuals *do* know what is best for them and are able to use that knowledge to self-direct their learning.

The second rationale is espoused by J. Roby Kidd, who reveals, with extensive documentation, the practicality of involving the learner in the educative process. He does this on the basis of that being, simply, the most effective learning strategy possible. Kidd states "the self must be committed or involved if effective learning is to happen."[11] He uses the term "engagement" to identify the learner's active participation in what he terms the "learning transaction." Engagement carries with it the concept that the quality and characteristics of both the learner and the educator work together in the learning venture.[12]

Both the philosophical and practical rationales are articulated by most of the basic authors in the field of adult learning. Although the weight of Rogers's presentation is on the value of involvement from a philosophical point of view, he gives specific techniques of a practical nature for enabling and encouraging learner involvement. Kidd, likewise, presents a sound philosophical and theoretical discussion in addition to his pragmatic approach. Others, such as Knowles, Miller, and Nadler, include both rationales and weave them together in their own individual approaches to adult education and human resources development.

Library educators also support the learner involvement approach. Joe Washtein declares that "full learner involvement requires learner participation,"[13] which implies its active and sharing nature. Martha Jane Zachert equates involvement with interaction and relates it directly with the ways adults learn: "The social psychologists demonstrate quite convincingly that, for adults, it is interaction that produces learning: interaction in relation to learner-identified problems; interaction based on the cumulation of individual experience represented in the learning group; interaction evoked by a peer who is himself in a learning/teaching stance."[14] Vincent Guilliano theorizes that the depth and effect of learning is directly relational with the type and amount of learner communication during the learner activity.[15] In short, the involved learner is participative, interactive, and communicative.

Thus, three major reasons can be specified for involving learners. The first is very pragmatic: it helps them to learn. How effectively individuals learn and apply their learnings is an important factor in the success of each activity and influences the overall success of the program itself. Learning effectiveness depends on the ability of the activity to motivate and stimulate the learner to learn as well as on its relevant topics, capable educators, innovative method, and smooth administration. Involvement of the learner links these in the learning process and enables in-depth learning to occur.

Involvement activates and intensifies learning, increasing the kinds of things that can be learned and deepening the impact of those learnings. Knowles places strong emphasis on this:

> The quality and amount of learning is therefore clearly influenced by the quality and amount of interaction between the learner and his environment and by the educative potency of the environment. . . . In fact, the main thrust of modern adult-educational technology is in the direction of inventing techniques for involving adults in ever-deeper processes of self-diagnosis of their own needs for continued learning, in formulating their own objectives for learning, in sharing responsibility for designing and carrying out their learning activities, and in evaluating their progress toward their objectives.[16]

Thus, the involved learner is likely to get more out of the learning situation. Not only do involved learners learn more, but also they are more likely and more able to do so on their own initiative. People actively involved in the process of their own learning do, then, assume more responsibility for their own learning process.

A second reason for involvement is that it increases the possibility that the individual learner, the activity, and the learning program each will achieve its goals in a more complete sense. When actively engaged in the learning process, learners generally feel more satisfaction from acquiring learning, from interaction with others, from their ability to apply their learnings. The learning activity also benefits through involvement, for it is more likely to be in concert with learner needs. And, the learning program benefits because, through involvement, it becomes a viable and permanent function, able to continue serving new needs of learners and the library.

The single most significant result for individuals is the movement from being passive to active learners. Gary Dickenson points out the obvious: "learning is an internal process, instruction is an external activity."[17] Activated by involvement, learners become responsible for their own learning, more aware of their potential for self development, more able to direct their own growth, and make the most of a wide variety of potential learning opportunities. In contrast to passive learners, involved learners are more likely to:

- become more highly motivated to learn,
- hold clearer and more accurate expectations of the activity,
- learn on more and deeper levels,
- develop deeper and more lasting commitments to the topic, the action, or the process of learning,

- recognize themselves and others as valuable learning resources,
- acknowledge and utilize everyday work situations as opportunities for learning and for applying previous learnings,
- learn which methods are most appropriate for their own learning,
- practically relate their own learnings to personal and work worlds,
- direct their own learning experiences toward personal goals,
- understand the results of their own learning efforts and feel satisfaction,
- be prompted to engage in further learning experiences.

Many of these are very personal benefits, extending beyond the learner's participation in a particular activity in a particular program.

Benefits are also possible in direct relation to the activity itself. An activity with substantial involvement during planning and implementation is more likely to utilize knowledge of and be responsive to learner needs. The activity design thus will be based more on accurate information than on untested assumptions. Involvement brings a wider range of resources to the learning environment and these will be contributed to, drawn upon, and shared by the entire participant group. Involved learners are supportive learners, and a successful learning activity is more likely to result from collaborative efforts from the educational staff, administrator, and learners than from just the educators and administrator. The impact of the activity is more substantially felt then because of the in-depth learning of the participants.

Impact can be broadened in yet another way. Involvement of learners in planning can be an effective method to develop well-informed leadership, aware not only of their own perspectives but those of others throughout the state, region or association. An advisory or planning and evaluation committee composed of learners is an excellent way to develop their knowledge and awareness of learning needs or the nature of programming efforts.

Benefits for the program as a whole are also significant. A program with active learner involvement built in during planning and evaluating the program, as well as during implementation of activities, tends to assure its close connection with the needs of the learners and with the educational methods they prefer. A pattern of successful activities, with part of the success attributable to learner involvement, strengthens the capability and credibility of the program. Involved learners become enthusiastic supporters of the program, promoting it with their colleagues and returning to engage in further activities for their own continued learning.

The third reason for learner involvement is its long-range effects through the application of learnings. The application of learnings is more natural, thus more likely to occur because, as Albert Wight declares and documents: "The process of participative, student-centered education more closely resembles the process of living, learning, and working in the real world."[18] Involved learners are able to weave the living and learning worlds together so that each reinforces and applies to the other and so that theoretical concepts and actual practice blend. Involved learners tend to become lifelong learners, learning and growing from life experiences and living more deeply from learning experiences. Involvement of learners in the educational process is an important route to encourage individual development and to assure individual freedom.

The process of being involved prepares the learner to use the skills and knowledge learned, to apply principles that have been presented, to relate learnings to the real world and to everyday problems. These linkages, when perceived and experienced by the learner, reinforce what has been learned and increase the possibility that it will be retained. Thus, involvement not only enhances the possibility of learning from the immediate learning activity, but it also better prepares the learner to become a self-directed lifelong learner, able to learn and grow from whatever experiences, contacts, and situations come. The individual who knows *how* to learn will approach each opportunity able to learn from it whether it is an official learning activity, a work experience, or a personal discussion. Such an individual accepts a personal responsibility for his or her own learning and is thereby less dependent on structured programs and activities. This allows the program more freedom and flexibility to incorporate creative approaches to help self-motivated staff members learn. A program that includes a substantial number of involved learners has more options to exercise in developing learning designs. The involvement of learners in the development of the program and its activities also offers access to more idea resources. Some of these will open up opportunities not thought of before; others will serve to test the feasibility of those ideas from a different perception of the situation. In short, the program with opportunities for involvement is one that offers more latitude in the kinds of activities it offers and more security in the acceptance that those activities will have and the benefits resulting from them.

The long-range result that benefits the library is, of course, that staff members learn more and can apply those learnings to their work situation. Learning through involvement builds relationships between those who learn and work together. Learnings, shared collegially, are likely to be reinforced collegially on the job. A non-involving lecture on communications is not likely to increase mutual understanding among staff members. However, an involving series of communication exercises will offer the opportunity to practice and experience how to communicate and, more specifically, how to communicate with colleagues. The experience gained from such involvement in learning can spill over into other areas, using the dialogue that has been established for the program and building on the relationships that have been especially beneficial. Once individuals become comfortable with their active involvement in learning, they will often seek that kind of involvement with other functions in the library. This implication deserves considerable thought by library administrators, for in some cases it would be advantageous and, in others, it might be viewed as a distinct disadvantage.

Those disadvantages to involvement must be considered as well, however. Involving learners in planning processes extends the time and cost factors, for it requires time for meetings, costs for communication, and skilled people to plan and accomplish such involvement. Involving learners through participative educational methods may limit the educational staff that can be considered, since involvement techniques require special skills. And, learners experiencing involvement are often reluctant to later engage in non-involving learning activities, thus either restricting the learning opportunities for those people, or restricting the program to library personnel with strong non-involvement preferences. These disadvantages must be considered and weighed against the strong advantages that support involvement.

Whether based on philosophical or practical rationale, though, the reasons for involving learners are significant. Involvement increases the amount and depth of learning. It makes more likely the achievement of goals of the individual learner, the activity, and the program itself. And, it enables greater application of learnings, thus increasing the long-range effectiveness of the process. The advantages resulting from involvement tend to prompt moves towards even greater involvement. When individuals see the value of involvement directly, they are more likely to seek it and to benefit from it. When those responsible for the program see evidence of strong linkage between learning and application to the work situation, due to involvement, they tend to increase the possibilities for further involvement. Throughout the library, where the results from involvement are seen as advantageous, functional, and beneficial in cost, participative approaches will increase.

Essential Factors

To assure that learner involvement is possible and can become realized, receptive attitudes are required on the part of the sponsoring organization, advisory groups, administrator(s), educational staff, and the learners themselves. This attitude, backed with a sense of responsibility on the part of each of these elements, will provide the opportunity for involvement. Attitudes and convictions must be present to endorse, encourage, and allow learner involvement. Without these, involvement is unlikely to be risked, tested, or accomplished. Belief in the value and appropriateness of involvement usually results from one or more successful experiences with it, from direct benefits from it, and from the opportunity to work or learn with others who are convinced and skilled in accomplishing it.

The library, agency, or association sponsoring the program must be open to a thorough examination of the values and benefits of learner involvement as well as to the costs of endorsing and actualizing this precept. Viewed with only immediate results in mind, learner involvement may not seem worth the time, expense, and effort. The sponsor has the responsibility for establishing learning for library personnel as a high priority, and showing recognition of its value by supporting it as an organizational function.

Advisory groups and planning committees must encourage and provide for learner involvement precepts in the program. They are responsible for maintaining involvement as a prevalent and persistent concern and for helping others be aware of its importance. The balance and interests of the membership of this group or committee may determine their awareness and stance in regard to learner involvement.

Backed by the organization and the advisory and/or planning group(s), the administrator must be open to implementing methods to involve learners and to discovering new benefits from that. An administrator must know his or her own personal beliefs in regard to learner involvement and be able to articulate those meaningfully. As the key decision-maker of the program, the administrator is able to see potential areas for involvement in the program as a whole and for individual activities, assuring that these channels for involvement are open and accessible to learners. The coordination of activity design, materials, preparatory and follow-up efforts, and on-going planning and evaluation functions offers involvement opportunities that can prove invaluable to the program. The administrator is responsible for seeing that program policies are developed to support the precept of learner involvement and that educators are engaged on the basis of their belief in and practice of it.

The program administrator must have a tested belief in the precept of learner involvement to be strong enough to build a program based on that belief, open enough to distinguish the situations that require compromises for necessary tradeoffs, and substantial enough to provide the patience to persist when the requirements for learner involvement rest very heavily on his or her shoulders. For the program administrator will often find conflicts between what is termed the manager role and the educator role. The one requires efficiency and the other requires effectiveness and sometimes those requirements conflict. The administrator is sometimes caught between differing attitudes of other elements, which will create stresses and a need for compromise. A strong belief in involvement can result from experiencing that involvement from various points of view: as a learner, as a program administrator, as an educator.

Educators require the intention, the effort, and the ability to construct inviting educational avenues with open and real points of entry for learner involvement. They have the responsibility that is perhaps most obvious—that of designing learning activities to stimulate involvement in relation to the activity's objectives. Such a design incorporates carefully a planned structure with flexibility and ready alternatives, an adept leadership sensitive to overt and covert issues, an approach that does not close off the possibilities of achieving personal learnings for learners, or for the educators themselves.

The educational specialist (content, method, or process) is in a position to enable involvement and, often, must articulately present a convincing and encouraging position to persuade others. During planning, educators must have a commitment and a belief in the value of involvement in order to plan the design of methods, techniques, and approaches to invite the learner to become involved. During implementation, empathy, patience, and persistence are needed to sustain the time and effort to learner interaction, communication, and participation, all the while realizing that without involvement, the task would be much easier. With the ability and conviction that come through study and personal experience, the precepts of involvement will be difficult to sustain, particularly in instances of working within or for organizations that do not hold that as a value.

Learners must be willing to risk and invest themselves, counting on adequate and satisfying returns. They have the responsibility to engage, participate, interact, and communicate as fully as opportunities allow and parameters permit, to explore and expand options for involvement, and to assist others to become involved. Learners should withhold judgment about not having opportunities to become involved until the available avenues have been tried. They can discover their preferred ways of being involved and then seek to broaden that repertory with deliberate efforts to try new ways. Aware of the value involvement has, they may encourage and support those who have not yet discovered or become comfortable with it.

The responsibility of learners is very significant. They are responsible for themselves and their decisions in relation to the amount and kind of involvement they wish. Zachert suggests the role of the involved learner within the learning situation as "a dynamic role, at once purposive, aggressive, and self-fulfilling . . . [able to] . . . move the cause and the reality of continuing education for librarians forward."[19] Learners must request or create the desired opportunities for involvement where they are needed but not apparent. The willing but unsure learner can be gradually involved through careful selection, sequence, and timing of the means of involvement. And, those who wish to remain uninvolved at a given time should be free to do so until they are ready to become involved.

Involvement requires the learner to be responsible to a large extent for his or her own learning, to have some grasp of personal goals, to be willing to risk a stance of opinion or action, to be aware of his or her need for predictability and certainty. The involved learner will need to be open in seeking help to achieve personal learning objectives and, in return, be willing to help others in their learning. The involved learner must be open to personal discoveries, such as the experience of personal growth and reward from increasing career competencies, and the all-important one: learning how to learn. The learner must be aware, through keen observation or personal experience, that the return will be well worth the investment of effort, energy, and risk.

If each of these essential factors is presented positively, learner involvement is assured. When resistance to learner involvement is encountered, strategies appropriate to the situation and circumstances will need to be devised. For example, in a situation with hesitant learners or a reluctant administrator, the practice of learner involvement might be introduced gradually for demonstration or testing purposes; as the results become accepted, it can be increased accordingly. Action taken at those points should seek the involvement of learners. Implementation is the most feasible point to initiate these efforts, for that is where the incentive, need, availability, and action are.

Cautions and hesitancy may be exercised by learners, educators, administrators, advisory and planning groups, or by the sponsoring organization. Such resistance may forstall or delay involvement. Also, reservations from a combination of these essential groups actually may outweigh the influences at work to encourage learner involvement. In such an instance, attempts at involvement forwarded by one of the essential groups acting alone will either be unlikely or will be unsuccessful. Careful ground work and persistent commitment by those convinced of the value of involvement can sometimes turn the tide, though.

The benefits and results possible from learner involvement serve to strengthen the organization, the program, and the learner. This assumption, however, may not be commonly shared in a particular situation. Some results are direct and some are subtle; some are immediate and some are long-range. Involvement can improve the relevance, the quality, and the results of each learning activity as well as increase the ability of the learner to learn from it. What actually occurs, of course, depends on a number of dynamic factors in the situation, including the commitment of the organization, the capability of the program, and the willingness of the learner.

Means for Learner Involvement

When the essentials discussed above exist, means will be found to involve learners. Anticipating involvement, then, program planners, educators, and the program administrator can plan ways to assure it. Opportunities for involvement exist throughout the program and for most learning activities. Involvement is possible during the actual learning activities, in preparation for them, and in follow-up. It can occur through information or through action, whatever seems appropriate to the particular situation.

Who is involved and how naturally will vary with the situation. Three means of involvement generally exist: 1) information in written or visual form, 2) personal contact, and 3) active participation in a learning task. The first of these offers less impact and less effort than the other two. It is also likely to be seen as less real than the more in-depth involvement offered, for example, by the third. Although specific possibilities for involvement can be described, creative and valuable ideas will often come from the learners themselves, based on their own interests and needs as well as their perception of those of others. In cases where learner involvement is a relatively new practice, however, many of the ideas may have to come initially from the program administrator, the planners, or educators.

When learners plan for their own involvement, three conditions are important to make that involvement relevant and real. They, the learners, must be assisted as well as encouraged to examine the ways in which their active participation will benefit them. They must be informed of the presently existing opportunities for involvement. And, they must be invited to create additional opportunities, bound only by their interests and needs and by the feasibility offered by the activity. Of course, any planning procedure to accomplish involvement must be supported by the conviction that it is a valuable, necessary component of the learning process and, thus, is worth the effort to achieve it.

Information and action both are required if involvement is to occur; information to provide expectations and action to fulfill those expectations are vital. For example, information prior to an activity can indicate what learners might expect, not only in relation to the objectives and nature of the activity, but also as to the expectations of and opportunities for learner involvement. Preliminary information can explicitly indicate that the learners will be deeply involved and responsible for their own learning. Specific mention can be made of the means of involvement prior to the activity and of the instructional methods to be used during the activity. This information, if clearly understood and honestly meant, will allow learners to know in advance that their involvement is considered important and will be expected. Prior awareness that involvement will be expected is important, since the element of surprise (when learners discover this only after they are in such a situation) is inappropriate and often counterproductive.

Notification of anticipated involvement, however, does not automatically mean that involvement is understood and agreed to. Open dialogue, discussion, and even demonstration to begin the activity help clarify that the promised involvement is indeed real and will indicate just what it entails. Consistent and direct communication from the educator(s) can actively encourage and reward learner participation. If expectations have been carefully built, the understanding of those expectations has been mutually achieved, and their fulfillment has been sincere and consistent, then continued involvement of learners is assured.

The best specific means to provide information and to actualize learner involvement depend a great deal on such factors as time available, physical distance between learners and educators, any previous experience of learners with involvement methods and results, and the potential offered by the topic and the educational approach. With each activity, many points of involvement can be planned and offered as options. This permits a choice and helps convince and encourage the less experienced and the less sure. The following means can be considered for application and use when appropriate and feasible. Each of them relies heavily on communications to build the concept of involvement and to stimulate and convince learners to become involved. Learner involvement runs as a theme throughout this book. Guideline 10 and the Models in the Appendix reveal specifics of how this might be accomplished, in addition to the following discussion.

Means of involvement that can be used prior to an activity:

- Criteria for selection can include those individuals interested and willing to become involved or those who have had previous satisfactory experiences of being involved.

- A needs assessment form or interview can request learner response to questions of preferred learning style and previous experiences with involvement. This procedure initiates the learner's active participation as well as provides useful information on which to plan. This can build credibility for the program as well as prompt learner interest and motivation.

- Written materials or personal contacts can explain the educational methods and the expectation of involvement, as well as the details of the living and learning logistics. Personal contact allows the potential learner the chance to ask questions and discuss concerns. Then, if these are settled before the activity, that individual will be more free to become involved during the activity.

- Materials or contacts can invite contributed comments, suggestions, and questions from learners, thereby offering an opportunity for early interaction during the activity.

- Involving some of the potential learners in planning or evaluating the activity will produce helpful ideas for involvement and is, itself, an excellent means, for these people can communicate accurately and meaningfully to their colleagues about the importance of involvement.

- An assessment of knowledge and/or skills can give the learner guidance in planning for the activity and his or her own learning emphasis. Self-assessments are increasingly available to help learners identify their prime needs before attending a learning activity. Whether done for oneself or for the planners or educators of the activity, such assessments elicit learner involvement.

Much of the success of each of these means for involvement depends on the response of the learner and, then, that of the administrator or the educator(s) to the learner's response. An absence of response will dampen further efforts. This, in turn, will not allow expectations formed earlier to be met, and the credibility of the program may be jeapordized.

Means of involvement that can be used during an activity:

- The opening moments of the activity are crucial for the manner in which the invitation to become actively involved is articulated or conveyed. Learner involvement can be communicated in many ways. Verbal description by the staff of the importance of involvement and the benefits that can be expected from it can relate involvement to the activity objectives. Interactive exercises can encourage learners to become acquainted with one another and to experience learning through involvement. An informal style of physical setting, comfort, and social climate will ease involvement. Supportiveness to learners from the staff, if sustained throughout and if genuine, will be perceived as encouragement to become involved.

- Skillful staff design and the use of participative educational techniques will demonstrate the value of involvement in learning. These techniques should not be used to mandate involvement but rather to invite and motivate learners to become involved. The staff's ability to reinforce the importance of each learner as an individual and as a resource is essential in order to sustain involvement and to draw the relationship of that involvement to learning.

- Involvement in the implementation of the design offers several opportunities to engage the learners in their own learning process. This might be as minor as helping to rearrange the meeting room or as major as helping to make a group decision to modify the design. Throughout this effort, the educator(s) and the program administrator must be sensitive to the comfort of the learners, adjusting means and/or style to provide relative ease without sacrificing the potential for growth.

- The feelings of risk felt by individuals being asked to involve themselves can present the staff with the opportunity to explain that the return on the investment is usually well worth that risk. This will offer sustained supportiveness and encouragement for those who are in transitional states, moving from passive to active learner roles.

- Periods of "free time" during the activity can foster social contacts, which add to the ease of learners and can increase their level of trust to the point where they become more open to shared participation.

- The group of learners can itself develop what Kidd defines as the "characteristics that need to be present in the group if effective learning is to take place [format changed somewhat]:

    —A realization by the members of the group that genuine growth stems from the creative power within the individual, and that learning, finally, is an individual matter.

—The acceptance as a group standard that each member has the right to be different and to disagree.

—Establishment of a group atmosphere that is free from narrow judgments on the part of the teacher or group members."[20]

These characteristics, plus the active intervention of the staff when needed can assure equitable participation and shared opportunities for involvement.

● The educational staff can very consciously initiate methods of involvement throughout the activity. Specific techniques include using small discussion groups, asking that each learner write his or her own thoughts prior to group discussion, turning questions addressed to staff back to the group for answers, sequencing elements of the design to move from less to more involvement, designing flexible alternatives to respond to the tolerance level of the group.[21] (Ten guidelines for involvement are suggested by Burke in *Conference Planning*.)

The degree to which involvement is possible during an activity will depend on such factors as: the objectives; the time span for the activity; the kind of group and their acceptance, ease, and skill with involvement techniques and methods; the methods selected for learning; and the educational staff's attitudes and skills.

Means of involvement that can be used following an activity:

● Evaluation can offer several opportunities for involvement, which is important to the learner, the staff, and the administrator. Forms or an evaluator can elicit ideas, comments, and suggestions from learners. A "feedback team" of selected learners from the group can be responsible for collecting and channeling learner opinions anonymously to the staff for design modifications. Feedback sessions can be held periodically to open up group discussion on any issues that need attention and possible remedy. On-going evaluation will be immediately and directly useful to the staff in relation to their responsibilities for the educational implications of the activity. Evaluation can also reinforce the learnings acquired during the activity.

● Follow-up activities after the group's departure from the learning site can also be a means for involvement. Additional correspondence, materials, and personal contacts can reinforce the learnings through involving the learner as an individual. Opportunities to reconvene on an informal and social basis can refresh the group spirit, offer continued assistance for the application of learnings to the work situation, and supply the opportunities to exchange information about personal accomplishments in relation to the acquired learnings. Often, learners are more motivated to read or use materials after the learning activity than before it.

Useful involvement after the learning activity increases and reinforces its effect. It continues the impact and helps the learner apply the results of the activity to everyday working and living situations.

In addition to each of these relatively specific suggestions for learner involvement, a few or, in some cases, all learners might also be involved in various administrative facets of the activity or program. This might entail planning or evaluation tasks or assistance of some kind during the activity. Sometimes this involvement could be through serving on an ad hoc group responsible for one or more activities. Staff development programs offer more possibilities for this kind of involvement than do continuing education programs. However, the range of possibilities is wide, depending on the creativity of the planners, the ability and inclination of the educators, and the willingness of the learners.

Self-Assessment

The tradition of adult learning has relied heavily on individual initiative and ability to find and select learning opportunities, to engage in and learn from those opportunities, and to apply the learnings to life and work. The right and privilege of individual learners to direct their own efforts has been one of the strengths and one of the weaknesses of the present pattern of adult education. This pattern has resulted in great diversification and individualization, lack of basic requirements, and inadequate dissemination of information about available opportunities.

The enthusiastic moves towards a nationwide continuing library education possibility, on one hand, offer the advantage of widely available information about assured programs and activities that meet prescribed standards of quality and accountability—a desirable outcome and a move toward greater consistency. It is also a move away from considering as important the ability of individuals to select the learning opportunities that they individually feel to be most important and relevant to their needs. Now, legislative and professional trends are appearing that seek to require continuing education in various professions, such as the health services, engineering, architecture, and librarianship. The major advantages of mandatory continuing education include quality control and accountability. Major motivators include accumulating credits, meeting certification requirements, and avoiding penalties. Agencies and associations are likely to serve increasingly essential roles in this growing institutionalization of continuing library education.

Within this broad view, involvement may provide learners at least one avenue for continued responsibility and direction. The individual use of self-assessment techniques, while possibly an answer to demands for mandatory continuing education, also opens new opportunities for direct, personal involvement in any learning activity. Essentially, basic forms can be supplied by the program to each learner at each activity within that program, or even through libraries to library personnel who desire to utilize opportunities outside of the program. The basic form, perhaps a very simple one as illustrated in Figure 12 [opposite], could be furnished.

For learners, particularly for "self-starters," the process of filling out such a form is a guidance function and a motivational device. Through it, each learner explores the meaning of his or her immediate learning experience and the application of his or her learnings on the job. Each learner is also urged to look ahead, to identify new learning needs, and to explore new-found interests. Thus, this personal assessment can assist the individual in seeking and selecting new learning opportunities as well as making the most of the present one. The individual may choose not only to use it for personal guidance, but also may place a copy in his or her personnel file for use in performance appraisals or include it as documentation in a resumé or vita. Although these forms are not widely used presently, greater application of them may be encouraged, based on the rationale of placing major initiative and responsibility on the individual.

Figure 12

Sample Self-Assessment Form

```
                              Name _____

CONTINUING EDUCATION ACTIVITY:   (Include title,
   date, place)

OBJECTIVES/FOCUS/TOPIC OF EVENT:

MAJOR TOPICAL RESOURCES IDENTIFIED:

MAJOR PERSONAL LEARNINGS:

DOCUMENTATION (i.e. EVIDENCE) OF LEARNINGS:


HOW LEARNINGS WILL BE APPLIED TO JOB RESPONSIBILITIES:

      Short-range

      Long-range


NEW LEARNING NEEDS IDENTIFIED:

      Immediate

      Future
```

Summary

Each learning activity can be seen as a room with many doors, each door being a single method of involvement. The room has been built by the program planners and/or the educational staff together with the administrator. These individuals, from the framework of their beliefs and ability, have locked some doors, closed but unlocked others, and left some ajar. The learners are in the building but not necessarily in the room. Those who do not want to be involved or do not know how to do so stand outside the open doors; those who find it difficult to initiate their involvement approach only the open doors; and those who are eager for involvement demand that the closed but unlocked doors be opened and challenge those doors that are locked. Both staff and learners are responsible for the construction and the use of the doors (i.e., means) of involvement.

Involvement of learners is stressed throughout this book because of the author's having been repeatedly in each of these roles and having repeatedly seen the value of involvement in its effect on learners and on learning activities. These personal experiences support and endorse the assertions of Kidd, Mager, Knowles, and Rogers about how adults learn. Zachert, however, brings this all home to the library world: "The ultimate success or failure of the efforts for continuing education may well rest not on how perceptively the planners and teachers understand the great perplexing problems of librarianship, but on their perception of how adults learn."[22]

The importance of learner involvement as Zachert emphasizes so rightly, is rooted in what is known about how adults learn. Current theory and technology of adult education emphasize the precept of learner involvement, and both philosophic and practical rationales support the many specific means that can be used to involve learners. From these rationales come three major reasons for involvement: (1) It helps people learn. Both the quality and amount of learning are improved, sparked by the learner's own initiative, and guided by the learner's own directions. (2) It enables the learner, the activity, and the program each to accomplish its aim. The learner benefits by moving from a passive to an active stance. The activity benefits from richer resources, learner support, better information. The program benefits from achieving what it was designed to do. (3) It has long-range effects through the application of learnings. The learner is prepared to apply what is learned and to learn from living and working situations.

Attitudes, responsibility, and opportunities are essential factors to enable learner involvement. Each key group must be willing and able to assume its responsibility for learner involvement: the sponsoring organization, advisory groups and planning committees, the program administrator, the educators, and the learners. Each stands to benefit from learner involvement even though the effort entailed to assure that may prove difficult. The means to achieve learner involvement are many and varied, both through being involved in the learning process itself, or in the process of producing learning activities. Learners must often be helped to understand the benefits from involvement, be informed of the opportunities that exist, and be invited to use those opportunities.

Specific means to involve learners depend on each situation. Generally, some means are relevant to use prior to an activity, while others can be employed either during or after the activity. Each of these has its own advantages and disadvantages, but an active effort to involve learners will utilize more than a single avenue. Both information and action are necessary to make involvement real and possible.

GUIDELINE 9—PROVIDE FACILITIES, EQUIPMENT, AND MATERIALS

Appropriate facilities, equipment, and materials support the learning process and can enhance learning significantly. If creatively selected, carefully coordinated, and skillfully used, these ingredients flavor and enrich the learning experience. Yet, no matter how up-to-date or glamorous they may be, these resources are not adequate substitutes for a good learning design that includes substantial content and appropriate methods. True, the design may be strengthened with these ingredients, but design consideration should rule their use rather than they dictate the design.

Anticipated during initial planning, the facilities, equipment, and materials for the various learning activities are actually chosen, assembled, and used by the administrative and educational staff during implementation. Physical facilities provide not only the housing of the learning activity, but also furnish environment for the learners assembled there. Equipment and materials supplement the various educational methods and techniques, making learnings concrete and thus more easily applied to real-life situations. Although such aids assist in achieving what might not otherwise be possible, learning activities can also be very effective without the use of expensive audio-visual equipment, numerous handout materials, and elaborate physical facilities.

When these ingredients are skillfully blended and carefully managed, their existence is assumed rather than observed, even by those directly affected. If, however, such adequate resources are lacking, faulty, or mismanaged, that fact becomes very visible and can adversely affect the value of the learning activity. This Guideline expands on the previously general discussion of resources in relation to planning (Guideline 4). Here, these resources, important to the complete and effective conduct of learning activities, are considered in greater depth and detail as steps closer to actual implementation are taken. Each category is described separately with its definition, purpose, and use. Criteria for guidance in selection and application of each are offered, as are checklists that can be adapted for planning and preparation of these resources in relation to specific learning activities. General sources of information are included to assist those people responsible for planning and producing learning activities. Guideline 10 then integrates these categories of resources with each other and with the other elements brought together in the implementation of learning activities.

General Description

These three ingredients: physical facilities, equipment, and materials, are often perceived as necessary in order for "things to go well," but often they are not thought to be as significant to learning as they indeed are. Although they need not be elaborate to be effective, they are not simply administrative necessities (and headaches). Rather, they are important adjuncts to the learning process and can be used:

●   to support, sustain, and reinforce learning,

●   to interest, stimulate, and motivate learners,

●   to clarify ideas, deepen understanding, and integrate concepts.

Wise use of these resources is governed by the design of the learning activity and must be relevant to its learning objectives, rather than dependent on current fads or glamorous gimmicks.

"Arrangements" is a commonly used term to describe the use of these resources, usually including the planning, logistics and follow-through essential for their effectiveness. Facilities include the physical space and its manipulation to provide the learning and, sometimes, living environment. Equipment and materials furnish that environment, often bringing the topic from the abstract to the concrete through the use of instructional aids. As with educational methods and staff, the best of what is available must be selected, with other alternatives held in reserve for use if needed. Many such resources can be used before or after as well as during a specific learning activity. Because of their possible complexity and detail, these "arrangements" usually require coordination through a single person.

The effort and expense involved in providing facilities, equipment, and materials are only justifiable if those resources are indeed appropriate for the situation. Thus, as alternatives are considered for selection, each may be tested for its appropriateness by asking:

●   Is it available?

●   Is it essential to the activity's design?

●   Is it relevant to the purpose(s) for which it is being considered?

●   Is it purposive to the learner's needs?

●   Is it suitable to the educator's skills?

These general questions provide an initial screening but then need to be followed with more detailed and specific criteria to fit with each category of resources.

Two important kinds of distinctions are also generally useful for program planners and implementors. One is the distinction between staff development programs and continuing education programs. For staff development, the facilities may be a meeting room in the library or at the work site itself. These facilities may restrict the use of instructional equipment, or, on the contrary, may make it more feasible than if held at another site. Continuing education activities, on the other hand, are characteristically held away from the work site, often in an environment assembled specifically for the learning activity. This, also, will affect the use of equipment. The same materials are usually equally suitable for both staff development and continuing education activities.

A second distinction is that between those resources used by the producers of learning activities and those used directly by the learners themselves (as discussed in Guideline 4). For example, physical facilities will be required for the group of learners as they learn from the educators. Facilities may also be required, however, for the program administrator and the educators to meet for planning purposes, or for assembling equipment. Materials may be instructions for the educator(s) or they might be handouts describing an intricate concept for learners. This second distinction will be made in relation to each of the three categories of resources covered in this Guideline, whereas the distinction made in Guideline 4, on the other hand, relies on each learner selecting what is pertinent for his or her own situation.

Facilities

Facilities are the physical quarters that accommodate a particular learning activity or event together with its equipment. Broadly used, the term can also include those facilities required for the learning program's administrative function. Guidelines 4 and 6 discuss these needs, while this Guideline is more concerned with those physical facilities required for the program's learning activities.

The setting for each learning activity should enable and encourage the learning process rather than prevent or inhibit it. Properly planned and selected facilities provide active learning assistance; mediocre facilities allow learning to happen; poor facilities impede learning. A very simple example can illustrate this: in a hot climate, the room where the activity is held needs good air-conditioning. This improves the ability of the learner to concentrate on learning. Merely adequate air-conditioning does little to help or hinder. A lack of air-conditioning or faulty machinery will distract learners, directing their attention to their comfort rather than what is to be learned. In most cases, whether the facilities are good or adequate, is not a prime influence. However, if they are poor or difficult, they will exert a negative influence that may counter-act an otherwise effective design.

Final selection of a particular site for a learning activity follows both a careful study of the advantages and disadvantages of various alternatives and a review of the facility with the needs of learners and educational staff in mind. Once selected, the site will probably affect the design of the activity to some extent, just as the activity's design may call for some adjustment of the site. When the design and the site are both sufficiently flexible and adaptive, the most satisfactory use can be made of the site. Sometimes, of course, no choice is possible. Often, for example, all staff development activities are held within the library. Even so, the selection of just *where* in the library an activity will be conducted may be aided by the application of the criteria for facilities.

Usually, compromises are necessary. The most desirable date or room may not be available. Insufficient electrical outlets may prevent the choice of an audio-visual "hands on" workshop. Living accommodations may be too primitive for a group of learners on a residential retreat weekend. The give and take between what is needed, what is feasible, and what is available often takes some time to resolve. In the meantime, the need to reserve a facility in order to publicize the activity may apply pressure to those responsible for a decision.

The decision, when made, should enable the design and the facility to produce together an effective, flexible, and adaptive learning environment. Several criteria are useful in making this decision. The purpose of the activity, its learning methods, and the number of learners determine the nature and over-all qualifications of the facilities. Of course, the facility must meet the needs of both the learner and the educational staff. The convenience and ease of accessibility of the learner should be considered, and the cost should be fair and reasonable, within the activity's budget. Sometimes, for example, conditions are included in the use of the facility, such as: "all group meals must be eaten in the hotel in exchange for free use of the meeting room." To be accepted, such stipulations should not exceed the value of the benefits they offer.

Site personnel should be knowledgeable and willing, within reason, to accommodate the needs of the group both before and during the activity. The learning space itself should be able to be occupied prior to the actual activity in order to allow time to set up and test the room arrangement or the equipment. For equipment not supplied by the site, nearby sources should be available. And, finally, the site should not have predictably negative connotations for learners because of past associations. In most cases, unique needs and requirements will undoubtedly mean additional criteria. Certainly, to evaluate a site in relation to these criteria, the facilities must be examined in person by the administrator and/or the educational staff prior to a final decision and commitment.

Figure 13 offers a checklist of criteria in a format useful for a program administrator to view and compare physical facilities to be held at a hotel or conference center.

Even more specific criteria can guide the selection of a room where a learning activity is to be held. In addition to the selection of a meeting room, these criteria may indicate its arrangement and layout.

- Size and shape of the room: is the room too large and distracting for its intended use? Is it too small for comfort? Do structural supports or its shape curtail the number of alternative training methods that can be used? Are the exits well situated and . marked?

- Atmosphere: What is the general feeling conveyed by the room? What is the initial impression it gives? Is that feeling in keeping with the intended tone of the activity? Are outside distractions, such as noise, light, traffic, and movement likely to be a problem?

- Flexibility: Are the furnishings and equipment alternatives functional, multipurpose, and in working order, able to adapt to changing learning formats relatively quickly and easily? How quickly and easily can shifts from one format to another be made?

- Lighting: Is the room able to be made light enough to enable reading and writing and dark enough to permit showing films or slides? Does glare from outside windows interfere with vision? Are electrical outlets numerous enough and easily accessible? Is video or audio recording possible?

Figure 13

Learning Activity Facilities Checklist—Meeting Site

Suitable	Not Suitable	Criteria	Comments—Qualifications—Special Instructions—Reminders
		1. Accessibility (public transportation? easy to find?)	1.
		2. Available (dates available? dates not available?)	2.
		3. Meeting rooms (see other sheet)	3.
		4. Living accommodations (if applicable)	4.
		appearance, cleanliness	
		lighting	
		desk/chair for study	
		reservation policy (minimum number? guarantee?)	
		late check out?	
		desk service—phone, messages	
		proximity to meeting room(s)	
		number of singles ___ number of doubles ___	
		price range:	
		food service—quality, schedule, cost	
		bar service	
		entertainment/recreation	
		5. Parking (free or fee? location?)	5.
		6. Maps/brochures	6.
		7. Special charges for special services (breaks? cleaning? damage deposit?)	7.
		8. Special accommodations for staff needs: meetings, storage, billing arrangements.	8.
		9. Suitable to meet learner expectations?	9.
		10. Is educational staff approval needed?	10.
		11. Special conditions?	11.

Who to contact for emergency: _____
Meeting/Conference manager: _____ ; Location of office: _____ ; Hours: _____ ; Phone: _____

- Acoustics: How well does sound flow within the room? Will a sound system be needed? Can bothersome outside noises be curtailed? Will folding room dividers prevent noise from adjacent spaces?

- Ventilation: Is temperature controllable? Are drafts or stagnant air likely to be a problem? Can needs of smokers and non-smokers be met?

- Storage and Security: Can materials and equipment be stored securely for brief times when the room is not in use?

- Convenience: Is the room accessible with ease to those expected to attend? Is the time convenient?

- Cost: Is the expense to be incurred fair and reasonable? Is it within the budget?

Since most facilities will not meet all requirements, selection should be based on the number of important criteria that are met for the intended activity. Figure 14 offers a checklist to use in evaluating the merits of various alternative meeting rooms considered for activities.

Once the selection of room(s) is set, the arrangement of furniture and equipment will be determined by the educational methods that will be used. Because decisions in relation to room arrangements are called for in relation to nearly every learning activity, and since many of those activities will have the educator(s) and a group of learners together in a single room, the following discussion may be helpful. [Other sources will assist those who wish to investigate this further: Burke's *Conference Planning* (1970), Davis's *Planning, Conducting, Evaluating Workshops* (1974), Knowles's *Modern Practice of Adult Education* (1970), This's *The Small Meeting Planner* (1972), and Warncke's *Planning Library Workshops and Institutes* (1976).]

For the presentation methods described in Guideline 5, rows of chairs (or tables and chairs) all facing the same way are usual. For interactive methods, chairs (or tables and chairs) should be facing each other either in a circle or semi-circle. For very informal sessions, sitting on the floor allows quick adaptation and change but should be used only if comfortable for all learners. Rooms with fixed seating arrangements fastened to the floor should be avoided. Tables or chairs with arm desks are necessary when extensive writing is required. Figure 15 (p. 148) illustrates basic seating patterns that can be used.

In general, a room 20 feet by 30 feet will be adequate for 50 to 60 people to observe or listen to a film or a speaker. The same size room will allow 20 to 30 people to participate in small group discussions without excessive noise interference, 30 to 35 people to be seated in a semi-circle arrangements with arm desk chairs, or 20 to 30 people to be seated in chairs at tables facing the front of the room. This can be used as a rough guideline in planning for different sized rooms. Additional room will be required for audiovisual equipment or for tables that will house exhibits, materials, or a registration process.

The room arrangement used for the opening period of the activity should accommodate the needs of the session satisfactorily; yet it should conform enough in appearance to existing norms and expectations to quiet any possible concerns

Figure 14

Offsite Learning Activity Facilities Checklist—Meeting Room(s)

Present or Available	Not Present or Available	Criteria	Comments—Qualifications— Special Instructions—Reminders
		1. Pleasant and comfortable	1.
		2. Suitable size and shape for group anticipated	2.
		3. Flexible arrangement and moveable furniture	3.
		4. Heating/cooling and ventilation (controls?)	4.
		5. Lighting, windows can be darkened	5.
		6. Adequate and convenient exits and entrances	6.
		7. Walls appropriate for newsprint/tape or exhibits	7.
		8. Electric outlets, sound control (where?)	8.
		9. Provision for screen projection	9.
		10. Black/white board (chalk, markers, erasers furnished?)	10.
		11. Stage or raised platform	11.
		12. Acoustics	12.
		13. Ceiling height	13.
		14. Noise level and traffic patterns	14.
		15. Storage and security	15.
		16. Cost	16.
		17. Additional rooms	17.

Contact persons: _____ ; Room key: _____ ; Heat, light, sound: _____
Room set up: _____

Figure 15

Basic Patterns for Seating Arrangements for Various Types of Activities

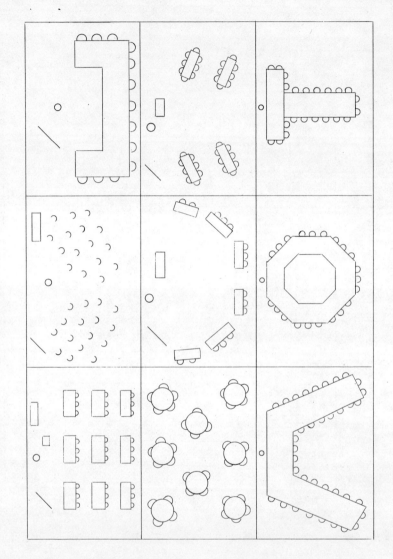

on the part of learners, particularly those entering a training situation for the first time. Subsequent shifts of room arrangement will depend on the methods to be used and the kind of verbal or physical activity those methods require. When the same room is used repeatedly for the same learners, rearrangements refresh perspectives and can change the mood and tempo. Rearrangements can also help learners break out of established, habitual seating patterns and to get to know new colleagues. Changes in room arrangement may need to be explained to the group, particularly if they are asked to assist in rearranging it.

The initial room arrangement should be clearly and carefully described to those responsible for setting up the room. A sketch is often the most effective way of assuring mutual understanding. Directions should describe the seating pattern for learners, the placement of equipment or exhibits that will be used, and the arrangement at the front of the room. Ordinarily it is advisable to make sure that no entrance to the room is on the same wall as the designated front of the room where the speaker, film or demonstration is situated.

Information about some basic logistics may need to be requested: When will the room be available and ready? Who will have a key? When must the room be vacated? What are the ground rules regarding smoking, eating, drinking? How can the room be secured during meal breaks? Where and how are lights, sound, and air controlled? Where are additional chairs if they should be needed? Who should be contacted in an emergency?

Just prior to the activity, the room should be checked thoroughly to verify that it has been arranged as requested. Last-minute details include setting up and checking out the equipment that will be used to assure it is in working order. The program administrator or educator responsible for the session are the logical individuals to double check all arrangements and equipment. The educator more often knows what is necessary to do the activity, but the program administrator should be present in case alternative arrangements are needed.

During and following the session, one person should be given responsibility to assure that the room is neat and organized, that changes in room arrangement are accomplished, and that the room is left as requested at the end of the session. Usually these tasks fall to the program administrator, who should be available throughout the session to attend to the comfort of the learners, any needs of the educator, and any changes in plans. Since most staff development activities will take place inside the library, some of these functions will be assumed by regular personnel. However, when an activity is planned outside the library, these concerns will be more essential to address.

Facilities arrangements involve a great deal of detail work, checking and cross-checking, frequent updating, and communications. After a number of activities, these various steps become second nature and no longer seem a tangled skein of details. Equipment and materials are equally detailed, requiring coordinative ability on the part of the program administrator.

Equipment

As used here, **equipment** refers to the educational media and devices used to support or enrich the activity's content or methods, that is, bringing special visual, audio, or tactile capabilities into the learning situation. Videotape cameras and monitors, sound systems for public address, projectors, and easels—all are considered equipment as are computers used for computer-assisted learning and satellites used for beaming special training programs. A growing and substantial trend indicates that the use of special educational media will increase in the future and that new varieties and applications will probably evolve.

A wide and tempting array of commercial technology is available, and an increasing amount of information is available about the applications of that technology. Currently, strong trends in libraries and in education are toward the use of audio-visual equipment. All these factors may influence the increasing use of these techniques, becoming in some cases almost a mandate. Availability plus salesmanship are strongly persuasive elements and have convinced many people of the value of these techniques. These converts, in turn, have developed many effective approaches to learning activities through extensive and skilled use of audio-visual equipment. Countering the enthusiasm of advocates is the resistance of some learners as well as some educators and program administrators to adjust to more extensive use of techniques that require equipment, or "hardware," as it is called. However, resistance to such equipment is being overcome by the enthusiasm and skill of those who have come to know and use it. Almost every group of learners now includes media advocates, and educational staff teams often include special resource people to bring that dimension to an activity.

Edgar Dale offers the classic tool for understanding the interrelationship among various types of materials. His "cone of experience" is a useful schema that displays the full range of learning experiences, such as field trips, simulations, and films in relation to the various types of materials they require, such as scripts, observation guides, manuals, and informational handouts. The cone presents a scale on the basis of the kind of sensory experience it produces—from the concrete to the abstract. For example, at the bottom of the cone, the learner is physically active, less so as the cone progresses upwards. At the upper levels, the learner makes mental associations of arbitrary symbols and visual images. Understanding this interrelationship is helpful to anticipate the kind of results that can be expected from using those different experiences in learning activities. Thus, the cone can be helpful in selecting the type of experiences and materials suitable for use in a particular situation.[23]

Yet media selection and use is still, for the novice, a difficult and frustrating experience, one that can become costly and can adversely affect learners through the use of inappropriately selected or ineptly handled equipment. Preplanning is essential when special equipment is to be used. Obtaining it is likely to take time and expertise. Use of some kinds of equipment will narrow the alternative sites that can be considered, since some sites may not provide the conditions necessary for proper operation of equipment.

Criteria that can help those responsible for the appropriate selection and use of special equipment include the following:

- The type of equipment selected for use should be essential to the educational methods in the learning design, assisting retention or application of learnings.

- The effort and funds required for equipment should be commensurate with its anticipated benefits to the learning experience.

- The selection of equipment should not close off the possibility of suitable and available alternative means that might meet the learning needs within the constraints of funding, space, or logistics.

- The equipment should be closely related to assumed or known learner needs and, if possible, to learner interest, acceptability, and level of understanding.

- The equipment should be up-to-date, operational, and handled by skilled personnel, technically adequate to accomplish the needed task(s).

- The room(s) selected for the learning activity should be able to accommodate the use of the desired equipment, or provisions should be made nearby for special use of equipped facilities for the sessions during which they are needed.

- Educational staff working with the equipment should be familiar with it as an educational tool and able to make the most of its use.

The most important of these criteria is the necessary correlation between the educational methods and the equipment. If this criterion is not met affirmatively, no further questions needs to be asked. Figure 16 (p. 152) is a chart of media equipment to consider. Each type is described in terms of advantages and disadvantages of their use. This overview, though brief, can open up alternatives in relation to the use of equipment in learning situations.

Investment in purchased equipment raises further considerations. Generally, equipment should be considered for purchase if consistent and long-term use of it is assured. Initial cost is not the only expense. Storage, maintenance, and handling are continued expenses. Some types of equipment also require licensed operators for each use, an important factor to consider before purchase. The ease and availability of sales, service, and software (programs to use with the equipment) are important factors as well. Of course, equipment requiring unique adaptations or permanent modifications for special use will have to be purchased. Special equipment for single-time or infrequent use might be rented or borrowed, rather than purchased. Often such equipment can be located and borrowed through schools, colleges, or businesses.

If purchase is to be considered, however, the following questions are useful to guide that purchase:

- What is the total cost of the original purchase, overhead, and hidden expenses over the period of its use?

- How available is equipment servicing?

- How soon is the equipment likely to wear out? become obsolete?

- Is sufficient software available to make the maximum use of this equipment?

Figure 16

Chart of Media Equipment with Advantages and Disadvantages of Different Types

EQUIPMENT	ADVANTAGES	DISADVANTAGES
blackboard/whiteboard (chalk/marker)	• good for small group visibility • can be modified and developed in full view of learners	• not suitable for large group visibility • writer must turn back to group • to be retained for later use, information must be transcribed
educational television	• immediacy, combines visual and aural impact • can reach large or small groups • does not require physical presence of resource people or particular sites	• passive rather than interactive unless especially planned • expensive to produce • utilizing equipment takes skill
film projector (8 or 16 mm film)	• simulated experience can have cognitive and affective impact • provides a common, shared experience	• requires skills to operate • equipment expensive and bulky • room must be darkened
flipchart (easel/pad/marker)	• good for small group work • sheets can be torn off, mounted on wall, or transcribed for retention	• writer has back to group • to be easily handled, sheets must be transcribed
opaque projector	• writer faces audience • visible for large or small groups • simple to operate • markings on sheets can be easily modified	• commercially prepared materials might be costly • unless being projected, materials are not visible to group • machine is bulky

(Figure 16 continued on page 153)

Figure 16 (cont'd)

EQUIPMENT	ADVANTAGES	DISADVANTAGES
overhead projector (pens/screen/ transparencies)	• prepared transparencies can be quickly and easily reproduced • otherwise, same as opaque except that material is transparent instead of opaque	• commercially prepared transparencies are costly • unless being projected, transparencies are not visible to group • machine is bulky
record player (records)	• simple to operate • appeals to auditory sense • moderate cost, durable	• learners may not have listening skills • little training material is on commercial records • few known and used teaching techniques
slide-tape/filmstrip-tape (slides, strip, cassettes)	• relative low cost and durable • simple to operate • illustrates concepts, presents visual data or simulated situation	• not as effective as film • takes time to select or prepare suitable material • hard to coordinate slides or film and tape effectively
tape recorder/player (cassettes and reels)	• can be used alone or with a group • simple and portable • prevents presented material from being lost	• possibility of poor quality sound • not usually as effective as visual • inadvertent erasure possible • must be transcribed or edited
videotape recorder/player (tape)	• same as film projector	• same as film projector • audience attention span shorter than for film

Often, needs for staff development equipment will tie in with other organizational needs, indicating that training needs can be met with minimal extra expense. For example, light colored walls can substitute for a screen. A flip chart can also be used for staff meetings and planning sessions, and it can display exhibits or displays between training sessions. Film or overhead projectors might be shared with another department with similar needs, or they might be used for library programming efforts. Equipment with an assured consistent use would be a good investment, whereas infrequent use might not warrant the expense.

Specific information on equipment, especially on audiovisual equipment, becomes rapidly outdated. Specialists within the fields of librarianship and education may be able to assist and guide selection for particular uses and may also be able to suggest available local sources for obtaining borrowed or rented equipment. Prime sources of information should be searched to determine the range of equipment available to meet a need when purchase is necessary. Current, reliable information is important before important decisions can be made about purchase or use of equipment. *Training and Development Journal* and *Training* both have frequent articles about the application of different audio-visual aids to specific training techniques and situations. Both periodicals also frequently review media books and advertise equipment. *Media and Methods* is a good source of information about media equipment, with critiques of capabilities and kinds of use. *Library Technology Reports* is a slower sources of such critiques. *Audio-visual Equipment Guide* is an annual that lists different kinds and makes of equipment. Creating a resource file, as described in Guideline 4, will be helpful for gathering information about equipment resources.

Figure 17 offers a checklist to help for planning and/or communicating purposes. It includes audio and visual equipment and miscellaneous supplies that are most frequently used for learning activities.

Materials

Special equipment often enables the use of unique materials. Together they can make complex, difficult, and abstract information and concepts more real, tangible, and concrete. As defined in Guideline 4, **materials** are the educational aids used to initiate, facilitate, or reinforce the learning process. They must be selected and used with some discrimination. Well employed, they can reduce barriers to learning, can deepen the learning experience, and can assist learners to apply their learnings. Often, they have a broad and long-range impact because they serve as reminders to learners and provide a means for them to tangibly share their learnings with others.

Because of their diversity, materials are difficult to categorize neatly, but two general groupings do seem possible. One includes those materials intended for direct use by the learner, such as informational or instructional handouts, schedules, or evaluation forms. The second group includes those materials used by the educator in conjunction with the educational method being used in the activity, such as a case study, a slide tape, or transparencies. Both types enhance

Figure 17

Learning Activity–Equipment and Supplies Checklist

Supplied By		Item	Comments–Qualifications– Special Instructions– Reminders
Site	Program		
		EQUIPMENT–AUDIO	
		1. sound system	1.
		2. podium mikes (number ___)	2.
		3. lavaliere mikes (number ___)	3.
		4. outlets (number ___ , location)	4.
		5. tape recorder	5.
		6.	6.
		7.	7.
		EQUIPMENT–VISUAL	
		8. slide projector	8.
		9. slide/tape projector (no. ___ kind ___)	9.
		10. movie projector (no.___ kind ___)	10.
		11. overhead projector	11.
		12. opaque projector	12.
		13. screen(s) (no. ___)	13.
		14. projection table(s)	14.
		15. electrical outlets (no. ___ location ___)	15.
		16. easel	16.
		17. playback monitor	17.
		18.	18.
		19.	19.
		20.	20.
		EQUIPMENT– MISCELLANEOUS SUPPLIES	
		21. lectern with light/sound	21.
		22. telephone (number: ___)	
		23. photocopy facilities	23.
		24. typewriter(s)	24.
		25. wastebaskets	25.
		26. extension cords	26.
		27. 3-prong adapter(s)	27.
		28. calculator or adding machine	28.
		29. clock or timer	29.

(Figure 17 continues on page 156)

Figure 17 (cont'd)

Supplied By		Item	Comments—Qualifications—Special Instructions—Reminders
Site	Program		
		30. scissors	30.
		31. directional signs	31.
		32. newsprint pads	32.
		33. masking tape	33.
		34. markers	34.
		35. spare bulbs for visual equipment	35.
		36. pencils/paper/pens	36.
		37. pencil sharpener	37.
		38. name tags/badges	38.
		39. transparent tape	39.
		40. cash/box change	40.
		41. receipt book	41.
		42. rubber bands	42.
		43. ruler	43.
		44. stapler and extra staples	44.
		45. staple remover	45.
		46. paper clips	46.
		47. small tools (screwdriver, pliers, etc.)	47.
		48. first aid kit	48.
		49. camera for candid photos	49.
		50.	50.
		51.	51.
		52.	52.
		53.	53.
		54.	54.
		55.	55.

● For purchase, replacement, repair, rental:

Address of nearest audio-visual supplier: _____

Address of nearest office/art supplier: _____

the learning experience by supporting the educational techniques being used, by supplying information to help learners make the most of the opportunity, or by building linkages with on-the-job application of learnings.

More specifically, typical materials intended for the direct use of learners include:

- preparatory materials, such as:

    —information about the topic and methods to expect,

    —assigned readings of content material or case studies to build a common ground of knowledge,

    —a self-assessment instrument to identify the specific needs that the session might attempt to meet.

- handout materials, such as:

    —illustrations or examples of concepts presented,

    —handbooks or manuals related to the skills or procedures to be learned,

    —directions and instructions for techniques to be used during the activity.

- follow-up materials, such as:

    —reading lists of sources related to the particular needs that were revealed during the activity,

    —copies of transparencies which were used during the activity,

    —forms for self-evaluation or program evaluation.

Materials distributed to learners in advance of an activity can provide them with a common base of knowledge, both in relation to the content area to be covered and to the activity itself: who is conducting it, what will be done, the time and place it will be held. Often assignments may be made to review in advance a case study or read an article or discuss an issue with others. This preparation can provide a foundation for a presentation or for group techniques. Preparatory materials can build the expectations of learners and are useful to interest and motivate those who are to attend. Well-organized and substantive materials also can impress learners as to the nature and the quality of the event.

Materials distributed during the training session can be used to reinforce or to clarify the topical presentations, or they can be used to give directions for exercises or techniques that will be the focus of the activity. Materials can save the distraction and effort of notetaking without sacrificing the necessary information. They can enable learners to concentrate on the session and yet have information to refer to after the activity is concluded. Some materials used during the activity are essential to the conduct of the activity, such as in-basket exercises, questions for discussion groups, or forms to fill out.

Materials distributed to learners following the training activity can be selected on the basis of findings during the session about the learners' level of understanding with regard to the topic. If asked during the session, learners often can suggest the kind of need they have for materials. For example, bibliographies, resource lists, and technical information can often be more pertinent if compiled after the session than before or during. Follow-up materials can reinforce learnings by reminding learners of essential points covered, and they can help learners to apply their learnings to job responsibilities. They also can help learners pull loose ends together, or may prompt rethinking an issue. Materials distributed at any of these three times can be used to relate non-library oriented presentations to specific use of library personnel.

In each of these phases, materials can be channeled to the learners. In addition, sometimes materials result from the training activity. For example, an action plan, a report, a list of recommendations, a videotape, or a cassette might have been developed by individual learners or by the group as a whole during the activity. Such tangible results are often a significant evidence of the learning that has occurred.

Other materials are used by the educator in conjunction with the activity's educational method(s). The following are typical examples with their major uses:

- Briefing materials are often necessary to give sufficient background to educators and help them plan soundly.

- Exhibits, charts, bulletin boards, displays, models, and mock-ups can be used to illustrate basic concepts, to picture procedural steps, to practice skills application or to reinforce information already presented.

- Films, filmstrips and slide-tapes can show how to do something, portray behaviors or attitudes, stimulate discussion and interaction.

- Instructional sheets and directions can be used to assure clear, sequential steps for an exercise, to enable the learner to practice a skill after the session is over, to convey what is important to observe in an interactive exercise, or to establish the situation for a simulation or role play.

- Programmed instruction or computer-assisted instruction materials are used to guide the learner through a given area of content or a prescribed procedure.

- Simulations are controlled enactments of realistic situations with materials that set up and maintain the simulation.

- Learning packages, usually professionally developed and commercially distributed, assemble a wide array of materials, guiding the learning process toward given objectives.

- Procedural manuals and policy handbooks are developed within the library and assist not only learning, but also application to the job.

A cautionary note needs to be sounded, for the variety of available types of materials may lead the program administrator and/or the educational staff astray, and thereby make the form and format of the materials more important than their function in the activity. Materials, as well as equipment and facilities, must be viewed primarily in relation to how effectively they can supplement the learning experience, not substitute for it.

Although the wide variety in purpose, type, and use of materials precludes detailed and specific criteria, some general criteria can be used to guide the selection and use of materials:

- The nature and use of the materials should be congruent with the objectives and educational methods to be used in the activity.

- Results from the use of materials should be predictable, for the most part, and they should fit with the objectives.

- Materials should address the level of interest and understanding of individual learners, spanning if possible the range of their differing abilities and experiences.

- Materials selected should be feasible in terms of their cost.

- Materials should be closely related to the real situation of learners and able to assist in the transfer of learning to application at the work site.

- Materials should be used to stimulate interest, to motivate reflection, and to prompt further learning.

- Instructional materials should be relatively simple to administer and utilize as well as able to produce the desired educational action.

- Guides, workbooks, and manuals should be practical and related closely to the learners' circumstances.

- Informational materials should be accurate, timely, clear, concise, explicit, and easy to understand; they should include the date and source of the information.

- The effectiveness of materials should be tested with evaluation measure and procedures.

- Materials to be used in conjunction with instructional media or specific methods should be developed by individuals informed as to the proper use of the media or methods.

- Pre-testing should be considered where it could build an awareness of the materials' clarity or effect.

- Dissemination patterns for materials should be planned ahead of time to make printing, reproduction, or ordering more efficient, and to assure that those who need the materials have them at the appropriate time and place.

Materials can be adopted, adapted, or developed. Adopted materials are most likely to be successfully applied in situations that closely parallel the original circumstances and objectives. Contacting others who have used the materials that are being adopted or adapted helps to make sure of the proper application and the implications possible from their use. Usually, the skill and experience of the educator is crucial to assure sound selection of materials to be adopted or adapted. Materials such as case studies, structured exercises, or handouts often can be adapted to new uses and different groups, modifying the materials to fit the objectives and the design of the new activity. Adaptation sometimes leads to overlooking important modifications, however, and thus may lead to unexpected outcomes. Both adopted and adapted materials should clearly credit and cite the original source on the material.

Developing original materials for learning activities is very demanding, and ordinarily not a task for the inexperienced. This often appears deceptively easy but becomes full of complexities and implications along the way. Developed materials have the advantage of being built to meet specific, perhaps unique, needs. As such, however, they may also reflect unintended perspectives and values left over from the original application. These leftovers are often significant and may affect learning. Materials must be designed based on the principles of adult learning and relevant to the specific plan for both the activity and the educational techniques to be used. Materials development is usually time-consuming and thus, costly. Whoever is engaged to develop original and specialized materials will need to know the nature of the activity, the desired results and the skills of the educator to be using the materials.

Materials, whether to be adopted, adapted, or developed, seem relatively easy to design, produce, and implement. To assure clarity and understanding, however, they should be pre-tested. Handouts, case studies, and direction sheets can be tested with potential participants or others to check how useful they are and how they can best be administered. When films or learning packages or programmed instruction materials are being considered, they should be previewed to assure their relevance to the topic and the techniques being used for the activity.

Pretesting materials, such as in an equipment dry-run or actually visiting the facilities prior to the learning activity, helps determine their relevance, check out their feasibility, identify problem areas, and discover potential surprises. The quality and workability of these resources is important to each learning activity, and thus, in the long run, to the program itself. The responsibility for each of these resources may vary with different activities and various educators, but their importance warrants close attention to their selection and management.

Procedure

The responsibility for selection and use of these resources is most often shared by the program administrator (or someone assigned the administrative tasks for the activity) and by the educator(s). The facilities choice, because it involves budgeting and many logistical details, usually falls to the administrator. Equipment and materials may be indicated by the educational design and thus become the province of the educator(s). The kind of equipment may be requested by the educator, but the task of arranging for it may reasonably belong to the administrator. Instructional materials may be developed by the educator, but the task of purchase, reproduction, or distribution of them is that of the administrator as is acquisition of the informational materials such as brochures and participant lists. Specific instances often vary in this regard.

When and where the activity will be held, and what materials and equipment will be needed are likely to be interrelated decisions. However these decisions are made, alternative facilities, equipment, and materials also should be reviewed or previewed and evaluated against the criteria listed above. Choices of facilities should be reviewed on-site and selected to obtain the most important advantages possible. Materials should be pretested; if the materials or methods selected require special equipment, that equipment should be set up and tested prior to the activity by using the actual materials intended for it. Each of these steps *must* occur prior to the actual event.

Then, during the learning activity, skillful transitions are essential to assist the learners in relating materials and media to actual on-the-job applications of their learnings. An introduction can inform the learner as to the purpose of the materials or media and what to look for or how to use it. For example, if a slide tape presentation is used to illustrate a particular procedure or technique, the learners might be advised why the slide tape is useful, the importance of the procedure it shows, which of the steps shown are particularly crucial, and which might be inapplicable under certain circumstances.

If discussion and questions are encouraged both before and after introducing and using materials or media, the depth and retention of learning is likely to be greater. Adequate time should be allowed during these transition points for discussion periods where learners talk with one another as well as question and discuss important points with the educator. Often, the most effective job of the educator in relation to the use of materials and media is to link the use of role playing film, or demonstration with actual application of what was learned to the job they have.

And, finally, evaluation measures should particularly focus on the effectiveness of the equipment and materials used. Feedback from learners and educators will also provide useful information to assist the incorporation in future planning of what has been discovered from utilizing these types of materials. Such feedback can have the immediate effect of bringing deeper awareness to people as to what they have learned with the help of the equipment and materials. In some cases, the specific materials must be considered again in later activities or for production and distribution separate from the activity.

Administrators and educators require useful sources of information about the kinds of materials and equipment available and how to make effective use of them in learning activities. The bibliography at the end of this book includes basic books and periodicals to consult. To keep current, materials reviewed in periodical literature in the fields both of adult education, and of training and development, as well as those in librarianship, are very useful. Articles in these periodicals describe specific applications of training techniques in various situations. Although not a valuable source in the past, library literature now has more information on staff development and continuing education resources. Libraries, agencies, and associations may have access to persons with knowledge and expertise, and these sources can often provide leads to other people as well as to existing resources.

And, finding or developing expertise in people is also a way of acquiring the needed resources. Workshops and seminars designed for the development of special skills are available through educational or training and development associations, such as the Adult Education Association, the American Society for Training and Development, the Association for Educational Communications and Technology, and such specialized groups as the Simulation and Gaming Association.

These organizations offer help for those responsible for design and management of learning, for preparation of instructional materials and audiovisual techniques, and for conference management. Thus, they become a source not only of the people and publications providing the expertise that may be needed, but they also enable program administrators and educators to build that needed area of expertise in themselves.

Information about specific training aids within a given type of method can be found in some of these same sources. However, this becomes more quickly dated than does the information about how to utilize types of resources or various methods. Commercial producers of materials advertise widely in training and educational periodicals and by direct mail. Training organizations, professional associations, and commercial businesses often package and market training aids to be used with their services, including films, filmstrips, audio cassette packages, programmed learning, and other learning packages. More and more, such aids are being developed by trainers and practitioners in the library field, and regular reading of library literature over a period of time will reveal many of these.

In general, the information about resources described in Guideline 4 will be helpful to those who seek information about facilities, equipment, and materials. Through these resources will come indications of useful aids or of other sources that will lead to useful aids. As with most areas of knowledge, individuals newly exposed may feel at a loss. But, as awareness grows through increased exposure to new areas of literature and activity and to colleagues with similar interests, knowledge about what is available will also grow. It takes time and contacts to build a repertoire of people, packages, sites, techniques and terminology. The resource file described in Guideline 4 will prove invaluable to record information about training aids and facilities, to list tools for finding specific techniques, and to file brochures and reviews describing specific materials and equipment. Such a file does not become invaluable overnight but is a source that can be relied on increasingly as it grows in size and scope.

Particularly with regard to materials used in training, the question arises concerning the value of non-library oriented materials. Some available materials and techniques are like supervisory training, leadership development, and public speaking, which seem to be readily adaptable to librarians and library educators directly. Others, less closely related to libraries or education, obviously will not readily ensure personal application by the learner in the work situation. Since the main purpose of learning is the application of learning to on-the-job situations and circumstances, more assistance and time must be provided to the learner in linking the principles and process with the local organizational base. For instance, supervisory training, or administrative principles illustrated in materials and media outside the library or library school context, will need specific, frequent, and definite linkages to the library situation. If the learners are not able to provide this link for themselves and are not assisted to do so, their learning will be blocked, and the application of their learnings will be frustrating and difficult.

Summary

Although sound selection and skillful use of facilities, equipment, and materials does not replace the need for good design, able educators, or capable management, it is important. Each of these three resources requires a review of alternatives in light of criteria for selection. Once the resources are selected, sound arrangements make the best use of each, relevant to the particular activity for which they were chosen. Facilities and equipment are necessary to house the activity and to enable educational methods and techniques to be used effectively. Materials can be used before, during, and after the activity to prepare, stimulate, and reinforce the learner. If well selected and used, these three resources will meet learner needs through the educational methods, thus helping to achieve the objectives of the activity. More specifically, these three resources are intended to: (1) support, sustain, and reinforce learning; (2) interest, stimulate, and motivate learners; and (3) clarify ideas, deepen understanding, and integrate concepts. To accomplish these purposes, elaborate or exotic means are not required. Rather, their relevance to the situation at hand and their effectiveness upon application are essential.

GUIDELINE 10–IMPLEMENT LEARNING ACTIVITIES

Implementation brings together the results of planning and preparation. The plan for the overall learning program determines the sequence of learning activities, and each of these activities has been somewhat defined as to need, objectives, topic, method, and perhaps, potential resources. These initial decisions then require subsequent planning and specific preparation before a learning activity actually can occur. Implementation of a single learning activity offers a focus within the learning program. Each learning activity assembles the roles and responsibilities of the administrator, the educational staff, and the learners into a common experience of living and learning together in a shared environment for a few hours a day or several days.

Within the learning program, a variety of activities employing educational resources and methods in different ways will interest and motivate learners. No single method or resource used repeatedly will yield all the desired results. Neither will one approach offer the most suitable learning style for each person, for each topic, or for each situation. Rather, an effective program results from a logical sequence of successful learning events, activities, and processes, each using the most relevant methods and techniques to achieve the established learning objectives.

Too often, however, considerable time and energy is devoted to producing an isolated training activity, this effort guided by the hope that the results will have significant impact on individual learners and the organization. Such an approach reveals little awareness that, for maximum impact on both learners and organization, each activity needs to fit within an overall learning program, building cumulatively to reach program objectives. Even so, each activity must still be produced with sufficient attention and focus to have meaning for its learners distinct from the rest of the program's activities.

This Guideline brings together the specific roles, responsibilities, and resources described in previous Guidelines. For those individuals responsible for producing the program's learning activities, a practical, action-oriented approach is suggested. Whereas previous Guidelines have detailed how to assess needs, set objectives, identify resources, and design a program, this Guideline describes two ways to implement an activity within the program. One is by offering a general tool that brings together and implements the specifics of an activity. This tool, an action plan, can aid the coordination, communication, and decision-making so essential for the implementation of a successful activity. The second way is by offering a specific, detailed narrative example of commentary on an activity, showing how implementation brings together each of the elements described separately in earlier Guidelines. Supplementing each of these ways are useful charts and checklists to aid implementors.

Action Plan

Implementation is the immediate and one-time fulfillment of an investment of a great deal of earlier planning and preparation efforts. Because of the unforeseen, the unpredictable, and the overlooked, success is not possible to guarantee. But there are ways of making the best use of preparation to keep the chance of mistakes to a minimum and to assure that needed modifications can be identified and made in time. The action plan, suggested for the needs assessment and evaluation, is also invaluable for planning and implementing each activity. Developed for an activity, it records what has to be done by whom and when, thus making the most of the time spent on the initial planning and meeting the need for dependable implementation. An action plan looks ahead during a period of relative calm and cool reasoning, protecting against the possibility that vital steps will be overlooked as decisions are required during the more pressured time when the activity is fully underway. An action plan approach is particularly useful for the person with limited experience, since planning "by second nature" is not that dependable until experience, sometimes repeated experience, has taught one what to look for, what to do.

An action plan has many potential uses. It is most effectively employed when several of its possible uses can be combined. Among these are the following:

- to employ a logical approach that will assure coverage of all the essential areas that must be considered and planned to ready the activity for its implementation,

- to provide a focus for joint planning that will elicit ideas and suggestions from the group and yet assure steady progress toward the goal of planning for implementation,

- to approach the assignments of tasks and the delegation of various responsibilities in an orderly fashion,

- to provide a useful mechanism to identify the points of communication and coordination that will be necessary to integrate the various components into the most appropriate sequence,

- to facilitate clear thinking and sound decisions made under pressure,

- to document the decisions and the progress made at each point during the planning and implementation phases (particularly useful if several learning activities are being prepared simultaneously, or if different people are responsible for various tasks),

- to reveal quickly what remains to be done at any point in the preparation for the activity,

- to record, after the event, the steps and processes that were accomplished and to serve as an aid in planning for similar activities.

Basically the action plan is a tool used to coordinate and direct the various roles and responsibilities of those directly concerned with the production of a learning activity.

Yet, the development of an action plan should not be interpreted as a means to make the activity rigid. Rather, an action plan can be of great value to uncover points where alternatives should be considered and to specify when final decisions will have to be made. Indeed, provisions for flexibility, identified in the plan itself, can often assure that that flexibility will exist, since it then prompts administrators and educators to innovate and adjust at appropriate times. Flexibility is tested by the extent to which evaluation findings are incorporated into planning and implementation and the extent to which this prompts adjustments and use of alternatives.

Figure 18, parts a, b, and c provide a model framework for an action plan. Specific tasks in relation to a particular activity can be fit into logical time frames, such as before, during, or after the event. Tasks can be designated in relation to the administrative role or the educational roles of the educator(s) or learners. To clarify the use of such an action plan, the three-part Figure 18 also exemplifies typical tasks within each of the roles in the sequence in which they might be done. These tasks are intended to be general enough to apply to a learning activity that might be a speech at a conference session or a workshop on book repair. Another example, an even more detailed approach, appears in Figures 19 and 20, (p. 169 and 170). Here, one illustrates a session using a presentation technique and one using an interactive technique. Both examples demonstrate the action plan approach on a more specific level. Use of these planning formats will require time and effort to adapt them to the needs and the style required by the given situation and the people concerned.

The greatest value of this action plan approach will be for the person responsible for producing a learning activity but lacking extensive experience or a near-by mentor. One caution in using these tools, however, should be directed to the administrator: the organization of the activity and the definition of roles and responsibilities is more clearly in the administrator's mind than anywhere else. Thus, assumptions may be made and expectations may be held that are not shared by others. This, in turn, can cause frustration and disappointment when these are not understood or fulfilled. For example, if the educators do not understand that they are to select the materials and indicate

Figure 18a

Sample Action Plan for a Learning Activity

	ADMINISTRATIVE STAFF	EDUCATIONAL STAFF	LEARNERS
B E F O R E — Administrative function: to coordinate, communicate, decide	Work with planning committee, with whom some or all of the following decisions may be made: Determine scope & depth of topic, the method to be used, the date & the location. Plan anticipated budget for activity. Identify & select educational staff &/or speaker(s) from available alternatives. Select site & reserve dates. Identify & invite target group of potential learners or disseminate publicity about the event to attract learners. Seek information about the nature of learner needs & problems in relation to the topic. Develop & disseminate informational & preparatory materials to go to selected/ registered learners, educational staff, library literature. Plan staffing arrangements for handling workflow, such as correspondence, recordkeeping, documentation. Order requested instructional materials. Arrange with site for rooms for learning sessions. Plan briefing session with educational staff for necessary logistics (i.e. arrangements); detailed sequence of events; timing; use of techniques, media, and materials. Arrange for exhibits, on-site library of resources, audiovisual equipment. Pack needed supplies, equipment, etc.	Educational function: to facilitate learning and application Make arrangements and commitment with administrator on fees & responsibilities. Communicate frequently with administrator to assure continued clear understanding. Provide biographical information and instructional or informational materials in relation to the focus of activity. Suggest criteria for selection of learners. Outline specifications for the space needs & arrangements at site. Request needed equipment & materials for ordering. Select & assemble first choice & alternate materials. Plan design of educational experience. Prepare informational presentation. Prepare interactive techniques & materials. Participate in briefing session & staff meetings during the activity. Request desired arrangements for living accommodations & transportation arrangements.	Learning function: to learn and apply learnings Register interest. Identify individual needs or problems in relation to the topic. Communicate those needs to the administrator. Prepare with background readings, discussions. Complete pre-activity assignments. Make arrangements for work & personal scheduling. Bring own experiences & information sources for sharing & learning with others who have like concerns.

Figure 18b

Sample Action Plan for a Learning Activity

	ADMINISTRATIVE STAFF	EDUCATIONAL STAFF	LEARNERS
D U R I N G Administrative function: to coordinate, communicate, decide	Make last-minute check to make sure all preliminary tasks and assignments are complete. Conduct briefing session with instructional staff present. Coordinate living & learning logistics. Serve as liaison with site for arrangements. Provide media & materials at the appropriate time for staff & learners. Assure that registration process is smooth, including room arrangements if necessary. Provide ready information about logistics where & when needed. Welcome learners, open session, & make introductions. Arrange for staff meetings to exchange observations & verify next steps, if activity is lengthy.	Participate in briefing with administrator & instructional staff in order to finalize arrangements & flow. Employ content & method within the schedule agreed upon, with provision for needed flexibility. Give presentation(s). Coordinate media & techniques & material used. Facilitate interactive techniques. Open with overview; close with wrap-up. Share responsibilities among all members of the instructional staff. Engage as a team with administrator in continuing planning, based on observations & knowledge of available alternatives. Educational function: to facilitate learning and application	Listen actively. Interact participatively. Ask questions for clarification. Comment from own experience. Provide feedback. Assist in on-site continuous planning if opportunity is offered. Learner function: to learn and apply learnings

Figure 18c
Sample Action Plan for a Learning Activity

		ADMINISTRATIVE STAFF	EDUCATIONAL STAFF	LEARNERS
A F T E R	Administrative function: to coordinate, communicate, decide	Return equipment & materials & supplies. Conduct post-activity "debriefing" meeting to elicit instructional staff perceptions of the activity and its possible results. Thank and pay instructional staff, site personnel, and others who contributed to the activity. Mail out materials & information that were promised to staff, participants. Prepare & disseminate final report. Follow through to see that all assigned tasks were done. Consider publicity about the activity— articles, speeches, presentations.	*Educational function: to facilitate learning and application* — Participate in post-activity "debriefing" to review & learn from how it went. Contribute observations & recommendations for follow-up or subsequent activities. Follow-up learner requests for information or materials. Prepare report if requested. Submit bill for fee and expenses.	*Learner function: to learn and apply learnings* — Apply learnings to job responsibilities Share learnings with colleagues and/or supervisors Respond to follow-up evaluation forms or interviews Encourage others to engage in continuing education efforts

Figure 19

Sample Action Plan for a Presentation Session

ACTION PLAN FOR PRESENTATION(S)			
	ADMINISTRATOR	**PRESENTER(S)**	**LEARNERS**
B E F O R E	Identify need to be met more specifically. Determine topic and special focus. Select date, time, place. Identify alternative presenters and contact them. Select site for climate desired. Select presenter(s) and inform of size and nature of group expected, purpose of session, specifics of content, and approach desired. Agree on fee, arrangements, write contract if desired, confirm. Test for further definition of need in subject area. Submit room sketch to site, confirm date, arrangements, food plans. Print handout materials. Submit info to appropriate media: date, place, person, time, etc. Plan evaluation and inform the presenter(s). Pack	Respond to initial contact with administrator, indicating interest, available dates, vita, fee, reference if requested. Continue to communicate with administrator on need. Submit outline of material for review and suggestions. Re-write outline to include suggestions. Specify necessary equipment and indicate materials to be reproduced and distributed. Prepare visual aids.	Register, if necessary. Do suggested preliminary reading.
D U R I N G	Conduct session to review and coordinate presenters and assure effective moderator approach. Check out room arrangement and sound and/or recording system. Set up media required. Monitor sound and media throughout to make sure heard/seen. Supervise registration, greet attendees, handle problems. Check for adequate seating for attendees. Arrange for evaluative forms/interviews.	Attend briefing session. Check room set up, sound and media, materials. Present information. Respond to questions from attendees following presentation or informally afterwards. Have materials distributed at appropriate time.	Listen actively. Take notes.
A F T E R	Thank and pay fee/expenses of speaker(s). Thank and pay site. Respond to follow-up inquiries from attendees, speaker(s). Return media and materials. Annotate Resource File on quality of site, speaker(s). Report as needed: 1) narrative, 2) evaluative, 3) financial.	Submit bill. Suggest follow-up activities that might be possible on basis of apparent reaction and response from group.	Read further in subject. Apply and share learnings.

Figure 20
Sample Action Plan for an Interactive Session

ACTION PLAN FOR INTERACTIVE TECHNIQUE(S)			
	ADMINISTRATOR	FACILITATOR(S)	LEARNERS
B E F O R E	Identify need to be met more specifically and test it with practitioners. Determine topic and special focus. Select date, time, place. Identify alternative facilitators and contact them. Select site for climate desired. Select educator(s) and inform of size and nature of group expected, purpose of session, specifics of content and approach desired, amount of time required, specific responsibilities, commitment to briefing session. Confirm fee, arrangements, accommodations in writing. Submit room sketch to site, firm date, arrangements, food plans. Print handout materials. Submit information to appropriate media: date, time, person, place, etc. Plan evaluation and inform educator(s).	Respond to initial contact with administrator with indication of interest, available dates, fee, vita, references if requested. Continue to communicate with administrator on need. Submit outline of design for review and suggestion. Re-write outline to include suggestions. Specify necessary equipment and indicate materials to be reproduced and distributed before or during the activity. Prepare visual aids if necessary. Coordinate activities with other facilitators involved.	Register, if necessary. Do suggested preliminary reading.
D U R I N G	Conduct briefing session to review and coordinate all parts of the design. Check out room arrangements and any media or materials required. Supervise registration, greet attendees, handle problems. Arrange for evaluative forms and interviews. Assure staff planning meetings are held when needed. Act as liaison with site.	Attend briefing session. Check room set-up, media and materials. Have materials distributed at appropriate time. Present basic context of information, principles and nature of technique. Work with group—problem-solving, learning exercise. Draw principles out of that experience. Prepare group for application of what they learned.	Listen actively. Participate: question, comment, react.
A F T E R	Thank and pay fee/expenses of facilitator(s). Thank and pay site. Respond to follow-up inquiries from attendees, facilitator(s). Return media and materials not used. Annotate Resource File on quality of site, facilitator(s). Report as needed: 1) narrative, 2) evaluative, 3) financial.	Submit bill. Suggest follow-up activities that might be possible on basis of apparent reaction and response from group.	Read further in subject. Apply learnings. Share with others.

the preferred room arrangement, reminders may be required, action may be reluctant—because of the conflicting beliefs of each person that the other was responsible.

Basically, the action plan approach to implementing activities assists the coordination, communication, and decision-making required. Other resources are available. They each approach implementation differently in format, although each attempts, in its own way, to bring together the various components that must mesh during implementation. Burke's *Conference Planning* (1970), Davis's *Planning, Conducting, Evaluating Workshops* (1974), Knowles's *Modern Practice of Adult Education* (1970), This's *The Small Meeting Planner* (1972), and Warncke's *Planning Library Workshops and Institutes* (1976) are additional aids in bringing together the many details and shared responsibilities for a given learning activity.

Narrative Example

Another way to clarify and describe just how those components are brought together to successfully launch a single learning activity is to profile a typical example. This example, a workshop in a library's staff development program, is first described in general terms briefly; then comments in more detail elaborate on how implementation assembles the elements described separately in other Guidelines. The Models in the Appendix are a similar attempt to describe how this happens with a program as a whole, making the principles more tangible by relating them to a particular example. The step-by-step detail here illustrates the necessary integration and relationship of the various elements of an activity.

At this point, however, several assumptions must be made explicit. The first, most basic assumption is that the goals and objectives of the organization's learning program have been defined. A second assumption is that the basic responsibilities for the program's planning, decision-making, and communication have been assigned. Third, the timing and sequence of the program's activities are assumed to have been planned to meet the needs of the learners and of the organization. The fourth assumption is that at least tentative objectives are established for the initial activities in the program, with the content and methods for these activities at least tentatively selected, based on the principles described in Guideline 6. Fifth, the principles of involvement and flexibility are assumed to be tenets of the program. And, finally, it is assumed that those with implementation responsibilities are honestly concerned with successful implementation through concrete, action-oriented efforts.

*****

As a result of the needs assessment results in a municipal public library, a workshop on supervisory skills was scheduled as the fifth learning activity in the newly instituted staff development program at the library. The administrator of the library assembled a representative group of staff members who were asked to serve as an ad hoc planning group to implement this supervisory skills workshop. At its first meeting, the group reviewed the staff needs, formulated the main objectives for the activity, and explored what kind of content and method would be most relevant to respond to the specified needs.

The general topic of supervisory skills was narrowed to two facets of that broad topic: 1) specific techniques of on-the-job instruction and 2) awareness of the responsibility for staff training as a part of the supervisory function. Within the given parameters of budget and schedule, the group specified the method to be used: a one-half day workshop concentrated on these two areas. A tentative date was selected two months in the future, based on the availability of the library's conference room and on staff scheduling factors. Various individuals were considered to conduct the workshop. The priority choice was a consultant from outside the library with experience in public library work and known training skills. Not having a staff development program administrator, the planning group selected one member of the group to coordinate this activity and, as a first step, directed that person to make initial contact with the preferred consultant and to indicate the results of this first planning meeting as the library's specifications for the intended workshop.

Contact with the consultant revealed that the specifications of topic, method, and scheduled date were all able to be met. Based on the initial, informally stated objectives and the specifications indicated by the first planning meeting, the consultant designed a four-hour workshop based on the indicated objectives. This information was sent by the consultant to be considered at the second meeting of the ad hoc planning group. In addition to the draft design, the consultant had supplied to the planning group a list of questions to elicit from them information helpful in further preparation. That discussion was recorded on a cassette tape and sent to the consultant who was unable to come to the meeting.

As a result of the taped discussion, the consultant changed the earlier priorities of the objectives, modified the design as suggested, determined the scope and depth of the content area to be covered, and selected materials for distribution to the participants prior to and during the workshop. The final, detailed workshop design and a list and directions for the needed equipment and desired room arrangement were sent to the coordinator of the activity. Written materials directly related to the topic of supervisory skills were prepared by the consultant, some to be used prior to and some during the workshop. Visual transparencies were prepared to illustrate some of the concepts in the presentations.

Two weeks before the workshop, an invitational memo was sent from the library administrator to each staff member with present or future supervisory responsibilities. The final workshop design and a thought-provoking preparatory sheet accompanied the memo. Just prior to the workshop, the library's conference room was arranged as requested by the consultant, with a semi-circle of chairs facing an overhead projector and a flip chart. Coffee and name tags were available as the thirty participants arrived.

The workshop went as planned, with some flexibility in the anticipated time blocks because of points of general concern that resulted in active discussion. An initial presentation by the consultant was followed by two role plays, which used real on-the-job situations enacted by volunteers. Each role play was followed by a critique from the group. The supervisory principles illustrated by these role plays were brought out in the discussion. After the mid-point break, a second a second presentation was followed by participants working in small groups on a case study. Recommendations from each small group were reported to the whole group. Principles revealed in the recommendations were high-lighted by the consultant in the general discussion following the group reports.

At the end of the workshop, the consultant initiated a general group sharing of how participants planned to apply and practice what they had learned. One part of the closure of the workshop consisted of a group interview that evaluated the workshop itself from the perspectives of those who attended it. A month later, a brief questionnaire was sent to all workshop participants asking them to describe how they had applied what they learned.

*****

This description of a typical library staff development activity provides a specific, tangible example with which to illustrate many of the elements necessary to implement a successful in-house learning experience. The following comment will amplify the description by detailing its step-by-step development.

The municipal public library conducted a comprehensive **needs assessment** a year ago in preparation for increasing its staff development efforts for the 80 people who staff the main library, the two branches, and the bookmobile. One of the prime needs revealed in the needs assessment questionnaire and interviews was in the category of "supervisory skills." In supplementary comments, some individuals indicated that they did not feel confident enough in their knowledge or ability to effectively supervise staff members for whom they were responsible. More specifically, many wanted to know how to do on-the-job training as part of their supervisory function. A few indicated that they knew that their future job responsibilities would probably include supervisory responsibilities and that they did not feel presently that they were adequately prepared.

Based on this indication of need, the library's recently revamped **planning** for staff development included, as its fifth learning activity, "a fall workshop on supervisory skills." Since no single individual was given charge of the staff development program, the library administrator usually provided the initiative and overview to start the wheels in motion at the appropriate time. For each activity in the program to that point, an ad hoc planning group and coordinator took major responsibility for implementing that activity. This approach, though not ideal, did offer centralized coordination and broad-based, meaningful contributions from representative staff members.

Guided by this pattern, the results of the needs assessment, the sequence indicated in the program's plan for staff development, the library administrator initiated and authorized a representative planning group to be responsible for this workshop. The group consisted of a branch supervisor, the person in charge of the maintenance staff, the personnel officer, the bookmobile librarian, a supervisor from the technical services area, and a public services department head. The first planning meeting was convened in mid-August. One result of that meeting was that the personnel officer agreed to assume the primary responsibility for coordinating this particular activity. Aware of the importance of that role, the personnel officer was alert throughout the meeting for key decisions as they were made, jotted frequent notes, and asked follow-up questions to assure that necessary action steps were made as explicit as possible.

The planning group used the needs assessment and the plan's designation of probable purposes, general topic, and suggested method as the point of departure for their planning. The main tasks of the planning group as addressed at its first meeting were:

- to view the relevance of the originally defined objectives to actual staff needs,

- to define the scope and depth of the subject treatment necessary to meet those needs,

- to review alternative instructional methods to accomplish the objectives,

- to identify those staff members most able to benefit from this activity as learners,

- to plan the next steps required for implementation.

The planning group engaged in a critical review of four key elements: the objectives, the topic, the method, and the learners. In final planning for implementation, these elements interrelate with one another in such a way that decisions concerning any one element could directly affect the others. For example, selection of one group of learners, only those who presently do on-the-job instruction, might require a different definition of the topic and a change in workshop techniques from what might meet the needs of learners who plan for training as well as those who do it. Careful definition of the four elements, evolved by those really in the day-to-day work situation, had a strong impact on making the workshop an integrated practical learning experience, thereby increasing the likelihood that participants would find their learnings relevant and would be able to transfer these learnings promptly into the work situation.

By far the most time-consuming of the group's tasks was that of developing the **objectives** for the learning activity. The group reviewed the identified needs, contributed their own experiences in seeking effective supervisory behavior, shared the comments and thoughts of other staff members about what was most needed, and pondered how to make the most of the four-hour time allotment. They tried with some difficulty to articulate and specify the results they might realistically expect from this activity.

Planning groups responsible for earlier activities had set the precedent of brief, simply-stated objectives indicating as specifically as possible what learning and behavior was sought. In the beginning of the staff development program, considerable discussion had centered on the advantages of establishing behavioral objectives for each activity, but staff ability and inclination for that were not strong. That, plus the argument that the staff would be affronted by behaviorally-stated objectives concluded that question, at least for that time.

As the discussion moved back and forth between the topic, the method, and the learners to be involved, changes and modifications were made in each element as well as in the original objectives. To facilitate their process, one member of the group used the blackboard to clarify and record the group's decisions. Vagueness about the content area posed a difficulty. Little was known formally about the topic, although almost all of the committee members had had considerable experience in supervising. Most helpful was that many individuals in the planning group knew and could describe what skills they wanted to improve. After weighing the advantages and disadvantages of who should participate in the workshop, it was decided that all staff members potentially responsible as supervisors and on-the-job instructors should be included as well as those presently responsible for those tasks.

Through their discussion on the originally defined "workshop to improve supervisory skills," the planning group evolved more specific objectives concerned with developing on-the-job training skills and the ability to plan for and to evaluate job-related instruction as part of the supervisory function. The overly broad topic of supervisory skills was honed to a more manageable definition that reflect more specifically defined needs and could be effectively covered in a four-hour workshop. A noteworthy serendipitous outcome from earlier activities—that of providing increased opportunities to know and learn with other staff members—was formalized as an additional objective. Finally, the activity objectives were compared with the overall program objectives to make sure the two were congruent and the activity was indeed supportive of the total program.

The fourth key element reviewed by the planning group was that of the **method**. The strengths and weaknesses of methods used in earlier staff development activities were discussed. The planning group re-evaluated whether the workshop method initially selected was the best means to achieve the kinds of learning needed. The most quickly and commonly identified instructional method for an in-house or an out-of-house activity is usually a workshop. Often, though, workshops are suggested more as a result of their current popularity than because of the method's assured relevance to all topics and all audiences. In this example, the workshop format offered the best opportunity for the needed topic and for the learner involvement and practical skill training that would facilitate application of learnings on the job. Other deciding factors in the selection of the workshop method were: the number of staff members with similar needs, the ability of a workshop format to help participants address real concerns, the value of an informal interchange with colleagues that would assist in the reinforcement and applications of learnings.

The library administrator, present at the planning meeting, helped keep an overall organizational perspective, including occasional reminders of the economic implications of what was being planned. A realistic look at the feasibility of implementing any staff development activity includes recognition of the costs incurred from staff involvement in planning, implementing, and attending learning activities, as well as professional fees for educational staff and the expenses of needed equipment, required facilities, and materials.

By the end of the three-hour planning session, the group had accomplished its major tasks and had a clear idea of their direction. Although time-consuming, the meeting was a sound investment, for the subsequent steps progressed steadily forward and none had to be retraced later. The objectives served as consistent guidelines for further planning, implementing, and evaluating. With the basic planning having clearly defined the activity, the necessary follow-through steps could be efficiently accomplished.

The personnel officer then contacted the consultant **(educational staff)** and explained what the library wanted, what preparatory work had been done; also discussed were the preferred timing for the activity and the fee. The consultant then asked questions about previous staff development learning activities, the methods used and content areas covered. Then, with a clear sense of what the group wanted, the consultant stated the experience and qualifications that seemed appropriate to this situation. The consultant and personnel officer jointly agreed that the consultant would conduct the workshop. After asking about the physical facilities that were available for the workshop, the consultant made some initial suggestions about workshop format and the scope of its content for initial reaction by the personnel officer. The consultant agreed to submit a draft **design** to be reviewed by the planning group's second meeting.

Within a couple of days, the consultant assembled the notes made during conversation with the personnel officer. The next step was to determine the necessary content areas to be covered, and to review the alternative instructional techniques most suitable for the objectives and topic. Then, the balance and sequence of these techniques had to be planned. Particularly sought were techniques to offer opportunities that involved the learners and helped them practice skills in the low-risk learning atmosphere, before they attempted new behavior in actual job situations.

The objectives described two basic content areas that would be needed: 1) the ability to instruct on-the-job, and 2) the ways to plan and evaluate on-the-job instruction for a department or branch staff. The consultant outlined the major topics within each of those areas to give some idea of the scope and depth that would be needed and possible. Sequence was determined on the basis that all participants had a degree of experience and could quickly relate to matters that concerned either the instructor or the learner roles in on-the-job instruction. These outlines composed the content blocks for the workshop. The consultant then balanced these with interactive blocks to provide a change of pace as well as an opportunity to involve the learner and to examine and perhaps practice those principles brought out in topical presentation.

After considering several alternatives, the consultant chose role play as the best technique to demonstrate in general the skills of instructing and the case to demonstrate to small groups the most desirable way to examine planning on-the-job instruction as part of the supervisory function. These choices appeared to be the most suitable considering the size and diversity of the group, the nature of the facilities, the limited time frame, and the apparent experience of the group with learning techniques requiring involvement.

To make sure that these four components would be able to be accomplished, the consultant estimated the time needed, figuring 20 to 30 minutes for each content presentation (or lecturette), 30 minutes for each of the role plays, plus discussion, and one hour for the case study and following general discussion. This, plus some time at the beginning of the workshop for introductions and some time at the end for evaluation and wrap-up—and a margin for flexibility— fit into the four hours available. Believing that written supportive materials can help reinforce and emphasize the most important learnings, the consultant explored informational sources to find appropriate handouts that might be useful and found several that appeared appropriate.

The consultant wrote a letter to the coordinator of the activity (i.e., the personnel officer) confirming the agreement regarding the workshop, including the date, time, place and fee. The letter included a statement of the expectations as to who was to do what prior to and during the workshop. Four enclosures accompanied the letter:

- the written objectives and design of content coverage and planned activities,
- a cassette tape of the consultant's discussion as to the design, including the rationale used to select the activities and the probable results that could be expected,
- a descriptive list of the selected materials that could be considered for distribution to the participants,
- a list of questions for the planning group to discuss and record in order to provide more information and preparation for the consultant.

The consultant asked that these four items be reviewed by the planning group and that their comments and reactions be taped and returned for further planning by the consultant.

The personnel officer distributed the letter, the plan, and the lists of materials and questions to the planning group members with a notice convening the second meeting of the planning group a week later. The group discussed and recorded their response to the consultant's questions concerning the group of participants generally—who do they instruct and for what tasks do they instruct others? what are their chief concerns? what problems do they have with the instruction they now do? what is the scope of their responsibility? how do they plan and schedule instruction? what specifically do you think they will want and need from the workshop? what would be the most helpful preparation for participants prior to the workshop? do they know each other well? The group then considered the design and the consultant's recorded discussion of content and techniques. Their comments and suggestions about the workshop design were recorded, and that cassette was returned to the consultant.

The consultant then considered the suggestions and responses to the questions and made appropriate modifications to the original plan. The outlines of content were altered to be more specifically relevant to the participant's experiences, problems, and responsibilities. The role plays and case study were retained as techniques, but the planning group suggested that it would be interesting and useful if each case study group reported on their recommendations before the general group discussion. This modification was made. The selection of supportive materials to be used was also guided by the planning group comments.

The consultant then sent the final design shown in Figure 21 (page 178) to the workshop coordinator along with the requirements for the physical facilities and materials for reproduction. The consultant suggested that a memo be sent to eligible staff members from the library administrator including the invitation; an explanation of how this activity fit into the library's overall personnel development program; details of the date, time and place; brief biographical information about the consultant; and instructions as to how personnel could be rescheduled where this was necessary. The memo was to be accompanied by the agenda for

Figure 21
Design of Staff Development
Activity: Supervisory Skills Workshop

SUPERVISOR'S TRAINING SESSION
Friday, October 18
8:30-12:30 a.m.—Conference Rm.

Objectives:
—to understand what job-related instruction is and why it is important for supervisors to do it well

—to know how to plan for and evaluate job-related instruction

—to increase instructional skills of supervisors who presently or potentially are responsible for job instruction

—to provide the opportunity for staff members to know and learn with other staff members

Opening:
Introduction of the consultant
Description of the plan for the workshop

Lecturette:
Job-Related Instruction

What it is
Kinds of on-the-job instruction
How adults learn (handout)
Principles of instruction
Techniques of instruction (handout)
Instructor/supervisor styles
General discussion, questions, comments

Role play:
Actual situations requiring effective on-the-job instruction. The role play is a tool for learning how to apply principles, followed by discussion.

Break

Lecturette:
The Training Function

Part of the supervisory job
The climate and leadership necessary
The training cycle: planning, preparation, presentation, application, evaluation
Requirements for successful training (handout)
General discussion, questions, comments

Case study:
Small group, each working on a realistic situation that illustrates training as part of the supervisory function. General group discussion.

What do you plan to *do* with what you have learned?

Group interview to evaluate the workshop.

Wrap-up comments.

the workshop and a one-page sheet of thought-provoking questions from a government document on training to help prepare the participants for the workshop. (The text of this sheet is reproduced in Figure 22.)

Other **materials** sent to be reproduced were to be made ready for use as handouts during the workshop. They included: a glossary of terms and descriptions of various training techniques applicable to job-related training, a two-page handout on "how adults learn," a helpful reminder (for later reference) what the instructor needs to remember about learners in general for effective on-the-job instruction, and a case study describing a situation where a departmental staff development effort needed to be planned and launched. Each of the handouts was directly related to the topic and included full bibliographic citations, not only to give proper credit but to provide individual participants access for their further study. The consultant also suggested that a selection of books and films on training and supervision be pulled from the library collection for the workshop session. Participants could browse through them during the break period and be aware of the resources easily available to them.

Also in the letter, the consultant specified the desired physical **facilities**: that the room be large enough to accommodate five or six small groups, that participant seating should be chairs in a semi-circle, that an overhead projector and flip chart be in the front of the room for use throughout the session. Coffee and juice was requested to be available in the room if possible, although there would be a mid-point break, and coffee could be confined to that one time if necessary to conform to the institutional rules. Coffee and juice available throughout the morning would add to the informality of the session as it could help people get acquainted and feel like meeting and talking with one another. Name tags were suggested primarily for the use of the consultant, although they were also useful to refresh the memories of staff members.

The coordinator of the activity drafted the cover memo suggested. The library administrator finalized the memo, and two weeks prior to the workshop date, it was distributed, together with the design and "questions" sheet, to all potential participants. These were intended to prepare the learners for the upcoming activity and to encourage them to come to it with some preliminary thinking on the topic in relation to their own job responsibilities.

The consultant arrived early on the workshop morning and was met by the personnel officer in the role of workshop coordinator. They checked out the meeting room for the arrangement and accoustics. The overhead projector and flip chart were checked for any unique characteristics that might prove surprising if discovered for the first time during the session. Many of the planning group members arrived a bit early and met informally with the consultant to get better acquainted, since they had known him (and he, them) only as voices on a cassette tape. The consultant asked the planners to actively seek feedback from other participants during the mid-point break, then pass on essential information so that any necessary changes could be made during the second half of the workshop.

About thirty participants attended. Others who were invited had scheduling problems or did not feel it met their needs. The library administrator arrived, opened the session by briefly describing the library's commitment to staff development efforts, and then introduced the consultant to the group. The library

Figure 22
Example of Preparatory Materials Supplied
to Participants in Learning Activity

Note: In preparation for the Inservice Training Session, it would be helpful to read through these questions and think about them in relation to your own training responsibilities.

QUESTIONS TO ASK IN APPRAISING THE
EMPLOYEE DEVELOPMENT PROGRAM

1. **Identification and Ranking of Learning Needs**

What is the difference between what is being done and what should be done?
Can the need be answered by other means than a learning situation?
Of the learning needs identified, which are the most urgent?
the most feasible in terms of the time and money available?
What portion of the total budget will be allocated to meeting these needs?

2. **Selection of Learning Objectives**

What are the tasks which make up the job?
What are the job performance standards that can be derived from the tasks?
What are the terminal performance objectives of the learning experience which will lead to adequate job performance?
What are the interim objectives leading to adequate performance at the end of the learning experience?

3. **Selection of Learning Content**

What do employees have to know or be able to do so that they can adequately perform the work?

4. **Selection of Learning Approaches**

Would some of the learning needs be better met through an educational program than through training, do they lend themselves best to classroom instruction, on-the-job training, or developmental assignments?

5. **Selection of Learning Resources**

What resources exist that could deliver the chosen approach?
Are those existing resources adequate to meet the need?
Will the use of the chosen resource be cost-effective?

6. **Selection of Participants**

Which of the employees available for a learning experience would benefit most from it?

7. Conduct of the Learning Experience

Are the instructional environment and time frame arranged to
facilitate learning?
Are the elements of learning presented in an order which encourages
thorough learning?
Does the instruction take advantage of up-to-date learning methodology and technology?

8. Evaluation and Feedback

Is the success of each step of the employee development program
being measured as it is carried out?
Can the contribution of the employee development program
toward the overall goals of the organization be assessed (i.e.,
achieving efficiency and economy in fulfilling its mission)?

Adapted from: U.S. Civil Service Commission. Bureau of Training. *Managing Employee
Development; A Step-By-Step Approach.* Washington, D.C.: Govt Print Off. 1976.

administrator arrived, opened the session by briefly describing the library's
commitment to staff development efforts, and then introduced the consultant
to the group. The library administrator chose not to be part of the participant
group since it might inhibit group discussion.

The consultant opened the workshop with brief mention of some of the
challenges and frustrations that occur with responsibilities for supervision,
illustrated by examples from personal experience. A few minutes were spent
asking participants what kind of instruction they did in their areas of responsibility and what kind of results they got from the instruction they did. This
gave the consultant a feeling for the level of understanding, experience, and
concerns of the learners. The consultant then described the workshop agenda
and asked if it would meet the needs they had. It seemed to, so that led into a
20-minute lecturette on the various kinds of job-related instruction, how to
select and when to use which method, instructional "styles" as related to supervisory "styles" and effectiveness, and recommended step-by-step procedures to
support the content presentation and to assure that sight as well as sound was
part of the learning method, thus increasing the ability of participants to retain
the essential information.

During the presentation, the consultant paused from time to time to ask
for questions or comments. The presentation was paced largely on observed
verbal and non-verbal feedback as "read" by the consultant. The kind of question
or comment that came from the group would give information about whether
the pacing was appropriate. At first, the group seemed more interested in listening
than in commenting. However, at the end of the presentation, several comments
and observations and some questions led to general discussion.

The consultant then described the usefulness of a role play to simulate
and dramatize a real situation in such a way that learnings can be more easily
observed and retained. The ground rules included a time limit and the responsibility
of the "audience" both to view the drama in light of the principles of instruction
presented earlier and to comment later. Responding to the comment that those

volunteering for the role play would be the individuals in the position to learn the most from experience, one participant was eager to volunteer, really wanting to know why his instructions on the use of a new form had not "taken" even though they had been thought to be clear and specific.

Before each role play, the consultant took care to interview the volunteers in front of the group in order to understand the problem that was to be enacted. The interview was complete enough so that circumstances were understood by the whole group and so that the players understood thoroughly their roles, the time frame within which they had to portray the situation, and the fact that the following group discussion would critique the interaction so as to help both the group and the individual volunteer. The imaginary set and props were described carefully during the interview. The role play proceeded and was terminated when time was called. At that time, the consultant again interviewed the "instructor" volunteer and the "learner" volunteer before the whole group. The first question related to how they each had felt during the instruction process—their feelings about themselves, their feelings about the other individual. The second question was: "how effective do you think the instructional process was?" Then, the consultant asked for group response to three questions:

- What was good about the instructional technique used in the role play?

- What could the instructor have done to improve the process?

- What could the learner have done to improve the process?

Throughout the discussion period, the visual transparency outlining the steps in how to instruct was displayed on the screen, so the group could relate their critique to the principles brought out in the presentation. Throughout the comments and questions, the consultant wove portions of the content material presented earlier. This discussion concluded, and volunteers for the second role play were requested. Several individuals volunteered and a different problem was selected, although the same process of interview, portrayal, and discussion was followed.

At the conclusion of the two role plays, the consultant drew that segment to a close with a five-minute description of observations on the role plays and the basics of on-the-job instruction. Interest in the role plays had been high with the discussion period providing a ready exchange of dialogue between participants, role players, and consultant. Now the consultant effected a transition to the next segment of the workshop, and since about half the time in the morning had been used, a mid-point break was announced before shifting to a new topic.

During the break, the consultant and the planning group members informally asked learners in one-to-one conversations how they thought it was going, what they were getting out of it, and what they might suggest changing. Shortly before time to resume the session, the consultant asked the planning group members for the feedback they had gathered and, on that basis, made some adjustments in the remaining part of the program. One suggestion had been to have copies made of a couple of the transparencies, so these were copied and distributed at the end of the session.

After the break, another 20-minute presentation covered on-the-job instruction as part of each supervisor's job, described the training function, and related it to other supervisory responsibilities. Again, comments and questions were requested from the group. This time, there were more than before. At the conclusion of the discussion, a random numbering by the consultant was used to assign participants to five smaller groups. The case study was distributed to each participant and time set aside to enable everyone to read the case carefully. Then, each group was asked to take twenty minutes to discuss the situation described in the case and to come up with recommendations of what they would do given the situation in the case. After the 20 minutes, the entire group reconvened and heard reports and recommendations from each small group. Again, the useful transparencies from the presentation were projected, so the group could relate their specific comments to the general principles given in the presentation.

At the conclusion of the reports and general group discussion, the consultant addressed one question to the whole group and invited individuals who wished to comment to do so: "What do you plan to do with what you have learned?" Several individuals had specific plans, some had general thoughts. Several did not comment.

Then, the consultant requested that some time be spent on an **evaluation** of the workshop, for this activity was an example of work-related instruction and all might learn from applying the general principles to the workshop they had just experienced. This process also reinforced the application of those principles in a commonly shared experience. Several questions were posed on the flip chart:

- To what extent did we achieve our objectives?
- What went well and was helpful?
- What should have been different/could have been better?

Several participants spoke freely, more were silent. Several good points were noted, and some suggestions were made for improvement. Some participants stated that they had discovered needs that they did not perceive before. In the wrap-up, the consultant gave a brief review of the objectives, topics, and activities of the workshop and then added a personal view as to what some of the strong points were and what did not work out as satisfactorily as expected. Additional sources for further help in training and development work were suggested for participants who wanted to explore the subject further and in greater depth.

Following the workshop, the planning group lunched with the consultant and discussed in greater detail their reflections on the workshop. At this meeting, the consultant suggested that a brief evaluative questionnaire be sent later to each learner to obtain second thoughts and perhaps comments from those who had not spoken during the evaluation interview.

*****

This detailed look at an illustration of a single staff development activity offers a perspective that may be useful for seeing the principles and guidelines at work in an actual situation. As a tool to assist effective implementation of learning activities, Figure 23 (p. 184) provides a brief checklist, listing essential reminders for some of the key components that need to be coordinated in planning and producing an activity. It cites references to the Guidelines that are most relevant

Figure 23
Checklist for Implementation of
Staff Development Efforts

NEEDS   (Guidelines 1 and 2)

____ Needs identified, analyzed, and priorities established?
____ Both individual and organizational needs included?
____ Learning is the most appropriate answer to identified needs?

OBJECTIVES   (Guideline 3)

____ Program objectives and activity objectives defined on the basis of identified needs?
____ Activity objectives state learning, behavior, or change sought?
____ Activity objectives congruent with program objectives?

METHOD   (Guideline 5)

____ Method selected appropriate for learnings sought?
____ Method appropriate and consistent with organizational style and learner acceptance?

LEARNERS   (Guideline 8)

____ Selection of learners on basis of need and interest?
____ Appropriate preparation and reward to motivate involvement?

ADMINISTRATIVE COORDINATION   (Guideline 6)

____ Clear and adequate flow of communication planned and done?
____ Well defined decision-making responsibilities?
____ Planning, implementation, and evaluation processes coordinated?

EDUCATIONAL STAFF   (Guideline 7)

____ Available and competent in relation to knowledge and method?
____ Responsibilities and expectations clearly outlined?

EDUCATIONAL DESIGN   (Guideline 5 and 7)

____ Content and process relevant to the activity?
____ Built-in means to assure feedback?

RESOURCES   (Guidelines 4 and 9)

____ Funding is sufficient to support the activity?
____ Facilities contain needed equipment and are adaptable to method?
____ Appropriate materials distributed at appropriate times?

EVALUATION   (Part III)

____ Results and on-going evaluation are assigned responsibilities?
____ Data is valid and usable?

to that component. Such a worksheet cannot eliminate the complexity, but it can perhaps provide a handy reference to keep track of the essential components.

The amount of time and preparation taken for a half-day workshop is extensive and expensive, more so than is usually realized ahead of time. Thus, the more benefits that can be obtained, the more the investment will pay off. In this example, there were several kinds of benefits, some of which were direct and some of which were incidental. The planning group benefited from the experiences of working together, of learning in a greater depth through inter-action with the consultant, of seeing the total picture of a learning activity. The individuals in this group then become a resource for the library, able to help others in planning learning activities because they were aware of the dimen-sions of such an effort and able to plan with fewer mistakes because of their experience. The participants benefited very directly from what they learned, applying it to their job responsibilities. Presumably staff members who are super-vised by the participants will benefit from improved instruction and, thus, will be able to do their tasks better. The library benefits from more effective and productive staff members and the public from better service from more compe-tent personnel.

For clarity, the example used here has assumed that the objectives for this activity refer to it alone. In reality, however, several activities might be planned to achieve a single program objective, implying that they would need to be more closely coordinated with each other than indicated here. For instance, a site visit, an in-house demonstration, and supervisory coaching might be three activities that could be combined to enable personnel to use new equipment such as a circulation charging system. Conversely, a single activity may work toward several program objectives, such as when a single seminar session is used to increase staff awareness of a community need, to learn how to inventory avail-able community resources, and to reinforce earlier learned skills in program planning and working with cross-cultural groups.

Another qualification to be pointed out is that a library with a compre-hensive staff development program will often make use of continuing education activities available outside the library for specialized needs or for opportunities that are too difficult or expensive to produce in-house. Smaller libraries may logically anticipate utilizing proportionally more outside continuing education opportunities than larger libraries that have more resources as well as more people with common needs. These outside activities might include packaged learning programs using self-instructional methods, a library management work-shop done within the local area by the state library agency, a networking con-ference at the state or regional level sponsored by a professional association, an affirmative action seminar done by the municipal or county government, or a site visit to a nearby organization using new equipment and procedures about to be introduced into the library.

Outside activities may not be as easily integrated into a staff development program as those activities developed within the organization. Outside learning opportunities, however, often offer unique specializations, renowned resource persons, or hard-to-get equipment or facilities. As with in-house activities, the objectives, the educational staff and methods, and the cost of the continuing education activity must be carefully reviewed before assuming that the anticipated results are realistic and that they will indeed meet library and personal learning needs.

The principles that are illustrated here pertain similarly to activities within a continuing education program of a state library agency or library association. There, however, the integration of learning and working is less possible to plan for, and often impossible to assure. The greatest challenge for the continuing education program lies beyond its ability to produce occasional activities of quality and substance. How can the program help assure that the learning gained during an activity will be conveyed back to the library and applied to job responsibilities? How can the program improve the possibilities that "improved library service through more competent library personnel" is an actual outcome as well as a stated intent? Developing responsive solutions to these very real questions would help to answer those who criticize continuing education based on the questionable degree of application of learnings in exchange for the funding spent on such activities. Several factors are important here: a thorough needs assessment to be sure activities that attract learners are based on real needs; instructional methods that enable in-depth learning and relate that learning to work situations; adequate communication with both the learner and the library to establish expectations about the kind of learning that is likely and the support that is necessary from the library to enable its application; linkage between continuing education and staff development efforts to weave their approaches and results more closely together. The ability to apply learnings on the job is a shared responsibility, and if each contribution is not made, the application is not as likely to occur.

Summary

Generally speaking, the ability of learners to learn is enhanced by access to topics through preferred modes of learning. When varied and relevant activities are available in a program and offer content and methods that motivate learners and enable them to learn, the probability that learning will occur is great. Factors such as awareness and accessibility of the activity, knowledge of the need(s), the ability and encouragement to attend, in addition to well-assembled components described in the previous Guidelines—these elements all contribute to the learner's capacity to learn. Inevitably, all these elements are not usually perfectly ordered and this draws the issue: the ability to provide for a quality learning program the funding to support it, the motivation to engage in it, the capability of producing it.

But, both staff development and continuing education programs can make good use of the action plan approach or other tools to insure that both management and educational functions are fulfilled. Implementation shows how well-managed and educationally sound the activity is, giving some indication of the learning effectiveness of the design, the skill of the instructional staff, the value of the methods and materials. A careful look at a particular activity can also help to improve subsequent activities and the program as a whole, if planning then incorporates the more effective components again and modifies those elements that did not meet expectations. Implementation links planning and evaluation, concluding the former and initiating the latter in relation to an activity.

Implementation brings together all the planning and preparation into a single focus in the program—a learning activity. Here, issues are raised, problems are resolved, learning occurs. Implementation is, at last, the "doin' part," and an action plan approach to implementing activities specifies what needs to be done. Especially useful for the inexperienced, an action plan helps to assure the all-important communication, coordination, and decision-making by activating the various roles and responsibilities necessary for the activity's planning and implementation. Although linked to the entirety of the learning program, each activity is also distinct, bringing together its own topic, method, learners, educators, and other specifics.

SUMMARY OF PART II

Implementation is the point where action occurs based on the plans made earlier, thus revealing the validity and importance of sound planning. As learning activities come to life, they offer tangible evidence of the roles, responsibilities, and resources that comprise the learning program. Initial planning identifies the learning needs and sets the program objectives, then outlines the learning activities with their objectives and methods. Implementation then brings these plans alive. How the components are assembled to implement each activity varies, depending on the situation and its opportunities, as well as on differing organizational and personal styles. Continuous planning and evaluation thread throughout the implementation of each learning activity, identifying and responding to the need for subsequent decisions.

Both educational and management decisions are necessary to produce each learning activity. The effectiveness of these roles and responsibilities in conjunction with one another is a major key to the success of each activity and of the program as a whole. Implementation brings these together to accomplish what is intended, to fulfill what is decided. Some decisions are from the management aspect of the program and some from its educational aspect, but a smooth blend of both kinds of decisions is necessary. Since these responsibilities are distinct and different, however, it is usually advisable to assign them to different individuals.

Most of the capability of the program rests with the abilities of the administrator, who is the central person responsible for the program and often the one to manage the specific learning activities as well. Although the program administrator's role varies depending on the situation, the program, and the individual, the administrator is primarily responsible for communication, coordination, and decision-making. Thus, the administrator is likely to have the most consistent, integrated view of the entire program as well as a keen eye on each activity. The main strength of an administrator is knowing what has to be done, when, and how—and then being able to accomplish that.

The educational staff, as "agents of learning," contribute their characteristics and expertise to the success of each activity. Their skills and knowledge lie in three areas: (1) presenting information, (2) designing and implementing educational methods, and (3) managing the learning process. Much of the effectiveness of the educational staff depends on their knowledge and abilities together with the administrator's ability to select and prepare appropriate educators to meet the activity's requirements.

A third major role and responsibility in implementation is that of the learner. Each individual learner must decide on his or her own personal and professional goals and develop effective strategies for learning that take advantage of available information and opportunities. A personal commitment to learning grows from the desire to be active, qualified and, satisfied from meeting work challenges successfully.

Involvement and flexibility are also both important factors for successful implementation. Involvement reinforces the learning process, assures the relevance of the program and its activities, and builds the program as an integrated organizational function. But involvement does not just happen. Ways to achieve it must be built into each activity, the job of the administrator and educational staff. Not only does learner involvement increase the depth of learning possible, but it also prompts an interest and motivation to learn. Further, it increases the likelihood that learners will make ready and apt application of their learnings on the job. Involvement also encourages the library, agency, or association support of the program. Although many points for involvement are possible in the planning phase, even more are possible during implementation.

Flexibility enables modifications necessary to achieve successful implementation of the objectives of the program and its activities. Original plans may become invalid due to changing circumstances or later information. If the program and activities are structured with effective ways to make adjustments, each will be more likely to be continuously relevant. The factor of flexibility assumes not only that such adjustments will be necessary, but also that alternatives have been considered, and that the willingness to change exists. The administrator, the educational staff, and the learners all benefit from being involved and from being flexible.

The key roles and responsibilities for each activity require resources to support the learning process. Although not a substitute for good learning design, appropriate facilities, equipment, and materials are important. Creatively selected, carefully coordinated, and skillfully used, these ingredients are chosen and assembled by the administrator and the educational staff for the activity's implementation. Several purposes are served by these resources: (1) to support, sustain, and reinforce learning, (2) to interest, stimulate, and motivate learners, and (3) to clarify ideas, deepen understanding, and integrate concepts. Often these resources make learnings tangible and more easily applied to real-life situations.

Implementation brings these roles, responsibilities, and resources together. The soundness of planning becomes apparent as the program and its activities are implemented. Planning built the framework; the finish work, the decor, and the furnishings assembled during implementation will determine the capability and character of the program. Implementation is the action part of the action plan and the point where the viability of the planning process is tested. Lynton states that for program planners, "the task is to find ways of relating theory and practice most usefully. . . . " When this task is well done, he indicates, the program will assure the individual competence in specific situations, with the ability to anticipate future situations.[24]

Implementation begins the payoff for the investment of time, funds, and effort. Indications of results become apparent: learners acquire new knowledge and skills, program administrators and educators see results from their preparations, the library, agency, or association sees the impact from their efforts. Implementing activities in a scattershot manner, however, will limit these payoffs. Without the coordination and direction of a program, the achievements of each single activity will be limited; such results likely will neither address the long-range needs of library personnel nor address issues in the library field with more than a temporary pallative. Such returns will be primarily short-range, not so substantial or lasting as a sound program could assure. Activities within such a sound program are deliberate segments, carefully chosen to work towards program-level goals as well as toward their own objectives. Evaluation will not only determine past successes and difficulties but also help plan wisely for future activities and programs.

NOTES

[1] J.R. Kidd, *How Adults Learn*, Revised ed. (New York: Association Press, 1973) [term used throughout].

[2] Leonard Nadler, *Developing Human Resources*. (Houston, Texas: Gulf Publishing Co., 1970), pp. 174-201.

[3] Rolf P. Lynton and Udai Pareek, *Training for Development*. (Homewood, Illinois: Richard D. Irwin, 1967), p. 8.

[4] Malcolm S. Knowles, "Separating the Amateurs from the Pros in Training," *Training and Development Journal* 30, no. 9:16-17 (September 1976).

[5] Cyril O. Houle, "The Educators of Adults," in *Handbook of Adult Education*, edited by Robert M. Smith, George F. Aker, and J.R. Kidd. (New York: Macmillan, 1970), p. 110.

[6] Charles E. Kozoll and Curtis Ulmer, eds., *In-Service Training: Philosophy, Processes and Operational Techniques* (Englewood Cliffs, New Jersey: Prentice Hall, 1972), p. 45.

[7] Ibid.

[8] Hedley G. Dimock, *How to Plan Staff Training Programs* (Montreal, Canada: Sir George Williams University, 1973), p. 2.

[9] Ibid., p. 46.

[10] Carl R. Rogers, *Freedom to Learn* (Columbus, Ohio: Charles E. Merrill Publishing Co., 1969), p. 217.

[11] Kidd, *How Adults Learn*, p. 269.

[12] Ibid.

[13] Joe Washtien, *A Guide for Planning and Teaching Continuing Education Courses* [Medical Library Association] (Washington, D.C.: Continuing Library Education Network and Exchange, 1975), p. 29.

[14] Martha Jane K. Zachert, "Continuing Education for Librarians: The Role of the Learner," Library Lecture, no. 24, University of Tennessee Library (April 20, 1972), p. 47.

[15] Vincent E. Giuliano, "Communication Levels Involved in Change," *In* Richard C. Huseman, Cal M. Logue, and Dwight L. Freshley, *Readings in Interpersonal and Organizational Communication* (Boston: Holbrook Press, 1969), pp. 177-200.

[16] Malcolm S. Knowles, *The Modern Practice of Adult Education: Andragogy Versus Pedagogy* (New York: Association Press, [1970]), p. 51.

[17] Gary Dickenson, *Teaching Adults: A Handbook for Instructors* (Toronto: New Press, 1973), p. 3.

[18] Albert R. Wight, "Participative Education and the Inevitable Revolution," *Journal of Creative Behavior* 4, no. 4:278 (Fall 1971).

[19] Zachert, *Role of the Learner*, p. 42.

[20] Kidd, *How Adults Learn*, p. 282.

[21] W. Warner Burke and Richard Beckhard, eds., *Conference Planning* [Selected Readings Series Six], 2nd ed. (Washington, D. C.: NTL Institute for Applied Behavioral Science, 1970), pp. 99-100.

[22] Zachert, *Role of the Learner*, p. 42.

[23] Edgar Dale, *Audio-Visual Methods in Teaching*, rev. ed. (New York: Dryden Press, 1954), p. 43.

[24] Lynton and Pareek, *Training for Development*, p. 109.

PART III–EVALUATING THE LEARNING PROGRAM

Planning and evaluation provide information, guidance, and decisions to direct implementation. Thus, successful implementation is most likely to result when both the planning and evaluation processes are effective and coordinated in a mutually helpful way. Evaluation is a means of discovering if and how objectives are being accomplished and what might be modified in order to assure the desired results. When systematically planned and done, evaluation provides timely knowledge of what is happening at present and the base for making appropriate decisions when preparing for what is likely to happen next. **Evaluation** is defined here as the planned process used to assemble and utilize that information necessary for effective, on-going decision-making and for accountability.

Basically, evaluation is a very common-sense procedure that people do, more or less effectively, in most facets of their personal and job lives: assembling and using information to judge a situation, first, to project possible impacts and implications and, finally, to decide on the most appropriate course of action. Yet, often these "evaluation" procedures are not realized as being what they are.

Likewise, the importance of evaluation is often unrealized by those responsible for planning and implementing learning activities. Perhaps this is the major reason for the lack of substantial evaluation efforts as an integral, significant component of learning programs and their activities. Good evaluation, however, can:

- furnish accurate information to assist further planning, to improve decision-making, and to document achievements,
- determine to what extent a program and/or activity is accomplishing its goals and objectives, and what impacts are occurring,
- identify program strengths and weaknesses and the reasons for specific successes and failures,
- assure more consistent quality in learning activities and efforts,
- reinforce learning and develop an awareness of growth and change,
- determine the cost and benefits of the program and its activities,
- justify the investment and answer demands for accountability,
- produce documentation that allows information to be shared with others.

Although few evaluation efforts are able to accomplish all of these possibilities at once, earnest and ambitious efforts, along with appropriate evaluation methods and techniques, can achieve many of them simultaneously.

In spite of these possibilities, evaluation tends to be the exception rather than the rule in relation to learning activities. Although the concept of evaluation is frequently endorsed as a significant precept and a desired procedure, actual evaluation is often makeshift and of little value or use. Ritualistic evaluation procedures, such as participant reaction forms, are often formulated at the last minute and have little depth or impact. Inadequate evaluation fails to meet the need, yet creates the illusion of doing so when it actually is not. Valid evaluation is more than just the means to channel impressionistic information into a required report form. Rather, consistent, purposeful, creative evaluation should be present throughout the learning activities and the functions of program management. Surely the practice of evaluation warrants as much exercise as its precept is advocated.

Even when exercised with a basic common-sense approach, evaluation requires thought and planning. After the purpose of the evaluation is determined, the most appropriate method to use in a particular situation must be selected. Methods of collecting and analyzing the information must be valid, reliable, accurate, and congruent with the purposes for which the evaluation is being done. Reporting and utilizing the information must assure that the appropriate people get the necessary information—the payoff of the evaluation process.

As an active and dynamic process, a pragmatic, common-sense evaluation might be planned around these key questions: 1) what needs to be known? 2) who has that information? 3) how can the necessary information be obtained? when? where? and 4) what is to be done with the information and when? Obviously such an evaluation will be concerned with the program or activity from beginning to end, and perhaps beyond. Most evaluations of present learning efforts, however, reveal the apparent belief that evaluation occurs only at the conclusion of the effort. Yet, information is certainly essential before that time to make decisions. Evaluation, planned systematically around these questions, is more likely to produce the kind of information that can be used for the important decisions that will need to be made throughout the program or during the activity.

In order to systematically plan and produce evaluation findings, several factors are important. When present, these assure that the evaluation process will occur and that, most likely, it will be appropriate and relevant to the purposes for which it is set forth. Learners, program planners, and administrators should have:

- an understanding of the importance of the evaluation function,
- a commitment to the evaluation function,
- open and honest contribution of information needed for the evaluation process,
- a knowledge of what kinds of decisions will be affected by the evaluation,
- access to resources with knowledge of how to plan for and get solid evaluation data,
- acceptance and use of the information obtained through evaluation.

When these factors exist, whether in relation to the learning program or in connection with other functions, thorough evaluation is likely to be of proven value. Where these factors do not exist, anything more than superficial evaluation will be difficult to establish.

At its two extremes, evaluation ranges from being non-existent "because it is not required" to being very esoteric, involving complex research methodology and statistical findings. Each of the many alternatives between these extremes can be tested for its relevance to a particular situation with such questions as: 1) What are the important factors in this situation? 2) What is the balance between the value received and the cost required? and 3) How does this alternative fit with evaluation methods and practices already in place in the organization? A suitable level for each specific situation can be found to fit the capabilities, resources, and requirements of both the program and the organization.

Evaluation is becoming more of a priority and a value, and, in some cases, a mandate. Governmental requirements, evolving professional norms, and internal and external demands for accountability are increasingly strong forces at work, creating pressures to evaluate competently and meaningfully. From the present indicators, this is likely to be a trend of some depth and duration.

The intrinsic importance of evaluation is being increasingly acknowledged also. The major results of evaluation is that this information can be used so that new actions can be taken, new decisions can be made, new behaviors can be implemented, new competencies can be practiced, and new questions can be answered. Learners find that evaluation reinforces their learning and helps them to pinpoint their needs for further learning. Program planners find indications of needed modifications in order to achieve greater program effectiveness and to cull what doesn't work well. Administrators find new strengths and resources within the organization and justification for extending or reducing program funding. People outside the organization find evaluation reports a source of new ideas to implement elsewhere, with caveats that assist in planning for adaptation and application of those original ideas.

Evaluation offers an opportunity for review and renewal—and for possible redirection for individual staff members and for the organization as a whole. As such, it is a logical check-point to encourage reflection: it prompts and "allows" introspection and self-examination. Growth, for individuals and for the organization, may be anticipated as a major outcome from the process of evaluation, for it becomes another point for learning. Awareness of this as a learning possibility is important because preparation for that learning may be important. Growth and change may bring difficulties as well as excitement, pain as well as achievement. Evaluation can catalyze the awareness of the changes that are occurring and can help in understanding the nature and direction of those changes.

In spite of the importance of these reasons, strong and consistent resistance to evaluation comes from a number of reasons. Several barriers may exist. A major one is the general lack of understanding of what evaluation is and how it can be used. This results in a lack of opportunities to design, develop, and practice evaluation. In turn, this creates few evaluation models or examples within the library field and, for those that do exist, there is limited visibility in library literature or conferences. Thus, for individuals with limited experience in evaluation, little opportunity is available within the library field to adapt and learn.

As a consequence of this situation, access to knowledgeable people who can help plan for and obtain solid evaluation information is difficult. Evaluation expertise available within librarianship is limited. This compound problem means that program planners, educational staff, and learners may not know and understand the importance of the evaluation function. They may not be committed to the precept of evaluation, or may not be willing to contribute openly and honestly to evaluation that is sought from them, or might not accept and use the information ethically and responsibly once it is obtained. One result is that there is presently no widely accepted or established norm affirming that evaluation is important and essential. Standards are just now beginning to be widely accepted for the evaluation of library service programs. Norms that encourage quality evaluation in learning programs may be some time in the future. The implications for pre-service, in-service and continuing education in librarianship are worth considering closely.

A frequently cited barrier is the cost of evaluation. Although, in some instances, cost is a valid reason for curtailing evaluation, cost is not usually a sufficient reason for totally disregarding the evaluation process. At times, cost may be a superficial reason used to justify ignoring evaluation. Or, cost may be a barrier based more on assumptions than on a real situation. In the long run, it may cost more not to evaluate than to evaluate, since part of the price of not evaluating is the cost of perpetuating ineffective practices. This can be expensive to the organization and exploitative of the personnel. The number of mistakes that a sound evaluation can prevent will offset a good share of the costs of it. Full use of evaluation information that can serve other purposes, such as identifying resources or problem areas for the organization, is another cost saver. The costs as well as the benefits of evaluation should be understood by both staff and administrators concerned with the program.

Another barrier to evaluation results from the complexity of people and of organizations. This makes it difficult to ascertain which effects and changes really result from the program or activity and which are due to other factors that may be entirely external to the program or activity. Consequently, most conclusions will be somewhat inexact, and completely reliable evaluation results in relation to the program will not be possible. Even well-planned evaluation with clear and well-defined program objectives cannot always isolate and discern the finer distinctions. Inevitably, a part of evaluation will necessarily be subjective judgement. Most evaluation is not intended to be a tightly controlled research study, but rather a functional, informational, and decision-making tool. Unrealistic claims made for the function or the results of evaluation can raise expectations, which may be later disappointed.

An important barrier is often the vested interests of those people involved in and responsible for the program. They may take its value for granted, resist "being examined," and be preoccupied with the demands of their regular workload. This may be the result of a reluctance to take time out to look at the program and its activities. Or, it may be a natural wariness or defensiveness, based on a sense that their assumptions are being challenged or that they are on trial. Most administrators, educators, and even learners have invested time, effort, and ego in the program, and evaluation may be seen by them as meddling, a waste of time, or interference with the normal activities. Generally, evaluation is concerned with long-range views and achievements, whereas administrators and educators look at the immediate "how to." Thus, a conflict of these interests may exist.

Related to this is another barrier. The word "evaluation" triggers past associations and meanings in learners, program developers, and administrators alike. Evaluation may be equated with a personal judgement, one that is usually passed downwards in the organization and often negative in tone. Thus, any data-gathering activity, whether focused on the program or on the person can be seen by some people as threatening. The results of such feelings can often be observed in the deliberate or unconscious distortion of evaluation information, in an intentional lack of response in those being evaluated, or in rejection of the program. This barrier is very difficult to overcome. It generally can be altered only with time and consistent, sincere efforts to help those responsible for evaluation and those whose learning or work is being evaluated to understand the purpose and use of that evaluation.

If these barriers delay or prevent evaluation, further planning and successful implementation may be inhibited, and continuation of the program may be jeopardized. Simple efforts at evaluation can grow with experience into more complex approaches addressing more concerns of learners, program administrators, educators, and the sponsoring organization. If never begun, however, the evaluation process has no chance to improve. Evaluation can determine the program's effectiveness in enabling learning to happen and its ability to produce learning activities efficiently. It can describe how far the program has come in relation to what it intended, what it accomplished in relation to what was hoped for. Evaluation brings to full circle the cycle of planning-implementing-evaluating and can, in fact, set into motion a new level of that cycle.

Evaluation is a means of obtaining a reading on some of the factors that are at work in a particular program or activity. Little assurance is possible that the findings will be comprehensive, conclusive, or helpful. Considering the complexity of human behavior and the factors that affect it, and considering the fact that evaluation procedures and instruments are not finely tuned, it is little wonder that, if seen as a panacea, evaluation will be likely to result in disappointed expectations than in a widely acclaimed and followed practice. However, if its limitations are understood and its potentials fully used, evaluation will provide ample return for the investment in it.

Aimed at obtaining and utilizing valid information, Part III presents Guidelines for deciding the purposes for evaluation, for framing an evaluation plan to collect and analyze needed information, and for the ways to report and use that information. The themes and precepts emphasized in earlier Parts continue here—broad-based participation, program flexibility, and the importance of integrated planning, implementing, and evaluating processes. A basic method is suggested in these Guidelines, but additional resources are indicated for those seeking more specialized methods and procedures.

GUIDELINE 11–DETERMINE EVALUATION PURPOSES

On approaching the process of evaluation, the first questions to be asked are: Why is the evaluation to be done? What is necessary to discover? What must be known? What decisions will hinge on evaluative information? *Why* the program and its activities are to be evaluated determines the appropriate methods and procedures to use. Only after "why evaluate?" has been answered can *how* to do it be logically decided.

Purposive evaluation protects the investment of time, effort, and funds that are part of the program and part of any evaluation function that is undertaken. To approach evaluation with little forethought, scant planning and random purpose presents a high risk for the evaluation and perhaps for the program itself. Early identification of the reasons for evaluating can aid in interrelating the planning and evaluation processes. Once the evaluation purposes are at least tentatively determined, planning can designate when and where evaluation will be needed to gather and supply information in order to make essential decisions or to fill necessary reports. In contrast, if the purposes for evaluation are not defined early, the range of options of how to evaluate will be severely limited, and the results may not, in the end, be able to satisfy the need for evaluation. If the reasons for evaluation are never determined, the evaluative strategies and techniques will not be sufficiently focused or integrated with the total program to make the most of the potential returns on the investment required for the evaluation.

Evaluation provides the opportunity to look critically and systematically at the learning program and to see to what extent it fulfills the expectations held for it. The means and methods to evaluate staff development and continuing education must be carefully planned. To some extent, evaluation occurs whether or not it is planned because people inevitably observe and draw conclusions from their observations, infer and make judgements from their inferences. Trice and Roman comment, however, that, "While such common-sense evaluation will occur 'anyway,' it is usually unsystematic, hap-hazard and impressionistic. Training specialists will be on much safer ground with systematic information, regardless of whether such data supports or refutes opinions generated via informal appraisals."[1]

When evaluation plans are laid early, better evaluation is likely to result as well as improved planning. For example, when program planners consider why they are evaluating near the time that they are determining program and/or activity objectives, those objectives are more likely to be able to be evaluated than if these two processes are separated. In other words, the measurability of objectives is more likely to be considered if planning for evaluation occurs simultaneously with the program planning process. Identifying the purposes for evaluation provides the basis for planning how that evaluation will be done. And, the means to accomplish it can be interwoven with planning for the use of the resources and the assignment of the roles and responsibilities, thus assuring that it is part of the fabric of the whole program and present at vital points throughout implementation of activities.

This Guideline is concerned with the range of purposes for evaluation, the criteria to use in selecting those purposes, and the procedures to choose those purposes. Examples illustrate the various types of purposes for evaluation. The word "purpose" is deliberately used here in relation to the objectives of the evaluation plan to help maintain the distinction between program objectives and activity objectives and those for the evaluation plan.

Diversity of Views on Evaluation

The number and nature of purposes can range widely once the decision to evaluate has been made. Purposes will vary with the needs to be addressed and with the attitudes and abilities of the program's decision makers. This choice of evaluation purposes is further complicated when the complexity of people and their views is added to the complexity of the program. I. L. Goldstein describes the spectrum of views on evaluation as typified by "the negativists, the positivists, and the frustrates":

> negativists are those individuals who feel that evaluation of training is either impossible or unnecessary—that the value of formal instructional programs cannot be demonstrated by quantitative analysis. . . . positivists . . .believe that scientific evaluation of training is the only worthwhile approach. . . . In the center of these two groups are the frustrates, who recognize that training programs must be evaluated but are concerned with the methodology necessary to perform the evaluation. This group recognizes that all programs will be evaluated either formally or informally; thus it is concerned with the quality of the evaluation rather than with the decision whether to evaluate or not.[2]

A major problem is faced when several individuals are responsible for program planning and evaluation and, among them, they present this entire spectrum.

A second spectrum is presented when the choice of focus for the evaluation must be made. Evaluation in some cases is directly of the program itself with a careful look at such things as the efficiency of the operation, adequacy of staff assignments, work flow, and the degree of accomplishment of the program objectives. Other programs focus on individual learning activities, viewing the learner selection, the educational staff performance, the evidence of applications of learnings, and the accomplishment of the activity objectives. Most evaluations seek information about both the program and the activity levels with various proportions of emphasis. Focus on the learner, a common approach for staff development, is less possible or frequent for continuing education efforts.

Depending on the objectives and the needs of a particular program, the focus of the evaluation may be on the learner, the program or activity as a whole, a specific activity, or the organization. All of these will need to be considered to some extent in most programs, although the emphasis may differ. For learners and supervisors, evaluation of the learner in terms of improved competencies, applied knowledge, and changed behavior will be the most important since most objectives address this kind of outcome. For program planners and the administrator, evaluation of the content, methodology, and educators will be essential to indicate the improvements and modifications necessary for further planning and implementation. For directors, evaluation of the impacts made upon the organization itself by the program or activities will be most vital. Evaluation of the effectiveness of the program in general will probably interest each individual and group affected by or involved in the program's efforts.

If a group is responsible for planning the program's evaluation, an internal tension may result if the full range of each attitudinal spectrum is represented. As in the first spectrum, the negativists will not want to evaluate formally at all, believing that what happens is self-evident and does not need complicated mechanisms to prove. The positivists will strive to incorporate a carefully planned scientific approach to obtaining and analyzing the information in order to prove the value of the learning activities in the program. The frustrates will want a way of knowing what is happening and what is being achieved but will want that to be pragmatic and timely, aimed at immediate use, documentation, or dissemination. If all of these are represented in the group, achieving balance and agreement may be difficult. If the determination of the purposes for evaluation is the responsibility of a single individual, the type and extent of the chosen evaluation will largely represent the point of view of that person. This will ease the initial decision-making, but may only delay the issue being confronted, as others involved in the program—educational staff, funders, and others—need evaluative information that may not be available because of the earlier choice of purposes.

In the second spectrum, that of emphasis, the purposes for the evaluation will differ. For example, in a state agency wishing a program emphasis, one of the purposes might be "to identify the impact of the continuing education program on other agency functions and services to the state's library personnel." Or, a library with a focus on activities might wish to "determine the degree of acceptance by library personnel of various instructional methods and types of learning approaches." An association emphasizing the program itself might propose "to determine if a decentralized program approach to continuing education is the most effective and feasible to use in producing learning activities for association members," whereas one with an activities focus might intend "to emphasize the use of appropriate evaluation methods in all activities and provide immediate and timely feedback to assure that the activity is meeting learner needs." Of course, the evaluation emphasis selected will likely be linked closely to the program and/or activity objectives, since one of the main evaluation purposes would be to determine the extent that the desired objectives have been attained and the amount of progress made in the intended direction.

Criteria

To guide the choice of evaluation purposes, three general criteria are useful. First, the evaluation must be planned to meet priority needs for information. That is, if the program administrator requires prompt, accurate readings on how effective or acceptable certain methods, educators, or materials are, the evaluation should be geared to provide that information, when available, so it can be used in subsequent planning. Or, appropriate evaluative information for the program should be timed to meet the schedule of organizational reporting periods concerned with planning and budgeting purposes, which, in turn, enables the program's needs to be met.

As purposes are being selected, several specific areas of need can be addressed: 1) Some facets of the evaluation must meet the needs of the organization. (Is the organization facing impending changes? Can evaluation help to anticipate and prepare for those changes; Is the organization under pressure for accountability? Can this evaluation be integrated with other organizational functions?) 2) Some facets of the evaluation must meet the needs of the program itself. (What activities and functions are anticipated most need to be modified? How can evaluation be linked with planning and implementation? What predictably weak areas will require close monitoring? What are the most crucial results being sought? Are evaluation purposes congruent with program objectives? 3) Some facets of the evaluation must meet the needs of the learners. (Will the evaluation help reinforce the learning? Can evaluation provide constructive self-awareness for learners?

Will evaluation interest and motivate individuals to engage in further efforts? What kind of evaluation do learners think is important?) Since each program and situation is somewhat unique, the specifics of these areas of need will vary. But, if evaluation meets real needs, it is likely to also meet the other two general criteria.

The second criterion is that the evaluation be planned to yield valid, useful information. For instance, if learner opinions are now recognized as valid information, that kind of information should not predominate until that attitude is modified. If an outside evaluator is to be the major individual involved in gathering, analyzing, and reporting information, that person will need to have the respect and trust of the organization, the program administrator, and others involved in the program. If an in-depth evaluation of the program and its activities would be blocked because of a fear of criticism and change, a less rigorous approach might be advisable. If the evaluation process or findings are not accepted or useful, the value of the effort and expense is questionable.

One measure of acceptability is often its congruency with the style of the organization. In other words, if an agency or an association uses a particular evaluation method for all programs, that method should also be used for the learning program if possible. This might be supplemented with additional approaches, however, if those are necessary in order to meet other criteria or requirements. Or, if a library is characterized by a participatory style, the evaluation approach selected should coincide with and utilize the strengths of that style. If, on the other hand, that does not fit the style of the organization, it would be an inappropriate and perhaps risky approach to select.

Thirdly, the evaluation must be feasible. The scope of the evaluation effort must be within the resources available. Since evaluation funding can sometimes be obtained separately from program funding, that possibility might be explored. If the desires for evaluation are enthusiastic, but the resources of time, money, and skills are limited, the nature of planning for evaluation will have to be realistic. In looking at such resources, Arden Grotelueschen cautions:

> Estimates of the costs of acquiring information should take into account hidden costs to the program. These include time lost to the program by evaluating; tradeoffs and alternative uses of funds; and human costs such as invasion of privacy, dangers of creating negative attitudes and reactions, sparking controversy, or generating pressure on program personnel. These may be compared with the costs of not evaluating.[3]

"Feasible" and "realistic" should not hinder vision beyond immediate and visible restrictions, however. As she proposes a model for quality control of continuing education, Julie Virgo stresses: "The important function of quality control when resources *are* limited cannot be overemphasized. The systematic application of quality control throughout the educational process will allow the best products to be developed by optimally using the resources available."[4] In other words, the investment in evaluation may, in view of the whole picture, enable the best management of program resources available rather than expending them in unproductive ways. Thus, evaluation may be most needed just when it seems least possible.

Purposes

These criteria can be helpful to develop or test the purposes selected for evaluation. Several purposes can often be simultaneously accomplished through the methods and techniques within an evaluation plan. Before the purposes are selected for a particular situation, however, it is useful to consider a wide range of possible purposes carefully. Setting forth the reasons why evaluation is to be done is a necessary first step to establish directions for a plan of evaluation and to build a foundation for getting the essential information. On the other hand, limiting the scope and number of puproses to some extent is often wise and encourages reasonable expectations for the evaluation.

As a help to those people seeking purposes for evaluation, Edward A. Suchman presents six considerations that "deal with basic questions that need to be answered in formulating the objectives of a program for the sake of evaluation": 1)What is the nature of the program objectives—what do the objectives set out to do? (This determines the content of the evaluation) 2) Who is the target of the program? 3) When is the desired change to take place? 4) Are objectives aimed at a single change or a series of changes? 5) What is the magnitude of effect? and 6) How are objectives to be attained?[5] Answers to these help to pinpoint, in fairly specific terms, just why a particular evaluation is needed, whether it is planned for a program or for an activity.

Approaching program evaluation more generally, Lawrence Severy defines program evaluation as intending "to indicate the ways in which programs or parts of programs are effective or ineffective and to indicate the findings in as scientific a manner as possible. This is not to say, however, that program evaluation can solve all problems."[6] Likewise, Knowles describes program evaluation as having two principal purposes: the improvement of organizational operation, and the improvement of its program. The first includes "such aspects as its planning process, structure, decision-making procedures, personnel, physical facilities, finances, recruitment, training, public relations, and administrative management." The second addresses the components of the program such as "objectives, clientele, methods and techniques, materials, and quality of learning outcomes." However, he goes on to caution: "In childhood education, evaluation is often used for still another purpose, namely, to assess the achievement of the students for the purpose of promotion from one grade level to the next—a purpose that is totally irrelevant to adult education."[7] Even so, many administrators, supervisors, and even learners continue to view evaluation primarily as an appraisal of the learner.

Of course, the measurement of the results of activities may indeed include discovering how much the learner learned and applied. But this area of exploration is intended to find out how effective the program's efforts have been, not to duplicate school protocol aimed at judging the learner's intelligence. Knowles indicates that this latter approach to the evaluation of training perpetuates the misuse that loads "evaluation" with negative connotations leading to feelings of resistance and resentment, which then become barriers to any evaluation process.[8] The program, not the learner, is being evaluated. Part of the evaluation of the program, of course, will probably require knowing how much the learner has learned and how that learning was effected.

It may be noted here that, with few exceptions, evaluation of learning activities and programs is not designed for the purpose of comparing activities or a program in one organization with those of another. Although a peripheral use of an evaluation may be to disseminate information beyond the immediate library, agency, or association, the purposes prompting the original effort are internal: within the organization, within the program, within the learner.

Chabotar and Lad broaden the scope envisioned by Severy and Knowles as they state: "Although the immediate purpose of evaluation is to determine how well the training program is achieving its assigned goals and objectives, ultimately it provides a source of information upon which a variety of decisions can be made and variety of purposes can be served."[9] Then, they go on to indicate five basic categories that include the reasons why an organization might want to evaluate its learning program, or, as he calls it, "training program." The five reasons are:

"1.   to determine whether the training program is accomplishing the objectives it was designed to accomplish, i.e. to determine the 'results' of training in terms of measured change in worker attitudes, skills, knowledge, and on-the-job performance.

2.   to identify the strengths and weaknesses of training activities, so that the quality of training can be improved in terms of curricula, instructors, method of presentation, the adequacy of teaching aids and facilities, and so on.

3.   to determine whether the 'inputs' of training such as time, effort and monetary costs are justified by the benefits or outcomes of the program—a look at the efficiency or cost/benefit side of training.

4.   to establish a data base which organization leaders can use as a public relations tool to demonstrate the productivity and efficiency of their operational procedures to funding agencies, taxpayers, and those persons benefitting from the services which the organization provides.

5.   to establish a data base or source of information which can be used by organization managers as a rational basis for making decisions."[10]

A more helpful addition to these broad statements would be a list of specific, tangible purposes for evaluating a learning program or its activities. For the convenience of those who face the task of planning an evaluation, the following are suggested for consideration:

●   to identify any intended or serendipitous results from the program as a whole or from any of its individual activities,

●   to specify the fact and nature of impacts made by program efforts on learners, on libraries, or in the library field,

●   to determine to what extent the program and/or its activities are accomplishing what was intended and the significant conditions that enable these accomplishments,

●   to discover the successes or failures of program management and to identify problem areas,

- to identify and provide points for quality control of the program's efforts,

- to assist planning and improve decisions by furnishing accurate information needed for decision making patterns,

- to discover the quality of the total educational process or the effectiveness of specific content, methods, materials, or educational staff in order to assure quality subsequent activities,

- to document the program's capability for reporting,

- to provide data and documentation to justify the program to the sponsoring organization, to its clientele, or to the library field,

- to make explicit the rationale and the policies that evolve through its implementation,

- to evidence and reinforce individual learnings,

- to improve learner motivation and morale,

- to provide an additional means for learner involvement and active participation,

- to identify new needs toward which the program must be directed,

- to be responsible and accountable for the personal and organizational resources expended,

- to establish or reinforce the importance of the evaluation process within the organization,

- to provide a basis for staff rotation or promotion through the library's reward and recognition system,

- to review program staff assignments of responsibility and the lines of authority.

Obviously, there is no shortage of valid purposes to evaluate. No one program should expect to adopt all these possible purposes, of course, but might select three or four on which to focus. These serve to prompt thinking and open up areas valuable for exploration while planning for evaluation. Though specific, these purposes will need to be even further defined if selected for use in guiding a given program evaluation. Evaluation purposes should be stated in written form to guide the planning for evaluation and to assure a consistent direction for that effort.

For example, the stated purposes of an evaluation plan for a staff development program in a fairly sizeable library might be:

1. to determine the prime learnings from training activities that have actually been applied to job responsibilities.

2. to discover which training activities over the past year were most acceptable and most successful from the viewpoint of

the learners, in terms of topic, instructional methods, and relevance to need.

3. to discover major effects of training results in relation to new or changed staff development policies.

4. to train selected members of the supervisory staff in the principles of program evaluation through the demonstration and practice of the evaluation of the staff development program.

These several examples of purposes for evaluation may be almost too numerous, but they reveal most of the reasons for evaluation.

Procedure

Who should determine the purposes for the evaluation? When should they be decided? How should they be evolved? These decisions of a procedural nature will be influenced most strongly, of course, by the factors and the individuals operating in the specific situation. The program administrator and planners are primary influences in formulating evaluation purposes, since the points of the program where evaluation procedures will be needed must be planned and implemented within the overall program structure. They are most likely to know the program both broadly and in depth, and to be aware of what information will be useful to measure and how that might be done.

Others can also be involved in suggesting the kinds of information that would be useful for their purposes. Individuals and groups from whom useful suggestions might be sought include: potential learners, staff members of the sponsoring organization, educators and consultants from the various activities, library school faculty, and other organizations concerned with staff development and continuing education for library personnel. Their ideas can strengthen the ability of the evaluation to capitalize on its resources and allow in the evaluation process itself for strategically planned multiple purposes. From the sponsoring organization might come an interest in the successful functions, activities, and problems that occured. Potential learners might suggest the possibility of some self-evaluation means to strengthen their own abilities to identify and reinforce their learnings. Educators for learning activities might wish to measure the acceptability and effectiveness of certain instructional materials or facilities. Other organizations concerned with learning for library personnel might want to know the effect of learners' experiences and backgrounds on the preferences they expressed for various learning methods or locales, the resources found especially valuable, or the relationship between results and the identified needs. Of course, the sponsoring organization, those people responsible for planning the program, or those assigned the separate task of evaluation will be the ones actually to decide on the purposes of the evaluation.

Ideally, the purposes of evaluation would be determined during the planning for the program and the various activities. At that time, those with assigned responsibility for the program would evolve the possible purposes of evaluation, then select a prime few on which to concentrate their efforts. At that point, other groups and individuals might well be asked for their ideas and needs in relation to evaluation. The purposes selected then form the basis for an action plan for evaluation, laying out the approach, methods, and techniques needed to collect and analyze the information and the ways in which it will be used.

Although the initial purposes should be fairly well defined, flexibility is important to accommodate emergent ideas or requirements for evaluation adding to, deleting from, or modifying the originally established purposes. External mandates or internal crises certainly can affect the purposes and the procedures for the evaluation. Usually it is advisable to have whoever is responsible for implementing the evaluation as such present and involved in establishing these purposes.

The ideal circumstances are often not possible, however, for one reason or another. Sometimes the evaluation purposes and plan are developed after most of the rest of the program is in place. Ironically, one strong advantage surfaces at that time: the need (s) for evaluation become(s) clear. However, two strong disadvantages also appear: 1) it is too late to get the information usually, and 2) it is difficult to dovetail evaluation as closely with implementation or with planning as it needs to be in order to be useful to both those processes. Thus, planning for evaluation at the time of initial planning is best in order to make the most of all the possibilities that good evaluation offers.

The purposes of evaluation, like the objectives for the program and its activities, will serve to guide the evaluation process throughout the program. The importance of forming them thoughtfully should not be underestimated. For the most part, evaluation purposes are directly dependent on the needs of the individuals and groups concerned with the learning program.

Summary

The decision that evaluation is advisable is a key initial decision to be made. If evaluation is indeed to be done, the next question is *why* is evaluation to be done? Only after this question has been asked and answered can consideration be given as to *how* to do it. The purposes of evaluation, once established, give direction and guidance to the evaluation process throughout the program. Purposes of evaluation and an evaluation plan, to be most effective, should be formulated during the planning process. In that way, needs for gathering, analyzing, and reporting information can be built into the learning program design, and the results can facilitate good decisions in educational and management functions. Purposive evaluation protects the investment of time, effort, and funds that go into the program. Evaluative purposes depend on the priority needs for information, on the ability to obtain usable information, and on feasibility of obtaining it in relation to the information's importance. In some situations, such purposes are implicit and informal. In other situations, detailed and exacting planning for evaluation will be called for. Evaluation should be designed to honestly serve the program and should not require the program to serve the evaluation.

GUIDELINE 12—DESIGN EVALUATION PLAN

"Why bother about formalized evaluation procedures?" asks Alan Knox. Then, he answers: "People associated with a program will make judgements about effectiveness even without formal evaluation procedures. The function of systematic and continuous program evaluation should be to provide more adequate evidence and to improve the soundness of the judgments."[11] Effective evaluation rarely "just happens." More often, the essential ingredients of a sound and useful evaluation include a clear-sighted vision of what is sought (i.e. its purposes), careful planning to assure that the tasks are feasible, and thorough follow-through to make the most of the evaluation function and findings.

Systematic planning for evaluation offers many advantages. It can assure that the most adequate method is selected to acquire the best information for full use. Planning reduces the risk of happenstance and increases the possibility that the necessary information will be collected at the appropriate time for its intended use. Planning designates the roles and responsibilities for the allocation of workflow as well as information flow. Egon Guba illustrates the problem of inappropriate evaluation that, he says, often results in "faulty designs and useless reports. If, for example, an evaluation design is selected solely upon the basis of reliability and validity, valid and reliable information might be produced at a time when it is too late to be of any use in an action program." Careful forethought can reduce the factors of wasted time and wasted data, with time and information spent unproductively examining factors of little use to the learning program.

Ideally, a plan designed for evaluation would meet known needs effectively and accommodate new needs successfully. Thus, it would be structured enough to be able to accomplish what is needed, but flexible enough to adjust to new requirements, emergent situations, or surprise findings. Evaluation is usually directed 1) to provide information for program planners and administrators and thus improve their planning and implementation, and 2) to justify or account for accomplishments and/or achievements. An evaluation plan systematically outlines how the purposes of evaluation will be fulfilled: who needs to do what in order to gather, analyze, and interpret the information; and when, where and how those actions will take place.

This Guideline emphasizes the value of systematic planning and describes the nature of an evaluation plan. Basic types of evaluation approaches are described briefly for those wishing to explore a given type more fully. A basic, non-technical approach is suggested to guide those not seeking a specialized approach. Each of these is discussed with its advantages and disadvantages. A few of the important issues raised by planning are outlined also to prepare planners.

Planning for Evaluation

The plan for evaluation will depend on the purposes for it, and identifying them is important, for they directly affect the plan. If the main reason a program is to be evaluated is to prove, disprove, or justify what it did or did not accomplish, the kind of information sought will be very different than if the main reason is to seek ways to improve the program's internal operation or its present services and products. The first instance would need to assemble the documentation that would prove or disprove initial assumptions and expectations. This type of evaluation might gather information throughout the program and might issue annual or quarterly reports, but it would fulfill its major mission with the conclusion of the overall program and the report of its judged accomplishments.

On the other hand, evaluation in the second instance would be planned to gather and utilize information throughout the program and/or its activities. The information would be considered and used immediately in making decisions about further efforts. Reporting, in this case, would be more immediate and usually less formal or definitive. The information would be analyzed soon after it was collected and would be disseminated and incorporated into the flow of program efforts without necessarily appearing in printed form. A "final report" might never appear other than the description of the methodology and comments on its effectiveness. The actual "results" of the evaluation would be very difficult to trace or account for, and the degree of success of the program that was due to the evaluation process would be nearly impossible to trace. Many program evaluations attempt to blend these two kinds of purposes, with some effort spent gathering information for the purpose of proving and some for the purpose of improving.

The process of deciding which evaluation is to be done and the planning of how that will be accomplished results in the evaluation plan. This plan then guides and directs the implementation, specifying the actions that have to be taken, when, and by whom, and designates the lines of communication together with the key decision points where evaluation findings need to be known and available. Without a plan, implementing evaluation becomes circumstantial, undirected, and often, to little avail.

Part I indicated the importance of addressing the function of evaluation during planning the program. Trice and Roman emphasize this also: "Within the training setting, evaluation is more effective when it is a normal and accepted part of program planning from the beginning. Along with identification of training needs, selection of training methods, and logistical planning, evaluation should be an initial consideration." They qualify this point to some extent, however, by indicating that although evaluation can be attempted near the end of an activity, or even after it is concluded, such evaluation "is sharply handicapped and usually fraught with difficulties."[13]

This is not to imply, however, that a plan for evaluation must be completely outlined in advance and then simply implemented at the indicated time. With evaluation, as with planning, the process must be evolving rather than locked into the limits of the original thinking and confined to what may be found later to be an inappropriate direction, unfeasible methods, or questionable results. In other words, the evaluation should be designed so it, too, can respond to feedback, review, and modification as well as to perform that function for the program.

The Plan for Evaluation

The plan for evaluating a learning program is, in most cases, neither elaborate nor separate. Rather, it is usually one segment of the total program design, weaving the necessary functions of the evaluation process into those for planning and implementation, usually in a time sequence that links all three processes. Speaking as a program planner, Grotelueschen states that "Evaluation is more an art than a science. It requires an ability to respond to a real state of affairs with an appropriate design, to create a plan out of the complexity of an educational program, and to respond to its many constituents."[14]

More specifically, the evaluation plan should outline:

- stated purposes for evaluating.
- kinds of information sought.
- when and where evaluation information will be obtained.
- methods used for obtaining and disseminating it.
- uses to which the information will be put.

No prescription for a "right" evaluation plan is proposed here, however, any more than any "right" program design was earlier. As in previous Guidelines, the "right" answers come largely from each situation and its unique needs, people, and perspectives. Consequently, criteria and questions are more valuable than definitive answers to obtain an appropriate and relevant evaluation.

Guba recognizes this lack of definitiveness as he acknowledges the lack of "a generalizable set of evaluation designs" and he states further:

> Programs to improve education depend heavily upon a variety of
> decisions, and a variety of information is needed to make and support
> those decisions. Evaluators charged with providing this information
> must have adequate knowledge about the relevant decision processes
> and associated information requirements before they can design
> adequate evaluations. They need to have knowledge about the place,
> focus, timing and criticality of decisions to be served. At present
> no adequate formulation of decision processes and associated infor-
> mation requirements relative to educational programs exists. Nor is
> there any ongoing program to provide this knowledge. In short,
> there are no adequate conceptualizations of decisions and associated
> information requirements or programs to produce them.[15]

Evaluation Models

This lack of definitiveness frees the evaluation planner from constraints that might be inhibiting. On the other hand, the planner is confronted with weighing the choices of what evaluation method to use. Evaluation models in the areas of program evaluation and educational evaluation do exist and can be helpful. These alternatives are described briefly here for program planners and evaluators to consider as they develop their own evaluation plans.

Brief profiles plus cited sources will offer a start to those who wish to develop an evaluation plan of some depth and complexity. Each of these models is most generally applicable to evaluating the program itself. Some application would be useful for individual educational activities, but, in most cases, their comprehensiveness would speak more to the needs of a program than to a single activity. A pilot test with an activity might be considered in order to practice with the method before it is applied to an entire program, however. Alternatives to the specifics of collecting the evaluation information, analyzing it, and reporting it are given in later Guidelines. These might be more helpful in planning for an activity's evaluation. The first few models described are more technically oriented, and the later ones are less so. A pragmatic, non-technical model concludes this section with a four-step approach.

Although no standard evaluation pattern exists for the library field, the CIPP model (Context, Input, Process and Product) has received a good deal of national exposure through special training programs sponsored by the U.S. Office of Education during the 1970s. Consequently, many state agency personnel and library administrators are familiar with this model. Thus, this offers the advantage of available and knowledgeable people in the library field. Actually, the full model is rather more complex than may be necessary for an evaluation plan for a continuing education program. However, other programs and functions within the library or library school may wish to also look at program evaluation, and the advantages of compatible evaluation plans may be desirable for the organization. The most extensive source of information on this evaluation model is Daniel Stufflebeam's *Educational Evaluation and Decision Making* (1971). Guba and Stufflebeam have issued an abbreviated version of this work as: *Evaluation: The Process of Stimulating, Aiding and Abetting Insightful Action* (1970). Brooke Sheldon's *Planning and Evaluating Library Training Programs* (1973) is specifically subtitled *A Guide for Library Leaders and Advisory Groups* (Tallahasse, FL: Leadership Training Institute, Florida State University, School of Library Science, 1973) and is directly concerned with the application of the CIPP model to educational programs in the library field.

Trice and Roman term the goal-attainment approach as "being the most traditional, the most widespread, the most obvious, and seemingly the most practical way to assess training."[16] It assumes that clear, specific, and measurable objectives have been formulated and that these are not subject to change. Criteria to use in measuring to what extent the objectives actually have been achieved must be defined and then applied to determine program success. The primary source of information on goal attainment methodologies is the Program Evaluation Resources Center, which publishes *Evaluation: A Forum for Human Service Decision-Makers*, a periodical with in-depth articles on various aspects of goal attainment. The Center also has published the *Bibliography on Goal-Attainment Scaling and Associated Methodologies* (June 1975) and Geoffrey Garwick's *Guidelines for Goal-Attainment Scaling* (February 1975). Instructional material, worksheets, and additional materials are available from the Center. The Center is also concerned with goal-free evaluation as conceived by Michael Scriven.[17]

George Aker and Wayne Schroeder, in their chapter on "Research for Action Programs" in Shaw's *Administration of Continuing Education* (1969) define action research "primarily as a means by which practitioners scientifically secure information to guide, correct, and evaluate their decisions and actions. . . . [Good] action research does indeed result in findings which directly and specifically influence decisions and actions."[18] Action research is flexible and developmental, with great ability to adapt subsequent decisions and actions to evaluation results. An important and relevant sources is McGill and Horton's *Action Research Designs for Training and Development* (1973).

Tools for management also assist in the planning and development of learning programs, either in conjunction with the practice of the organization or as a separate effort. Each includes strong evaluation components. Management by objectives (MBO) is one approach that has been mentioned earlier. Program Evaluation and Review Technique (PERT) blends planning, implementation, and evaluation with a graphic means of describing program management and functions in a time sequence. Planning-Programming-Budgeting System (PPBS) views the application of limited resources to the achievement of defined objectives, ranked by priority. The Cost-Benefit approach concentrates on fiscal accountability and looks at results in relation to their cost to obtain. A variant is the Educational Program Audit, which is an outside audit based on cost/benefit principles of the internal evaluation that must be in place and working before the audit is done.

A major overall source of different types of educational models is Worthen and Sanders's *Educational Evaluation: Theory and Practice* (1973). Each of these methods, models, and sources approaches evaluation in its own way, specifying the what, who, how, when, and where that is relevant to that approach. General materials in the areas of program evaluation and educational evaluation will yield additional references and information.

Some pragmatic sources are less technically oriented, lying between the simple four-step method and the intricacies of very specialized evaluation. The balance that program planners and evaluators will strive for is to have enough substantial evaluation to determine results and to improve the present situation, yet not to run the program solely for the sake of evaluation. The following references and descriptions might provide the necessary middle ground for the many people who are responsible for evaluation of continuing education programs. They require more common sense than technical know-how.

Chabotar and Lad suggest in their *Evaluation Guidelines for Training Programs* (1974) "a conceptual framework to make some evaluative sense out of the many facets of training that might be studies," explaining that "good evaluations account for the relationships among these variables and focus attention upon measuring both trainees' actions and attitudes." They argue that "planning is the key, not only to a successful training program, but also to an accurate evaluation of that program's effectiveness."[19] Many examples define and specify strategies for the evaluation of program functions and outcomes, and special emphasis is given to both planning and implementation of these strategies.

In *The Modern Practice of Adult Education* (1970), Knowles advocates formulating evaluative questions that include "the criteria by which the evaluation data will be judged." Several pages of examples of such questions are helpful and stimulate ideas. He suggests that "a good deal of the value of engaging in an evaluative process comes from involving key people in figuring out for themselves the important questions to ask about a particular program at a given time."[20]

Wentling outlines and defines the general design features of an evaluation system in his *Evaluating Occupational Education and Training Programs* (1975). These are clearly described and applicable to other kinds of educational programs. Groteleuschen's entire *An Evaluation Planner* (1974) is a step-by-step workbook, again based on questions, that is useful for planning an evaluation of adult basic education programs. The procedure and questions are easily adaptable to other situations. He states: "Evaluation efforts are usefully organized around selected issues; once issues are selected, search for evidence may begin."[21] The outline and presentations are easily understandable.

A relatively simple, four-step approach is especially useful for either planning groups or individuals with limited experience in evaluation or for situations wherein restricted time and funds prevent working with the planning and application of more elaborate evaluation techniques. For example, associations using member groups for program planning may also have frequent changes in the persons responsible for planning and implementing either the program as a whole, or the evaluation portion of it. They will find such simple but useful methods more easily passed on to new groups and individuals. In turn, this advantage can increase the possibility of program evaluation being sustained and of its having continuity. Libraries and agencies sometimes require a specific evaluation method for all organizational functions, as do some funding sources. In such circumstances, the question of which method to use is moot.

The four-step method illustrates the information necessary in nearly any plan for program evaluation. It can be used as well with individual activities that are parts of the program. How can such a plan be developed? In particular, how can it be developed by individuals without extensive training and experience in evaluation methodology? The answers to a few basic questions asked in a preferred sequence can lead to a plan for evaluating the learning program or activity:

Step 1	*What* needs to be known?
Step 2	*Who* has that information?
Step 3	*How* can the necessary information be obtained? *Where*? *When*?
Step 4	*What* is to be done with the information, and *when*?

Responses to these questions provide a framework that relates evaluation to each individual situation with its unique characteristics. Although the sequence is flexible to a certain extent, in that some answers will be more quickly and easily available, each question should be fairly completely answered before moving on to the next.

Developing a plan for evaluation defines what needs to be known as specifically as possible, using as a basis, the objectives of the program and those for the specific learning activities and events. Working through "what needs to be known" will, to a certain extent, automatically answer the "who," "when," and "where" questions. The "how" may require some basic knowledge about and experience with techniques of evaluation, in addition to a basically practical common-sense approach. In general, the evaluation will seek to identify what changes did occur as a result of the program or the activity—those that were planned for and those that weren't. The evaluation provides means for the use of this information for accountability reporting (verbal or written) or for further planning.

What needs to be known? This is tied in closely with the reasons and purposes for evaluation; those, in turn, are closely related to the objectives of the program or the activity itself. Maintaining a focus on the hard question of what needs to be known is difficult. Usually, ideas about where the information should come from and how it might be obtained flow easily well before the question of what should be evaluated is clearly identified. When this definition is difficult to formulate, the list of possible purposes in Guideline 11 might provide a starting place to prompt definition, within the requirements of a specific program or activity, of just what needs to be known.

For example, the evaluation of a library's staff development program aimed primarily at making specific impacts on the organization could be planned to identify just what impacts were being made and how. For a program aimed at increasing on-the-job performance of selected staff categories in the library, the evaluation would be planned to focus on the persons involved in the program and how their competence was altered. If the evaluation were planned mainly to critique the nature and sequence of activities within the program, then an evaluation would be designed to look at these activities. In each case, information relevant to what needs to be known must be collected, analyzed, and utilized.

Actually, the definition of what needs to be known must be specific enough to permit constructing measures and strategies that will gather the evidence needed. In determining to what extent the program's objectives were accomplished and what methods were most effective in achieving the gains made, information would be sought from learners, supervisors, and educational staff about the information and skills that were learned and could be demonstrated, and about the most effective methods used to help that learning occur. The question of "what" needs to be known often has to be worked with at some length in order to determine with sufficient specificity to permit sound evaluation.

Defining in global terms what is to be evaluated is not useful, except as a beginning point to go further. Although the results to be evaluated are not necessarily confined to objectives, if these have not been clearly identified and written down, meaningful evaluation will be almost impossible. Without objectives, there is no way to tell the original intention and no way to determine success or a lack of it. A common error in program and activity objectives, for example, is the indication that "attitude and behavior changes" are sought as results, without describing what specific attitudes and behaviors are intended to be changed by which groups of learners and under what circumstances. For meaningful evaluation, the program and activity objectives will have to specify what performance is sought, under what circumstances, and what evidence would show that. Thus, evaluation is closely linked with objectives.

But, the dilemma of defining what needs to be known may persist. If so, this may help: almost all evaluation information falls into one or both of two categories. One group is the information that indicates what has resulted from the staff development efforts, what changes were made, or what results are evident. Another group is the information that gives a reading of what happened or is happening, an indication of issues and problems. Scriven has distinguished between these two types, terming them formative and summative evaluation. **Summative evaluation** gives evidence of the results of training activities and provides an assessment of them. **Formative evaluation** yields information that can be used for the development or improvement of the on-going program or activity. Scriven discriminates between these two types on the basis of their intent. Summative evaluation intends to "add up" the results. Formative evaluation intends to weave information back into the program or the organization so that it can be used in decision-making for the next steps.[22] Both intents can be realized by a single evaluation plan, or a plan might address only one or the other of these intents. For the pragmatic approach to evaluation, Scriven's distinction is basic, simple, and comprehensive.

This first step is the most difficult of the four. It often seems easy and straightforward, but when initial assumptions are clarified and put down in writing, further definition is called for. Yet, once "what" is determined, the other steps flow fairly smoothly. Too often, Step One is not fully clarified before the later, easier steps are determined. Then, much later, this is discovered and backtracking is necessary, unless, of course, it is too late.

Who has that information? "Who" can generally be described as including those who are affected by the program's efforts or the results of those efforts. For evaluators deciding to focus on the effectiveness of learning activities, the "who" would include the learners themselves as a prime source of information. That information source might be cross-checked by supervisors, library directors, those who use the library's services, or the activity's educational staff. The information might be known through experience directly or through observation of the learner's behavior. In the example used here, the learners would report what they know through experience, the supervisors what they have observed. Although most information is usually asked for directly, it may be deliberately sought through a number of sources to offer a variety of perspectives. For some evaluation plans, a control group without the opportunities to learn may be compared with a group with specific training. Then, a measure is made to determine the effects of that training.

Precautions in handling sensitive information may be necessary in an evaluation plan to reduce the possible feelings of threat or exposure that result from seeking such information. People from whom information is gathered and those to whom it goes may need assurance about how the information they give will be used, how the privacy of individuals is being protected while helpful evaluation information is being collected to evidence results or demonstrate accountability.

How can the necessary information be obtained? This includes the design, methods, and techniques used to accomplish the plan. To be useful, these must be appropriate to the situation and the evaluation purposes. Guidelines 13 and 14 detail the specifics of collecting and analyzing evaluation information. Considering how to obtain evaluation information inevitably raises additional questions: What is possible? What is feasible? What degree of depth and scope are intended? How detailed and accurate must the information be? How much control is required? Are adequate resources available to do what is needed? Are both formative and summative information sought?

"How" involves both substance and procedure in that it identifies the action part of the evaluation plan by indicating who is to be responsible for doing just what, when, and where to acquire the desired information. For example, learners might be asked to demonstrate their knowledge or skill while at the learning activity or to evidence it later by developing a model, plan, report, or proposal that would utilize and evidence some of the learning resulting from the activity. To be significant and valid, of course, this would have to be compared with the degree of knowledge and skill the learners had prior to the activity.

When? The evaluation plan must include the sequence and frequency to assure accurate timing in relation to when the information is needed and when it is available; it must also reflect whether that information is intended for personal goal setting, for organizational problem-solving, or for program modification. Planning a schedule begins at the end—looking at the point the information is needed, working backwards to reach the time when it is first available to be collected, then allowing time to develop forms, interviews, or documentation procedures.

For example: When will the information be needed? In time to assemble a report, to make a decision, to provide documentation for a presentation, to provide a needs assessment for a new series of activities. When will the information be available? When follow-up interviews are completed, when mid-point forms are returned, following the planning meeting, when the learner applies the new skill on the job, just before a new series begins. When will it be analyzed? In time for the next planning meeting, soon after the form deadline, after the seasonal holidays. These time frames must be incorporated in the evaluation plan, and they are often displayed in chart or outline format.

Where? "Where" is closely related to when and should also be included in the plan. Information is often gathered on-site at the learning activity because of its convenience, being an accessible and controlled situation, and because of the fact that learners will anticipate and accept it as part of routine procedure. On-the-job application of new knowledge, skills, or attitudes can best be determined after the learning activity and the return to the workplace, however. Observation of individual and library behaviors related to regular routine work can only be seen accurately where those functions are usually performed.

"Where" can often condition other factors. For example, a pen and paper pre-test may require a quiet, private place. A group interview would require a room where people could speak freely. And, if schedules or facilities are not appropriate, the findings may not reflect accurately what was being sought. Then too, the comfort level, physical and emotional, of those giving evaluation information must be considered in relation to the place. This factor can condition the amount or tone of the information if the place where it is obtained is uncomfortable to the person being asked.

What is to be done with the information, and when? The advantage of planning for a systematic evaluation is to assure that information is gathered at the appropriate time and channeled, in time, where it is needed in order to accomplish the intended purposes. For example, information about program strengths and weaknesses may go to the program planners to review and modify subsequent activities or program management. Information may go to the organization's directors to be considered in conjunction with broader issues or future planning. Some information may be returned to learners and their supervisors to help them plan how to best use the new abilities they acquired through involvement in the program. Evaluation purposes specify the intent of the plan and indicate the direction and use of the information collected and assembled. The evaluation plan outlines what information goes where, when, and in what form, from whom and to whom.

The plan must specify the method of information dissemination together with the points of communication and decision-making that are used or affected. For example, if an oral presentation is to be given to the program planners at each quarterly meeting, that needs to be specified in the plan. If a written report is required to the general staff meeting on an annual basis, that should be defined. If feedback is to be elicited from learners during an activity and given to trainers during staff meetings held regularly, that should be clarified. If documentation of planning meetings and other program functions is required, designation should be made of the kind of information required and the person who should direct that process.

In considering what is done with the information, the large question of responsibility in connection with the dissemination of the information will need to be addressed. Concerns arise around the issues of the "ownership" of the information, the right to privacy, and the ethical use of information. How information is disseminated is a key element in building or eroding the credibility of both the staff development program and the individuals connected with it. Inept or unthinking distribution of information may be perceived as exposure from the learners' viewpoint, as threat from the viewpoint of training staff or program planners, and as revelation of unanticipated but needed change from the administrator's viewpoint. In gathering information, there is an implicit responsibility to share the general findings with those who have contributed their responses to the evaluation. The evaluation plan should recognize and accommodate these issues.

Information often is disseminated through some method of documentation. Documentation is a particular concern at the point of evaluation, since careful records aid the evaluation process and may provide the best evidence available in relation to the program and its activities. Documentation is the act of collecting and recording information in order to communicate and/or preserve it. Methods of documentation are most often written reports, minutes, and notes, which may stand alone or may accompany other existing written records. Oral and visual records such as tape and video cassettes are becoming more used for documentation as the equipment improves and people's skill and comfort with these procedures increase. Once a record—written, oral or visual—is made, the information can be inserted into the regular communication channels and decision-making structures of the program or of the library or library school. If the evaluation information is intended to influence the decisions to be made, it must be in a form that can be communicated effectively and must be accessible to those responsible for making present or future decisions. Depending on the need and the capability, documentation may be straight reporting (such as the results from returned forms, statistics, or decisions of a meeting) or it may include some degree or analysis, interpretation or recommendations. Usually documentation is an assigned responsibility of one or more people who may be part of the group.

Another important part of the plan for evaluation, one often overlooked, is the provision for evaluating the evaluation. When evaluation is considered a serious and worthwhile endeavor, it must continue to be relevant and justifiable. Just as the program and personnel may need to modify their direction, adjust their priorities, be alert to changing circumstances, so must the evaluation function be open to review. Chabotar and Lad specify three criteria "on which most evaluations can be judged: 1) validity, 2) reliability and 3) usability."[23] The specifics on how best to do this will vary with the situation, but generally speaking, the following aid evaluating the evaluation: provide time to be used in evaluating the evaluation; designate periodic check points for such review; assess those to whom evaluation information is disseminated to see if it does indeed meet their needs; assign the review of the evaluation to a specific individual or group; reassess the purposes for evaluation at each point of significant change in the program or in the organization. Wentling and Lawson offer, in *Evaluating Occupational Education and Training Programs* (1975), additional specific ways for such evaluation.

But, it must be remembered that evaluation should be designed to assist, not to run, the program.

The four-step method proposed here is but one alternative of many, suggested because of its simplicity for use in planning for evaluation. The selection of how best to approach evaluation involves a choice among the evaluation approaches and methods. Those described in this Guideline are but a few basic ones of the many that are available. A distinct, and sometimes invaluable, advantage of the last method described is that people can be involved in evaluation, even without calling it evaluation. The process described here can clearly be seen as a decision-making aid and, using it as such can reduce feelings of threat or wariness that often result from an evaluation process. This may alleviate a strong resistance to evaluation sufficiently so as to get it done.

Other alternatives, not before mentioned, exist. One is to adopt or adapt a presently existing evaluation plan from a similar learning program elsewhere. Another is to utilize a packaged system selected from those available and apparently able to obtain the information desired. Still another is to hire an outside consultant to do an evaluation. Each of these alternatives offers the advantages of relieving the organization's personnel of the evaluation task and of obtaining evaluation expertise perhaps not available within the organization. Each of these alternatives will pose the same three disadvantages: 1) each will require answering question one anyway (to determine what needs to be known) and will be necessary before being able to wisely select or make use of the apparent convenience of the alternative. If question one is by-passed, the essentials of the staff development situation at hand are not defined and a very high risk exists of inappropriately selecting ready-made resources that may not be able to produce a useful evaluation. 2) The effort required to "fit" the specifics of the alternative being considered to the unique aspects of a given situation may take as long as proceeding through the suggested four-step process without considering the alternative. 3) The use of most "convenience" packages or outside people does not usually, by itself, offer the benefit of training the organization's staff in the practical principles of evaluation, which they could then apply to other organizational functions.

Evaluation Issues

As planning for evaluation develops, some key issues and questions are raised. Unique circumstances may create issues additional to these, but the following frequently confront program planners and evaluators:

- the most effective use of available resources to achieve the desired evaluation.
- the responsibility for evaluation.
- maintaining the relationship between evaluation purposes and program objectives.
- the distinction between evaluation and research.
- the use of internal evaluators versus those from outside.

Fortunately, for most programs, not all of these issues must be faced at once. But, they are frequent issues that come up.

Resources of personnel, energy, and funds to channel into evaluation may be limited, for that commitment entails planning and preparation as well as the process of collecting, analyzing, and reporting the information for use. The interest and skills of those involved in administrative or educational roles in the program may need to be supplemented by outside assistance. Very real constraints may exist to curtail current efforts. Especially when initiating a new program, it may be apparent that perhaps program evaluation will need to evolve as the program develops rather than being considered with planning. Even though this is not recommended, it is sometimes essential to initiate a new program with some activities to show the intent of the organization; then, later, a more feasible planning/evaluation process can be constructed that may not have been possible in the beginning. Whenever evaluation is delayed, it is important to preserve careful records, so a retrospective view is possible, and to be aware that evaluation is a priority, even if a postponed one. Another approach can be used for an on-going program that seeks to build more reliable planning and evaluation procedures than have been possible in the past. That approach is to begin by evaluating the activities now produced as activities. The results found through the evaluation can then help evolve an improved program design. A third approach is to use stop-gap measures, such as wide involvement of staff and/or advisory groups in frank feedback sessions that, though informal, can lead to modifications and improvements before a comprehensive evaluation plan can be begun.

Beyond planning the evaluation, resources can be carefully surveyed in order to determine what could be used in implementing evaluation. Special funding sources can be sought from government, business, foundation, or private groups who are interested in study or research projects in education or librarianship. Even if short-term, these can offer a help, especially for a start. Contacts with individuals or groups having special interests or a commitment to furthering the efforts of a learning program can be helpful. These individuals or groups are not necessarily confined to the library field, so the search should be outside as well as within the library world. Graduate library schools or adult education schools might provide names of student groups able to develop a special project. This could help establish a program or could be used to help conduct activities evaluations, but would be time-limited. A specially designated group of participants in a learning activity might seek deeper learnings and be willing to undertake commitments of involving themselves in designing the activities or assisting with the evaluation procedures during the activity. A final option is the special training of program staff in evaluation methods and techniques, and to them employ an internal evaluation process. Other options for making the most effective use of available resources will emerge from creative thinking about each particular set of circumstances.

The question of responsibility for evaluation has two parts. The first concerns who is going to do it. The program administrator is often the one with the final decision as to whether evaluation will be a strong element and priority in the program or not. The organization's precepts and practices will influence that decision, as will the perceptions and understanding of that individual. Whether the evaluation is to be conducted from within the program or from outside, the function itself needs clear definition and assignment, with the authority and responsibility of that position spelled out. Whatever the nature of the evaluation plan decided upon, it will need to be closely coordinated with the particular continuing education program and to take into account the individuals and the organization involved in making it come alive. There is usually some controversy over whether a program can be fully evaluated from within the program itself or, for objectivity, whether it requires an outside evaluation.

The second part to this question of responsibility concerns the program's part in aiding self-evaluation by the learners. One of the greatest potentials for approaching evaluation remains largely undeveloped and not widely used. In continuing education the initiative and choice of the learner or employing library usually determines who attends a given learning activity, if any are to be attended. In some ways, that responsibility implies the validity of the individual's personal needs assessment process or the insight of the library. If that point of view can be extended, the personal or library responsibility would logically include evaluation of what has been learned. Up to now, however, self-evaluation procedures have not been extensively used.

Yet, self-evaluation offers a promising area for evaluative efforts. Such an approach prompts individual learners to personally test the results of their learning in their application of those learnings to their jobs and in relation to what they actually needed or wanted to learn. The self-evaluation possibility can deepen the ability of learners to become self-directed in their educational efforts in general and can also increase their ability to learn from specific activities produced by the program. Although the responsibility for engaging in self-evaluation belongs to the individual learner, the activity and the program can provide the means for this to be done. "Learner contracts" have been found to be a successful learning catalyst and provide for evaluative evidence and criteria to be developed by both the educator and the learner, and then carried out by the learner. Guideline 13 covers this topic more thoroughly.

The third issue concerns maintaining the relationship between evaluation purposes and program objectives. One of the precepts stressed in earlier Guidelines is that objectives should be flexible and may change with more awareness of learner needs or available resources. Obviously, when objectives for the program or its activities change, the evaluation purposes may be affected. But what if the evaluation plan is partially completed, and changing objectives makes those efforts obsolete and calls for new measures that may not be possible? The evaluation should guide but not run the program, and if evaluative information and procedures are no longer valid, and have no other use, they must be set aside. Often the activity objectives evolve somewhat in the minds of the implementors of each activity. But changes may not be made in the written wording, or the information may not be passed on to the evaluators. This lack of communication can result in a gradual split between the purposes of the evaluation and the objectives of the program or activity. Thus, communication is important to keep the two congruent with each other. Personal relationships also often enter into the picture.

The evaluation process can be of great assistance to an evolving program, or to one anticipating renovation or renewal. However, it can also be perceived to be a threat or an obstacle to be bypassed. When this happens, the evaluation process becomes more and more isolated, and the information that it yields, even if relevant, is not used. Eventually, the information is not accepted and the process of program evaluation may be jeopardized. Both administrator and evaluator need clear concepts of the value of evaluation, and both need to approach the process in a collegial fashion to assure that the evaluation is closely related to the program and its activities.

The fourth issue weighs the distinction between evaluation and research. This issue is raised when, in developing a plan, some choices will have to be made between alternatives: Is the focus of this evaluation on evaluation or on research? The two are not exclusive of one another, but Severy accentuates the difference in his analysis of program evaluation and research. He indicates this as one of the major problems confronting those people trying to approach problem evaluation as research: "Evaluation research deals with people and programs in real life · action environments; therefore, the program is considered the primary activity, and research must become secondary. When it comes to choosing between perfect research design and meeting the needs of the program, priority is usually given to the program."[24] For those seeking research opportunities and techniques, this choice of focus may be viewed as unfortunate. However, for action-oriented program planners, this choice will be seen as logical and reasonable.

Lack of a research-oriented approach may be subject to criticism from knowledgeable researchers, particularly those from outside the program. Educators and program planners are more "apt than evaluators to be concerned with immediate, specific use of knowledge while evaluators think more in long range, problem solving terms." This is the distinction that Trice and Roman make, adding that educators tend to believe that "everyday experience and practical judgments are far more realistic than results generated from 'scientific methods.' "[25] The stance presented in this book is a pragmatic one, focused on the usefulness of evaluation (tied to the discovery or exploration of what can be improved) and the examination of results from continuing education efforts. The emphasis throughout these Guidelines has been operational rather than research oriented, concerned with the doing rather than the study of what is being or has been done.

Looking at the purpose of program evaluation, Severy states that it is to "indicate the ways in which programs or parts of programs are effective or ineffective and to indicate the findings in as scientific a manner as possible."[26] Program planners and evaluators will benefit by utilizing relevant research methods and techniques to achieve as "scientific a manner as possible." Unsound evaluation procedures should not be perpetuated simply because they might be justified on the grounds that they are not "research." This use of applicable research strategies can help build the credibility as well as the soundness of program evaluation, from a view inside or outside the organization that sponsors the program.

The pull toward research technology should not cloud the view of program planners or evaluators to the fact that, especially in relation to educational programming, evaluation is part of the learning process. In some instances, it deepens the learner's awareness and integration of knowledge or skills within the activity. In other instances, it becomes a "meta" learning, a learning about programming, about evaluation and planning, for the individuals and groups most closely involved with the program. Viewed as an educational process rather than a research study, the choices of emphasis and procedure in the evaluation plan may be different than if the evaluation is primarily to defend, to prove, to be accountable, or to produce research.

For those who wish to explore research methodology within an educational program context, two sources are helpful. Both strongly advocate experimental designs. Lawrence Severy, in his *Application of the Experimental Method to*

Program Evaluation: Problems and Prospects (1975), provides a wealth of further resources on the subject. Chabotar and Lad, in *Evaluation of Training Programs* (1974), advocate the experimental approach for training programs, and they include self-instructional exercises for beginning with simple and proceeding to complex designs. They stress research criteria such as validity, reliability, and usability.

The final issue, that of using internal versus external evaluators, is often encountered. Many people are involved in evaluation to some extent. Some plan and carry out evaluation procedures; others will respond to collection procedures; still others will make decisions based on that information. But the basic responsibility for the evaluation must be assigned. If not assigned to an individual or a group, it may be overlooked. Turning the evaluation task over to someone outside the organization is often seen as desirable, particularly if it is thought to be complex and difficult, requiring special abilities plus "objectivity." Sometimes a more real reason for using outside evaluators is that no one inside wants the responsibility or the difficulties that can come to one in such a position.

Thus comes the point of deciding whether to use internal or outside evaluation resources. Each route has its advantages and disadvantages. Most of the advantages of using an internal evaluator are based on that person's being a normal part of the organization: easily available; apparently less expensive (though evaluation would be an additional responsibility to an existing job); broader knowledge of the organization, the program, and the people involved; awareness of what aspects need evaluating and how the results can be used; and, in most cases, more ready acceptance by staff. The disadvantages of the internal evaluator include: inevitable biases; perhaps vested interests in the results; tendency to highlight successes; usually little expertise or experience with evaluation; the difficulty of that person in relation to his or her colleagues (including superiors, "equals," and subordinates).

For the external evaluator, the advantages are: objectivity; experience with evaluation methodology; lack of involvement with internal factions; low vested interest in evaluation results; no distraction by other responsibilities within the organization, less exposure and vulnerability to pressure that encourages compromise, and the ability to see those aspects of the program that those more intimately connected with it may take for granted. The disadvantages include: lack of full and balanced information about the program and organization; expensive direct and indirect costs; less aware of how disruptive evaluation may be or of the practicality of recommendations resulting from the evaluation; may be perceived as threatening to program planners; may not agree with program values or intent established; may be regarded as an "outsider" or even a threat by staff. Of course, these general advantages and disadvantages do not always pertain. The pros and cons of a given situation will depend on that situation and the people involved.

The choice between an internal and an external evaluator is a difficult one to make and depends to a great extent on the resources available, including the interests and capabilities available within the organization, the primary reasons for the evaluation, and the anticipated value of the evaluation. Several alternatives have proved workable in various situations. One is to have an outside evaluator work with the planning committee to evolve the plan of evaluation in the beginning. The evaluator can then "stand by" to give advice when needed and intervene at crucial points, although the actual implementation is done by the in-house staff. This alternative gives the advantages of technical expertise, credibility, and a back-up resource. That outside evaluator might also be responsible for analyzing and reporting some of the data. At the same time as serving as an evaluator, that person can train local in-house staff in the processes and the procedures of evaluation. A critical point is to be able to select the appropriate outside evaluator—one who is willing to be involved in this way, is able and available to do these tasks, and is congruent with the organization, its program, and its personnel.

A second alternative is to select one or more individuals from the program staff and to develop a technical evaluation expertise in them. Available study programs and reading materials would need to be strongly supplemented by the chosen person's interest and willingness to be involved. This expertise would then be introduced internally in the library, agency, or association and made available for use in developing other programs and doing other evaluations. The difficulty of the individual in this unique position in relation to her or his peers and colleagues is not eliminated, although it may be alleviated somewhat by the special training.

A third alternative is to explore the possibility of utilizing evaluation personnel available from the larger organizational context, that is, the municipality, the university, or the state or federal government. This alternative makes the most of the advantages and offsets many disadvantages of both internal and outside evaluators. It also opens up the possibility of a team of one internal person and one outside person from this larger context working together. For example, the inside person, perhaps relatively inexperienced in evaluation, might define and formulate evaluation purposes and the major points to be evaluated. Then, the outside person might critique that, raising questions to help direct the focus, and designing the evaluation study for implementing with the least disruption. The internal team member might help plan and share in the data gathering responsibilities. The outside person might analyze the information and present the results, and the inside person then would make recommendations for application. This alternative brings many important advantages.

Also, involving the planning committee with either an internal or external evaluator can help them to learn about and practice new skills in evaluation. This can be very revealing to the members of that group, for essentially they would be in the position of learners in any part of the program, and would have a greater understanding of the problems that might be encountered. This type of involvement also provides those involved an added dimension, increasing their knowledge of the function and value of evaluation as well as their practice with its techniques. Such an effort can be rewarded by the increased awareness and ability of those involved in the evaluation. But, this is a long-range goal requiring a different investment than the typical short-range evaluation aim of "get it done and reported."

In selecting and contracting with an outside evaluator, the expectations, the role(s), and responsibilities should be clearly indicated. That person can help make these realistic because of past experience with similar situations. Whether from inside the organization or outside it, an evaluator's involvement depends greatly on the depth of commitment to evaluation and the level of understanding held by those making the decisions of whether, how much, and when to evaluate.

Suchman illustrates the importance of this understanding: "Quite often the evaluator will be called in to evaluate a program only to find that the objectives of this program, much less its criteria of success, have never been clearly defined. What is more serious, he may find that there are wide differences of opinion among practitioners as to what they are trying to accomplish."[27] Or, an evaluator may be asked near the end of the effort to "come and evaluate it." Such an evaluation precludes formative evaluation entirely, curtails summative evaluation severely, and is inadequate if evaluation is intended to be a part of the learning experience or a valid basis for accountability. Creative evaluation, well designed and implemented, can enhance learning, motivate involvement, and increase the benefits and rewards from the learning program.

A different, though equally fundamental, difficulty concerns differing value positions of the evaluator and the administrator or program staff. It, too, is described by Suchman:

> In general, the evaluator will seek to measure achievement, while the program personnel will be more likely to emphasize effort or technique. The evaluator will be more concerned with higher level or ultimate objectives, while the practitioner will be more involved with lower-level or immediate objectives. To the evaluator, the criteria of success will deal more directly with improvement in the status of the recipients of services, while for the staff, the tendency will be to seek criteria which reflect the smoothness and efficiency of the services themselves rather than their effect upon the people to whom the services are provided."[28]

The influence of this situation is often more subtle than the lack of clarity and depth of understanding.

Summary

Because each of these issues frequently confound planners for evaluation and sometimes evaluators themselves, those people aware of such difficulties will be better prepared to forestall that potential. And, as Severy says so neatly: "Program evaluation obviously is not a simple thing to accomplish. However, it seems clear that one might as well begin by approximating the ideal method as closely as possible."[29] Effective evaluation does not occur automatically but is more often the result of a clear-sighted vision of purpose, careful planning to assure that the task is feasible, and thorough follow-through to make the most of the evaluation function and findings. Awareness of these issues can help.

The importance of integrating the evaluation process with those of planning and implementation has been emphasized earlier. In spite of its importance, though, it only rarely happens. Usually the urgency of busy planning and implementation crowd out looking ahead for evaluation. Evaluation becomes an afterthought. Makeshift arrangements and last-minute actions assemble available information to meet the need for "evaluation." Evaluation is often not determined to be a priority until the program is in difficulty or when it has completed a cycle or an activity. Then it becomes apparent that information is needed. Evaluation, at that point, looms as a large priority, but may not then be possible.

From gathering information to making use of the information found, the plan for evaluation integrates evaluation with planning and implementation of the total program, its activities and its administrative functions. Thus, planning for evaluation must be developed during the initial and continuous planning process that guides the production of activities and the program management. Evaluation itself may, like the program, start simply and grow in effectiveness and complexity. Simple, straightforward evaluation may be useful and satisfactory for a long time before more elaborate endeavors are thought necessary.

The plan defines information needs and timing in order to make the decision necessary to direct necessary decisions and action. It outlines systematically how the purposes for the evaluation will be fulfilled: who needs to do what to gather, analyze, and report the information; when, where, and how those actions will take place. The plan includes: 1) stated purposes for evaluating, 2) kinds of information sought, 3) when and where it will be obtained, 4) methods used for obtaining and disseminating it, and 5) uses to which it will be put. The plan also designates roles and responsibilities, allocates workflow as well as information flow, and guides the timely accomplishment of the evaluation.

In addition to the most suitable evaluation method, key issues and questions are discussed during planning for evaluation. These include: best use of resources, responsibilities for evaluation, the relationship between evaluation purposes and program objectives, the distinction between evaluation and research, and the use of internal vs. external evaluators. Evaluating the evaluation can help to assure its relevance to the objectives and make adjustments if it is not closely enough related or helpful to the program. Sometimes, though, the importance of evaluation is not perceived until it is no longer feasible to accomplish it.

GUIDELINE 13–COLLECT EVALUATION INFORMATION

The first step in implementing the evaluation plan is to collect information to be analyzed and used for the purposes determined earlier. Those purposes determine the selection of approaches to use to collect information before, during, and after the various learning activities and then to analyze it. Some collected information will evidence accomplishments; some will signal problems in the making; some will suggest needed changes. Evaluation information can be collected from learners, supervisors, educators, and outside observers, and it might pertain to a single learning activity or to the program as a whole. Methods and techniques can be carefully planned ahead of time or can be used at the last minute. The plan can involve those who were part of the activity or program, or it can assemble expert opinions from assigned observers and available documentation. But, somehow, evaluation information must be collected in order to be interpreted and reported to whomever needs to have it. If collected according to a plan, such information probably can be used to its fullest extent, because it is known to be needed and will be more efficiently collected.

Collected information helps check out assumptions, increases awareness of prospects and problems, and provides for action. The information can reveal whether commonly held assumptions and expectations are accurate in relation to what is actually occuring, or whether those assumptions may need to be changed. Awareness, particularly if it is an early alert, can be useful to identify problems before they become crises, to know about serendipitous results that were unanticipated but might be encouraged (or discouraged), and to keep track of external factors likely to affect the program. And, on-going planning and decision-making need to be guided by information that is sufficiently specific, timely, and valid.

This Guideline identifies categories of information particularly useful to collect for a learning program and the criteria to guide the collection of that information. The sources to get data from and the typical methods and instruments that can be used to do so are described. Often, though, collection techniques are blocked. This Guideline describes these various blocks and suggests bypasses to circumvent them.

Criteria

With the overview of an evaluation plan, evaluators are more likely to make the most of efforts to collect only viable information and to be able to channel it promptly and effectively where it is needed. Also, with an overview, little time and effort are wasted in collecting information that leads nowhere in particular. The collected information will be used to evaluate a specific activity or the program as a whole, to determine what impacts have been made on the organization, or to measure the knowledge, skills, and attitudes acquired by the learners.

Four criteria are important to guide the collection of evaluation information:

- The information sought should relate to the purposes and address the issues. Careful definition of purpose sorts the relevant information from the irrelevant, assuring that primarily needed information is collected. Excessive and irrelevant information is expensive to collect and to analyze. It also leads to frustration and confusion and, further, it may exploit those people asked to supply the information.

- The information to be collected should be available, possible to collect, and obtained in time to be used. Collecting the information must be acceptable to those from whom it is sought and acceptable to those who will use it.

- The information obtained should be as valid and reliable as possible, using dependable techniques. Although both objective and subjective information can be valuable, a clear distinction must be made between them. Definitive conclusions regarding results from learning are usually not possible because of the many variables. Inevitably, some subjective judgement will have to be used.

- A variety of techniques should be used. This assures that the information can be cross-checked, offers the opportunity to tap individual preferences and abilities, and improves the ability to identify unanticipated results.

Criteria for the collection of information should be considered while the plan for evaluation is being developed, for the plan specifies the points where evaluation information is to be collected and the people from whom it is to be collected.

Categories

Defining evaluation information by categories is more useful in the collection of information than in other evaluation tasks. Neither the analysis nor the reporting functions would be well served by such divisions. Doing so is more procedural than substantive, helpful in planning how to collect the information and allocate specific responsibilities to different people. For example, the statistical information might be gathered by someone with experience in that area; opinions might be gathered through interviews done by an individual with that experience and those skills; observations could be made by someone in a position to do that. No matter how collected, however, all types of information will be brought together for analysis and reporting.

At least three categories are possible. One is on the basis of the focus of information—that is, on the learners, on the activity as such, or on the program as a whole. Another is on the basis of the source of information—that is, the learners, supervisees/supervisors, program planners, educational staff, or others affected by or involved with it. A third is determined by the techniques used to collect the information and the logistics they require—that is, the type of information, the timing or locale, or the assignment of responsibility. Those responsible for planning the evaluation must determine if one or more of these groupings would be useful.

Some specific examples in each of these categories may clarify how they might be used. The focus of the information presents a profile of that component in the three categories.

- In regard to the learner, they are revealed:

    a. demographically—where they come from, what library positions they hold, their responsibilities, age, race, and sex,

    b. on the basis of their knowledge and/or experience—comparisons of their initial abilities and those at the end of the activity, their perspective of what they need/want to know or do, their present competency in relation to that level required by their jobs, their self-perceived serendipitous learnings,

    c. by their individual and collective expectation—how many want to hear about the subject, how many want to be able to do something new or differently, how many just want to "get away from the routine,"

    d. by the application of learnings—how they have qualified in their library's reward and recognition system, what follow-up steps they plan as a result of their learnings.

- The learning activity may be drawn on the basis of its:

    a. content—coverage, relevancy, accuracy, repetition,

    b. design—appropriateness, skill, sequence, timing, acceptance of methods,

    c. use of resources—educational staff, instructional aids and materials, funding, and facilities,

    d. results—adequate, relevant to need and expectations, amount in relation to the effort and cost required.

● The learning program as a whole might be sketched in terms of:

    a. cost/benefit ratio—what trade-offs were necessary to provide for the learning program? are the impacts worth the cost? what are the long-term or short-term benefits?

    b. effectiveness—how many learners have participated and to what effect? what side-effects have been noted?

Information for each of these profiles would be obtained from a number of sources perhaps. In other words, information would be sought from sources other than the learner, as well as from the learner directly, to create that profile.

● The gatherer of information would seek the learner's opinion:

    a. about his or her own learning,

    b. about the relationship that a specific learning activity had with those learnings,

    c. about the effectiveness of the program in general.

● Educational staff might be tapped for:

    a. their perceptions of the learnings gained by participants,

    b. their opinions of the efficiency of the program personnel in planning for the activity,

    c. their view of their own performance,

    d. critique of the learning design.

● The program administrator might be asked about:

    a. the effectiveness of the learner selection process,

    b. the skills of the educational staff members,

    c. the adequacy of the activity designs,

    d. the problems of the educational delivery system of the program.

At a later point, these perceptions could be cross-checked and correlated to draw a more complete picture of the operation and results of the program.

The third category is logistical, being dictated by the techniques used and, often by the timing and locale of how opinions are collected. For example, they may be gathered by interviewing both learners and educators as to their perceptions of the effectiveness of a particular learning activity's design. These interviews may be done early in the activity, at mid-point, and at the end of it. A single person might handle all the interview data. Then, this might be correlated statistically with similar or different activities to see if any conclusions could be drawn about design factors. Another person might be responsible for the statistical work. This category is, for the most part though, valid for logistics rather than for substance.

At the point of analysis, each of these categories would be brought together, their earlier division into categories of focus, source, or logistics no longer relevant.

Techniques

For the most part, evaluation techniques evolved from the common-sense practice of "if you want to know, ask." Questions asked in sophisticated ways become scientific inquiries or dissertations with prescribed rules and procedures. Much less refined techniques are in more common use. Even so, techniques over the years and through repeated use have developed several patterns that range from informal to formal. Those described here are typical.

Techniques to collect evaluation information may be used in various combinations to meet the needs of a single evaluation purpose. Or, a single technique may be designed to answer multiple purposes. Techniques may be used to find evidence of results from the program's learning activities (i.e., summative evaluation). Or, the information may be channeled into modification of direction or method, clearer articulation of the present situation, or future planning (i.e., formative evaluation).

Most techniques used to collect evaluation information utilize instruments. **Instruments** are prepared tools designed to elicit the desired type of information from the relevant source. Two factors influence the extent to which instruments can be effective. One is the quality of the instrument, that is, its ability to do the job expected of it. The second is how adequately the instrument is administered, including effective communication about the instrument and its directions. An important qualification is the credibility of those who administer the instrument in the eyes of those to whom it is administered. Instruments must be tailored to the issue and situation, but they also need to be fashioned to fit the people from whom information is being collected. Yet, often the strongest influence in the choice or development of instruments is the fact that they are readily available or that the evaluator is familiar with that particular instrument.

Tests are often the first thought in relation to evaluation techniques. The use of tests throughout the schooling process as the major means for evaluation may be the reason for this prompt response. The school pattern assumes that tests, used both before and after a specific learning activity, are valid, reliable measures of learnings. Heavy use of tests in school probably is also the cause of the predictably strong resistance to them from adult out-of-school learners. Thus, the general lack of acceptability of this technique often reduces its feasibility. In fact, sometimes the use of tests affects learner acceptance of the program's efforts and learner willingness to be involved in either the activity or the evaluation. "Tests," Knowles warns, "should be used with caution and preferably with the participants' full participation in the decision, administration, and analysis."[30] Evaluators who consider tests must be aware of their potential dangers as well as their strengths.

- Standardized tests can, for the most part, be assumed to have the advantage of high validity and reliability. They may or may not fit well with the specific situation in which they are used, however. Selection from the array of available tests must be carefully done. Their feasibility, when met by strong resistance factors, reduces their acceptability to those to whom they are to be administered. As continuing library education becomes more institutionalized, it is likely that more and more tests relating directly to library proficiencies will become standardized. New fashions in education—such as requirements for performance-based learning, competency-based education, criterion referenced instruction, and adult performance levels—are also influencing the trends towards standardized tests by making the developmental procedures for such tests more accessible.

- Performance tests are demonstrations of what was learned, a gauge of applied knowledge and of the problem-solving ability gained through learning activities. Although usually conducted at the work site, sometimes this test is held at the learning site, with case study problems that pose practical examples of typical problems found on the job, but with some control of the topic and situation by the evaluator. These tests are primarily measures of what was learned and how well it is being applied. Long acceptable as a demonstration of skills learnings, some are constructed to test knowledge and attitudes. Supervisory observation is an informal adaptation of this test. Under most circumstances, constructed performance tests are a relatively reliable and valid means to find out how well a skill may have been learned and how successfully it can be applied.

- Tailor-made tests are often developed for a specific situation and can incorporate the awareness of the content and method actually used. They require extensive time to design, test, and administer. Depending on their format and approach, they often give rise to strong resistance attached to testing in general. They usually have not been validated through rigorous protocol, so their reliability is often questionable.

- Tests for self-assessment or self-evaluation can be supplied for a particular learning activity or might be designed by learners themselves. They help learners determine for themselves what they have learned and how well they can apply it. The self-directed nature of these tests increases their acceptability, and they are the exception to the general resistance felt toward tests. On the contrary, they often prompt strong motivation for learning. They not only supply needed information, but promote an in-depth understanding of the value of evaluation. The best sources of forms and procedures for these tests are in adult education literature on contract learning and self-directed learning, most notably Knowles's *Self-Directed Learning; A Guide for Learners and Teachers* (1975).

The range of test possibilities is wide. Difficulties of using tests may lie in the reliability of the test, the capability of the test response to meet the purpose set for it, the difficulties of administering it, and the feelings of those taking it. When these difficulties are minimal or nonexistent, tests can offer solid data that can be strong evidence of the accomplishments of the learning program. Testing with a representative sample can sometimes deal with some of the difficulties that arise with testing generally.

Questionnaires are the most frequently used (and abused) method of collecting evaluation information. Usually, they are designed to be used for a particular activity, with specific questions relating to facets or results of that event eliciting opinions, evidences of learnings, or reactions. At times, their frequent use and poor quality wear out their advantages. Used before an activity, they can identify learner expectations, self-perceived ability, knowledge, and needs. Used during an activity, they can test the learner's knowledge or can elicit opinions and reactions to the methods or the educators. Post-activity forms can identify personal feelings or define what the learners thought were their most significant learnings. Follow-up questionnaires may be sent to the learner, a supervisor/supervisee, or colleagues to ask for their observations of the learner's actual behaviors in relation to the recent learning opportunity.

Questionnaires usually combine several types of questions on a single instrument that is distributed and collected at pre-determined times. The responses are then tallied, analyzed, and channeled to those who need the information. The following types of questions are likely to be found on questionnaires:

- scales to rate the training activity, personnel, facilities, materials, attitudes and opinions, such as "Rank the value of this activity to you on a scale of 1-10, using 1 as low, 10 as high."

- ratings of various components to determine which were most effective or acceptable, such as "Rate the five most significant sessions of this workshop using 1 for most important, 2 for next most important, and so forth."

- forced choice questions to give a limited option in expressing opinion, such as "I found this training session to be __ excellent, __ good, __ fair, __ poor."

- open-ended questions that guide the respondent in regard to the type of information being sought, but leave the choice and terminology free, such as "What were the most helpful learnings you gained?"

Questionnaires are more often used than are tests or interviews, for the common perception is that they can be devised with less expertise than that required for other methods. Since most people are experienced with responding to questionnaires, their level of acceptability is generally high. Supplementing the home-developed variety, standardized package questionnaires are now available for such subjects as prejudice, leadership, and human relations topics and can be used for pre- and post-views.

Often questionnaires bring forth subjective information despite consistent attempts to "objectify" the forms and the responses. Perhaps the most used evaluation technique is the typical end-of-the-activity/how-did-you-feel-about-it? form. This procedure has its advocates and its opponents. The former indicate that such a process gathers spontaneous, immediate reactions from learners fresh from the experience of the activity, when they can pinpoint problem areas, suggest modifications, or identify unmet needs. Opponents of this practice discount the information it yields as "happiness" data, indicating more about the internal feelings of the learner than about the quality of the program. Thoughtful questions can indeed elicit information with some validity. But often, questionnaires become a ritual with no use made of the information they produce. If only used at the end of the activity, the information will not produce changes or modifications in that activity, although, at that point, they may provide insight about what happened.

Being very flexible in format and approach as well as content, questionnaires can be designed to focus on the learner, the activity, or the program. The information is usually quick to administer and analyze and can be easily distributed where needed in time to modify an activity, change emphasis of a program, or fill a gap in subject content. Their quality depends on whether they elicit the information sought. Pre-testing can often eliminate lack of clarity or the most inappropriate questions. Questionnaires are sometimes anonymous to enable respondents to be more open and frank with their answers. A series of questionnaires used during a single activity (or a number of coordinated activities) can be very helpful, not only to test but also to reinforce what has been learned by asking that it be internalized and communicated through the form. When such a series is used, each learner can select an anonymous designation to identify and "track" individual changes or growth evidenced during the series.

Interviews can elicit information not obtainable through testing or questionnaires, and, at the same time, can reinforce learnings. The flow of conversation brings forth information of more depth and substance than pen-and-paper procedures. Informational statements give a better indication of the internalization of learnings than do other methods, with the exception of the demonstration test. The validity and accuracy of the information can be affected by the interpersonal relationship between the interviewer and interviewee(s) and by the degree of skill possessed by the interviewer. The information itself is highly subjective and difficult to efficiently record, but useful where those factors are not drawbacks. Interviews are particularly useful to report results or to give opinions and reactions concerning activities. Interviews can be an expensive procedure due to the amount of time required first to conduct the interviews and then to analyze the wealth of information they produce. They may be informal or structured, group or individual.

- Informal dialogue can reveal valuable information about a program or perceptions of training activities or of the organization. Often, real in-depth concerns are revealed during the informal exchanges with educators, supervisors, or colleagues, as well as with learners. Particularly useful during breaks in an activity, informal conversations may yield much information that can be used to modify that activity. The information is very subjective and thus sometimes not acceptable to those in a position to use it, but the process is often very acceptable to those being interviewed. The procedure is usually feasible and flexible, requiring only that the program planners, educators, or evaluators be aware of the opportunity and responsibility. In some cases, a reaction panel or a feedback team made up of learners can be used to give both their own opinions and those that they have heard from others.

- Structured interviews consist of carefully pre-planned questions designed to gather specific information. Questions may be asked of an individual or of a group by the interviewer. Less dependent on random conversation, structured questions are intended to produce more uniform types of information than is possible through unstructured situations. The information is subjective but more directed toward specific subjects and issues. The interviews are usually pre-arranged, and the interviewee(s) know the purpose. Feasibility often depends on the time required to interview, to analyze, and to report the information in time for it to be useful. The results of interviews are improved if the questions are carefully selected and if the interviewer is skilled.

- Individual interviews can be informal or structured. They yield primarily subjective information and are more useful for unearthing opinions, reactions, and suggestions than for reporting hard evidence of results. The time of the interviewer and the interviewee(s) is expensive.

- Group interviews offer several advantages: inter-stimulation of ideas, less time required of the interviewer, a wealth of information yielded. The disadvantage is that they are very difficult to document, and the information can't be channeled to those who need it rapidly. Group interviews can be conducted during regularly scheduled meetings before, during, or following learning activities. Meetings such as staff or faculty meetings can often profit from sharing the information gained through a group interview focused on a given subject.

Interviews, when used often over a period of time, can keep track of a dynamic situation, for example, the one that often occurs when a learning experience is regarded positively (or negatively) at first and then opinions gradually change over a period of time following the experience. Interviews may focus closely on a single activity, or they may be fairly broad in their scope. Often they identify emerging needs as well as the results from activities.

Documentation, another source for collecting evaluation information, can reveal the results and impacts of learning programs. Personal or organizational documentation results from recording information in order to communicate or preserve it. Personal documentation can include the tangible products produced by learners as a result of learning experiences or training exercises (such as an action plan, a new procedure or file, a learner diary of experiences and learnings, a report of recommendations, an analysis of a procedure). Organizational documentation includes reports, plans, memoranda, personnel appraisals, and statistics of production, accuracy, or work flow. Over a period of time, these records can reveal the growth of an individual or changes in the organization. More effective and accurate organizational planning, better decision-making at meetings, or more staff involvement in organizational issues might evidence organizational impact. More favorable personnel rankings, new interests or endeavors, observed improvement in skills, and fewer errors or complaints might indicate individual learner achievements. Records and files could provide the evidence for each of these.

Documentation can be used for cross-checking other evaluative information or for establishing a benchmark to check against or develop other measures. If documents are available, analyzing them may be more rapid and less costly of time than gathering the same or similar information through other measures. Tangible documentation produced by learners may benefit both the learner, who learns while producing the product, and the organization, which has a report or plan that can be used directly in organizational functions.

Observation inevitably occurs and people form judgments on the basis of their observations. As a valid means to collect evaluation information, however, observation must be deliberately and carefully structured. Those who observe need to be trained in what and how to observe, those being observed need to know they will be observed. And, means to record observations are essential with those written methods most commonly used. Often, the informal approach to observation is thought sufficient, but this is an unwise assumption and, in some cases, may be unfair. Prepared observers must possess the skills of seeing and recording information without personal bias or misinterpretation of behavior. Whether the observer actively engages with the learner in the demonstration of learning, or whether the observer is unobtrusively watching, the observer is the key to accurate and reliable information. The observer's skills must be well enough developed to assure quality and fair data.

The techniques used to collect evaluation information range from commonsense to scientific inquiries. Those that are selected for a particular activity or program should be able to bring strong advantages to that situation, and ways to cope with the possible disadvantages should be sought as well. Basically, these techniques seek to determine what the learner has learned and how that happened through measures taken at the learning or work sites. Often a sample may be drawn about the entire group. Chabotar and Lad's *Evaluation Guidelines for Training Programs* (1974) is helpful in selecting and using samples in evaluating learning programs, as are more technical sampling sources.

Blockages and Bypasses

Collecting evaluation information is sometimes impeded either deliberately or inadvertently. The implication of this is serious for, if the information cannot be collected, it cannot be used. Then, initial assumptions and expectations continue untested. When a blockage is detected, however, bypasses are sometimes possible and can be employed to reduce the amount of blockage to then enable the information to be collected. Or, bypasses can be built in as a preventative measure when potential blockages are suspected.

One of the most frequent blockages results from a lack of understanding and acceptance of the evaluation process. When this happens with the program planners, the administrator, or the educational staff, the result may be that no plans or provisions are made for evaluation. The consequence, then, is that evaluation is not done or, if done, is likely to be superficial and perfunctory. When this lack of understanding and acceptance occurs on the part of the learners from whom information is being gathered, the result is a lack of information—for example, questionnaires not returned, interview appointments not kept, or distorted information supplied. With any of these circumstances, the resulting evaluation is likely to be inaccurate and may misdirect analysis.

The bypass for this blockage is to involve those who do not understand the importance of evaluation more deeply in the process of it, so they might understand from direct personal experience what evaluation can do and why it is valuable. Emphasis on gathering feedback type of evaluation that has immediate and often obvious practical uses may help, since the resistance may come from believing evaluation to be solely judgmental. Also, information about the evaluation plan might be shared more fully among learners, educators, and administrator. For learners, written materials prior to the activity could include an explanation of the evaluation, or a session at the activity could be devoted to evaluation both in general and as it applies to the particular activity, with time for questions and responses. The planning period, bringing administrators and educators together, provides a way to inform them of the evaluation's purpose and to incorporate evaluation procedures into the design.

A second common blockage is the lack of willingness to participate in evaluation, even though the principles and practice may be understood. If a number of individuals show strong unwillingness to evaluate or be evaluated, others who were previously neutral may be swayed to join the resistance. The result then will be much less complete information than may be needed to fulfill evaluation purposes. Collecting evaluation information is particularly difficult if the educational staff are resistant or defensive about being evaluated, for this will influence learners also. Lack of willingness may be due to disinterest in the activity, lack of time, or the presence of more pressing priorities. Unlike school and academic situations, compliance cannot be enforced in adult learning; punishment and censure are not effective. Knowing just how the individuals and the activity or program will benefit from accurate, complete evaluation information may be sufficient to convince the resistors to contribute to it. The personal influence of the administrator, educators, or evaluators is sometimes effective, as is increasing the awareness and possibility of motivational incentives, such as certificates or other forms of recognition. This, of course, assumes that such benefits as rewards and recognition and/or improved activities will actually be part of the evaluation results.

The "lack of appropriate evaluation instruments and procedures" is cited by Guba as being a fundamental impediment to adequate evaluation information.[32] Whether using prepared materials and designed methods, or whether developing those that will meet a particular situation, the use of inappropriate or inadequate evaluation procedures will result in inaccurate or unusable information. A certain amount of evaluation knowhow is required for any but the simple approaches that rely on common sense more than expertise. Bypasses for this dilemma include discovering just what techniques are available and how they can be used. This can be done through self-study by those responsible for evaluation or by using a consultant to assist with the more sensitive aspects of the evaluation process. Careful pre-testing of all techniques is one way of working directly with the technique to see how applicable it is in a specific situation.

One blockage that is rarely intentional is that of timing. The amount of time to plan or implement collection may be inadequate, not in the appropriate sequence, or not correlated with the needs for information or with its availability. One common result when the evaluation process is sidetracked in favor of other activities is that the availability of evaluation information is curtailed. Two related bypasses are possible. One is to assure that those responsible for evaluation are strong advocates of the process; the second is that they are involved in the general planning for the program and/or activities.

A difficult block to bypass is when there is a conflict of priorities that confuses and frustrates individuals involved with implementing the evaluation processes. For example, the need for rapid and low-cost techniques for collecting evaluation information may collide with the need for accurate and valid information. This conflict may result in a stalemate that essentially prevents sound collection of the information needed. The bypass is to have a clear and common understanding about all priorities at any given time.

Finally, after the program and/or activity design has been set and the plan for evaluation has been laid, changes may be needed (or may just happen). Sometimes the objectives may need to be changed. This may make the present evaluation plan invalid. Perhaps the type of information to be gathered or the methods to be used in collecting it are no longer relevant. Then, new decisions are required for adjustments to assure the continued validity of the evaluation. Those decisions must be informed and sound. The bypass for this blockage is the deep involvement of those responsible for evaluation in the general planning process; this will help them be aware of the reasons for such changes and the need for the evaluation plan to be flexible to accommodate the changes.

These blockages are not infrequent or uncommon. Each situation is unique in its mixture of personalities, decisions, problems, and resources. Immediate and potential blockages will be found within each situation, as will the bypasses. In instances where the commitment to evaluation is perfunctory, any one of them can be cited as a reason why evaluation is not being done. However, where evaluation is believed to be valuable, creative bypasses will be found around the blockages, no matter how many may be present. Often an initial resistance to evaluation will change into acceptance or even enthusiasm when resistors observe that the use of simple but effective evaluation measures has a direct and tangible return, whether useful to the individual learner, to the implementation of the activity, or the operation of the program.

General Concerns

Program planners and evaluators confront the question: How can evidence about learnings and how they occurred be obtained in such a way that the information is adequate and reliable and yet is obtained by acceptable means? This question does not become clearly apparent until it is time to collect evaluation information. Then, resistance or challenge may be encountered in the form of some of those blockages described earlier. One reaction to resistance is to make evaluation mandatory. This may obtain the information but will often generate negative feelings on the learner's part, thereby affecting his or her willingness to learn and become involved. Another reaction is to withdraw the requirement for evaluation. This may avoid negative feelings, but it will also yield no information for evaluative purposes and may set an undesirable precedent.

Library staff development and continuing education efforts are based on the precept of individual responsibility for making the most of the learning opportunities in an adult, ethical fashion. But, presently, there is no generally accepted norm or standard for measuring the gains made by learners from a program's opportunities. Yet, the need continues, the need to know what was learned and how, so that learners, program planners, administrators, and funders will know what is effective and what is not. This need, however, is sometimes countered by the unavailability of acceptable methods to discover that information.

To raise this concern is not necessarily to answer it, however. Both Knowles and Davis address the situation to some extent, and both advocate approaching evaluation as "a mutual undertaking" although in different ways. Knowles "prescribes a process of self-evaluation, in which the teacher devotes his energy to helping the adults get evidence for themselves about the progress they are making toward their educational goals." His reason for this approach is that:

> Probably the crowning instance in incongruity between traditional educational practice and the adult's self-concept of self-directivity is the act of a teacher giving a grade to a student. Nothing makes an adult feel more childlike than being judged by another adult; it is the ultimate sign of disrespect and dependency, as the one who is being judged experiences it.[33]

He extends this early concept in his later *Self-Directed Learning; A Guide for Learners and Teachers*, which proposes procedures and forms to help the self-evaluation process, on the basis of demonstrated proficiency in relation to defined criteria.

Davis, like Knowles, advocates the measure of performance based on established objectives as the only real testing of what has been learned. Davis describes the discomfort of some adult educators in asking learners to demonstrate their competencies. Further examination reveals that these discomfitted individuals have usually not involved the learner in setting the objectives, in diagnosing their own needs; thus, to involve them in the evaluation proves awkward. But, he emphasizes, "Evaluation by objectives is not an imposition on adults when they have freely 'contracted' on the objectives."[34] His answer to rightfully claiming demonstration of competence as a major measure of learning is to involve the learner in evaluation as well as in earlier processes through a "learner contract."

The need for demonstration of learned competence is not simply to "show what you have learned" at the end of the learning activity. It involves determining what the learner was able to do before exposure to the activity; that is then measured against what the learner was able to do after that learning experience. Obviously this can be linked with needs assessment procedures, since that process would have determined what knowledge or skills were necessary, and thus were lacking. The evaluation procedure also reveals needs that still exist or new ones now apparent. Often, in looking at what parts of the activity were successful and what parts were not, individual evaluation may not be necessary at all.

Methods of involving the learning group may be used to give a picture of progress and will reduce the pressure on the individual to exhibit personal competence and "prove" knowledge.

What is wanted and needed in the way of evaluation information must be balanced against what is feasible to obtain. Often, initial evaluation plans are overly ambitious, promising more than is possible. This usually becomes apparent when evaluation information begins to be collected. When the time to evaluate is insufficient, evaluation knowhow is limited, or access to individuals with information is impossible, however, the original evaluation plan may then have to be redrafted. Three areas are most involved in such revisions: 1) priorities must be reset, 2) the means to collect and handle information must be modified, 3) a greater effort is required to inform key people of the value and use of evaluation.

Redrafting the original plan will usually involve compromises, some difficult for program planners and evaluators to accept. But, the dilemmas posed by compromise will be frequent ones throughout the program, for not everything wanted to needed will be feasible. Cutting back on the planned evaluation will, of course, restrict the available information, but rarely are circumstances so severely limiting that evaluation is simply not possible at all.

Summary

The plan for evaluation is first implemented with the collection of information. According to the plan, various kinds of information will be needed and those will be collected in specified ways. For the purpose of collection, three groupings are possible: by focus, by sources, and by technique. The relevancy of each of these is closely tied to the needs and the capability of the unique situation.

Evaluation information collected according to a plan will be useful to its maximum extent and will likely be more efficiently collected. Criteria can help guide the selection of techniques used to collect the information needed. The techniques include tests, questionnaires, interviews, documentation, and observation. Most evaluations blend a combination of these techniques to obtain the information needed. Blockages may impede the collecting of information. They include: lack of understanding and acceptance of evaluation; lack of willingness to participate in it; lack of appropriate instruments and procedures; timing; conflict of priorities; and the need for changes in the evaluation to accommodate changes in the program or activity design. Preventative and prescriptive bypasses to each of these are possible.

The key question surfacing at the time of collecting the information is: how can evidence about learnings and how they occurred be obtained in such a way that the information is adequate and reliable yet is obtained by acceptable means?

GUIDELINE 14–ANALYZE EVALUATION INFORMATION

Evaluation information that has been collected is of little value until it has been organized and analyzed. Then, it can be used by individuals concerned with the program in general or those with a specific task, role, function, or activity within the program. Analyzed information can be interpreted to reveal effectiveness and results, and, thereby, to influence subsequent decisions. Although the plan for evaluation included the collection, analysis, reporting, and use of evaluative information, even a very thorough evaluation plan cannot predict the results of the analysis. But it can specify the kinds of analysis procedures to be followed and can indicate potential uses and users of the results of it.

Analysis links the collected information and its use. The substance of the analyzed information must be both practical and usable, as must the form used to report it. One program may use the information to document any gain in learners's skills and to identify the impact that those improved competencies make on the library. In another program, the information may be directed towards improved program planning and structural changes in the library, including realigning jobs and extensive training for new skills. Yet another program may use the analysis to report the effectiveness of the program to its membership. For each use, analysis is necessary to make the information usable.

This Guideline describes several factors that influence the organization and its interpretation of evaluation information. It outlines the procedures necessary to this process. It also explores the advantages and disadvantages related to who is responsible for analysis and suggests the importance of setting priorities.

Key Factors

Decisions must be made concerning both the extent to which analysis can feasibly be done and the allocation of responsibilities made for accomplishing the necessary tasks. Two general questions may be asked:

- What is the desirable balance between the cost of analysis and interpretation (i.e., the time and the money) and the benefits that are anticipated from that analysis (i.e., information for planning, documentation for accountability)?

- What parts of the analysis require common sense, logic, and knowledge of the program, and what parts require evaluation expertise to obtain the information needed?

These questions may be usefully addressed at the time of planning for evaluation. But even so, they often have to be considered again after initial implementation of that planning has begun. Often the real scope of evaluation is more extensive than what was originally envisioned. And, equally often, that fact first becomes apparent only after the information has been collected, that is, before it is analyzed.

In responding to these two guideline questions, their more specific ingredients must be explored. Several factors are essential to successful analysis. The importance of each of these in a given situation may vary, but, in most programs, each is significant. The specific factors that must be taken into account include:

- a perceived need and value for the analysis,

- established priorities,

- the kind and amount of information to be analyzed,

- the skills and knowledge of those responsible for the analysis,
- the availability of resources, such as time, funds, facilities, and equipment.

Each of these elements is interrelated with the others. For instance, skilled personnel may be available to deal with a large amount of statistical evaluative information. If the needed computer time and equipment are not available, however, such procedures will not be possible to enable the needed interpretation. Or, if all the needed human, technical, and financial resources are available to do a credible analysis and skilled interpretation of the collected information, but if decision-makers are not interested in the findings or have chosen to ignore the evaluation process entirely, it is unlikely that those resources will be released. The interrelationship of these factors is important, for a single negative factor may cause a need for alternative approaches or redesign of the evaluation plan.

Building favorable perceptions of the need for and value of analyzing collected information begins early in the planning and evaluation phases. Token sanction and encouragement of evaluation may be easily obtained, and planning for evaluation is also usually possible. But, during collection and analysis, tensions not present before may begin to rise, resulting in overt or covert resistance that forestalls the actual evaluation. Often sensitive and personalized situations develop, requiring diplomacy and tact. When the plan for evaluation addresses the needs of analysis realistically and when the key decision-makers have been involved in the earlier decisions about the evaluation, the value of an appropriate evaluation will probably be understood.

Several steps can be employed to raise the level of awareness of the need for analyzing information or to convince those who resist evaluation in general or the processing of the information in particular. A basic step is to select from the available evaluative information those findings of immediate applicability and use. If essential and timely, the information itself can then demonstrate its own value. Another possible step is to circulate or discuss similar situations in which evaluation has played an important role. These may serve as examples of the possibilities that exist in the present circumstances. Both of these suggestions use the approach of exhibiting benefits from analyzed information. A more fundamental step would be to search for the objections and barriers blocking an understanding of the need for and value of analysis. If the resistance is rooted in fear of negative findings, that issue may have to be confronted very directly. Or perhaps it is possible and still helpful to shift the focus or to stress the positive.

Since it is not possible to evaluate everything that may be important, priorities must be established to determine what is to be evaluated. Then, information is collected on that basis. Typically, however, more information results from collection than was originally envisioned or can be utilized, and it may not be feasible to organize and interpret all the information that has been collected. For instance, the many possibilities for the results of one questionnaire are usually not exhausted before both time and personnel are spent. Given that situation, priorities may have to be reestablished for analyzing the collected information once its implications are seen.

In establishing this second level of priorities, it is important to again look at the expected use of the information, so that the analysis most suitable for the intended use and the most crucial needs will be done. Other criteria for selecting topmost priorities at this point would be:

- information most quickly and economically analyzed,
- information most needed for immediate use,
- resources most available to handle the collected information,
- information most likely to go out-of-date.

Other, more specialized criteria might supplement this more generalized list with considerations related to a particular situation. The fact that priorities may change between the time of planning for evaluation and the time when the information is available to be analyzed and reported. The evaluation plan must be able to accommodate that kind of change and decision-makers should remain alert to this possibility.

A third factor influencing analysis of information is the kind and amount of it to be analyzed. Some kinds of information may need special expertise or processing to interpret, and sometimes resources beyond those available to the program may have to be tapped. When the range of different kinds of information to be collected has been foreseen in planning, many of the collection instruments can be specially designed to allow ease of analysis. The physical amount of information is less apt to be accurately predicted, however, and file drawers may fill with collected but unanalyzed evaluation forms or tapes of interviews, with everyone lacking the time or special expertise to analyze it. Lack of analysis will, of course, prevent use.

Usually the possibilities of kinds and amount are simply not predicted accurately. Sometimes, however, this may be a deliberate effort in order to produce enough information to be selective in what will be analyzed and reported. Then, the information that is most necessary and important is actually analyzed, the rest discarded or held. The main disadvantage to this approach is that a portion of the time and effort spent to plan for and collect the information is, essentially, wasted; the approach is not economical. This can also be viewed as an imposition on those from whom the information is collected.

The skills and knowledge necessary for analysis may be tapped internally, that is, among those actively involved in the program. Circumstances such as funding, timing, or convenience often make internal arrangements the most feasible. If the plan for evaluation has been confined to limited, relatively unspecialized methods, a common-sense and relatively unsophisticated approach may be sufficient. If just a few areas require special knowledge or expertise, outside advice and consultation may be sought. If, however, the plan requires technical expertise beyond the capabilities present capabilities within the program, an outside consultant might be sought just for the analysis and, perhaps, the reporting responsibilities.

If evaluation of depth and sophistication develops along with the program, the results and funding are more predictable, capable of handling more esoteric evaluation approaches. Gradual growth plus commensurate staff development efforts in evaluation will strengthen the program's ability to continue to meet its own needs effectively. Where organizational resources and commitment permit, however, the possibility of engaging an outside evaluator might well be considered, either for the analysis or for the whole evaluation.

Ordinarily, an experienced evaluator will accomplish those functions more efficiently than individuals with less experience. Along with a special expertise, an evaluator may also bring a perspective (and maybe a bias) about what kinds of results can be expected from continuing education programs. Objectivity is one of the advantages to be expected from the use of an outside evaluator. But there are disadvantages: the cost, if not planned for, can be a barrier; the outsider's lack of in-depth knowledge of the program and the organization can take time to remedy; limited availability and accessibility on an inconsistent basis may pose difficulties. An outside evaluator for a continuing education program, however, may bring a credibility and exposure to the program to a greater degree than would be possible with only an internal evaluation by program staff.

Another alternative is that of using a group, perhaps a committee serving as advisors or planners for the program. The main advantage to this is that these individuals presumably know what information they need because of their familiarity with the program. If the plan for evaluation produces a flow of useful information, they can make prompt and appropriate use of the findings. The major disadvantages of this approach include the possibility of bias, the time and effort required to work effectively as a group, and the mix of evaluation knowledge, skills, and preferences. There is also the possibility that evaluation may not rank as high on the priorities as does planning and, thus, may be set aside.

Some programs and some activities have used a panel of participant/practitioners who are charged with reviewing program activities and functions. These individuals know first-hand their own impressions and experiences with the program, can see possible on-the-job applications, and often contribute their services because of either a commitment to improving the program or a realization of the personal learning that can result from serving on such a panel. Panel members may monitor individual activities or review the total continuing education operation. The disadvantage of this is the lack of evaluation expertise in using lay individuals. However, this may be offset by their knowledge of organizational needs and a pragmatic view of how effective the learning experiences were. Usually, such a panel would be assigned the activities and products of the program rather than its management and internal operation, although, in some cases, they might be useful with both aspects.

The final factor is that of the availability of those resources that analysis requires, in addition to the necessary skills and knowledge. The availability of time, funds, facilities, and equipment may dictate the direction and completeness of analysis even more than the actual requirements of processing the information. Allocation of staff time, funds, and facilities needs to be anticipated at the point of planning for evaluation. However, often the demands of analysis are difficult to know how to predict and plan without prior experience. If these provisions have not been planned for adequately, the anticipated procedures for analysis may be curtailed when the full scope of the task is seen after the information has been collected. Then, if the program is a high priority within the organization, and if the evaluation is a priority within the program, the prospect for obtaining the needed resources may be favorable.

These five specific factors are important to sound analysis of evaluation information. They are ingredients that, put together, enable planners, administrators, and evaluators to answer the questions of balance between cost and benefits and of need for expertise raised earlier. Once these factors are considered and the questions are answered satisfactorily, the analysis can proceed with more specific procedures and tasks.

Procedures

Procedures for collection and analysis are the most technical ones of the evaluation function. This also may be one of the main reasons that more evaluation is not better done. If planning for the collection has included preliminary thinking about the analysis to follow, the instruments and procedures can more easily be organized. And, those to whom the information will be sent can be alerted and reminded of the kinds and use of information they will receive. Information for formative purposes must be promptly analyzed and reported. That for summative purposes may await further information before being reported.

Three tasks make up the procedures for analysis:

1) review of the original information, such as the forms, scores, documentation, notes from interviews, observations,

2) coding of that information to bring it together in a single place,

3) interpretation of the information to extract its meaning and to answer the questions asked of the evaluation.

How usable the result of this process will be depends on how clear and feasible the purpose(s) for the evaluation is/are, how adequate the collection of information has been in relation to those purpose(s), and how useful the collection procedures were. Finally, the quality of the result will also depend on the ability of the people and procedures used to organize and interpret the collected information.

The review of the original information includes assembling all the information available that relates to what is being evaluated. This is to assure an awareness of the scope of information available and to see what range of useful information can be gleaned from what is available. Further, this review provides cross-validation from different sources that might help to verify and substantiate the findings from any single source. For example, the review of the information available from a one-day training session might include participants' questionnaire forms turned in at the conclusion of the session, notes from interviews conducted with participants' supervisors following the session, and documentation of the reports and projects undertaken by participants subsequent to the training session but related to the topic of the session. The review of information from various sources offers an overview of what is available and helps in planning for the next step.

The second task, coding, consists primarily of organizing information in categories for purposes of counting or interpreting. Categories should be well-defined, mutually exclusive, and as exhaustive or detailed as necessary to get at the information indicated to be needed. It is important to have good, well-defined categories in order to make accurate and useful assignments of information. Coding is facilitated if, at the time of designing the collection instruments, advance thought was given to how coding might be done, and if those thoughts were incorporated into the collection instrument to make the task of coding easier.

Information available from all sources in relation to the focus being evaluated will need to be organized, grouped, and recorded in order to interpret it. Some will be easily quantifiable and recorded. From questionnaires, for example, the questions involving scaling, ranking, and forced choice are easily recorded with tally marks for each response and later totaled. A blank copy of the questionnaire can be used for this purpose. Total numbers and percentages can easily be figured. The open-ended questions from questionnaires and structured interviews can be recorded by key words and phrases, grouped (after being listed on a common sheet of paper) into patterns that will surface. From the first third of the total responses, those patterns and natural groupings usually emerge to guide the remaining tallies. This process is generally termed content analysis and defines the kinds of responses in terms of what they said.

Another approach to content analysis also results in both frequency indication and groupings. It pre-determines the groupings, such as: positive/negative; content suggestions/method recommendations; problem identification/resource identification; concerns/satisfactions/needs. Again using a blank copy of the original instrument, columns may be made for each category selected and tally marks then made for the number of times each category is mentioned, (or keywords written, where appropriate). As in the earlier approach, categories should be clearly defined and mutually exclusive.

Other information is not so easily categorized, however. In-depth interviews, open-ended questions eliciting long discursive responses, and information from widely disparate documentation sources are difficult to neatly tabulate. Individual and group interviews produce immense quantities of information, much of it hard to categorize. Performance tests may be recorded with notes of observations supplemented perhaps by indications of self-evaluation. Self-assessment forms and performance learning contracts indicate criteria and evidence in relation to those criteria, and these require in-depth individual scrutiny. Usually the type of information and the purposes for which it has been collected will indicate how it should be treated to bring it into sufficient organization. To be interpreted when statistical interpretations are to be made, some of the information may be more easily worked with if displayed in tables, chart form, or other graphic formats.

The first result of coding is lists, numbers, and words. Tendencies and trends then begin to show through the frequencies and the groupings. The feasibility of cross-checking and correlating the information can also be initially tested at this point, and statistical determinations can be done at this time. The most used of these are frequencies; percentages; proportions and ratios; measures of central value, such as mean, median, and mode; and the measures of variability. Chabotar and Lad's *Evaluation Guidelines for Training Programs* (1974) has an extensive section on statistical analysis in regard to training programs, with self-testing exercises to develop skills for people with little experience in statistics or training. Guilford and Frutchter's *Fundamental Statistics in Psychology and Education* (1973) covers a wide range of enumeration and measurement types of statistical data. This source also has self-testing exercises and clear, pragmatic explanations. Its focus is not on training programs, but it is a basic source on statistics. Jum Nunnally's *Introduction to Statistics for Psychology and Education* (1975) covers descriptive statistics and inferential statistics and describes how to compile and interpret information for practical use from statistical data. These resources help in instances where coding is beyond being simple and self-evident.

Interpretation occurs when meaning and significance is extracted from the collected and organized evaluation information. The accuracy of the conclusions that are drawn, the implications that are made, and the recommendations that are formulated depend, to a great extent, on the quality and accuracy of the previous steps. Interpretation is the point where a close review and examination of the available information provides some results and direct effects a definition of relationships perhaps not seen before, a basis for generalizations to be at least tentatively made, an anticipation of side-effects and trends, and a picture of issues and problems.

Considering the potential importance of the interpreted information that will be forwarded to the learners, the program planners and administrator, and other organizational personnel, several factors are important to emphasize. Interpretation must be as balanced, honest, and complete as time and information can make it. Different interpretations are usually possible on the basis of the same information. Alternative explanations are possible given the same data. Judgement, experience, awareness, and understanding alter the perspective of each person and shed a different light on the available information in each situation. Care must be taken to assure that the interpretation is not biased to support a previously held position when the information could also be read in other ways. When individuals or organizations have much at stake in the results of a program, the interpretation of evaluation information may become vulnerable to being slanted, even though perhaps unwittingly, to support a desired stance.

Interpretation poses the need for a balance between internal perspectives and external ones. On the one hand, involvement of learners, those responsible for the program or activity, and administrators of the organization is important to broaden understanding of the findings, to balance different perspectives, to reduce the threat that is often felt when findings are announced, and to promote change. If the responsibility for interpretation of evaluation information rests with a single individual, and if that individual reports only one possible interpretation of the information available, strong reaction and resistance may rise to counter the recommendations suggested on the basis of that single interpretation.

On the other hand, independent interpretation from an outside evaluator often gives a different, broader view from wider experiences and more astute and objective observations than may be possible from inside the organization. Yet, an outsider's perspective will be limited by lack of intimate knowledge of the organization's workings. The need for technical expertise and that objective view may justify engaging outside expertise. But that view should be balanced by that of those people within the organization who may know and express the nuances, the subjective impressions that may not have been incorporated in the statistical analyses, charts, and conclusions drawn on the basis of "hard" data.

Also to be considered in interpretation is the understanding, acceptance, and explanation of the degree of accuracy and precision that is actually present in the findings. Of course, the information will need to be as accurate as possible considering the effectiveness of the collection instruments and procedures, the capability for analysis, and the available expertise of those who have worked with it. But, realistic qualifications should clearly state how exact the information is believed to be and thus how reliable the interpretation is. Overly high expectations are often held concerning the conclusiveness of evaluation results. With the possible exception of very research-oriented types of evaluation, the interpretation will probably give more of an indication than a definitive prediction.

Time and timing affect the interpretation of the information. The time needed to collect the information is wasted if no commitment is made to invest more time to organize and interpret it. Analysis requires time, a cost factor, as will the reporting and dissemination of it. Timing refers to the scheduling of both the analysis and the reporting. Some evaluation information will need prompt analysis and reporting, while other data will not depend significantly on timing of the analysis. Since the purpose of collecting and analyzing evaluation information is its use, the timing of the analysis should be appropriate to those who will be using it.

A final consideration is important in interpretation. From whom does the information come? To whom does it go and for what purposes? Who owns it? Those who fill out forms and take tests and respond to interviews have a right to know who will be using what they say and how. Those who collect the information and those who analyze it have a responsibility to be aware of the use of the information they have assembled. When desirable, anonymity can be assured, either at the point of collecting or of analyzing the information. This can protect the right of privacy and thus increase the chances that future evaluation efforts will be accepted and trusted. Information should be handled with necessary precautions and respect for individuals as well as with attention to the need for information to improve the program.

Summary

Analysis makes the collected evaluation information usable; it links collection and use. Findings must be organized and interpreted before they can document results or provide useful information for future planning. Although the plan for evaluation cannot predict the results of analysis, it can specify the analysis procedures to be followed and can indicate the potential uses and users of the interpretation resulting from the analysis.

Several significant factors influence the analysis, such as the perceived need for analysis, the priorities, the information itself, the skills and knowledge of those responsible for analysis, and the availability of resources. Analysis procedures include: 1) review of the collected information, 2) coding it, and 3) interpreting it. Differing interpretations can, of course, be drawn from the same information.

GUIDELINE 15–REPORT AND UTILIZE EVALUATION INFORMATION

Planning for evaluation and the efforts of collecting and analyzing evaluation information are wasted if no provision is made for reporting and utilizing that information. Evaluation discovers what has been accomplished, what remains to be done, and what changes for improvement are indicated. Reporting these discoveries then builds the connections necessary for action. Although reporting is usually done at the end of an activity or as a cycle in the program is completed, the usefulness of the information occurs at the point where both the information availability and need coincide. Regular and frequent reporting provides the required flow of information, guiding modification and improvement of program effects and documenting present results. The plan for evaluation outlines how the evaluation information will be reported and utilized, assuring that the information gets to the right place at the right time.

Each point of reporting can be a catalyst to solve problems, confront issues, highlight feelings of satisfaction and achievement, motivate further learning and involvement, and guide implementation of personal or organizational changes. Timely, regular feedback keeps track of progress and enables better decisions about next steps. Well-constructed final reporting can initiate action as well as conclude it. On the other hand, negative results can also come from reporting evaluation information: fear or resentment at the findings; impaired credibility for individuals, for the evaluation itself, or for the program; disinterest and lack of follow-through on recommendations. But, fair and full reporting is essential to enable use of evaluation information.

This Guideline points out the value of utilizing evaluation information and the importance of reporting it in order that it be utilized. Various aspects of reporting are described here, including who is usually responsible for it and where reports go, as well as what is reported and when. Criteria for reporting information are given and alternative methods of reporting are suggested. Ideas on how to best utilize evaluation of staff development and continuing education through the reporting process conclude the Guideline.

Kinds of Reporting

Using the definitions developed earlier in this Chapter, the two basic types of information to be reported include: 1) information about the results from the program or activity efforts (i.e., summative information), and 2) information giving a reading about what is or is not happening, and the possibilities of why (i.e., formative information). The first type usually requires the kind of reporting that concludes a major effort, wraps-up a demonstration period or project, or documents achievements during a given time period. The second, usually termed feedback, requires prompt collection, analysis, and reporting since it is utilized for decisions made soon afterwards.

Ideally, these two types of evaluation are consistently and effectively used throughout any program. An example of such an ideal situation in a staff development program is one where frequent reporting, perhaps a system of written and oral progress reports, is incorporated into existing communication channels. Information, both formative and summative, is collected in relation to staff development throughout the library as a regular and accepted practice. For the most part, evaluation tasks are shared by various staff members in accord with their staff development responsibilities, degree of involvement, and level of interest. Information that can affect on-going program planning or implementation is sent promptly to the staff development committee for their review and, if necessary, their action. Information that may be useful in personal self-assessment is forwarded, under cover, to the person concerned.

As they become available, summative information findings are sent to the staff development committee for review and discussion, then forwarded with their recommendations to the head of the library, with copies to the staff association, oral presentations to meetings of department heads, plus a write-up in the staff newsletter. Here, both types of information from the evaluation process are actively involved in the library routines, responsibilities are shared, and the information is disseminated throughout the library. This sharing of responsibilities and information broadens the evaluation awareness and skills of the entire staff.

A similar ideal example to illustrate how evaluation is reported and used in a continuing education program is less cohesive, perhaps, but nonetheless effective. Each learning activity is, to a certain extent, treated as a single entity, and well-defined information is collected from each one, with formative information then directed to the educational staff for immediate modifications, summative information becoming part of the report of the activity itself. Provision is made to help each participant engage in self-evaluation. The responsibility for activating that possibility belongs to each participant individually, and sometimes to others at the work site.

· From time to time, program evaluation meetings bring together the planning and advisory groups, the program administrator, key educational staff members, and selected past participants to review general program effectiveness. This review is on the basis of reports of individual activities, feedback received after the activity, and evidences of long-range and delayed effects. Recommendations then go to the agency or association management to account for current budget expenditures and to justify next year's requests.

Each of these examples reveals that the information must be made available, that is, collected, analyzed and reported, before it can be utilized in whatever way is most appropriate for the situation. Planning for evaluation must take this into account and assure that the bigger picture is not lost in the smaller, perhaps more intense, aspects of evaluation process and procedures.

Dissemination

The dissemination of evaluation information is essential to enable timely and appropriate use of it. The channels used for the flow of formative information are identified in the evaluation plan and in the program design. Regular checking is often necessary to make sure that the channels continue to operate, that the information received is useful and accurate, and that the amount of information is sufficient. Sometimes, the information may be accurate and useful but poorly timed. If, for example, learner feedback about workshop content is not received in time for planning the next series of activities on the same topic, the schedule for collecting and analyzing or for reporting will need to be adjusted. Since program management is so dependent on formative evaluation, the primary responsibility for checking that flow often rests with the program administrator, or, if the learning program is closely interrelated with other organizational programs and functions, with the director of the library, agency, or association.

Similarly with summative evaluation. Unless people have the information, they cannot be expected to act upon it. This fact is more easily seen in formative evaluation, less obviously perhaps in relation to summative reports. If a summative report is produced for a particular audience, for the learners or program planners, for instance, it naturally would be disseminated to that audience for their use. With some adaptation, however, a summary or selected sections might, at the same time, be disseminated to the educational staff or other groups perhaps outside the library, agency, or association. Even if a report is developed to meet requirements for a university or governmental body and a certain style and format are mandated, this same information can be repackaged, using the same basic findings, for other audiences.

As with each of the components of the evaluation function, the decisions about dissemination should be guided by the purposes for the evaluation and the evaluation plan. Those, in turn, will be based on who needs what information, when, and how. Certainly the costs of dissemination will be an important, and sometimes limiting, factor. The amount of effort and number of methods used to disseminate the information must be justified by perceived benefits. This consideration must be balanced by the awareness that dissemination is necessary to enable utilization of the information.

Reporting

Just as dissemination enables use, reporting enables dissemination. Reporting evaluation information is often the most tangible evidence of the value of the evaluation. A sound report can bring to light what, to that point, has been only a hazy impression of a vaguely understood function. In those individuals from whom information has been sought, reporting makes the process come full circle and the collection of such information then often makes more sense to them, motivating their later cooperation in that process. Conversely, an ineffective report can distort information, thus risking poor decisions, damaged credibility, or sidetracking of sound recommendations no matter how well supported they may be with solid evidence.

General direction for those responsible for reporting the results of learning programs and efforts can be provided by the following criteria:

- Reporting should present information that is useful, valid, honest, and based on solid and documented evidence.

- The report should present information that is understandable to the audience for which it is intended, using a method/media appropriate to both the information being reported and that audience.

- The report should include adequate but not excessive information, qualified with its assumptions, constraints, and limitations.

- The report should be timed to correlate with the need for the information and directed to those individuals and organizational components that need the information.

- The information should be presented in such a way that the privacy of individuals is preserved.

- The report should be disseminated to those involved in or affected by the program and those involved in the evaluation process.

- The information reported should be closely related to the purposes for which the evaluation was done.

- The report should describe the methodology used as well as the findings, conclusions, and recommendations.

- The manner and means used to report and disseminate information should be congruent with the intent of the program and the style of the organization.

Different organizations, different programs, and different individuals will each bring unique approaches to reporting. The reasons for an evaluation's being done will be perhaps the strongest influence on the kind of information presented in a report,·whereas personal approaches and styles will most influence the manner of its presentation.

Reports

An evaluation report compiles the evaluation information intended for dissemination and use. Selection of the most appropriate means to use in reporting will depend on the kind of information to be reported and on where and how the information will be used. The most common method of reporting evaluation information is the written evaluation report usually required as a major measure of accountability. Often, this is a typed or printed document distributed through routine organizational channels to the people in administrative levels of the sponsoring library, agency, or association, or, in some cases, to a separate funding agency.

But this limited concept of reporting can be usefully broadened to include any combination of the following audiences and methods:

- a capsule version of the formal evaluation report, to be distributed to all educational staff and learners of an activity.

- articles, in an association journal or agency newsletter directed to practitioners, describing the content area of the learning activity and its major results.

- interim progress reports on planning and follow-up actions as well as on the implementation of an activity or the program in general.

- verbal presentations to association members at their conference.

- media reports, such as slide tape or videotape, that can be shown to library personnel within a system, state, or region.

- demonstration teams of learners who show what they have learned to colleagues on the library staff or to those attending a library association meeting.

- draft copies can be submitted for review as a test of the initial analysis and to balance perspectives and draw additional conclusion to seek further evidence of results.

These possibilities will increase the number of people who can benefit from the program and its activities. Each point of reporting and dissemination can provide a catalyst for someone else to begin new learning activities, can give reinforcement to individuals and groups with a commitment to continuing library education, or can boost the awareness in practitioners (and potential learners) of the efforts of the organization.

Reports are often prescribed by guidelines and specifications or by tradition. Even if mandated as to content and form, reporting can be useful to fulfill other purposes of direct value to participants in the program as well as to the sponsor or a separate funder. And, it can do so simultaneously, with multiple benefits at a single cost. Normally, reporting requirements are not inflexible, often permitting more information than the designated limits when that would be useful and desirable. Restrictions on dissemination patterns are also usually flexible. For example, sometimes an evaluation report is specified to be a document separate from the descriptive or narrative report. Often, however, it is more helpful to integrate the two kinds of reports, and this is usually possible when sound justification can be made for it.

There are three basic methods of reporting: written, oral, and audiovisual. No matter what method is selected, it should be matched with the criteria listed earlier. The content of evaluation reports will, of course, vary with the purpose for reporting information. Generally speaking, most summative reports, giving only results, are more formal than those that forward formative information to where it is needed. Typically, a summative report occurs at the end of a cycle of learning activities, or at the end of a specified time period, such as a year. Formative evaluation information, on the other hand, is usually designed to fit into the regular channels of communication and decision-making within the organization, in particular, within the program management area. Often, this fit is so smooth that it is not clearly identified as evaluation at all. Since this naturalness may enhance its usefulness, it is a desirable state of affairs under most circumstances.

In addition to being expected, written reports have several advantages. Such a report can be easily disseminated and preserved for as long as needed. It also serves as an excellent basis for modifying the evaluation information into other methods of presentation. On the other hand, disadvantages include its being only one-way communication and its rather ordinary approach, which may prompt its being set aside, unread.

Often, written reports are only produced as administrative documents when the possible interested audience might actually include all those involved in or affected by the program and its activities. In such cases, reports done in a journalistic manner will have more popular appeal than will a stuffy, traditional administrative style. Reports may be planned to: present the rationale to advocate a particular value or point of view, utilize questions and answers written as dialogue to hold interest, describe detailed statistics to convince, display testimonials to sway opinion, flaunt technical jargon to impress. No matter how written, recommendations made in the report should be responsibly put forward, well documented with real evidence, and within the realm of feasibility. Carefully produced charts, pictures, and illustrations can make a written report easier to understand and read.

Other information useful to include would be background information about the program or activity, with descriptions of its general approach and methodology, participants, planning process, and basic assumptions. The rationale, plan, and procedures used for the evaluation itself are important to explain as well. The report would include overall comments about the successes and the failures (all programs have both), together with documentation of the personal or organizational changes in behavior that did occur, the conclusions and the recommendations that flow from those observations, and any suggestions for follow up endeavors. Often, these core components are pulled together in summary form and presented at the beginning of the report, followed by the evidence, documentation, explanations, and descriptive detail later in the report. Sometimes implications are outlined to indicate what is likely to happen if the recommendations presented are implemented, or not implemented. Bibliographies, copies of instructional materials, lists of resource people or participants, and evaluation forms are often included in appendices. Vital information for any report, the date and names of persons responsible, is, of course, essential to include.

Oral reports or presentations are another method of reporting. They may give the same information as the written report, using audiovisual aids to supplement the individual or group making a personal presentation. The advantage of such a presentation is that it enables a dialogue between the audience and the presenter and permits the presenter to "read" the degree of interest and understanding in the audience. Disadvantages include the lack of easy or convenient replication without the person(s) making the presentation. Audiovisual tools, such as flannel boards, newsprint, overhead transparencies, or charts, can liven and clarify a presentation.

The third method is the audiovisual report or presentation. Presentations using audiovisual means exclusively offer the same advantages as the written report, plus the fact that a kinetic medium may make more of an impact than the printed word. The need for special equipment and the cost of producing the presentation are chief disadvantages. Slide tapes and videotapes are the most immediately useful methods. They can be employed to portray learning activities in progress, learner performance at the work site, or statistics and graphic materials. Multi-media approaches increasingly are being used for descriptive reporting of projects and programs, and often these weave evaluation information into the narrative.

Depending on who the report is from and to whom it is directed, the reporting process might blend all three methods for different approaches to different groups, even within the same organization. For example, the evaluation committee might make an administrative report through the usual required channels, offer an oral presentation to the staff association, and develop a slide-tape presentation for use with other libraries in the system. The basic information in each would be the same, but it would be tailored differently for different purposes and audiences.

Reporting formative evaluation is generally less visible or apparent than summative reporting and often achieves its purpose even more effectively because of that. Often ephemeral, subjective, and qualified, a permanent report may not be an advantage. At times, however, highlighting formative evaluation as such may be useful for one purpose or another, lest the information get misplaced or overlooked. Decision-makers may require occasional reminders that regular channels of feedback bring them evaluation information for the decisions they make. In such cases, utilizing some of the methods of reporting usually employed for summative evaluation may be effective in presenting formative information more forcefully or in assuring that the value of evaluation itself is known. Perhaps because of its formality and format, summative evaluation usually tends to be seen as more significant and conclusive, although it is no more important in terms of the decisions that it actually affects.

Memos, written and oral briefing reports at meetings, staff or faculty conferences, position papers and action plans—all can convey or rely heavily on formative evaluation information available in direct or indirect forms after collection and analysis. The content is very directly connected with the use to which it will be put. For example, feedback indicating that the material used to prepare learners for an activity was misleading, when forwarded to the person responsible for that task might assure that such a situation did not occur again. Or, strong indications that the needs of the clerical staff were being overlooked in the program would go to the program administrator either to elicit an explanation or to adjust the program. Generally speaking, the more widely available that formative evaluation information is throughout the organization, the more different channels it will flow through automatically and the more different purposes it can address.

Whether formative or summative, whether written, oral or audiovisual, the intent of the evaluation report is the key factor in determining just what it should include and how the information shall be presented. No matter what the method, the content, or the style, the report must communicate the information needed about the program or activity to those individuals and groups who can use it for information or for action. Generally, the better developed the plan and the more clearly defined the purposes for evaluation, the easier the reporting and dissemination will be and the more likely the information is to be utilized.

Utilization

Evaluation information can be utilized for accountability and for enabling sound decisions to adjust, improve, or modify the program or activity being evaluated. Finding ways to make the most of the evaluation information available for these purposes requires commitment to see that the information is used, the vision to see just how it can be used, the initiative to take the necessary steps, and the skill to plan and carry through those necessary steps. Utilization requires that the information be connected with the decision-making and communication channels of the program so that the information is accessible and can be fit when and where the decisions must be made. For example, if a regional series of management seminars elicits negative reactions through a questionnaire, the program administrator may wish to interview selected participants by telephone to discover the reasons for their reactions. If the reason appears to be that participants were not adequately prepared for the depth or the approach, the program administrator may want to make changes before the series is finished, perhaps by asking the educational staff to alter content or method, by clarifying the advance publicity to build more realistic expectations, or by establishing more stringent criteria for the selection of future participants. Most often, as in this example, feedback must be collected and analyzed early, then reported appropriately so that necessary remedies may be determined and action taken.

But, feedback is not always negative. Perhaps, as in the series described, the learners from early seminars were strongly inclined to form on-going study groups in their own libraries following the seminars. In this case, the instructional design for later seminars could be strengthened to provide those skills needed to organize such groups, and more extensive bibliographies and materials could be provided to facilitate and supplement their efforts. Most of all, it is important to use the information.

Evaluative information that is not utilized does not serve any program well. It provides no benefits but, rather, may be wasteful of the program's resources. One reason that evaluation information is not more frequently used fully is that there are few examples of programs that describe explicitly their attempts to collect and use information for program management and instructional design purposes. Many programs use evaluative information automatically and effectively without second thought. But for a new or a revamped program, it will be important to build in clear, workable means for assuring that the information gets to the right place for it to be used. Certainly the pressures of limited time and the need to produce program activities often inhibit the available information being fully used in a timely and effective way.

When openly and creatively approached, however, reporting evaluation information can have widespread benefits connected directly with its utilization. The analysis and interpretation can lead program planners and the administrator to a critical, reflective review of the program. Often, this useful procedure is bypassed because of the pressures of time. But such a review can serve to bring into closer correlation the objectives and the action of the program, both of which are looked at in the reporting process. Reporting encourages planners and evaluators to focus on what happened and to compare that with what was anticipated. Thus, reporting can help a program stay "on track."

This review process is not only true of final reports but also pertains to the procedures for regular and interim reports, those used to channel feedback to where it is needed or to orient individuals and groups newly involved in the program or the activity. Regular use of reporting helps accustom individuals to the evaluation process and provides a view of the usefulness of evaluation procedures that would otherwise perhaps be viewed with suspicion. If carefully constructed, and if some explanation is included for the methods and procedures used, the reporting mechanisms themselves can help individuals learn about evaluative functions as such and their usefulness to the program, in addition to furnishing needed information about that program. Also, weaving evaluation information into the reporting processes throughout the program will increase its usefulness and will reinforce the possibility that those involved in the program as learners, educational staff, program planners, or staff will be able to accept and understand the evaluation function.

Reporting is particularly helpful to encourage and allow the library, agency, or association to share with other organizations not only what is being done in the learning programs but how effective various efforts are and what improvements might be suggested for those who adapt the ideas elsewhere. This serves to share more widely what is found about different approaches to learning programs. It broadens the awareness of what is being done in the field, what effects are possible, and gives the organization useful visibility. In turn, this visibility can also attract new resources, others interested and active in working with learning programs, into contact with the reporting program.

A report that includes evaluation information with adequate data and description will provide reliable and directly usable models that might be more easily and effectively replicated elsewhere. Evaluation information is needed to support the claims of success and accomplishments often reported widely about staff development and continuing education activities. A careful examination of such reports, however, will reveal which ones incorporate actual evidence to back up the enthusiastic claims of success. The present trend to develop and publicize working examples as models has limited effectiveness if those examples have not been tested in some way in relation to their ability to bring problems to the surface and respond to them. In presenting models, problems or difficulties may be hidden, leading others to adopt the new, disguised problems along with the "model" solution to other problems.

Reporting on programs and activities is usually accepted procedure for most libraries and state agencies. For a library association, reporting serves the very direct, pragmatic function of providing continuity during the necessary transfer of the continuing education function, which may be done frequently. This is especially true when the association's continuing education efforts are offered through a committee structure with transitional membership. In these instances, individuals may assume responsibility for the learning program without knowledge of the efforts of past efforts, the successes and the failures. Reporting leaves a record of the history and results and can provide useful information to assist those with limited experience about their association's continuing education endeavors.

Reporting can stimulate more and better programs when it is disseminated beyond the sponsoring organization as well. The introspection and self-examination are useful to stimulate modifications and improvements within the program itself, but then sharing that knowledge beyond that single organization prompts the spread of innovative ideas or tested approaches in new settings. Dissemination can lead to cooperative efforts with other organizations having similar interests and can increase the available resources, including enlarging the number of potential learners. Reporting fosters sound planning, spreads ideas, encourages more evaluation, and is often part of the educational process.

Utilization of evaluation information has been mentioned throughout this Guideline directly, by inference, and by example. But that is not to imply that it happens automatically. Specific ways help to assure that the reporting and dissemination does lead to utilizing the information. The most real and lasting of these ways is to involve various elements of the learning program and of the library, agency, or association throughout the evaluation process. If accustomed to regular reporting and aware of the value of the evaluation process, individuals will be interested in reports as well as in contributing actively with their own evaluative responses or in helping collect, analyze, or report future evaluations.

An important consideration in planning for maximum utilization is that data does not speak for itself. To be used, it needs a context, a direction, and a channel that will make it meaningful to those who are expected to know about it or who could use it for some purpose. Sound, thoughtful reports with well-documented recommendations can help people think of logical follow-through actions that will meet their needs. A well-presented, dynamic description of what has been accomplished can motivate and interest people previously uninvolved.

When feedback and reporting become habit, a significant summative report then will be perceived as important but not regarded as an undue threat or concern.

Frequent and regular reports are like signposts guiding the traveler dependably in a normal and helpful fashion, providing information about distance and direction. As long as these signposts continue to be seen as aids to the traveler in his journey, they will be accepted and utilized. If, however, there are only few but impressive signs, each a landmark of large proportions, they will be regarded with awe as threatening and definitive—more so, perhaps, than they actually are. Often, such landmarks denote an infrequently traveled road rather than guide a number of travelers along a comfortable route.

Regular patterns of decision-making and communication use evaluation information. Evaluation information also can be utilized to motivate interest and involvement in the program as well as to increase acceptance and understanding of the evaluation process as such. Ways to promote such use on a regular, practical basis can be encouraged by making the information accessible, demonstrating how it can be used effectively, building reporting into program activities and functions, and involving potential users of information in planning to collect, analyze, and disseminate it. After the investment is made to collect, analyze, and report evaluation information, then enabling full utilization of it makes the most of the library's or agency's investment.

Summary

Once evaluation information has been collected, organized, and analyzed, it must be reported so that it can be disseminated and used for the purposes that prompted it to be gathered originally. Effective and timely reporting does not always mean a document produced at the end, however. Indeed, it is often not a concluding statement but an initiating action, since reporting it enables evaluative information to be used. Once communicated, findings can be put to use in practical and often immediate ways. This utilization is the payoff of the entire evaluative function in the program. Reporting summative information gives an indication of results, the point from which new directions may be taken. Reporting formative information prompts and facilitates decision-making by program managers and educators.

The evaluation report itself is a means of communication whether written, presented, or audiovisual. Its intent is the key factor in determining just what it should include, and how that information will be presented. Usually an accepted procedure, reporting may require effective and built-in ways to assure that the information actually is reported and utilized.

SUMMARY OF PART III

Sound evaluation can assure that quality staff development and continuing education efforts will be available to the individual learners and to the library, agency, or association. Without an evaluation process, it is impossible to know if the organization's investment in the learning program actually is gaining a return in benefits. Evaluation offers the opportunity to discover what is happening as a result of the program's efforts, to review how well the program functions, and to indicate appropriate directions for subsequent decision-making and action.

More often a spoken precept than an actual practice, the decision to evaluate the learning program is a key one; and, since evaluation is closely related to both planning and implementation, this decision should be made early. The decision itself must rest on a careful, thorough consideration of the benefits expected from evaluation and the costs likely to be incurred. Evaluation must be an integral part of the program from the beginning, structured yet flexible, and viewed as an essential component rather than as a frill, since, without it, the risk of poor decision-making is very high.

Some of the factors that lead to an effective evaluation include: an understanding of the importance of the evaluative function, commitment to it, open and honest information, access to resources to plan for and obtain useful information, and acceptance and constructive utilization of the information. When these essentials are present, the evaluation process is likely to occur and to be appropriate and relevant to the specific needs for evaluation as defined by the purposes set forth for the evaluation.

Several barriers can prevent evaluation from being a common, quality practice, however. Cost is often cited as a reason. Other reasons, less often stated but more often real, include: a wariness of the process because of its esoteric and specialized nature, lack of confidence and competence with the process, dearth of existing examples of use for adaptation and practice, lack of norms endorsing evaluation, and past negative associations with evaluation. Until these problems are modified or overcome, evaluation may continue to be largely token and pro forma for many programs. Each of these barriers has possible bypasses where evaluation is really desired.

Once the decision has been made to evaluate, planning for evaluation is the next major step. Evaluation is very demanding of time, effort, and resources. If it is purposive, however, it is more likely to make the most of that time and effort and to return useful information in exchange for the investment. Defining the purposes for evaluation lays the basis for planning how it will be done. These purposes then will guide the evaluation process throughout its implementation.

Once the purposes have been determined, a systematic plan is needed. The plan is a blueprint of how to fulfill the purposes: who is to do what to collect, analyze, and report the information; and when, where, and how those actions will take place. It also specifies who will use the information and how. This systematic, planned approach protects the investment that evaluation will require. It increases the possibility that the most effective methods will yield the most usable information. The plan for evaluation includes: 1) the stated purposes for evaluating, 2) the kinds of information sought, 3) when and where evaluation information will be obtained, 4) the methods to be used for obtaining and disseminating it, and 5) the uses to which that information will be put.

Following the outline of the purpose and plan, the implementation of the evaluation includes three basic actions. First, the needed information must be collected. Techniques such as questionnaires, interviews, and tests acquire the information from various sources. Those techniques and sources must be feasible, appropriate, valid, and reliable in order to assure full use of the collected information.

Secondly, the information collected will need to be organized and analyzed in order to be communicated and used. Since the information will not speak for itself, it will not be useful until some interpretation has been made or some conclusions have been drawn. The amount and method of analysis may be simple or complex depending on the factors of the needs of the organization or learners, the resources available, the type of plan, and the techniques used. Analysis includes reviewing the available information, coding and interpreting it to extract its meaning and to answer the questions asked of the evaluation.

The final action is to report and disseminate the information for use. If this step is not fully performed, much of the value of evaluation is lost. Evaluation information must be reported in a usable form, at the appropriate time, and in the appropriate place for those who need it. Some of the information may need to be promptly relayed to program planners to change or make new decisions. Some of it may need to be documented with evidence from various sources and formalized in a periodic written report. Full utilization of available evaluation information requires the belief that it can be useful, the ability to see how it can be used, the initiative to take the necessary steps to use it, and the skills to carry through those necessary steps.

Utilization of evaluation findings can affect the program by directing timely attention to problem areas or serendipitous results. It can have an impact on learners, for they are often directly involved and can relate evaluation to their own needs and ideas. It can benefit the organization that sponsors the continuing education program, for the information can help strengthen the program and can provide for close correlation of the program and organizational aims. And, reporting evaluation results can benefit the library field by sharing the knowledge and experience that has been gained and from which others might profit.

Regardless of the nature of the learning program or its planning process, results from learning programs are often expected immediately, even when this expectation is unrealistic. Although skills training in the use of audio-visual equipment or new reference tools can be quickly applied to present job responsibilities, the administration of the library, the staff of the program, and the learners in the activities all need to recognize that some results will necessarily take a long time. Some results are simply long-range, for example, developing critical abilities for book selection, understanding the library as an organization, and overcoming resistance to the use of new equipment or procedures.

A good evaluation can strengthen and enrich both the program and the organization. It can serve to identify and deepen the growth of learners. It can provide foresight for careful planning. It can build in flexibility and responsiveness. Evaluating the program and its activities brings full circle its development, completing its implementation and fulfilling its plan. Evaluation is more of a beginning than an end, for it is the basis for new efforts, improved processes, and revitalized energies. When threaded throughout the program, this revitalization can develop and sustain staff development or continuing education far beyond original dreams, for each evaluative effort identifies new needs—of learners, of libraries, of educators, and of librarianship.

NOTES

[1] Harrison M. Trice and Paul M. Roman, *Evaluation of Training: Strategy, Tactics and Problems*, ERIC Clearinghouse on Adult Education [Training Information Sources, no. 3; June 1975] (Syracuse, NY, Syracuse University, 1973), p. 3.

[2] I. L. Goldstein, *Training: Program Development and Evaluation* (Monterey, CA: Brooks/Cole, 1974), pp. 67-88.

[3] Arden D. Grotelueschen, et al., *An Evaluation Planner; A Guidebook for Developing Evaluation Plans Responsive to a Variety of Contexts, Audiences, and Issues Within Adult Basic Education* (Urbana, IL: Office for the Study of Continuing Professional Education, University of Illinois, 1974), p. 49.

[4] Julie A. Virgo, "Quality Control in Professional Continuing Library Education: A Model " (A paper presented at American Association of Library Schools program, January 1974, Chicago, Illinois.) (mimeo, 1975).

[5] Edward Allen Suchman, *Evaluative Research; Principles and Practice in Public Service and Social Action Programs* (New York: Sage, 1967), pp. 39-41.

[6] Lawrence J. Severy, *Application of the Experimental Method to Program Evaluation: Problems and Prospects* [TM Report, no. 47] (Princeton, NJ: ERIC Clearinghouse on Tests, Measurement and Evaluation, Educational Testing Service, 1975).

[7] Malcolm S. Knowles, *The Modern Practice of Adult Education: Andragogy Versus Pedagogy* (New York: Association Press, [1970]), p. 223.

[8] Ibid., p. 235.

[9] Kent J. Chabotar and Lawrence J. Lad, *Evaluation Guidelines for Training Programs* (East Lansing, MI: Public Administration Programs, Michigan State University, 1974), p. 19.

[10] Ibid., p. 20.

[11] Alan B. Knox, "Continuous Program Evaluation." In Nathan C. Shaw, ed., *Administration of Continuing Education; A Guide for Administrators* (Washington, DC: National Association for Public School Adult Education, 1969), p. 372.

[12] Egon G. Guba and Daniel L. Stufflebeam, *Evaluation: The Process of Stimulating, Aiding and Abetting Insightful Action* [Monograph Series in Reading Education, no. 1] (Bloomington, IN: Indiana University, 1970), p. 12.

[13] Trice and Roman, *Evaluation of Training*, p. 4.

[14] Groteleuschen, *An Evaluation Primer*, pp. 3-4.

[15] Guba and Stufflebeam, *Evaluation*, p. 10.

[16] Trice and Roman, *Evaluation of Training*, p. 7.

[17] Susan Salasin, "Exploring Goal-Free Evaluation," *Evaluation; A Forum for Human Service Decision-Makers* 2, no. 1:9-16 (1974).

[18] George F. Aker and Wayne L. Schroeder, "Research for Action Programs." In Shaw, Nathan C., ed. *Administration of Continuing Education; A Guide for Administrators* (Washington, DC: National Association for Public School Adult Education, 1969), pp. 347-48.

[19] Chabotar and Lad, *Evaluation Guidelines*, pp. 25-26.

[20] Knowles, *Modern Practice of Adult Education*, p. 226.

[21] Groteleuschen, *An Evaluation Planner*, p. 60.

[22] Scriven, M. "The Methodology of Evaluation." In R. W. Tyler, R. M. Gagne, and M. Scriven, eds., *AERA Monograph Series on Curriculum Evaluation* no. 1. (Chicago: Rand McNally, 1967). pp. 39-83.

[23] Chabotar and Lad, *Evaluation Guidelines*, p. 15.

[24] Severy, *Application*, p. 14.

[25] Trice and Roman, *Evaluation of Training*, p. 37.

[26] Severy, *Application*, p. 14.

[27] Suchman, *Evaluative Research*, p. 159.

[28] Ibid., pp. 158-59.

[29] Severy, *Application*, p. 15.

[30] Knowles, *Modern Practice of Adult Education*, p. 235.

[31] The most useful aid is: Eugene Webb, Donald Campbell, Richard Schwartz, and Lee Sechrest, *Unobtrusive Measures: Nonreactive Research in the Social Sciences* (Chicago, IL: Rand-McNally, 1966).

[32] Guba and Stufflebeam, *Evaluation*, p. 8.

[33] Knowles, *Modern Practice of Adult Education*, p. 143.

[34] Larry Nolan Davis and Earl McCallon, *Planning, Conducting and Evaluating Workshops: A Practitioner's Guide to Adult Education* (Austin, TX: Learning Concepts, 1974). p. 277.

APPENDIX:
MODELS OF LEARNING PROGRAMS IN
STAFF DEVELOPMENT AND CONTINUING EDUCATION

Models contain principles and components described in tangible terms, either verbally or graphically. They translate the general into the specific, the abstract into the tangible. This, in turn, can spark insight, stimulate ideas, and open up possibilities. Models can prompt learning and aid planning and implementation. They assist learning by illustrating and clarifying principles with depth and texture. In addition to helping the learning process, models offer alternative patterns that can guide application of principles and practices in new situations.

Thus, models are particularly relevant here, since the intent of this book is to prompt and enable individuals and organizations to initiate or to strengthen learning programs for library personnel. Models encourage new applications of current ideas and extend innovative approaches to situations known for traditional patterns. Here, they are included to give a more extended and wholistic idea of learning programs and the type of activities such programs might include. The various components are woven into a single extended example within a given context rather than treated only briefly, as under each topical Guideline.

Generally, two types of models are possible. One describes the essentials in functional terms, such as: select need, develop instructional strategy, measure results. Often this type of model outlines the recommended sequence of tasks and represents their interrelationship with schemas or flow charts. A second type of model describes the typical tasks, functions, components, and processes in a narrative flow, often in chronological order.

Here, three narrative models set the precepts, principles, examples, and suggestions from the fifteen Guidelines into specific action contexts. The first model is that of a staff development program in a medium-sized public library. The second is a continuing education program in a regional library association, and the last is a state library's continuing education program. None replicate any existing program, although most of the components described are typical and may be found a number of places. Since they offer somewhat different opportunities and constraints, the differences between those learning programs in libraries and those conducted through library associations and state library agencies are intentionally highlighted here.

In a very real sense, all descriptions of staff development and continuing education efforts, activities, and programs can be viewed as models. Thus, many available sources indicate patterns or prototypes helpful to furnish inspiration as well as ideas and people resources to tap. These reports often describe a single activity, such as a workshop or an institute or a job exchange, rather than a multiple-activity program approach to address the learning needs of various library personnel. Although these reports of activities can be very useful in planning similar ventures, they mislead if they overlook building the planning and delivery system of learning that will produce not only a single activity but will also sustain a learning program beyond the more limited activity dimension of a single activity.

Often, however, such reports exist as internal administrative documents and are not disseminated beyond their own organization. Creative new service programs, outreach efforts, or budgeting procedures are more likely to be topics for conference programs or in conversations among colleagues. Continuing education models are more prevalent and available than are staff development models. Staff development is often so thoroughly integrated into the various ongoing organizational functions that it is not easily identified or communicated as a discrete program. Thus, it is less often published, less widely disseminated, considered less generally applicable in other situations. Continuing education, however, is more often seen as a distinct function or role of the agency or association. Thus, it is more likely to be described as such and is more often found written in reports or journal articles. Staff development and continuing education are on the increase; if more were known about what is being done successfully or unsuccessfully, the stimulus of shared ideas would be more widespread, and the application of those ideas would be less limited.

Once made, most reports of staff development programs rest in file drawers and administrative cabinets. Brief mention may be made of them in annual reports or in library newsletters, and the few articles scattered through library literature usually describe isolated activities rather than programs. Two published sources present staff development models in library settings. One is the conceptual model for staff development in the *Library Trends* issue devoted to personnel development and continuing education (volume 20, number 1; July 1971). The second is Conroy's *Staff Development Model Book: Program Designs for Library Personnel* (1976). This compilation includes twenty-one models. In addition to these published sources, in his unpublished research paper *A Model for Library Staff Development* (1971), Thomas J. Alrutz (Graduate School of Library Science, Catholic University of America) offers a schematic model for library staff development for general application to any type of library.

Staff development models outside the library field are also useful to consider. For library schools considering staff development, for example, "Comprehensive Staff Development," by Ernest L. Bentley, Jr., in *TIP: Theory into Practice* (Volume XI, number 4; October, 1972) is useful with many applications for faculty development. Silvern's *System Engineering Applied to Training* (1972) illustrates the technique of flowchart modeling to plan and conduct staff development. The Havelocks's *Training for Change Agents* (1973) describes in detail models for training those people involved in systems change. It is hoped that future efforts will result in more published descriptions of more programs, thus making them more accessible as sources of ideas.

Michael's bibliography, *Continuing Professional Education in Librarianship* (1975) contains annotated references to both staff development and continuing education sources in the United States and other countries. This basic and current resource includes theory and philosophy as well as practical application sources. Its coverage is broad, embracing fields other than librarianship. Similarly, Stone's *Continuing Library Education as Viewed in Relation to Other Continuing Proffessional Education Movements* (1974) relates the major aspects of continuing library education with other fields, thus introducing for study continuing education models beyond librarianship. The final report to the National Commission on Libraries and Information, also by Stone, on *Continuing Library and Information Science Education* (1974) describes applicable concepts from a number of models. These concepts were then combined to form the proposed nationwide structure that later became the Continuing Library Education Network and Exchange (CLENE). Three alternative continuing education models were also presented in the report.

CLENE, in turn, has published *Continuing Library Education Needs Assessment and Model Programs* (1977) by Virgo, Dunkel, and Angione. This work focuses on medical librarianship and introduces models that blend a specific content area with the strong organizational supports necessary to build and sustain a successful program. *Continuing Professional Education* (1975) is more broadly focused and, as a bibliography, leads to models of continuing education in professional fields. The *Proceedings of the HEA Title II-B Institute on Continuing Education Program Planning for Library Staffs in the Southwest* (1975), edited by Foos, reports both general and specific models for programs and describes the Kontinuing Education Game (KEG) developed for the Institute. Models and resources were also a prime result of the CLENE/USOE Institute for State Library Agency Personnel Involved in Continuing Education (1976-1977). The *Continuing Education Resource Book* (1977), edited by Elizabeth Stone, was published by the Continuing Library Education Network and Exchange.

These various sources of models are useful to review if a new program is being planned or if a current one is to be redesigned. Often, models offer ideas and tools to assist program developers. Thus, recommended resources are listed, with full citations, and the models appropriate to the theoretical discussion in this book follow.

BIBLIOGRAPHY OF STAFF DEVELOPMENT AND CONTINUING EDUCATION MODELS

Alrutz, Thomas J. *A Model for Library Staff Development.* Washington, DC: Graduate School of Library Science, Catholic University of America, 1971.

Bentley, Ernest L., Jr. "Comprehensive Staff Development." *TIP: Theory Into Practice* XI, no. 4 (October, 1972).

Conroy, Barbara, ed. *Staff Development Model Book: Program Designs for Library Personnel.* Boulder, CO: Western Interstate Library Coordinating Organization, 1976.

Continuing Professional Education. (Informal Bibliography, no. 8) ERIC Clearinghouse in Career Education. DeKalb, IL: Northern Illinois University, 1975.

Foos, Donald D., ed. *Proceedings of the HEA Title II-B Institute. Continuing Education Program Planning for Library Staffs in the Southwest. March 17-28, 1975.* Baton Rouge, LA: Graduate School of Library Science, Louisiana State University, and the Southwestern Library Association, 1975.

Havelock, Ronald C., and Havelock, Mary C. *Training for Change Agents: A Guide to the Design of Training Programs in Education and Other Fields.* Ann Arbor, MI: Institute for Social Research, University of Michigan, 1973.

Silvern, Leonard C. *Systems Engineering Applied to Training.* Houston, TX: Gulf Publishing Co., 1972.

Stone, Elizabeth W. *Continuing Library Education as Viewed in Relation to Other Continuing Professional Education Movements.* Washington, DC: American Society for Information Science, 1974.

Stone, Elizabeth W., ed. *Continuing Education Resource Book; Compilation of Selected Continuing Education Resources and Products Developed by the Participants and Staff in the 1976-1977 CLENE/USOE Institute for State Library Agency Personnel Involved in Continuing Education.* Washington, DC: Continuing Library Education Network and Exchange, June 1977.

Stone, Elizabeth W., ed. "Personnel Development and Continuing Education in Libraries." *Library Trends* 20, no. 1 (July 1971).

Virgo, Julie A., Dunkel, Patricia McConaghey, and Angione, Pauline V. *Continuing Library Education Needs Assessment and Model Programs.* (Concept Paper, no. 5) Washington, DC: Continuing Library Education Network and Exchange, 1977.

MODEL 1

The Midwestern, medium-sized city included a community college and a state university. Each of these had a library to serve their students and faculty, and each was also accessible to local residents. The public library was a city and country-wide system with one main, centrally located building, four branches, and two bookmobiles to serve the county. For several years, interlibrary cooperation among the three library systems grew, primarily through the initiative and commitment of the three library directors. Frequent contact between staff members from each library was achieved through a local librarians' association that met periodically but informally for planned activities.

Staff development efforts in the public library had been sporadic and uncoordinated until two years ago, when, through the efforts of an enthusiastic staff member at the middle management level, an interest group developed. These staff members met frequently during their lunch hour to discuss how they might improve their own job satisfaction and performance. The interest group included staff members from all levels, and they began to explore some of their on-the-job needs and to address the possibilities for staff development. As the originally broad interest became more focused, the group developed a written proposal and took it to the library director. The proposal requested consideration of a staff development program, describing the results that could be anticipated, outlining some of the most needed activities, and recommending that coordination of staff development efforts be assigned to one of the assistant librarians.

The director's response, in turn, was to designate six members of the interest group as a staff committee with three charges: to identify staff development efforts presently being made, to explore in greater depth the training needs in the library, and to make recommendations for priorities and action on the basis of their consideration. These recommendations were to be supported by solid rationale and evidence. The director further appointed the recommended assistant librarian to the committee.

A needs assessment was planned. Individual and group interviews with selected staff members, plus a questionnaire sent to all staff, enabled committee members to identify how individuals learned their present jobs. They discovered that most of the on-the-job training was done through instruction by the immediate supervisor, and staff perceptions indicated that this was done with varying degrees of skill. Gathered opinions further brought out what staff thought was important in order to address those needs unmet to that point. An unexpected result of this needs assessment process was that some important resources were unearthed—staff members knowledgeable in areas other than those that their present job assignments might indicate. The information gathered was analyzed by the committee and presented to the library director as requested. It was also distributed to all departments and branch heads, and a brief abstract of the report was run as an article in the staff association newsletter. Copies of the full report were put in the staff room for further use.

Staff development then became topical, an agenda item at most staff meetings and at supervisor's meetings. In addition to the written needs assessment report, members of the committee made oral presentations at meetings, responded to questions, and invited comments and suggestions. Catalyzed by the committee's action, staff interest began to build. More staff members evinced new interest in using the training opportunities available and requested other efforts to meet the needs they felt. Then, the library director allocated a modest amount of money to support a one-time training activity to be planned and implemented by the committee working closely with the circulation unit.

Now, several months later, the staff development committee is an active, formal group responsible for the planning and evaluation of staff development efforts. They meet four times a year as a group, incorporating new members every two years. Each on-going or one-time training activity is guided by a team composed of two committee members and the assistant librarian responsible for coordinating the library's staff development efforts. The committee as a whole is responsible for developing the learning program as a whole, integrating it as a regular function of the library's management, and coordinating its various aspects.

The committee has identified a group of continuing needs: supervisory skills, reference tool updates, new staff orientation, and sessions on library and departmental procedures and forms. Of these, the latter is considered primarily the responsibility of the supervisor and is recommended to be done consistently through on-the-job training activities. Short videotapes were made for routine procedures and the use of forms used throughout the library system. These standardize the approach, assure on-demand access, and save time.

Responses to the other three needs (supervision, reference, and orientation) are planned throughout the year on a regular schedule. This year, besides these continuous needs, two one-time needs required special training as the result of organizational changes: new circulation equipment and procedures plus a new method for referring inter-library loan requests. Each of these required special efforts over a relatively short time span for the staff affected by these changes. During the year, a new need emerged: more adequate communication patterns throughout the library. This need was, of course, much broader than training alone. The structures used for the staff development efforts, however, seemed the most logical and useful for fully addressing the situation, and training became a significant part of the solution to the identified communications problems.

Based on these identified needs and some tentative ideas for activities, the committee formulated a goal statement and objectives to guide further planning and evaluation, and to direct their implementation of the program. The first year of the program was anticipated to be somewhat tentative in nature in order to test the viability of the program itself and the feasibility of its being conducted by the committee.

Goal: Improved library service through increased staff competencies.

Objective 1: Initial orientation will prepare new staff members to understand their individual assignments within the context of the library and the community.

Objective 2: Regular high quality staff development activities will enable staff members to build and maintain the skills they need.

Objective 3: Staff development efforts will prepare an increased number of professional and para-professional staff to assume flexible job assignments with new areas of responsibility.

Objective 4: Current needs of the library and the staff will be specified through a timely and appropriate on-going needs assessment process.

Objective 5: Information about available staff development efforts and continuing education opportunities will be disseminated to staff on all levels.

Objective 6: Personnel policies regarding staff development opportunities will be established and modified as needed, drawing upon experiences with the program.

Then, based on the needs and these objectives, the staff development program (see chart) was planned to include the following activities and efforts:

1. *An orientation series* that consisted of a one-day briefing, a tour, and a follow-up refresher. The initial briefing included a presentation of information about the community, the library's role in the community, the library's organizational structure and personnel policies, as well as discussion of the additional means available to use in learning more about the library. Organized by the personnel office, this briefing included a tour of the main building, one branch, and a bookmobile. The format and procedures were outlined for consistency in replication and coverage, but ample time was allowed for questions. After about two months, a second orientation day focused more specifically on library

Staff Development Program Schedule Chart

Program Activities	JAN	FEB	MAR	APR	MAY	JUNE	JULY	AUG	SEPT	OCT	NOV	DEC
Orientation	○			○		○		○		○		○
Reference Updates	‖‖	‖‖	‖‖	‖‖	‖‖	‖‖	‖‖	‖‖	‖‖	‖‖	‖‖	‖‖
Supervisory Workshops		⬡			⬡			⬡			⬡	
Circulation Training		Staff Meeting Session	Unit Trng.		Re-fresher							
Organizational Communication								Needs session		Work session		Plan
Committee Meetings	☐		☐			☐			☐			

policies and more in depth on each department and branch. This refresher of the briefing session responded to further questions and was planned around the needs identified by supervisors as well as by new staff members themselves. Requested areas were given special emphasis.

2. *Reference tool update sessions* were held once a week, before the library opens for public service. The subject areas and tools to be featured in a given session were communicated to each department and branch a week ahead of time. Various staff members prepared the presentations and demonstrated the use of the tools. These sessions were also open to library staff members from the local community college and university, who often reciprocated with presentations of their own new or noteworthy tools. Thus, each library's staff increased its knowledge of and access to a wider range of resources than any one of the libraries could have provided alone.

3. *Supervisory skills workshops* were held quarterly, each time on a specific facet of supervision: planning, delegation, personnel appraisal, interviewing, on-the-job training techniques, evaluation of services. Intended for both present and potential supervisors, these workshops were planned in coordination with resources available through the city/county government. The use of library staff as interns or apprentices working with the major trainer provided opportunities for developing training resources within the library itself.

4. *Special training activities* were designed and presented to meet the training needs that arose when a new circulation system was initiated in the library. The change included not only equipment and procedures but some rearrangement of physical space and personnel responsibilities. Three activities were presented: A general information session was held as part of an all-staff meeting regularly held twice a year. A second session was held for all personnel affected by the change-over and the new system. This session involved a more detailed explanation and demonstration and a "walk-through" of the new procedures. A third session was designed to train all supervisors and staff members at the main building, branches, and bookmobiles who would be using the equipment. The planning for this latter session involved library staff people and training personnel from the equipment manufacturer. Following these sessions, the circulation desk staff was urged to keep a diary of problems and questions that arose. These, then, provided the basis for a refresher session a month later.

5. *New interlibrary loan referral procedures* were introduced to the staff with a simple step-by-step instruction booklet. The instructions were pre-tested twice with several staff members to assure that the wording was clear. The need at first was seen as one for training; later, it was perceived to be a need for clear communication through intra-organizational channels. Plans were outlined to make a videotape for use in on-the-job instruction about the procedures. Those plans were held in abeyance until the instruction booklet proved to be satisfactory or not. In the meantime, the implementation of procedures was carefully monitored.

In planning for this last one-time need, that of the new referral procedures, a more urgent organizational priority was found: a better system for intra-organizational communication was found to be crucial. Although this was not solely a training need, especially at the beginning, the library administrator requested that the staff development committee design a one-half day problem-solving session on the library's internal communication. They were given a budget to identify and select an outside expert in organizational communications. With the consultant, they worked out a method to involve all levels of the staff, discovering what kinds of problems they most frequently encountered and what kind of information was needed where and when. Using this information to give some focus to the problem-solving session, the consultant designed the means of refining the issues and working out solutions that would work. One of the main results from the session was an outlined procedure and a strategy for presenting that procedure to each segment of the library. The plan was to be tested for six months, carefully monitored by the staff development committee, and then refined in light of findings from a careful review at the end of that test period. Throughout this sequence, the consultant, when not actively involved, was available for back-up advice.

The committee developed a chart of the development activities, which was reproduced and disseminated with the staff newsletter and was posted on the staff bulletin board with a reminder that outside continuing education opportunities were also part of staff development. The board was the central place for posting notices of available local, regional, and national opportunities. Committee members also made a point of keeping alert to the various offerings of library associations, community groups, and self-study learning packages distributors. These were then brought to the attention of the various interested groups; for example, supervision and management opportunities were mentioned in the monthly supervisor's meetings.

The evaluation plan for the library's staff development efforts was very simple but viewed as very important. The committee did not include any members with much experience in evaluation, but two members were particularly interested in becoming more proficient in that area, so they engaged in some self-directed study to learn more about it. First, they considered activity evaluation, and for that, they planned means for immediate feedback from participants at the conclusion of each activity. This was supplemented by a follow-up interview at a specified time, after some application of learnings would have been possible. The two individuals, together with the assistant librarian, did the analysis of these activity evaluations and presented them to the whole committee along with their recommendations as to what needed to be considered for an improvement of procedures, a change of policy, or a modification of the program design. The entire committee looked at the findings in the overall context of the program— its anticipated direction, the achievement of its objectives, and the degree to which the needs it sought to meet were real.

The committee felt it important to develop a means for each staff member to be able to do a self-assessment that would help the individual to know his or her own needs and to chart any progress toward meeting the priority needs through staff development. Such a system should be able to provide a basis for staff mobility to new responsibilities in line with interests and abilities. Although contemplated and endorsed, this was not possible during the first year. In some ways, the delay proved beneficial as the staff became used to the fact of activity and program evaluation before addressing more personal evaluation measures.

The committee also gave some attention to reviewing their own functioning. They found that their decision making improved with the experiences of working together and sharing tasks that needed to be done. They found that they reached peaks of enthusiasm and energy in planning and implementing the activities. These peaks were, in most cases, followed by valleys after an activity, and time was needed to re-group their personal and collective efforts. Once they realized that this was a natural sequence, and could be anticipated, it was easier to deal with. At first, however, it was very disconcerting.

The committee was also responsible for evolving policies for staff development. They considered a thorough revision of the policy statement on continuing education that existed before the staff development program was put into effect. This included statements on the rewards and recognition that could be expected from participating in staff development, the eligibility requirements for educational leaves, and the responsibilities of the library, the committee, the supervisory staff, and the staff members. These policies, in draft form, were submitted to the library director and the staff association for comments as they evolved into more formal policy statements.

The first year saw heavy responsibility, and much time commitment, on the part of committee members. These individuals were hopeful that, as time passed, their responsibility and initiative will become more widely shared throughout the staff. The assistant librarian was an effective coordinator, a central and supportive figure who brought organizational skills to the group. The first year served to clarify roles and responsibilities, to move staff development into forward gear, to alert the staff to and interest them in their own growth, and to integrate the staff development function within the library organization.

*****

MODEL 2

This regional library association is broad and varied in all respects: extensive rural areas as well as concentrated urban sections; several large libraries with 75 to 130 employees, and many with one and two person staffs; some of its six states with sophisticated library standards, and others struggling to catch up to minimum standards for library service. Open to all library personnel and trustees, the association's membership includes 900 of a potential 3,500 eligible to join. The history of the association is respectable: many years of stable activities, a reputation for conservative and quality endeavors, a balance of viewpoints and tensions about present and future directions of library work and association activities. The last three years brought new, articulate leaders, ones having strong linkages with the past but seeking to increase membership and provide new services to meet the needs of libraries and library personnel in the region.

One of the association's increasingly important functions is that of continuing education. Always a standing committee of some stature, continuing education now is planned by the new leadership as one of the major means to produce self-supporting membership services and to provide a valuable motivational factor for potential new members. However, recent organizational changes altered all standing committees somewhat. In this scheme, each committee chair is to be appointed for two years on the basis of demonstrated competence and interest, as shown through previous service as a member of the committee. This, it was thought, would give the continuity and substance necessary to increase quality committee activities.

The interest and demand for regional continuing education activities is strong at the present time, having increased dramatically in the past few years. The continuing education committee now produces three events annually to meet identified priority needs: an all-day activity (usually a workshop on a single theme) at the annual conference and two sub-regional workshops at other times each year. These activities are well attended and have a reputation for quality and relevance to problems. The methods used are usually traditional, although more experimental approaches have been tried with mixed success. The continuing education committee operates with limited funds to engage the resource people necessary for their activities. This amount is supplemented by modest registration fees to cover expenses of materials, facilities and equipment, and publicity. Non-member registration fees are double those for members to provide an additional incentive for membership.

Each of the activities is planned and produced by a subcommittee guided by advice from the committee as a whole and by the policies already established. Subcommittees meet as often as necessary. Often, they incorporate individuals outside the group's membership or an ad hoc planning and/or evaluation group with a particular interest in the topic or method to be used or in the geographic area where it will be given. Twice, subcommittees have co-sponsored activities with other divisions in the association.

The committee meets as a whole three times a year, their travel for such meetings partially subsidized by the association budget. At each of these three meetings, time is committed to analyzing needs assessment and evaluation information, modifying the present program where needed, sharing information about newly-discovered resources that might be used for future activities, bringing subcommittee information up to date, and having a presentation or exercise in relation to educational techniques or program planning and evaluation methods. This presentation or exercise is an important motivational factor for committee members and, becuase of it, association members interested in serving on the continuing education committee are not in short supply but, rather, wait for appointments. In some cases, committee members themselves prepare a presentation or introduce and lead an exercise that will meet an evidenced committee need. Usually, however, an outside expert is invited to explain or demonstrate to the committee a speciality that may add to the expertise of committee members in either their committee or library responsibilities.

The committee consists of four present subcommittees and one newly-formed task force charged with examining the feasibility of a new subcommittee. One subcommittee is responsible for the day-long activity sponsored by the committee at the annual conference. This group plans and produces the activity and has one or two members who serve liaison functions with the conference program committee to pool ideas and suggestions and to assure continuity with the conference's theme. A second subcommittee plans and produces one sub-regional workshop, as does a separate and third subcommittee. The fourth subcommittee is responsible for general needs assessment and evaluation functions for the whole committee, publicity for the three activities each year, and an awareness of potential new developments in the region that might have an impact on continuing education needs.

The newly formed task force is looking into the possibility of establishing a clearinghouse function for continuing education resources and activities that have been identified in the region. If this would be a useful service, it may be offered to association members as part of the continuing education function of the association. The feasibility study, among other things, will include an indi-cation of the potential scope of such a service and the cost and alternative ways of providing it, one of which may be through the committee. There has been some talk of another task force in the future, which would look into the possibility of providing the opportunity for individuals on the committee to serve as consultants to other groups in the region who wish help with planning continuing education activities. Action on this has not yet been taken.

The objectives for the committee are regularly reviewed every two years. Although there has been some modification in the recent past, they have proved very durable and, though they do not spell out the anticipated results of the program, they do indicate the operational responsibilities of the committee:

- to respond to identified priority needs of library personnel for continuing education opportunities.

- to produce moderately priced educational opportunities for the region without duplicating the activities of other organ-izations.

- to provide for in-depth growth in educational techniques skills (such as planning, implementation, and evaluation) of committee members.

These three objectives outline the major committee responsibilities and are understandable to all association members. The first two focus on the production of learning activities and services. The first objective also identifies another committee function, that of continuous needs assessment for continuing educa-tion. The second objective qualifies the range of committee activities. This, of course, implies the need to know what other continuing education efforts are going on and prompted the clearinghouse idea. In addition to the committee's objectives, each continuing education activity is planned with its own, more specifically focused set of objectives. These are reviewed and discussed by the whole committee after being drafted by the subcommittee responsible for that activity. Final plans are made after committee review and then are implemented by the subcommittee.

In addition to its objectives, the committee has developed a few policies and procedures to guide its efforts with some consistency. For example, some of the committee's time and effort are allocated to the needs of the committee itself and some to the production of continuing education for others. To a large extent, the committee is self-supporting through the fees for activity registrations and the allocated association funds for continuing education. Committee members, however, often contribute their travel expenses, and their libraries sometimes take care of incidental expenses. When resource people or consultants are engaged to produce an activity, they are requested to work closely with the subcommittee through planning, and, in some cases, to provide opportunities for some sub-committee members to serve functional and supportive roles during the activity or the preparation for it. This provides an incentive and an in-depth learning opportunity for subcommittee members, many of whom go on to develop a particular interest into a speciality. This is a major reason for a low committee drop-out record and for a high degree of personal commitment, as well as for the reputation for high quality activities done with enthusiasm.

Committee meetings and sub-committee meetings are the main means of direct communication. Each meeting is guided by an agenda and includes time for discussion and exchange of ideas on topics relevant to the committee's responsibilities. Often, pre-meeting mailings are used to introduce plans and proposals for activities or to ask for thinking or action prior to the meeting. Minutes of each meeting are sent both to all committee members and to members of the association's executive board following each full committee meeting. Subcommittee meetings follow a similar pattern, but minutes are sent to subcommittee members and the individual chairing the committee. Where necessary, telephone contact supplements face-to-face meetings and correspondence.

The decision-making pattern is largely consensual within the committee structure, with compromise sometimes necessary to get an implementable decision within the time available. With only occasional suggestions from the executive board, the committee is largely autonomous but informs others affected by its decisions promptly and fully. Likewise, subcommittees are autonomous while working on the tasks and activities, but only after plans have been discussed by the whole committee. The chairman of the full committee takes responsibility for managing the program, for coordinating necessary communications, and for convening and chairing committee meetings. Subcommittee chairmen are responsible for implementing their plans but report regularly to the full committee.

Continuing education is seen presently as one of the major roles and functions in the association. A currently popular demand for activities is being responded to with tangible services to the membership, services with value to the individual learners and their libraries. This also strengthens the association. The effectiveness of this committee is largely dependent on the commitment and skills of its members and on the quality of the activities and efforts that they produce. Strong incentives have, so far, not only attracted interested members to the committee, but have also increased their skills as they serve. A serendipitous result from the last few years of work has been the development of an informal information and referral network relationship of past committee members, as they share ideas, techniques and opportunities among each other even after they no longer serve on the committee.

*****

MODEL 3

A year ago, a new state librarian was appointed to head the state library agency of a midwestern state. The agency itself has a staff of 90 persons. The state's eight systems are designated by reason of geographic and demographic compatibility. Each system director is considered part of the state agency staff, as are various specialized support staff. Other field personnel include consultants who, for the most part, assist with problems and programming within the systems structure; they sometimes work with individual libraries as well. The agency has a statutory responsibility for all types of libraries although the actual depth of responsibility assumed varies among the library types, with services to academic libraries more limited than those to public or school libraries. Special libraries, however, particularly institutional libraries, avail themselves of a number of services ranging from specialized materials to consultant help.

When first appointed, the state librarian met with library personnel within each systems area and requested their recommendations for top priority efforts to be addressed by the state agency. The most frequently indicated needs and hopes were: more adequate state-wide use of library resources, more attention to upgrading library facilities and collections, improved communication between the state library and the state's library personnel, and more and better continuing education opportunities to improve the capabilities of library personnel. Based on these recommendations, plus the state librarian's own personal view of the state's needs, then, the agency's direction, personnel, and budgeting were reorganized. One of the results of this effort was the acceptance of the state agency's role and responsibility to produce continuing education activities and to endorse and encourage that continuing education for library personnel produced by others.

With regard to this continuing education responsibility, the state librarian assembled an advisory council on continuing library education. This group is composed of 15 members with broad representation from the libraries in the state: types of libraries, positions in libraries, trustees, and liaison people from library associations. These members have two-year overlapping terms. They meet twice a year for two-day meetings at which they both review the previous year's continuing education accomplishments and problems and draw up recommendations for the future program efforts.

The beginning of the continuing education effort of the reorganized state library consisted of the appointment of the advisory council. The council's first meeting was a 4-day retreat where they got acquainted and explored the chief problem areas related to learning needs of library personnel in the context of the library needs of the state's citizens. Key state library agency staff members were also present during the meeting. Together the two groups evolved the focus for continuing education as being a systematic approach to further state agency goals through continuing education. This was to be done by 1) upgrading the competencies of library personnel; 2) helping personnel keep up with changes in technology, society, and librarianship; and 3) providing consistent and assured quality in continuing education activity.

The retreat work sessions were facilitated by a consultant who guided the group through a simulation that led to a plan for the continuing education program now in place. The simulation, called the Kontinuing Education Game (KEG), helped the group understand and practice principles of program planning as well as experience working together on a very real task. This prepared them for the two years they would be working together on continuing education and, at the same time, produced a plan for continuing education that reflected the representative nature of the advisory council and the expertise of the agency staff.

Guided by the results of the retreat and the council's recommendations, the agency administrator sought a capable staff person for the continuing education position. The director of library personnel development is responsible for designing, implementing, and managing the agency's continuing education program, guided by the advisory council's recommendations. The director reports directly to the state librarian and meets with other divisional and systems heads to assure close linkage with other agency functions. This organizational structure for the program took a total of 9 months to fully implement, with the first 6 months taken up in the state librarian's surveying opinions and needs from library personnel throughout the state. The selection of the advisory council took about two months, and the selection of the continuing education director involved another month following the retreat.

The first tasks that were taken on by the director included becoming familiar with the state library's organizational structure, procedures, and personnel; reviewing what past continuing education had been done through the agency and in the state by other groups; and analyzing the current needs information already available that related to the problems and issues of library personnel and that had implications for learning. Guided by the recommendations of the advisory council and the outline developed in the KEG exercise, the director laid out a tentative three-phase plan of activities. It consisted of two-year cycles, which could be lengthened if progress was slower than expected or if adequate resources were not available.

The overall goal came from the advisory council: to meet the continuing education needs of library personnel in the state. Two conditions were attached to this goal: 1) the needs the state agency is responsible for are those related to the agency's mission and those that will improve the quality of library service for the state's citizens, and 2) systematic planning is the method to be used in developing the agency's continuing education efforts.

Three broad program objectives were also recommended by the council: 1) The state library will facilitate continuing education activities throughout the state. This will include disseminating information about existing programs offered by other groups as well as those produced by the state agency. It will include co-sponsorship and other means of encouraging incipient efforts, and enable the participation of library personnel. It will include the purchase of the necessary quality learning packages, which can then be distributed and made available. This will include making resources available within defined guidelines, including full or partial funding when that is essential.

2) The state library will perform an active leadership role in relation to continuing education for all types of libraries and for all levels of library personnel. This includes working with planning groups and committees as well as assisting with advice or resources. Part of this leadership role will be to raise the level of awareness of continuing education's importance as well as enabling it to occur. It will include linking continuing education closely with statewide library concerns. It will include publishing and disseminating information about continuing education. It will include an exploration of the continuing education incentives that are important to library personnel.

3) The state library will develop the personnel of the agency itself, through staff development efforts using outside continuing education opportunities to raise the level of competency and commitment. This will include counseling for personal educational planning, tuition reimbursement, and travel funds for job-related study.

Implementing these objectives through a program of activities and planned program functions is the responsibility of the director. The director's first task was to do an initial needs assessment. This was approached in a general fashion, using available needs information from each system's monthly reports, from agency field personnel, and from the agency's established priorities on inter-library cooperation and instituting a statewide reciprocal borrowing service. The director attended several systems meetings to become known and to informally ask library personnel about their needs, and at these, found wide levels of experience, education, and job requirements. These findings affected the director's identification of topical needs for activities significantly, and to some degree influenced the selection of methods of delivering the education. Trustee education and that of the lay public was also found to be important.

The advisory council recommendations and the information about continuing education needs among the state's library personnel were woven together by the director in an action plan outline for the program's three phases. Impressed by the number and variety of needs expressed, in the *first phase* the director placed top priority on disseminating information about educational opportunities that already existed in the state and region. A calendar was developed and sent to every library for posting in a place accessible to its staff. Updated and sent every month, each calendar includes four months of listed events, indicating topic, place, date and contact person. The director's office acts as a "hotline" service to provide additional information when requested. Many planning and evaluation meetings are also included on the calendar, in addition to association meetings, library school courses in the state, workshops and institutes of special interest to library personnel, and adult education courses on such topics as interpersonal relations, communications, and problem solving. The director gleans this information from library and community contacts, information received from mailing lists, and library literature sources.

The state agency became a member of the Continuing Library Education Network and Exchange (CLENE) to gain access to nationwide learning opportunities and assistance in program planning. This led to the discovery of the ACCESS videotapes, several of which were closely tied to the patterns of needs that emerged from the assessment. Four tapes were bought: on vertical file, preschooler programming, censorship, and using volunteers. These were then provided through system facilities or directly to a requesting library. These sources, plus a couple of commercial learning packages, gave quick response to some of the most frequently cited needs. It also gave visibility to the continuing education program. Systems communications, the state library newsletter, and other library-related publications carried frequent mention of the program's present efforts and future plans.

A combination of LSCA and state library funding was commited to continuing education and was given in small grants to individual libraries or through systems. The proposals that were part of the application for the grants had to demonstrate a systematic approach to staff development or continuing education activities and had to include both needs assessment and evaluation components. Four or five grants are awarded each year, and the results of funded projects are disseminated through state agency channels. Many of the projects have resulted in activities that are, with some adaptation, applicable to other locales and libraries.

Two activities were produced directly by the state library. One was a workshop prior to the state library association conference. Its focus on interlibrary cooperation was intended to allow library administrators to explore the advantages and difficulties that increased cooperation would bring. It was selective but included many of the key decision makers in the state. It was produced by the entire state library staff, and their efforts were aided by an outside consultant from a similar state that had engaged actively in interlibrary cooperation for the first time five years ago.

The second activity was a traveling area institute, given four times in the state and focused on materials selection policies and practices. This was intended for the small-staffed library and included selection tools, weeding principles, and ways to share resources to meet demands. This activity required sound planning to produce the first time; improvements were worked in for each successive presentation. The director served at each presentation in both administrative and coordinative functions, which allowed further knowledge of the state, its libraries, and its librarians. The design and materials for this activity were filed at the state library and could be used by any system wanting to replicate it.

Two traditions were begun that effected the continuous needs assessment, which, in turn, would assist future purchases and productions. One was the practice of holding open hearings on continuing education at the state library association conference each year. These generated constructive criticism of the program itself, elicited unmet needs, and sought to identify new educational resources that could be tapped. The second tradition was instituting forms and interviews as part of evaluating each activity, including viewing videotapes or using self-instructional learning packages. These evaluation forms not only gave information about how each activity was perceived but also were designed to help participants identify further needs. These completed forms were analyzed and digested by the director; they also were provided to the advisory committee for consideration.

The activities for this first two-year program were financed adequately but not abundantly through LSCA and state funding available through the state library. This first phase revealed both the need and opportunities for additional funding (or for stretching current funding) with more co-sponsored efforts. Had continuing education not been designated a priority, funding would be difficult to justify, and if the program had not produced some immediate activities of value, it would have been impossible to extend.

The second phase is still in the planning stages, as new efforts are felt to be needed in several areas. More encouragement is needed to prompt systems efforts toward internal staff development and to share some of those activities across systems lines and with the libraries that are not members of a system. More sequenced learning opportunities are needed to offer topics and issues at different levels of interest and experience. This would enable an individual learner to start with a beginner course or workshop, then later to take an intermediate level activity in the same topic, and finally to engage in an advanced effort with the desired level of competency. To strengthen the state's resources, a sequence for training trainers is envisioned. This would permit libraries and systems to do more of their own internal staff development rather than rely so heavily on the state library or other outside resources. State consultants, in the beginning, would be available to help with educational design and the delivery of educational services, audiovisual techniques, evaluation methodology, and assistance in writing proposals to apply for state and other funding. Although this kind of help would be needed often in the beginning, its use would diminish and level off later, when local resources had developed.

The second phase would not bring changes to some of the functions of the state library. The calendar would continue with some improvements; notably, its dissemination is now to every person working in libraries, not just to the library in general. Packages are continually being assessed when their topic or method seem relevant to expressed needs. Now, criteria and standards are more firmly known and more rigidly applied. Some state library-produced workshop, seminars, and courses will be produced, but they will cover subjects that cannot be done at the local level or are important to do on a statewide basis. Quality rather than quantity is stressed in the production of these activities. These activities will broaden their instructional approaches as they answer widely general needs or selected specialties.

A search is presently being conducted, in this first phase, for a means to identify the competencies needed in the state's libraries. That will then be used during the second and third phases to guide the development of activities, which will be planned on a more sound basis than personally perceived needs or assumed ones. This will probably be an extensive effort that will take considerable planning and coordination to accomplish, but it would be helpful to libraries for selecting, hiring, and evaluating personnel. It would be helpful to the state library for setting standards realistically and for educational programming.

The third phase seeks to develop a human resource directory of capable in-state people able and willing to plan, produce, and evaluate continuing education activities and staff development programs. This would include both identified and developed resources, the former with broader awareness of the state by the director and the latter from the trainers' training program. Counseling for continuing education planning is a prospect either through the individual systems or through the state library agency. Evaluation of continuing education efforts will be even more strongly emphasized in the third phase. Although done throughout, an overall evaluation of the total program is planned at that time. Continued efforts to publicize and disseminate information about available opportunities is envisioned, as are the initiation of efforts where needed but not presently done and the provision of planning help and access to training resources.

The beginning of the first phase has not given conclusive results yet, but the working relationship between the director and the advisory committee has been good. And the state librarian, though the responsibility is fully delegated, continues an interest in continuing education and watches closely to make sure that those efforts are integrated with other state library functions and responsibilities and that the program remains accountable for its funding and its charge. Problems will undoubtedly occur in the future, but the basic communications and decision-making processes have been provided for, and this is an assurance that the program will be able to cope with crises as they arise.

BIBLIOGRAPHY:
BOOKS AND DOCUMENTS,
PERIODICALS, AND
CURRENT INDEXING AND ABSTRACTING SERVICES

BOOKS AND DOCUMENTS

This selected list includes current material about adult and continuing education; training and development; and program planning, implementation, and evaluation. With few exceptions, most listings are since 1970 and published in the United States. The list intentionally highlights resources outside the field of librarianship. Citations listed here cover every Guideline and each major topic in this book. Additional references from the field of librarianship or from areas beyond the scope described above may be found in citations in the notes or in the text itself.

Aker, George F. *Adult Education Procedures, Methods and Techniques; an Annotated Bibliography, 1953-1963.* [Syracuse, NY]: Library of Continuing Education, 1965.

American Society for Training and Development. *Professional Development Manual.* Madison, WI: American Society for Training and Development, 1974.

Anderson, Ronald H. *Selecting and Developing Media for Instruction.* American Society for Training and Development. New York: Van Nostrand Reinhold Co., 1976.

Anderson, Scarvia B., Samuel Ball, and Richard T. Murphy. *Encyclopedia of Educational Evaluation; Concepts and Techniques for Evaluating Education and Training Programs.* San Francisco, CA: Jossey-Bass, 1974.

Apple, Michael W., Michael J. Subkoviak, and Henry S. Lufler, Jr., eds. *Educational Evaluation: Analysis and Responsibility.* Berkeley, CA: McCutchan Publishing Corp., 1974.

Argyris, Chris and Donald Schön. *Theory in Practice: Increasing Professional Effectiveness.* San Francisco, CA: Jossey-Bass, 1976.

Atherton, Pauline. *Guidelines for the Organization of Training Courses, Workshops and Seminars in Scientific and Technical Information and Documentation.* Paris: Unesco, 1975.

Berdie, Douglas R. and John F. Anderson. *Questionnaires: Design and Use.* Metuchen, NJ: Scarecrow Press, 1974.

Bergevin, Paul E., Dwight Morris, and Robert Smith. *Adult Education Procedures: A Handbook of Tested Patterns for Effective Participation.* Greenwich, CN: Seabury Press, 1963.

Bloom, Benjamin S., et al. *Handbook on Formative and Summative Evaluation of Student Learning.* New York: McGraw, 1971.

Borich, Gary D., ed. *Evaluating Educational Programs and Products.* Englewood Cliffs, NJ: Educational Technology Publications, 1974.

Bradford, Leland P. *Making Meetings Work: A Guide for Leaders and Group Members.* La Jolla, CA: University Associates, Inc., 1976.

Brown, F. Gerald and Kenneth R. Wedel. *Assessing Training Needs.* Washington, DC: National Training and Development Service Press, 1974.

Brown, James W., Richard B. Lewis, and Fred F. Harcleroad. *A V Instruction: Technology, Media and Methods.* 5th ed. New York: McGraw-Hill, 1977.

Brown, James W., Kenneth D. Norberg, and Sara K. Srygley. *Administering Educational Media: Instructional Technology and Library Services.* 2nd ed. New York: McGraw Hill, 1972.

Bullough, Robert V. *Creating Instructional Materials.* Columbus, OH: Charles E. Merrill, 1974.

Burke, W. Warner and Richard Beckhard, eds. *Conference Planning* (Selected Readings Series Six) 2nd ed. Washington, DC: NTL Institute for Applied Behavioral Science, 1970.

Byers, Kenneth T., ed. *Employee Training and Development in the Public Service.* (Public Sector Human Resources Management Series, vol. 1) New ed. Chicago: International Personnel Management Association, 1974.

Chabotar, Kent J. and Lawrence J. Lad. *Evaluation Guidelines for Training Programs.* East Lansing, MI: Public Administration Programs, Michigan State University, 1974.

Continuing Education: A Guide to Career Development Programs. Neal-Shuman Publishers, Inc., comp. Syracuse, NY: Gaylord, 1977.

Continuing Education Unit; Guidelines and Other Information. Atlanta, GA: Southern Association of Colleges and Schools, Commission on Colleges, 1974.

Continuing Professional Education. (Informal Bibliography, no. 8) ERIC Clearinghouse in Career Education. DeKalb: Northern Illinois University, 1975.

Conroy, Barbara. *Staff Development and Continuing Education Programs for Library Personnel: Guidelines and Criteria.* Produced for ERIC. Boulder, CO: Western Interstate Commission for Higher Education, 1973. (ED 083 986)

Cooley, William W. and Paul R. Lohnes. *Evaluation Research in Education.* New York: Irvington Publishers, Inc., Wiley and Sons, 1976.

Craig, Robert L., ed. *Training and Development Handbook.* Sponsored by American Society for Training and Development. New York: McGraw-Hill Book Co., 1976.

Davies, Ivor Kevin, et al. *Organization of Training.* New York: McGraw, 1973.

Davis, J. Ronnie and John F. Morrall. *Evaluating Educational Investment.* Lexington, MA: Lexington Books, 1974.

Davis, Larry Nolan and Earl McCallon. *Planning, Conducting and Evaluating Workshops: A Practitioner's Guide to Adult Education.* Austin, TX: Learning Concepts, 1974.

Delbecq, Andre L., et al. *Group Techniques for Program Planning; A Guide to Nominal Group and Delphi Processes.* Glenview, IL: Scott, Foresman, 1975.

Denova, Charles C. *Establishing a Training Function.* Englewood Cliffs, NJ: Educational Technology Publications, 1971.

Dickinson, Gary. *Teaching Adults; A Handbook for Instructors.* Toronto, Canada: New Press, 1973.

Dimock, Hedley G. *How to Plan Staff Training Programs.* Montreal, Canada: Sir George Williams University, 1973.

Engle, Herbert M. *Handbook of Creative Learning Exercises.* (Building Blocks of Human Potential Series.) Houston, TX: Gulf Publishing Co., 1973.

Ford, LeRoy. *Using Problem Solving in Teaching and Training.* (Multi-Media Teaching and Training Series) Nashville, TN: Broadman, 1972.

Furst, Edward. *Constructing Evaluation Instruments.* New York: Longmans, Green, 1958.

Goldstein, I. L. *Training: Program Development and Evaluation.* Monterey, CA: Brooks/Cole, 1974.

Gorman, Alfred H. *Teachers and Learners; The Interactive Process of Education.* Boston: Allyn and Bacon, 1969.

Grabowski, Stanley M., ed. *Adult Learning and Instruction.* ERIC Clearinghouse on Adult Education and Adult Education Association of the U.S. Washington, DC: ERIC, 1970. (ED 045 867).

Gronlund, Norman E. *Stating Behavioral Objectives for Classroom Instruction.* New York: Macmillan, 1970.

Gropper, George L., and Zita Glasgow. *Criteria for the Selection and Use of Visuals in Instruction.* Englewood Cliffs, NJ: Educational Technology Publications, 1970.

Grotelueschen, Arden D., et al. *An Evaluation Planner; A Guidebook for Developing Evaluation Plans Responsive to a Variety of Contexts, Audiences and Issues Within Adult Basic Education.* Urbana: University of Illinois, Office for the Study of Continuing Professional Education, 1974.

Guba, Egon G. and Daniel L. Stufflebeam. *Evaluation: The Process of Stimulating, Aiding and Abetting Insightful Action.* (Monograph Series in Reading Education, no. 1) Bloomington: Indiana University, 1970.

Guilford, Joy Paul and Benjamin Fruchter. *Fundamental Statistics in Psychology and Education.* 5th ed. New York: McGraw-Hill, 1973.

Havelock, Ronald C., and Mary C. Havelock. *Training for Change Agents: A Guide to the Design of Training Programs in Education and Other Fields.* Ann Arbor, MI: Institute for Social Research, University of Michigan, 1973.

Hendershot, Carl H. *Programmed Learning and Individually Paced Instruction. Bibliography.* 5th ed. Bay City, MI: Hendershot Programmed Learning Consultants, 1973. [Four supplements bring this cumulation to 1977.]

Horn, Robert E. *Guide to Simulation Games.* Cranford, NJ: Didactic Systems, Inc., 1976.

Johnson, David and Frank Johnson. *Joining Together; Group Theories and Group Skills.* Englewood Cliffs, NJ: Prentice-Hall, 1974.

Johnson, Stuart R. and Rita B. Johnson. *Developing Individualized Instructional Material.* Palo Alto, CA: Westinghouse Learning Press, 1970.

Kaufman, Harold G. *Obsolescence and Professional Career Development.* New York: Anacom, 1974.

Kaufman, Roger. *Educational System Planning.* Englewood Cliffs, NJ: Prentice Hall, 1972.

Kemp, Jerrold E. *Instructional Design; A Plan for Unit and Course Development.* Belmont, CA: Fearon Publishers, 1971.

Kemp, Jerrold E. *Planning and Producing Audiovisual Materials.* 3rd ed. New York: Thomas Crowell, 1975.

Kidd, J. R. *How Adults Learn.* Revised. New York: Association Press, 1973.

Kirkpatrick, Donald L. *A Practical Guide for Supervisory Training and Development.* Reading, MA: Addison Wesley, 1971.

Kleis, Russell J. *Bibliography on Continuing Education.* East Lansing: Office of Studies in Continuing Education, Michigan State University, 1972. (ED 078 242).

Klevins, Chester, ed. *Materials and Methods in Adult Education.* 2nd ed. New York: Klevens Publications, Inc., 1976.

Knowles, Malcolm S. *The Adult Learner: A Neglected Species.* Houston, TX: Gulf Publishing Co., 1973.

Knowles, Malcolm S., ed., *Handbook of Adult Education in the United States.* Washington, DC: Adult Education Association, 1960.

Knowles, Malcolm S. *The Modern Practice of Adult Education: Andragogy Versus Pedagogy.* New York: Association Press, [1970].

Knowles, Malcolm S. *Self-directed Learning; A Guide for Learners and Teachers.* New York: Association Press, 1975.

Knox, Alan B. *Adult Development and Learning.* San Francisco, CA: Jossey-Bass, Inc., 1977.

Knox, Alan B. *Helping Adults to Learn.* (Concept Paper, no. 4) Washington, DC: Continuing Library Education Network and Exchange, 1976.

Koberg, Don, and Jim Bagnall. *The Universal Traveller; A Soft-System Guide to: Creativity, Problem-Solving and the Process of Reaching Goals.* Rev. ed. Los Altos, CA: William Kaufman, 1974.

Kozoll, Charles E. *Staff Development in Organizations: Cost Evaluation Manual for Managers and Trainers.* Reading, MA: Addison Wesley, 1974.

Kozoll, Charles E. and Curtis Ulmer, eds. *In-Service Training: Philosophy, Processes and Operational Techniques.* Englewood Cliffs, NJ: Prentice Hall, 1972.

Lauffer, Armand. *Practice of Continuing Education in the Human Services.* New York: McGraw Hill, 1977.

Lawson, Tom E. *Formative Instructional Product Evaluation: Instruments and Strategies.* Englewood Cliffs, NJ: Educational Technology Publications, 1974.

LeBreton, Preston P., ed. *The Assessment and Development of Professionals: Theory and Practice.* Seattle: University of Washington, 1976.

Leonard, Edwin C. *Assessment of Training Needs.* Fort Wayne, IN: Midwest Intergovernmental Training Committee, 1974.

Levin, Jack. *Elementary Statistics in Social Research.* New York: Harper and Row, 1973.

Lovin, Bill C. and Emery R. Casstevens. *Coaching, Learning and Action.* New York: American Management Association, 1971.

Lynton, Rolf P. and Udai Pareek. *Training for Development.* Homewood, IL: Richard D. Irwin, 1967.

Mager, Robert F. *Developing Attitude Toward Learning.* Palo Alto, CA: Fearon, 1969.

Mager, Robert F. *Measuring Instructional Intent, or Got a Match?* Belmont, CA: Fearon, 1973.

Mager, Robert F. *Preparing Instructional Objectives.* 2nd ed. Belmont, CA: Fearon Publishers, 1975.

Mager, Robert F. and Peter Pipe. *Analyzing Performance Problems.* Palo Alto, CA: Fearon, 1970.

Maier, Norman. *Problem-Solving Discussions and Conferences: Leadership Methods and Skills.* New York: McGraw-Hill, 1963.

Maier, Norman F. R., Allen R. Solem and Ayesha Maier. *The Role-Play Technique: A Handbook for Management and Leadership Practice.* La Jolla, CA: University Associates, 1975.

Mamoureus, Marvin E. *Marketing Continuing Education: A Study of Price Strategies.* (Occasional Papers in Continuing Education, no. 11) Vancouver, Canada: University of British Columbia, Centre for Continuing Education, 1976.

Mayhew, Lewis B. *Changing Practice in Education for the Professions.* (SREB Research Monograph, no. 17) Atlanta, GA: Southern Regional Education Board, 1971.

McCallon, Earl. *Workshop Evaluation System Manual.* Austin, TX: Learning Concepts, 1974.

McGill, Michael E. and Melvin E. Horton, Jr. *Action Research Designs for Training and Development.* Washington, DC: National Training and Development Service Press, 1973.

McLagan, Patricia A. *Helping Others Learn; A Handbook for Adult Educators.* St. Paul, MN: The author, 1976.

McLagan, Patricia A. *The Learner's Guide to Efficient Information Processing and Learning in Changing Times.* St. Paul, MN: The author, 1976.

Miles, Matthew B. *Learning to Work in Groups.* New York: Bureau of Publications, Teachers College, Columbia University, 1959.

Mills, H. R. *Teaching and Training—A Handbook for Instructors.* New York: John Wiley and Sons, 1972.

Minor, Ed and Harvey R. Frye. *Techniques for Producing Visual Instructional Media.* 2nd ed. New York: McGraw-Hill, 1976.

Nadler, Leonard. *Developing Human Resources.* Houston, TX: Gulf Publishing Co., 1970.

Nadler, Leonard and Zeance Nadler. *The Conference Book.* (Building Blocks of Human Potential Series). Houston, TX: Gulf Publishing Co., 1977.

Nixon, George. *People, Evaluation and Achievement.* (Building Blocks of Human Potential Series) Houston, TX: Gulf Publishing Co., 1973.

Nunnally, Jum C. et al. *Introduction to Statistics for Psychology and Education.* New York: McGraw-Hill, 1975.

Nylen, Donald, Robert Mitchell, and Anthony Stout. *Handbook of Staff Development and Human Relations Training.* Washington, DC: National Training Laboratories, 1967.

Odiorne, George S. *Training by Objectives; An Economic Approach to Management Training.* Toronto, Canada: Macmillan, 1970.

Otto, C. P. and R. O. Glaser. *The Management of Training: A Handbook for Training Directors.* Reading, MA: Addison Wesley, 1970.

Payne, David A. *The Assessment of Learning: Cognitive and Affective.* Indianapolis, IN: Heath, 1974.

Peters, John M. and Curtis Ulmer, eds. *How to Make Successful Use of the Learning Laboratory.* Englewood Cliffs, NJ: Prentice Hall, 1972.

Pfeiffer, J. William and John E. Jones, eds. *A Handbook of Structured Experiences for Human Relations Training.* Vols. 1-5. La Jolla, CA: University Associates, 1969-1975.

Pipe, Peter. *Objectives—Tool for Change.* Belmont, CA: Fearon Publishers, Inc., 1975.

Polette, Nancy. *In-Service: School Library/Media Workshops and Conferences.* Metuchen, NJ: Scarecrow Press, 1973.

Popham, W. James. *Evaluating Instruction.* Englewood Cliffs, NJ: Prentice Hall, 1973.

Popham, W. James and Kenneth Sirotnik. *Educational Statistics: Use and Interpretation.* 2nd ed. New York: Harper and Row, 1973.

Rauch, David B., ed. *Priorities in Adult Education. A Publication of the Adult Education Association of the U.S.A.* New York: Macmillan, 1972.

Roberson, E. Wayne, ed. *Educational Accountability through Evaluation.* Englewood Cliffs, NJ: Educational Technology Publications, 1971.

Romiszowski, A. J. *The Selection and Uses of Instructional Media.* (Halsted Press Book) New York: Wiley, 1974.

Saint, Avice. *Learning at Work: Human Resources and Organizational Development.* Chicago: Nelson-Hall Co., 1974.

Sattler, William M. and W. Miller, eds. *Discussion and Conference.* 2nd ed. Englewood Cliffs, NJ: Prentice Hall, 1968.

Seymour, W. Douglase. *Skills Analysis Training: A Handbook for Managers, Supervisors and Instructors.* New York: International Publications Service, 1968.

Shaw, Nathan C., ed. *Administration of Continuing Education; A Guide for Administrators.* Washington, DC: National Association for Public School Adult Education, 1969.

Sheldon, Brooke and Blanche Woolls. *Developing Continuing Education Learning Materials.* (Concept Paper, no. 1) Washington, DC: Continuing Library Education Network and Exchange, 1976.

Silvern, Leonard C. *Systems Engineering Applied to Training.* Houston, TX: Gulf Publishing Co., 1972.

Smith, Robert M., George F. Aker, and J. R. Kidd. *Handbook of Adult Education.* New York: Macmillan, 1970.

Steele, Sara M. and Robert E. Brack. *Evaluating the Attainment of Objectives in Adult Education: Process, Properties, Problems, Prospects.* (Syracuse, NY: Syracuse University Press, 1973.

Stephenson, Robert W., and James R. Burkett. *An Action Oriented Review of On-the-Job Training Literature:* Washington, DC: American Institutes for Research in the Behavioral Sciences, 1975.

Stufflebeam, Daniel L., ed. *Educational Evaluation and Decision Making.* Phi Delta Kappa National Study Committee on Evaluation. Itasca, IL: F. E. Peacock Publishers, 1971.

Suchman, Edward Allen. *Evaluative Research; Principles and Practice in Public Service and Social Action Programs.* New York: Sage, 1967.

Taxonomy of Educational Objectives: The Classification of Educational Goals: Handbook I, The Cognitive Domain. ed. Benjamin S. Bloom. New York: David McKay Co., 1956; *Handbook II, The Affective Domain.* ed. David R. Kratwohl. New York: David McKay Co., 1964. 3 volumes.

Teachey, William C. and Joseph B. Carter. *Learning Laboratories, A Guide to Adoption and Use.* Englewood Cliffs, NJ: Educational Technology Publications, 1971.

This, Leslie E. *The Small Meeting Planner.* Houston: Gulf Publishing, 1972.

Tough, Allen. *The Adult's Learning Projects.* Toronto, Canada: Institute of Studies in Education, 1971.

Tracey, William R. *Designing Training and Development Systems.* New York: American Management Association, 1971.

Tracey, William R. *Evaluating Training and Development Systems.* New York: American Management Association, 1968.

Tracey, William R. *Managing Training and Development Systems.* New York: American Management Association, 1974.

Trice, Harrison M., and Paul M. Roman. *Evaluation of Training; Strategy, Tactics and Problems.* (Training Information Sources, no. 3; June, 1974) Compiled by ERIC Clearinghouse on Adult Education. Syracuse, NY: Syracuse University, 1974.

U.S. Civil Service Commission. *Administration of Training.* (Personnel Bibliography Series, no. 51) Washington, DC: Government Printing Office, 1973.

U.S. Civil Service Commission. Bureau of Training. *Managing Employee Development; A Step-by-Step Approach.* (TLP-302) Washington, DC: Government Printing Office, 1976.

U.S. Office of Education. *Preparing Evaluation Reports: A Guide for Authors.* Washington, DC: Government Printing Office, 1970.

U.S. Public Health Service. *Training Methodology. An Annotated Bibliography. Part I, Background Theory and Research; Part II, Planning and Administration; Part III, Instructional Methods and Techniques; Part IV, Audiovisual Theory, Aids and Equipment.* (Publication 1862) 4 volumes. Washington, DC: Government Printing Office, 1969.

U.S. Social and Rehabilitation Service. *A Trainers Guide to Andragogy; Its Concepts, Experience and Application.* Rev. ed. Washington: Government Printing Office, 1973.

Van Maanen, John. *The Process of Program Evaluation.* Washington, DC: National Training and Development Service Press, 1973.

Verduin, John R., Jr., Harry G. Miller, and Charles E. Greer. *Adults Teaching Adults.* Austin, TX: Learning Concepts, 1977.

Veri, Clive C., and T. A. VonderHaar. *Training the Trainer.* St. Louis: Extension Division, University of Missouri, 1970.

Walberg, Herbert J. *Evaluating Educational Performance.* Berkeley, CA: McCutchan, 1974.

Walker, Scott B. *Conference Planning.* Washington, DC: National Training and Development Service Press, 1974.

Wallace, Everett M. and Robert V. Katter. *Research and Development of On-the-Job Training Courses for Library Personnel.* Final Report. Santa Monica, CA: Systems Development Corp., 1969 (ED 032 085).

Warncke, Ruth. *Planning Library Workshops and Institutes.* (Public Library Reporter, no. 17) Chicago: American Library Association, 1976.

Warren, Malcolm W. *Training for Results: A Systems Approach to Development of Human Resources in Industry.* Reading, MA: Addison Wesley, 1969.

Warren, Virginia B., ed. *Second Treasury of Techniques for Teaching Adults.* Washington, DC: National Association for Public Continuing and Adult Education, 1970.

Washtien, Joe. *A Guide for Planning and Teaching Continuing Education Courses.* (Medical Library Association) Washington, DC: The Continuing Library Education Network and Exchange, 1975.

Wentling, Tim L. and Tom E. Lawson. *Evaluating Occupational Education and Training Programs.* Boston: Allyn, 1975.

Williams, James G. *Simulation Activities in Library Communication and Information Science.* (Vol. 6 of Communication Science and Technology Series). New York: Marcel Dekker, 1976.

Wilson, Vivian. *Concise Planning for Training Meetings.* Princeton, NJ: Brandon Systems Press, Inc., 1969.

Wittich, Walter A. and Charles F. Schuller. *Audiovisual Materials, Their Nature and Use.* 5th ed. (Exploration in Education Series) New York: Harper and Row, 1973.

Worthen, Blaine R. and James R. Sanders. *Educational Evaluation: Theory and Practice.* Worthington, OH: Charles A. Jones, 1973.

Yaple, Henry. *Programmed Instruction in Librarianship: A Classified Bibliography of Programmed Texts and Other Materials, 1960-1974.* (Occasional Papers, no. 124) Champaign: University of Illinois, Graduate School of Library Science, July 1976.

Zalatimo, Suleiman and Phillip J. Sleeman. *A Systems Approach to Learning Environments.* Roselle, NJ: Meded Projects, Inc., 1975.

PERIODICALS

This selected list includes periodicals useful to those individuals and groups producing activities for library staff development and continuing education. Intentionally, this list does not include library or library education periodicals. It should be noted, however, that many regular publications from state library agencies and library associations contain current listings of available continuing education activities, as does CLENE's *Continuing Education Communicator.* Except for occasional articles or special topic issues, only the *CLENExchange* and the *Journal of Library Education* regularly contain technical assistance, book reviews, references, and research reports directed toward library education producers.

Administrator's Swap Shop Newsletter. National Association for Public Continuing and Adult Education; 1201 16th St., NW; Washington, DC 20036.

Adult and Continuing Education Today. Today Publications and News Service, Inc.; National Press Building; Washington, DC 20045.

Adult Education: A Journal of Research and Theory in Adult Education. Adult Education Association; 810 18th St. NW; Washington, DC 20000.

Adult Leadership. (This was discontinued in August 1977; see its successor, *Lifelong Learning: The Adult Years.*)

AEC Newsletter. Adult Education Clearinghouse, Montclair State College; Upper Montclair, NJ 07043.

Audio. North American Publishing Co.; 134 N. 13th St.; Philadelphia, PA 19107.

Audio-Visual Communications. United Business Publications, Inc.; 750 3rd Ave.; New York, NY 10017.

Audiovisual Instruction. Association for Educational Communications and Technology; 1201 16th St. NW; Washington, DC 20036.

Audiovisual Journal. Audio Visual Library Services. University of Minnesota; 3300 University Ave. SE; Minneapolis, MN 55414.

AV Communications Review. Association for Educational Communications and Technology; 1201 10th St. NW; Washington, DC 20036.

AV Guide: The Learning Media Magazine. Trade Periodicals Inc.; 434 S. Wabash; Chicago, IL 60605.

Bits & Pieces: A Monthly Mixture of Horse Sense and Common Sense about Working with People. The Economics Press, Inc.; 12 Daniel Road; Fairfield, NJ 07006.

Business Screen. Harcourt Brace Jovanovich Publications; 757 3rd Ave.; New York, NY 10017.

Canadian Training Methods. Canadian Training Methods; 542 Mt. Pleasant Road; Toronto, Ontario, Canada.

CLENExchange Newsletter. Continuing Library Education Network and Exchange. P.O. Box 1228; 620 Michigan Ave. NE; Washington, DC 20064.

Continuing Education. Pennsylvania Research Associates, Inc.; 1428 Ford Road; Cornwall Heights, PA 19020.

Continuous Learning. Canadian Association for Adult Education; Corbett House— Sultan St. 21-23; Toronto, Ontario, Canada.

Continuum. National University Extension Association; One Dupont Circle NW; Washington, DC 20036.

Convergence; International Journal of Adult Education. International Council for Adult Education; 252 Bloor St. W; Toronto, Ontario, Canada.

Correspondence Education. Western Gulf Publishing Corp.; 3090 N. Lincoln Ave.; Pasadena, CA 91103.

Dean and Director. Bureau of Business and Technology, Inc.; 101 Park Ave.; New York, NY 10017.

Educational and Industrial Television. C. S. Tepfer Publishing Co., Inc.; 607 Main St.; Ridgefield, CN 06877.

Educational Broadcasting. Brentwood Publishing Corporation; 825 S. Barrington Ave.; Los Angeles, CA 90049.

Educational Technology. Educational Technology Publications Inc.; 140 Sylvan Ave.; Englewood Cliffs, NJ 07632.

Education–Training Market Report. Box 795 Westbury; New York 11590.

ETV Newsletter. Tepfer Publishing Co., Inc.; 607 Main St.; Ridgefield, CN 06877.

Evaluation: A Forum for Human Service Decision Makers. Program Evaluation Resource Center; 501 Park Ave. So.; Minneapolis, MN 55415.

Evaluation Quarterly: A Journal of Applied Social Research. Sage Publications, Inc.; P.O. Box 776, Beverly Hills, CA 90213.

Group and Organizational Studies; The International Journal for Group Facilitators. University Associates, Inc.; 7596 Eads Ave.; La Jolla, CA 92037.

Human Resources Management. Bureau of Industrial Relations. Graduate School of Business Administration, University of Michigan, Ann Arbor, MI 48104.

Improving Human Performance Quarterly. National Society for Performance and Instruction; P.O. Box 266; Charlestown, WV 25414.

Instructional Technology. Girard Associates, Inc.; 399 Howard Blvd.; Mt. Arlington, NJ 07856.

Journal of Applied Behavioral Science. NTL Institute of Applied Behavioral Science; P.O. Box 9155; Arlington, VA 22209.

Journal of Cooperative Education. Cooperative Education Association; Drexel University; Philadelphia, PA 19104.

Lifelong Learning: The Adult Years. Adult Education Association; 810 18th St. NW; Washington, DC 20006.

Mass Media/Adult Education. 2116 No. Charles St.; Baltimore, Maryland 21218.

Media and Methods: Exploration in Education. North American Publishing Co.; 134 N. 13th St.; Philadelphia, PA 19107.

Meetings and Conventions. Gellert Publishing Corporation; 1 Park Ave.; NY 10016.

Mountain Plains Journal of Adult Education. Mountain Plains Adult Education Association; University of Wyoming; Laramie, WY 82071.

NAVA News. National Audiovisual Association News; 3150 Spring St.; Fairfax, VA 22030.

NSPI Journal. National Society for Performance and Instruction; P.O. Box 266; Charlestown, WV 25414.

People Watching; Curriculum and Techniques for Teaching the Behavioral Sciences. Behavioral Publications Inc.; 3852 Broadway; Morningside Heights, NY 10025.

Personnel. American Management Association; 135 W. 50th St.; New York, NY 10020.

Personnel Administrator. American Society for Personnel Administration; 19 Church St.; Berea, OH 44017.

Personnel and Guidance Journal. American Personnel and Guidance Association; 1607 New Hampshire Ave. NW; Washington, DC 20009.

Personnel Journal. Personnel Journal, Inc.; Box 1520; Santa Monica, CA 90406.

Personnel Psychology. Personnel Psychology, Inc.; Box 6965, College Station; Durham, NC 27708.

Public Personnel Management. International Personnel Management Association; 1313 E. 60th St.; Chicago, IL 60637.

Simgames; A Canadian Guide to Simulations and Games. Champlain Regional College; Lennoxville Campus; Lennoxville, Quebec, Canada.

Simulation and Games. Sage Publications; 275 S. Beverly Drive; Beverly Hills, CA 90212.

Sloan Management Review. Alfred P. Sloan School of Management; Massachusetts Institute of Technology; Cambridge, MA 02139.

Supervision. National Research Bureau, Inc.; 424 No. 3rd St.; Burlington, IA 52601.

Supervisory Managment. American Management Association; 135 West 50th St.; New York, NY 10020.

Techniques for Teachers of Adults. National Association for Public and Continuing Education; 1201 16th St. NW; Washington, DC 20036.

Telephone in Education Newsletter. Instructional Communications Systems; University of Wisconsin–Extension; 975 Observatory Drive; Madison, WI 53706.

Training and Development Journal. American Society for Training and Development; Box 5307; Madison, WI 53705.

Training; The Magazine of Human Resources Development. Lakewood Publications; 713 Hennepin Ave.; Minneapolis, MN 55403.

What's Ahead in Personnel. What's Ahead in Personnel; 20 N. Wacker Dr.; Chicago, IL 60606.

CURRENT INDEXING AND ABSTRACTING SERVICES

Abstracts of Instructional and Research Materials in Vocational and Technical Education. Center for Vocational and Technical Education; Ohio State University; 1900 Kenny Road; Columbus, OH 43210.

Business Periodicals Index. Wilson Company; 950 University Ave.; Bronx, NY 10452.

CIRF Abstracts. CIRF Publications; International Labor Office, CH-1211; Geneva 22, Switzerland.

Comprehensive Dissertation Index. University Microfilms International; 300 N. Zeed Rd.; Ann Arbor, MI 48106.

Current Contents: Social and Behavioral Sciences. Institute for Scientific Information; 325 Chestnut; Philadelphia, PA 19106.

Current Index to Journals in Education. CCM Information Sciences; 886 Third Ave.; New York, NY 10022.

Dissertation Abstracts International. A. The Humanities and Social Sciences. University Microfilms International; 300 N. Zeed Rd.; Ann Arbor, MI 48106.

Education Index. Wilson Company; 950 University Ave.; Bronx, NY 10452.

Manpower Research Inventory. Superintendent of Documents; Government Printing Office; Washington, DC 20402.

NICEM Media Indexes. National Information Center for Educational Media; University of Southern California; Los Angeles, CA 90007.

Personnel and Training Abstracts. Institute of Personnel Management; Anbar Publications, Ltd.; Box 23; Wembley, England.

Personnel Management Abstracts. University of Michigan; Graduate School of Business Administration; Ann Arbor, MI 48104.

Psychological Abstracts. American Psychological Association; 1200 17th St. NW; Washington, DC 20036.

Public Affairs Information Service Bulletin. Public Affairs Information Service; 11 West 40th St.; New York, NY 10018.

Resources in Education. Educational Resources Information Center; Superintendent of Documents; Government Printing Office; Washington, DC 20402.

Social Sciences Citation Index. Institute for Scientific Information; 325 Chestnut St.; Philadelphia, PA 19106.

Social Science Index. Wilson Company; 950 University Ave.; Bronx, NY 10452.

Sociological Abstracts. Sociological Abstracts, Inc.; P.O. Box 22206; San Diego, CA 92122.

Work Related Abstracts. Information Coordinators, Inc.; 1435 Randolph St.; Detroit MI 48226.

GLOSSARY

Activities. Discrete but coordinated components of a program designed to produce results that help to achieve program objectives as well as more specific educational objectives.

Activities Objectives. *See* **Objectives, Activity.**

Continuing Education. Those learning opportunities utilized by individuals in fulfilling their need to learn and grow following their preparatory education and work experiences.

Content Specialist. *See* **Educator: Content Specialist.**

Continuous Planning. *See* **Planning: Continuous Planning.**

Design (verb). Planning a sequence of learning events, activities, and processes in such a way that the established program or activity objectives can be accomplished effectively and appropriately.

Design (noun). The outline or plan resulting from the process of developing a program or activity.

Educator (Educational Staff). Individuals with the prime responsibility for conducting the learning experience; those who enable learning through skilled and deliberate efforts; "agents of learning."

   Content Specialist—Individual responsible for presenting information on a given specific topic.

   Methods Specialist—Individual responsible for designing and implementing particular methods and techniques that adults use in learning.

   Process Specialist—Individual responsible for managing the process of learning using the principles and practices of applied behavioral sciences and/or adult education.

Evaluation. The planned process used to assemble and utilize information necessary for effective, on-going decision making and for accountability.

   Formative Evaluation—Yields information that can be used for the development or improvement of an on-going program or activity.

   Summative Evaluation—Gives evidence of results and provides a measure of the program or activity results.

Equipment. The educational media and devices used to support or enrich an activity's content or methods by bringing special visual, audio, or tactile capabilities into the learning situation.

Facilities. The physical quarters that accommodate a particular learning activity or event together with its equipment. Facilities, broadly defined, can also include those quarters and equipment required for the program's administrative function.

Formative Evaluation. *See:* **Evaluation: Formative Evaluation.**

Goal. *See:* **Purpose.**

Instruments. Prepared tools, usually in written form, designed to elicit the desired type of information from a relevant source.

Involvement. The active inclusion of individuals as participants in the various stages, activities, and functions of the learning program.

Implementation. The process of assembling the decisions and ingredients essential to accomplishing what is intended. It is the action taken to help people learn, the production of events, activities, and processes that, when fulfilled, will achieve the program's objectives.

Initial Planning. *See:* **Planning: Initial Planning.**

Learning Package. A collection of focused resources to help people learn.

Materials. The educational aids used to initiate, facilitate, or reinforce the learning process.

Method. The mode of procedure, the form and format, or the type of approach to learning that is employed for the various activities in a program.

Methods Specialist. *See:* **Educator: Methods Specialist.**

Needs. A lack of essential knowledge, skills, or attitudes that prevents satisfactory job performance or interferes with an individual's potential for assuming different or greater responsibilities, now or in the future.

> **Knowledge**—The awareness of facts, ideas, and concepts relevant to a task, a function, or an organization.

> **Skills**—The ability to apply knowledge proficiently in a manner appropriate to the situation.

> **Attitude**—A position, and often behaviors, that indicate an opinion, disposition, or manner with regard to a person, a thing, or a situation.

Needs Assessment. Systematic process used to identify needs including both gathering and analyzing the information.

Objectives, Activity. Statements that specify the kind(s) of behavior expected to occur in learners and/or the changes expected in the library as a result of one activity.

Objectives, Program. Statements that describe the intent, function, and results expected from the total learning program.

Planning. Decision-making process leading to implementation by developing the means to accomplish a desired end.

> **Initial Planning**—Produces a flexible outline of the situation, needs, and objectives of the program and an action plan of steps and activities. It may include provisions for an evaluation process and for continuous planning.

> **Continuous Planning**—Incorporates the discoveries and results from program implementation and evaluation in on-going decision making.

Process Specialist. *See:* **Educator: Process Specialist.**

Program. A coordinated variety of learning activities that are sequentially planned over a substantial time span and are directed toward defined objectives.

Program Objectives. *See:* **Objectives, Program.**

Purpose. An intended direction or aim, a goal; an overall definition of what a program or activity is to accomplish.

Resources. The means needed, available, and/or used to produce a program or its activities. Resources include information and financial support, people, facilities and equipment, materials and supplies.

Staff Development. A purposive effort intended to strengthen the library's capability to fulfill its mission effectively and efficiently by encouraging and providing for the growth of its human resources.

Summative Evaluation. *See:* **Evaluation: Summative Evaluation.**

INDEX

[N.B.: Models in Appendix are not indexed here.]